AF692310

Footprints of Enterprise

Indian Business Through the Ages

Footprints of Enterprise

Indian Business Through the Ages

Federation of Indian Chambers of
Commerce and Industry
New Delhi

Delhi
Oxford University Press
Calcutta Chennai Mumbai
1999

This volume is a celebration of fifty years of India's Independence

Editorial Board

S. S. Kanoria, *Chairman*
Amit Mitra
P. Murari
Vijay Topa
Kishore Singh, *Managing Editor*
Kokila Rangachari, *Managing Editor*

Advisors

Prem Shankar Jha
Nitish Sengupta
S. K. Singh
Nazeeb Arif

Oxford University Press, Great Clarendon Street, Oxford OX2 6DP

Oxford New York
Athens Auckland Bangkok Calcutta
Cape Town Chennai Dar es Salaam Delhi
Florence Hong Kong Istanbul Karachi
Kuala Lumpur Madrid Melbourne Mexico City
Mumbai Nairobi Paris Singapore
Taipei Tokyo Toronto
and associates in
Berlin Ibadan

© Federation of Indian Chambers of Commerce and Industry 1999
Tansen Marg, New Delhi 110 001

ISBN 0 19 5647742

All rights reserved. No material from this book may be reproduced
without the written permission of FICCI

Book design and typeset by Arrt Creations
45 Nehru Apartments, Kalkaji, New Delhi 110 019

Photo research by FICCI and Arrt Creations

Typset in Stone Serif 13 pt. and Labyrinth 8.5 pt.

Photograph captions by Kishore Singh

Processed and printed by International Print-O-Pack Limited
B 204-205 Okhla, Phase I, New Delhi 110 020

Published by Manzar Khan, Oxford University Press
YMCA Library Building, Jai Singh Road, New Delhi 110 001

Contents

राष्ट्रपति
भारत गणतंत्र
PRESIDENT
REPUBLIC OF INDIA

MESSAGE

I congratulate the Federation of Indian Chambers of Commerce and Industry(FICCI) for bringing out a publication "Footprints of Enterprise: Indian Business Through the Ages" to commemorate the 50th Anniversary of our Independence.

I am sure that this volume, a valuable addition to the corpus of literature on Indian commerce and industry, not only surveys the past but also sheds light on the directions that Indian business must take in the future.

I wish the publication every success.

Narayanan K.R.

(K.R. Narayanan)

New Delhi
August 27, 1998

देहि मे ददामि ते नि मे धेहि नि ते दधे।
निहारं च हरसि मे निहारं नि हरामि ते॥

A mutually beneficial business relationship can be forged only on the basis of truthfulness and reciprocity.
Yajurveda 3/49

योगो ज्ञानं तथा सांख्यं विद्याः शिल्पादि कर्म च।
वेदाः शास्त्राणि विज्ञानमेतत्सर्वं जनार्दनात्॥

Yoga, knowledge, numbers, learning, crafts, effort, the scriptures, implements, and science, all these have originated from the Creator, Vishnu.
Mahabharat, Anu parva, Vishnusahasranama 139

Introduction

S.S. Kanoria

Civilization is a stream with banks. The stream is sometimes filled with blood from people killing, stealing, shouting and doing the things historians usually record, while on the banks, unnoticed, people build homes, raise children, sing songs, write poetry and even whittle statues. The story of civilization is the story of what happened on the banks. Historians are pessimists because they ignore the banks for the river.

Will Durant

As we trace the footprints of human enterprise over the sands of time, one recurring theme presents itself millennium after millennium. This is the story of the indomitable spirit of man, his tireless quest for knowledge and to benefit from such knowledge. From the moment our ancestors learnt to walk upright, the story of human evolution is, in fact, a saga of human enterprise. From the tools that prehistoric man carved from stone to the silicon chip that runs the world today, it is indeed the unconquerable spirit of enterprise that has shaped history and civilizations.

The world as we know it today — with computers, automobiles, aircraft, telephones, television, and so on — is a reflection of scientific enterprise of perhaps only the last 150 years. These path-breaking inventions, which are so integrated with our life today, form only a micro-speck in the total canvas of human enterprise and evolution. The human species, as we recognize it, emerged 35,000 years ago, although man-like creatures have been in existence for over 14 million years. When one considers that the earth's crust was formed 4500 million years ago, the evolution of mankind itself looks a recent phenomenon. And this, perhaps, is why we must acknowledge the infinite acts of enterprise that man has undertaken to bring us to the current level of development.

The journey from prehistory to the twenty-first century is filled with innumerable milestones — the fruits of man's enterprise and quest for knowledge. Prehistoric man sharpened poles, the first spears, in 5,00,000 BC; stones were shaped and used as tools and weapons by 2,50,000 BC. The use of fire to warm, protect, and cook evolved around that time, though man learnt to make fire only 12,000 years ago. Work with metal began around 5500 BC; around this time, the spindle was developed for spinning. The wheel and the kiln to make bricks were invented. Around 3500 BC, the first form of writing emerged in Sumeria, one of the earliest civilizations. From symbols to syllables to the alphabet, writing traversed many milestones on media: from stone to clay to papyrus and, finally, paper.

▲ Early civilization took long periods of time to evolve, moving across periods of hunting with sharpened stones to the discovery of fire for cooking and protection, to the wheel and its use in turning pottery. These were the first steps towards bulding a civilization that, in the stride of only a few decades, can now change the way the world thinks and believes.

◀ The river Indus, which lent its name to the Indus Valley Civilization that flourished in South Asia 4500 years ago, is symbolic of a history, culture and tradition that gave the world among its earliest planned cities and advanced skills in commerce and business.

But for it, the literature of generations would not have been preserved, and man's horizon of knowledge would be limited.

It is overwhelming to discover the extent of human enterprise that has been at the root of every conceivable development in the world. In this story of mankind can we then label any one achievement as the most important? Is it the development of mathematics, science, architecture, or medicine? What about achievements such as the introduction of the calendar, the drawing of the map of the world, or the discovery of planets? Are they any less important? The invention of electricity, the first wireless message, the steam locomotive, the flying machine, the printing press, the thermometer, the battery, the human heart transplant, the conquering of space, the test-tube baby, the cloning of cells: which of these milestones is less important? What about the arts,crafts, music, songs; the epics, the wonders of the world, the conquests? Are they not yet another facet of human endeavour and enterprise? Indeed, mankind's evolution is a mosaic of countless forms of human enterprise, each symbolizing a step forward in man's quest for excellence. In this journey through millennia, civilizations have emerged to survive or to die, as willed by the people who created them; nations have been created and divided by the designs of men; and countries have progressed or left behind due to human effort or the lack of it.

We have been no different. India, today, is considered one of the foremost nations of the world. This is in no small measure due to her people, her rich heritage, and the values enshrined in the learning of thousands of years. Four thousand and five hundred years

ago, in 2500 BC, the Indus Valley Civilization resulted in settlements that left an indelible imprint on our land and its people, and was perhaps one of the most progressive the world has ever seen. Today, the ruins of the cities at Mohenjodaro, Harappa, Lothal, Surkotada and Dholavira speak of an age when urban planning was in evidence, cities had proper sanitation, goods were produced and sold abroad, and even ports were constructed for the transportation of men and cargo by sea. Imposing citadels were built in an architectural style that is enviable even today, houses used burnt bricks unlike the sun-dried forms of Mesopotamia, and there is strong evidence of high levels of organizational, administrative, and technological skill. A glimpse of the ancient past in India is provided by Himanshu P. Ray and Jagatpati Joshi in Section I of this volume. India's civilizational span, and the enterprise of its people, is evident in the forms of business and trade that existed even then.

However, the romance of the Indus Valley Civilization, for those who have cared to glance at this period in the infinite past, is not merely the display of the signs of a modern society. It is also the aura and mystery that surround its death. Just a few centuries past 2000 BC, that great civilization came to an end. Why this happened remains, to this day, unknown. However, speculations have given rise to theories of a man-made disaster wiping out the civilization, or perhaps an environmental catastrophe, even, maybe, war or disease. The lesson this has for us should not be lost sight of, that the greater the degree of human enterprise, the greater the need for caution; and still greater the need to enhance our knowledge to withstand forces unleashed by adverse, unforeseen circumstances, whether caused by environment, disease, war, or by the evil design of men.

Be that as it may, the spirit of India lived on, as did its spirit of enterprise. Tan Chung, in this volume, takes us back on a journey along the famous Silk Road that affected India. B.D. Chattopadhyaya takes us back to an age when the Buddha and Mahavira lived in the middle Ganga valley, and refers to Buddhist texts that contain the first references to different types of traders and bankers such as the *vanik, sreshthi,* and *sarthavaha.* Trade continued to develop, and later rulers in the Mauryan empire even evolved measures to ensure optimum revenue to the state. India's foundation for business is reflected in the early Dharmasastra texts attributed to Manu, Yajnavalkya, and Narada.

▲ India in an Asian setting. From the very beginning, India was important for her natural resources, her technological advancements, and was strategically placed on trade routes that shaped the nature of Indian enterprise and was responsible for the spread of Indian culture.

(previous page):

▲▼ Jewellery from south India *(above)* and silver coins from the Gupta period *(below)* are as indicative of a flowering of arts as of growing affluence, a result of trade practices that spread across much of Asia.

As we move on in history, India came to occupy a dominant role in world commerce. Shireen Moosvi, in her article on trade in Mughal India, refers to a quote by Bernier, a French traveller, who noted that 'gold and silver, after circulating in every quarter of the globe, came at length to be swallowed up, lost in some measure, in Hindoustan'. By this time, Indian merchants controlled large sectors of trade in the Red Sea, Iran, Central Asia and South East Asia. Indian entrepreneurship thus became an acknowledged force not only within the country but across the seas as well. India's bounties attracted traders and business from several parts of Europe, and thus the seeds of the British Raj were sown with the arrival of the first traders of the East India Company on the shores of India.

The transformation of a trading body into the Government of India by the mid-nineteenth century ushered in a new era in a country where numerous business communities existed with long traditions of trading and manufacture. Indigenous big business was gradually suppressed, 'taking a subordinate place under the domination of British business interests in India', claims Sabyasachi Bhattacharya who also points out that 'it was business that *became* the British Raj'. However, it is a tribute to Indian entrepreneurship that this dominance did not obliterate the Indian business spirit; if anything, it strengthened its resolve, as history tells us, and perhaps prepared it for the challenges of building a new, independent nation in the years to come.

The British never intended to industrialize India beyond the demands of their colonial needs, and the economic policies pursued by them clearly point towards this. Infrastructure was created more to exploit India's resources than to develop the country, though, unintentionally, it helped in bonding the country later. Despite domination and the adverse policies of the Raj, India's industrial enterprise began to bloom within the realm. The foundation of a steel plant by Sir Jamshetji Tata, the textile mills established by Cowasjee Davar, the pioneering industrialization led by Ghanshyam Das Birla, these ushered in new business confidence in India.

Premier Indian business organizations like FICCI were formed to serve indigenous Indian interests. Eventually, the business community played a major role in supporting and attaining India's independence, as it moved, shoulder to shoulder, with the political leaders to demand economic and political freedom. As Aditya Mukherjee points out, strong nationalistic sentiments led businessmen to shelter freedom fighters against British rule and its policies, and even bear with strikes in their own factories, voluntarily granting full wages to workers for the duration of the strike. The task of rebuilding India was begun in

▲ Advertisement from *The Times of India* annual, 1930 for Burmah Shell. Even though Indian entrepreneurship was dwarfed by European companies, it created its own niche in the markets of commerce. The British, meanwhile, were able to bring in technologies and products into India as a result of their own industrialization, seeking opportunities for them in the country.

◀ The Europeans first came to India in search of spices, and were also lured by her excellence of crafts skills. India, at that time, had a well-organized heirarchy of skilled workers, and strong trading systems, but fell prey to political upheavals and came under colonial domination.

right earnest, and India's business fraternity rose to the occasion with customary entrepreneurial zeal.

Today, fifty-one years after India's Independence, we as a nation have much to be proud of. Perhaps it is also true that we have a large section of the economy that strikes at our collective conscience and mocks at the claim that India has achieved several milestones in these five decades: India certainly does not belong to the rich league of nations following a half century of self-rule and independence. It cannot boast of widespread literacy, or housing and medical care for all. However, it would be naive to brush away the remarkable achievements that it has notched in developing a self-reliant economy, the most important of which has been the ushering of the Green Revolution, in creating and sustaining our scientific and technological temper, and in protecting the growth of a vibrant democracy where the rule of law exists and freedom is valued.

After five decades of Independence, India may not have reached the top of the ladder, but Indians certainly have. Indian scientists, technologists, and engineers are developing cutting edge technologies in global firms around the world that base their leadership on such advancements in research and development. It would perhaps be difficult to name one Silicon Valley company that does not have an Indian in its core team. If India has produced distinguished Nobel laureates in the past, it today produces global CEOs. Indians

▲ Prime Minister Jawaharlal Nehru with industrialist and prominent FICCI member S.S. Kanoria. Nehru fettered the spirit of free enterprise by promoting the public sector, and it is the public sector that is in need of liberalization today.

have conquered space, and recently took pride in seeing their first lady astronaut at NASA. Success stories of Indian businessmen who have ventured into the unknown in unfamiliar surroundings and have emerged as global leaders in their fields abound and some are told in the pages of this book.

The phenomenal success of Indians in several economic and business sectors is indicative of the inborn Indian spirit of enterprise and the tradition of business it has fostered. If anything has constrained India's development, it is only the fetters that we have cast around ourselves in following, in the past, certain restrictive policies. It is unfortunate that instead of trust, cooperation, and effective partnership between government and industry, the government in post-independent India pursued a policy that treated the private sector as adversary while adopting the public sector as its favourite child.

Today it is widely acknowledged that these restrictive policies prevented Indian industry from developing a core competency, and from becoming competitive in the global context. Without these fetters, India's spirit of enterprise would have ensured that the private sector would grow beyond the confines of the domestic market and venture into developing skills that would make it a world class player by the start of the new millennium.

The turning point of 1991, when crisis forced reforms upon us, has certainly changed the rules of the game for business in India. Fortunately, at that time we had a bold and imaginative government that converted a situation of adversity into a milieu of opportunity. However, liberalization has been confined to the private sector, and does not take the public

▲ The greening of India in the post-Independence decades has been largely responsible for the economic stability of the country. With enough stock of foodgrains, the country has set about the challenge of keeping its tryst with destiny as the fourth most industrialized nation in the new millennium.

sector into account. We are still awaiting the moment when, along with a bold and just labour policy, the country will become one single economy with neither artificial barriers nor different rates of taxation between states.

The shift from a controlled economy to a highly liberated one has opened up significant new vistas of growth. At the same time, it has also posed a strong challenge to traditional Indian industry which, over the years, had become somewhat resistant to change, and is now being forced to restructure because of the onslaught of competition from within and outside. However, the development of India's entrepreneurial spirit through thousands of years of history, gives us confidence that we have the resilience and the capability to take up pioneering challenges as we have done since times immemorial. Indians, as history points out, are not just survivors, they are winners. Some of the remarkable achievements recorded in this volume only provide testimony to the dedication, commitment, and capability of the Indian entrepreneur. As Nitish Sengupta rightly points out, India was set on an irreversible path of economic reforms that, despite political obstacles, was to lead her to a high growth trajectory. Sanjaya Baru, in his essay, says that Indian entrepreneurial and professional skills are as good as the best, and S.K. Singh asserts that India will be among the global leaders in trade, industry, science, and technology. Ashok Desai has dealt with the changing relationship between government and business, whereas Prem Shankar Jha describes the challenges of the twenty-first century. Gita Piramal, in her characteristic style, comments on the rise and fall of business empires. The other eminent authors of this volume have drawn attention to several other aspects and dimensions that mark this spirit of enterprise, and which are deserving of your attention.

▲ The industrial revolution was late in coming to India, the result of subversive colonial politics. After Independence, however, the country has marched in to take its rightful place in the infotech revolution where, instead of being a follower, it has proved itself a leader.

How do we see India in the next millennium? The pace of technological change and greater integration of the world economy will result in an entirely new economic order. It is obvious that we shall see a very big shift towards the development of the services sector. Swaminathan S. Anklesaria Aiyar asserts in his article, 'Make no mistake, the future lies in services much more than industry ... India's greatest comparative advantage lies not in manufacturing, the scope for which is quite limited, but in services.' The services to GDP ratio for high-income countries was 58 per cent in the 1980s, and by mid-1990s the share went up to 66 per cent. The market for global service exports is estimated at US$ 1200 billion. We have to prepare a concerted strategy to take advantage of this market. India has the most important asset required to position itself at the cutting edge of international competitiveness: its skilled human resources. Once again, it will be India's human enterprise that will take it to the top echelons of growth in the world.

It is also obvious that individual states in the Indian federation will play a much more important role in facilitating development in their regions. Today we have leaders like Chandrababu Naidu, chief minister of Andhra Pradesh, who is more comfortable in his role as CEO of Andhra Inc., a role he plays with considerable professionalism in promoting investments in his state. His vision statement compares to those that multinational companies make to tackle the challenges of the new millennium. It will be such proactive and visionary leaders that will shape the new face of India and carry the processes of liberalization, modernization, and innovation directly to the people of India.

▲ Today, India is not isolated from world affairs in business. If it stands shoulder to shoulder in the comity of nations, the day is not far when it will lead the way in new directions in the service of mankind.

The private sector will emerge as an important driving force in the new millennium. Corporates will increasingly benchmark international standards of quality and pricing to sharpen their global competitiveness. History provides ample evidence that, given the opportunity, Indians can take on any challenge, however daunting. The enduring values and rich heritage that shape our culture, and the basic spirit of enterprise that India represents, will lead us to the dawn of a new era of development.

Amit Mitra has rightly pointed out that the gigantic web of the infotech revolution will facilitate the birth of a new strata of 'home knowledge workers' and release latent 'women power' by eliminating the need of conventional offices, and will make the concept of contemporary trade unions obsolete. Anuradha Rajivan, Kanika Goswami, and Suresh Achar, in their contributions, describe only a few such new generation Indians, men and women, who have taken upon themselves the task of taking the country to new entrepreneurial heights.

India has always looked forward, and in the twenty-first century, it is uniquely positioned to emerge as one of the foremost economic superpowers of the world. The challenge is for the people and leaders to respond to this opportunity. Today, as we tread the footprints of Indian business over the decades, we cannot but take pride in our past. It is heartening that the new generation of business people continues the Indian legacy of excellence, and the future that it weaves together will certainly bring greater prosperity and stature to our nation. This volume is a humble tribute to this quest for excellence in human enterprise, and our endeavour in presenting this rich tapestry will bear fruit if these experiences inspire and unleash a spirit of enterprise in our nation that will give our people a much higher quality of life. In the words of Ralph Waldo Emerson, essayist, poet, and philosopher:

> As long as our civilization is essentially one of property, of fences, of exclusiveness, it will be mocked by delusions. Our riches will leave us sick, there will be bitterness in our laughter, and our wine will burn our mouth. Only that good profits, which we can taste with all doors open, and which serves all men.

Section I

The Pre-Colonial Era

Overview

Networks of Indian Enterprise

Himanshu P. Ray

The letter of my lord, the most illustrious elder, arrived; I read and understood it, and I was happy to learn that you were well and your affairs in order, for which I thanked God very much ... Please give Sus Siti and Kinbati [and Isha.] and Ishaq the Banyan my best regards, and tell them of my longing for them. Inform them in my name that as for pepper, in this coming year its value, [that is] the price per *bahar*, will be thirty dinars, and more, and as for refurbished iron, a *bahar* will be [worth] not less than twenty dinars, and that the *raqs* [shining, glittering iron], which was in the city, is completely exhausted. [Tell them also] to dispatch a ship from Mangalore, if they can, and to send in it any available pepper, iron, *cubeb*, and ginger; it should set out at the first opportunity for al-Dyyb [Diu], taking some coir [coconut fibre], fine aloes wood, mango and coconuts, because all these are selling well.
If they are equipping a ship in Aden, and they want me to take part, I will share [in it] with them. If there were a ship sailing from Mangalore this year, I would send them gold, sugar, raisins and [other] goods. Be sure to inform them of all this, and do not be remiss, for you take the place of a letter of mine to them.

These are excerpts from a letter in Arabic written by Madmun bin Hasan bin Bundar, the representative of the merchants and superintendent of the port of Aden, on 11 September 1149. Like his father, he was also a shipowner and a middleman between the Mediterranean Jews and those in India. The addressee of the letter was Abraham bin Perahya Ben Yiju, a learned Tunisian Jew who operated a brass factory on the Malabar Coast. The term *banyan* or *bania* mentioned in the communication was the usual appellation for an Indian merchant.

The letter is a lucid example of the interaction among the ancient trading communities of the Indian Ocean and is no mere isolated instance, for travel to distant lands formed an intrinsic part of the early trading networks. Merchants from various regions are referred to as 'tax farmers' in the inscriptions from Java

▲ Boat panel from a terracotta temple of Bengal. Bengal has often been described as 'boat country' on account of its active waterways and an extraordinary inland navigation system. It was along these that goods and commodities were transported, till at least the eighteenth century, as is evident from the accounts of James Rennell, the first Surveyor-General of India.

dated between the ninth and fourteenth centuries AD. These included groups from lower Burma, Cambodia, east coast districts of what are now Andhra Pradesh and southern Orissa, or from the western Konkan coastal region already dominated by the Ayyavole merchant association. Inscriptions in Arabic from the Indian subcontinent dated between 1218 and 1291 refer to traders and shippers from Arabia and Persia resident in the towns of Gujarat. There is evidence of maritime networks across the western Indian Ocean as early as the third millennium BC. A triad of names that figures consistently in Mesopotamian texts includes those of Dilmun (the Bahrain archipelago), Magan (the Oman peninsula), and Melukkha (identified with Harappan settlements). An early reference appears in the boast by Sargon of Akkad (2334–2279 BC) stating that

> The ships from Meluhha
> the ships from Magan
> the ships from Dilmun
> he made tie-up alongside
> the quay of Akkad.

Early literary sources, such as the *Arthasastra* and Jataka texts dated to the beginning of the Christian era, provide graphic details of several aspects of trading activities. The *Tandulanali Jataka*, for example, narrates the story of the Boddhisattva who was a valuer of horses, elephants, jewels and gold for the king of Varanasi. Commodities for city dwellers were transported and traded by merchants in caravans. A narrative describes how a Boddhisattva, born in a family of caravaners in Varanasi, journeyed to different parts of the land with 500 carts drawn by oxen. To escort such caravans across the desert, merchants relied on desert pilots well versed in the knowledge of the stars, and on guides for journeying through forest tracts.

The Jatakas describe how, on the arrival of a ship, merchants would converge there to buy the goods, and often had to pay money in advance to secure a share in the cargo. This was a practice not only in the ports of the Indian Ocean but also of the Mediterranean Sea. When a convoy of foreign ships reached a harbour, some local merchants would try to monopolize all the imports and thus drive up prices, a practice against which Muslim law books fulminated.

Alternatively, a merchant could procure goods by mutual agreement with another in a neighbouring

▼ A painting in Ajanta Cave depicting the voyage of Kalyanakarin and his brother. It is the third of the seafaring tales painted at Ajanta and is particularly significant as a representation of ancient sailing vessels.

region, by transporting local goods to the correspondent merchant and bringing back goods received in exchange. A third way was by directly approaching the producer, and there are several references to traders journeying for trade purposes to villages specializing in a particular craft. In contrast, in the *Arthasastra,* much of the trade is described as being under the control of the state, supervised by the *panyadhyaksa.* It was he who regulated the prices of various commodities to allow a certain percentage of profit. Goods are categorized as *svabhumija* or those produced indigenously, and *parabhumija* or those imported from different lands. Indigenous goods could be sold only at one centre such as the capital, while those goods not produced indigenously could be retailed at various outlets.

The largest single group of shipowners was the merchant community. Panini, the famed Sanskrit grammarian, refers to terms indicating merchants with two boats or those sailing with five ships. One of the frequently encountered hazards was shipwreck, though other perils of the unknown were also dreaded. A theme that figures prominently in early Buddhist literature and in the sculpture and painting of Buddhist monastic sites from the second century BC to AD seventh century, is that of a 'saviour' from dangers associated with travel. A painting in cave II at Ajanta depicts the story of a merchant ship that journeyed to an island to

▲ Coins from the Chola-Rajendra period (AD 1012–44) showing the spread of monetized trade.

▼ Terracotta sealing with a boat symbol from Bengal. In the ancient period, large pots were frequently used for transportation of commodities. The mouths of these vessels were covered with cloth and tied with a string, the knot being then sealed with a lump of clay which was stamped with a seal and hardened by exposure to heat.

▶ *(facing page):* Printed coloured cotton, eighteenth century, Burhanpur. Cotton textiles were an essential part of trade both within the subcontinent, as also across the Indian Ocean. The earliest surviving examples of this trade between Egypt and Gujarat date from the eleventh to the fifteenth centuries. Often complex scenes were depicted indicating a narrative function, reminiscent of a tradition of theatrical painted scrolls with religious themes, such as the Ramayana.

▲ Ear pendant in gold, Taxila, first century AD. Indians were as fond of gold jewellery in ancient times as they are now. The level of craftsmanship remained of high quality, through the centuries.

▶ *Swastika* from Taxila, first century AD. Taxila was situated on the trade route leading to Balkh and occupied a position of singular commercial importance as is evident from the finds of large numbers on uninscribed and inscribed coins minted locally.

collect a precious cargo of sandalwood, but was threatened by a demon. The vessel's owner, the merchant Darukarnin, called on his brother Purna, a Buddhist monk, to help pacify the demon.

An important aspect of interaction between the polity and maritime trading groups related to protection provided to incoming vessels by the state. Significant in this regard is the Motupalli pillar inscription of king Ganapatideva of the Kakatiya dynasty dated to the thirteenth century. The inscription is engraved on four sides of a pillar of the *mandapa* in front of the Virabhadrasvami temple at Motupalli on the south-eastern fringe of the Krishna delta. It records an edict of the king promising protection for sea traders whose vessels may have been wrecked off the coast. While earlier rulers confiscated such cargo, Ganapatideva provided an assurance that only the usual customs duties would be levied on it. The items of import and export mentioned in the inscription included sandalwood, Chinese camphor, pearls, rose-water, ivory, zinc, lead, silk thread, corals, perfumes, and pepper.

The charter of Visnusena, dated AD 592, from Lohata in the Gujarat–Kathiawar region, provided a detailed list of 72 trade regulations or customary laws to be followed by the community of merchants. The charter assured them protection and endorsed their continued functioning. For instance, it specified that merchants away for a year were not required to pay an entrance fee on their return. Other clauses specified duties that were to be paid. A boatful of utensils had to pay twelve silver coins, but if these were for a religious purpose then duty was reduced to the worth of only one and a quarter silver coins. A boat carrying paddy paid only half this amount. Commodities mentioned included dried ginger sticks and bamboo.

The general pattern found in early South and South East Asia was that while internal trade was often monetized, long distance trade was conducted on a barter basis. The *Periplus Maris Erythraei,* a first century AD Greek text refers to ports on the coast of India, one of the principal ones being Bharuch at the mouth of river Narmada. Here was a market for wine, copper, tin and lead, coral, raw glass, and Roman

money. Roman gold and silver were exchanged at a profit against local currency.

In ancient India, the earliest coinage was punch-marked silver coins struck from the sixth to second centuries BC. Up to the fourth century BC, these coins were produced locally by tribal states or *janapada*s in a variety of weights, styles, and fabrics. The coinage of Magadha formed the prototype for the series issued during the rule of the Nandas and the Mauryas. Silver punched-marked coins continued in circulation in the post-Mauryan period and have been found in association with Roman coins and Satavahana objects in the Deccan. The evidence from inscriptions further supports the widespread occurrence of Satavahana coins. A majority of the donations at the Buddhist monastic site of Kanheri near Mumbai were in the form of perpetual endowments of money. There are references to money being invested in guilds and the interest used for various purposes.

Textiles were among commodities that could be used as an investment, handed down from generation to generation. These included a wide range from coarse cottons to fine silks. Furnishings in Asia consisted mostly of carpets, cushions, canopies, and draperies, all the produce of the textile industry. Inscriptions dating to the early centuries of the Christian era refer to guilds in the western Deccan trading in different varieties of textiles. It is not surprising then that the first European accounts of life in Arab and Asian ports mention the presence of trading craft that carried large quantities of textiles.

More recently, attempts have been made by radiocarbon methods to date textile collections in museums, such as the Newberry collection at the Ashmolean Museum, Oxford, and to study the designs and patterns for information on the clientele as also the origin of the textiles. Several specimens in the Newberry collection have been found to bear close stylistic similarities to eleventh-century painted wooden book covers of early Jain manuscripts. An interesting contrast is evident in the use of textiles in the western Indian Ocean as opposed to that further east. While the fabrics travelling to South East Asia were stored or ceremonially displayed as signs of wealth, those that went to Egypt were transformed by being fashioned into garments and furnishings.

Merchants were major donors who contributed towards the construction of religious monuments. In the south, generous donations for the building and maintenance of temples came from the powerful Manigramam and Ayyavole associations of traders who controlled both inland and transoceanic trade under the Cholas. Records of these temples now form an important source for the reconstruction of the history of these guilds. In Tamil areas prior to the twelfth century, there is inscriptional evidence of Jain participation in Ayyavole association and donations made to Jain religious establishments. Similarly, in Kannada areas, Jain influence is discernible in the several inscriptions of the Ayyavole traders located in or near Jain temples, which relate to gifts to Jain establishments, particularly in the twelfth and thirteenth centuries. Among important records of the Manigraman is the ninth-century Takuapa inscription found together with a group of stone sculptures in

▶ Purchase of Jetavana, relief on a railing pillar from Bharhut dated to the second century BC, depicting the purchase of the grove of prince Jeta with as many punch-marked coins as would cover it. This grove was then gifted by the merchant Ananthapindika to the Buddha. An inscribed label below the medallion reads: 'Ananthapindika dedicates Jetavana purchased with a layer of crores'.

south Thailand and probably located earlier in a shrine. The inscription refers to the digging of a tank and the stationing of armed soldiers for its protection.

This connection between trading groups and religious establishments was not restricted to local merchant communities: foreign communities also made donations to Buddhist monasteries and Brahmanical temples in order to gain acceptability into local networks. The *Yavanas* (the term *Yavana* initially meant Ionian Greeks, but by the beginning of the Christian era was broadly used to denote any foreigner) donated generously to Buddhist monastic centres of the western Deccan in the early centuries of the Christian era. This is evident from their inscriptions on pillars of the *chaitya* hall at Karle and the Sanskritic names of donors that are in marked contrast to those in records from the north-west where *Yavana* donors retained their Greek identity. The indigenous trading system was gradually transformed with the entry of Europeans in the Indian Ocean from the fifteenth century onward. This expansion of European mercantile activity was paralled by the rise of powerful states such as the Mughal in the subcontinent.

Two far-reaching developments took place in the Mughal period. First, there was growing interaction between Indian business houses and European trading companies. Especially noticeable was that Indian technology, though cheaper in terms of production costs, was, by and large, on a par with that in Europe. Thus increasing use was made of Asian shipyards by Europeans for shipbuilding in the sixteenth and seventeenth centuries. Second, there does seem to be evidence for clearly increasing official involvement in trade with West Asia from the mid-seventeenth century onwards. In fact, Shah Jahan's ships monopolized trade between Surat and the Arabian coast. Trade between Central Asia and India too received a boost under the Mughals.

◀ Silk brocade, sari border, seventeenth century, Chanderi. Textiles, especially silks, were crucial signifiers of social status and were also treasured as heirlooms to be passed on from one generation to another.

▼ The Dilwara temples in Rajasthan were built by Jain merchants to propitiate their gods.

Perspectives of Harappan Economy and Trade

Jagatpati Joshi

The remarkable discovery of the Indus Valley Civilization in 1921–2 in the north-western part of the subcontinent proved an important landmark and pushed back the antiquity of its culture to the third millennium BC. Confined more or less to the limits of the Indus basin, the Harappan civilization, named after the first site discovered, showed signs of 'stagnating' diagnostic cultural traits.

The Indian sites provide a plethora of information regarding environmental factors, regional adaptation, and variability in settlement patterns, and its social and religious fabric based on material evidence. The last eight decades have thrown up over 862 pre-Harappan, Harappan, and late-Harappan sites, most of them clustered around the Saraswati river system, leading some archaeologists to designate new nomenclatures such as the Indus–Saraswati Civilization or the Saraswati–Hakra Civilization. The area

▼ An artist's perspective of the citadel and residential complex at Surkotada in Kutch, Gujarat, site of the Indus Valley Civilization (2500–1900 BC).

of its distribution in India and Pakistan covers of 2.5 m. sq. km. Following radiocarbon testing and calibration, the dates for the settlements range from c. 2900–1900 BC.

While pre-Harappan and Harappan sites are located along major rivers, late-Harappan sites are found along the upper reaches of their tributaries. The area covered by the civilization can for convenience be divided into six zones — Punjab (type site: Harappa); Rajasthan and Haryana (type site: Kalibangan); Bahawalpur (type site: Ganweriwalla); Sind (type site: Mohenjodaro); Baluchistan (type site: Kulli Harappan); Gujarat (type site: Dholavira, Lothal).

Of these, the first four tend to have a number of sites that are termed pre-Harappan or early Harappan in the formative stages of antecedent culture. In every case, there are examples of the three representations: where there is a clear cut stratigraphic break between pre-Harappan and Harappan cultures, although the two complexes are found in mixed form through a number of layers subsequent to the layer marking a break, as in Kot Diji and Kalibangan; where the stratigraphic break is not clearly marked and an overlap exists, as in Banawali, Kalibangan, and Dholavira; and where Harappan culture never reached the site of pre-Harappans, such as at Jalilpur and Sarai Khola.

How the civilization developed has remained a subject of scientific study and romantic speculation, for though 'death from an unidentified source is understandable, unnatural birth is an unnatural phenomenon'. Several theories regarding its 'origin' and

▲ Map showing the extent of the Harappan civilization.

▼ Port view, an artist's conjecture of the harbour at Lothal, Gujarat, part of the Indus Valley Civilization, showing that seafaring activities enjoyed prominence in the socio-economy of the settlement.

'form' have been propounded but not one explains it fully, either through 'colonization' or 'acculturation'. The pattern of cultural contacts in the plains of the Indus and the adjoining western region varied in accordance with both time and space. Evidence from sites such as Dholavira, Banawali and Kunal in India, and Naushreo, Balakot, Mehergarh, Leewan, Rehman Dheri, Amri, Ghazishah and Kot Diji in Pakistan, veer towards their independent growth, with the exception of economic interaction between them, spread from the seventh to third millenniums BC. Recent pre-Harappan excavations at Kunal, in Haryana's Hissar district, have brought to light crowns, armlets, bangles, necklaces, and pendants in precious metals (gold and silver), 12,000 carnelian beads, and steatite seals that are Harappan in shape and style but without the typical animal and pictographic script.

The early Harappans knew how to build citadels, were familiar with pottery, and acquainted with 'fish scale' and 'pipal leaf' designs, and appeared to operate some kind of trade mechanism over long distances. The 'horned design' and 'pipal leaf' are depicted in pre-Harappan settlements at Kalibangan and Banawali and may even be precursors to the horned deity of Indus Valley seals.

▲▼ Popular seals from Mohenjodaro depicting Pashupatinath *(above)* and the bull *(below)*. Scholars speculate that these seals, possibly religious in nature, may also have been used by traders, since they also have pictographic markings.

Excavations reveal Harappan settlements built in combinations of mud brick, burnt brick and chiselled stone in a growing phenomenon of urbanism. Despite architectural variations, the settlements had an impressive topography. Kalibangan, for example, had a citadel with an imposing gateway and a flight of steps. The citadel had platforms on one side and a residential complex on another, the two separated by a partition wall. The Harappans at Banawali built a citadel and a town secured by fortifications designed like an irregular trapezium. At a later stage, a deep, broad moat was dug around the town. Lothal had a dockyard, a warehouse, a granary, a high acropolis, and a city located at a lower height. Surkotada had a citadel and a fortified residential annexe. The citadel had an imposing gateway complex. The citadel and residential annexe had an inter-communicating ramp and, later, a gateway. Excavations at Dholavira have brought to light an acropolis, middle town and lower town, the first two strongly fortified. The acropolis had a remarkably elaborate layout, and used highly polished stone blocks and pillars. At the centre of the citadel is a water reservoir with a feeder channel covered with slabs and provided with manholes. Besides, there are two lapidary workshops. The most outstanding discovery is a large inscription of ten Harappan signs: could it have been a signboard? Excavators of Rojdi in Saurashtra, are of the opinion that it was 'not an agricultural settlement but appears to have been a centre for procuring raw materials and processing them into finished

▲ A Mohenjodaro seal shows a boat with a cabin, its presence a testimony to the possibility of long distance sea travel.

▼ Bronze dancing figure, Mohenjodaro. The use of metals points to a sophistication in metallurgy which has been a characteristic trait in the development of trade practices in the subcontinent.

products primarily for exporting them to Sind and West-Asia. The settlement was a port and a manufacturing centres'.

The Ghaggar river system with its network of tributaries, along which lie hundreds of Indus sites, was a more stable river system than the Beas, Sutlej, and Ravi. It provided a consistent line of communication through the Sirhind Nala between Punjab and Rajasthan for obtaining timber from the areas of present Himachal Pradesh. The Ghaggar–Saraswati–Hakra system had three major economic pockets. The first was on the north along Sirhind where, in an area of 120 sq. km, in Mansa district, Punjab, 7 cities, 6 towns, and 14 villages have been located, indicative of commercial interaction around an urban complex. The second or central pocket was in the Bikaner/Bahawalpur area where 400 sites have been located over an area of 1000 sq. km dating to pre-Harappan and Harappan times. The third, southern one, in Kutch, which is geographically midway between Sind and Gujarat, has a concentration of fifty Harappan and late-Harappan sites.

The urban phase of the civilization had, therefore, the technological potential, resources, builders, planning and engineering skills, instruments and the manpower to create them. Twenty-one rural Harappan sites have been identified in Mehsana district, Gujarat, besides Valabhi, which have yielded evidence of cattle breeding centres dating back to Harappan times. The Kutch mounds, in comparison to those in Saurashtra, indicate larger, thicker deposits of habitation. The Harappans at Daimabad, in Ahmednagar district, Maharashtra, used the typical late-Harappan pottery and Indus script, and today represent the southernmost limit of the Harappan spread.

Paleobotanical studies carried out on excavated samples of grain from sites in Sind, Punjab, and Gujarat have thrown a flood of light on the food habits of the people. The discovery of a ploughed field at Kalibangan indicates the pattern of ploughing: two sets of furrows cutting at right angles, similar to the system still prevalent in Rajasthan where two crops of mustard and horse gram are grown in the same field. Terracotta models of ploughs from Banawali and Kalibangan suggest ploughshares shaped not very differently from those in current use.

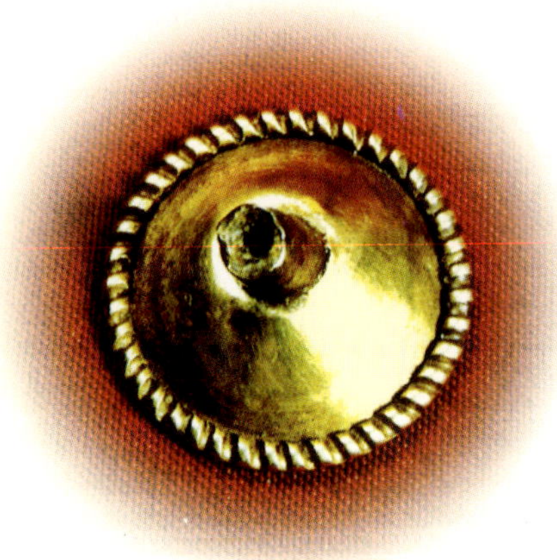

While the staple food of Harappans in Punjab, Haryana and Rajasthan was wheat and barley, those in Gujarat grew rice, millet, *ragi* and jowar. Evidence from granaries in Mohenjodaro, Harappa, and Lothal indicates surplus food produce. The practice of methods of irrigation has led to the Harappans being referred to as 'master hydraulic engineers'. The availability of water tanks at Dholavira suggests reservoirs for potable drinking water and *bund*s for small irrigation.

The Harappans supplemented their diet with the flesh of domesticated and wild animals: cattle, buffaloes, sheep, goat, pig. Animal husbandry and poultry farming were practised. Animal remains of camels, elephants, horses and asses at these sites testify to their use for transport of men and material. Bullock carts and animal packs were used. A variety of cart frames and wheels with or without hubs suggest that the bullock cart was the most popular mode of transport. Small models of boats from Lothal and the depiction of a boat on a seal from Mohenjodaro and on a potsherd from Dhulia suggest that boats, with or without sails, and a cabin for the crew, were common.

A number of industries flourished in Harappan towns: bead making, copper smelting, shell, pottery, jewellery, and seal making. Bead making was practised at Lothal, Surkotada, and Kuntasi. Copper smelting was done at Lothal where a coppersmith's furnace has been found, besides copper ingots; copper was melted in crucibles at Chanhudaro and Harappa; casting and hammering was undertaken. The dancing figure from Mohenjodaro, a copper bull from Kalibangan, and a chariot from Daimabad show the high perfection of indigenous sculpture in Harappan and late-Harappan times. At Harappa, separate rows of workmen's quarters have been unearthed. In Lothal, bead makers and coppersmiths inhabited areas in the lower town. Copper tools include a curved saw found at Lothal. At various settlements, there are remains of the shell industry, and fragments of ladles, bangles, and inlay. Cotton was grown by the Harappans, a piece of cotton cloth was found at Mohenjodaro, and cloth impressions are available from Lothal and Kalibangan. Evidence of ivory working is available from Lothal, Kalibangan, and Surkotada. Spindles and spools suggest the manufacture of yarn. There was a great centre of steatite seal making at Chanhudaro where a large number of unfinished, incomplete seals in various stages were found along with engravings and the metallic equipment required for the industry.

It is evident that this industrial base required both the raw material and the market for finished products, suggesting both internal and external trading. Rajasthan supplied copper to the industries in Gujarat. Rajpipla supplied semi-precious stones to Lothal and Chanhudaro for its bead industry. Barley and wheat

▶ Painted earthen jar, Mohenjodaro. The quality of pottery testifies to the sophistication of the civilization.

◀ The use of ornaments with precious metals and stones was in fashion during the Indus Valley Civilization as can be seen in the finds from excavations. Part of a gold girdle/bracelet (top), an ear stud (middle), and a bead necklace (below).

were supplied by Punjab and Haryana to Gujarat which supplied bajra, jowar, and cotton. Similarly, Baluchistan supplied woollen goods to the rest of the area, and Gujarat cotton. Copper implements, beads, and shell bangles came from sites in Gujarat, and from Allahdino and Balakot in Sind. Steatite seals were supplied from Chanhudaro to all Harappan sites. Internal trade was carried out by guilds that had their own seals, a large number of which have been discovered at Mohenjodaro, Harappa, and

▲ Coin: Uninscribed Cast, (3rd-2nd century BC) made of copper, weighing 8.49 gms and 2.3 cms in diametre. Obverse: Six-arched hill with crescent.

▼ Chariot, late Harappan period, Daimabad in Maharashtra. Evidence of exotosis and ancylosis in cattle bone remains excavated from Surkotada suggests their use for draft purposes.

Lothal. A standard system of weights and measures was followed for uniformity.

The third and second millenniums BC witnessed the growth and flowering of some of the great Bronze Age cultures from Mesopotamia to the Indo-Pakistan subcontinent, particularly from the Euphrates via Makran, Sind, and the Gujarat coast up to the Saraswati valley. During the Bronze Age, Bahrain played a vital role in transmitting cultural cross-currents from the east to the west. Archaeological evidence of maritime activities, docks and ports in India is available since the middle of the third millennium BC. The tidal dock at Lothal bears testimony to this. A Bahrain type seal found at Lothal is evidence of early trade contacts. Other port towns were Kuntasi, Shikarur, and Prabhas Patan on the Gujarat coast.

As far as trade with West Asia is concerned, archaeologists have postulated three theories: direct trade through Harappan colonies in Mesopotamia; a central place of exchange through entrepots like Tepe Yahya; or an agency system in which local authorized agents and foreign resident agents played a decisive role. According to Mesopotamian records, they traded in the east with Dilmun, Makan or Magan, and Meluhha. The identification of these areas is disputed, though the area of the Persian Gulf is identified with Dilmun, Magan has been identified with Oman, Makan with the Makran coast, and Meluhha with Kutch and Saurashtra. During Akkadian times, boats from Meluhha brought carnelian, ivory, shells, timber for building, textiles, and copper. These were goods that came from the Harappan ports.

That the Harappans had trade links with West Asia is testified to by the number of Harappan objects, or those produced under its influence — seals, beads, terracotta figurines, objects of shell,

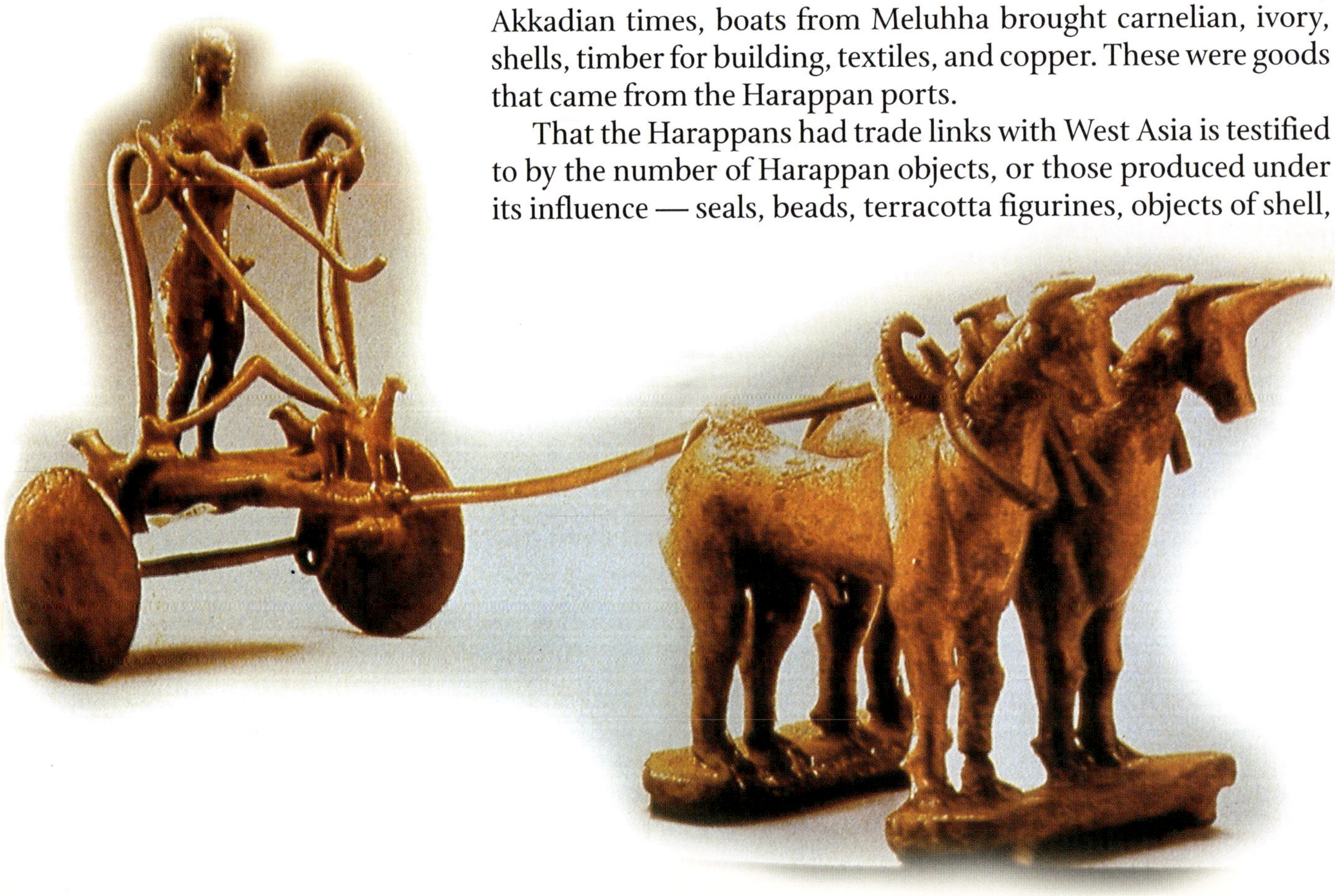

▲ Terracotta spools, Lothal, Gujarat. Their possible use can be determined when fitted, as here, into a modern charkha. Remains of cotton cloth from the Harappan civilization have been unearthed.

▼ Terracotta model of a boat, Lothal, Gujarat. Boats, with or without sails, were common.

ivory, and dice — found at Ur, Tell Asmer, Kish, Lagash, Umma, Nippur, Tepe Gawra, Tell Agrab, and Ashur. The impression of Harappan seals, the bull with the Harappan pictographic script, from Jokha, a site in southern Mesopotamia, is interesting since it is on a container in which cloth was wrapped. Sixty-five such pieces were also found in Lothal. In the Indo-Mesopotamian trade, Harappan carnelian and etched beads from a number of sites like Tell Asmer, Tape Gawra, Nittur, and Ur are worth a mention.

In Bahrain, six stone weights of the Harappan type and a dozen seals of the Persian Gulf type, have been found in one house, indicating a partnership between Harappan and Persian Gulf merchants. At Hammad, a Harappan seal with the engraving of a Harappan bull (in a charging stance), a peacock, and five pictographic letters have been found. Since the sequence of letters on the seal is similar to that on seals from Mohenjodaro, it is likely that the merchant in whose grave it was found originated from the Indus Valley. In Oman, at Rasal Junyaj, a Harappan seal and potsherd with four Harappan letters has been found. Pottery from Hili, particularly some of the painted motifs such as the pipal leaf and peacock, show Harappan influence and trade contacts as far back as the third millennium BC. At Shortugai on the Oxus in Afghanistan, a Harappan settlement has been discovered. The Badakshan mines of lapis-lazuli attracted the Harappans who exploited these and supplied the semi-precious stones for the bead industry at home and abroad.

The Harappans had contacts with Turkmania where Altyn Depe and Namazga Tepe have provided definite evidence of Harappan interaction in the form of a seal. Tepe Yahya has yielded a stamp of a Harappan seal impression on a potsherd.

The Persian Gulf seal from Lothal, a terracotta model of an Egyptian mummy and a Syrian head from Lothal, some West Asian hairpins from Chanhudaro, Harappa, Manda and Banawali, copper ingots from Mohenjodaro and Lothal, and the reserved slipped ware found at Surkotada, Lothal and other sites help show, although in a limited way, West Asia's trade contact with the Harappan civilization. Sumerian clay tablets from Ur prescribe the nature of contracts and the degree of risk undertaken by merchant financiers, sailors and captains, details about merchandise, and the amount of tax paid. These could as well have belonged to its contemporary Harappan settlements in their interaction with Sumer.

How this highly sophisticated urban civilization declined to die into obscurity until its discovery in the early twentieth century is a subject matter of another essay. Suffice to say that antecedents to Indian commercial links with the outside world date to this remote past.

The Silk Road and India

Tan Chung

Although the term was coined by a German scholar in the nineteenth century, in reality the Silk Road (or Silk Route) refers to the ancient intercontinental intercourse which was the result of Chinese initiative. Chinese scholars have conceived three such Silk Routes: the cross-border Eurasian road linking Europe with eastern China, the maritime route between Chinese ports and the eastern coast of Africa, and a southern Silk Road linking south-west China with South Asia and extending further west from eastern Indian cities and ports over land and sea. This essay deals with the Indian connections on this international highway.

From the early times of its existence, India was a seafaring country and a hub of international networking. Its contacts with China are testified to by references to China *(cina)*, Chinese dresses of silk *(cinamsuka)*, and bundles of Chinese silk *(cinapatta)* in the *Arthasastra*, composed by Kautilya in the fourth century BC. This ancient Indian text is the earliest reference to knowledge of foreign lands, and of Chinese silk. Indo-Chinese trade, over land and sea, can be documented from early Chinese records such as the official histories of the Han dynasty. The powerful Han emperor Wu (140–87 BC) sent Zhang Qian (also spelled Chang Ch'ien) to Central Asia to conclude alliances against the Hun tribes who had been engaged in prolonged hostility with China. To the surprise of Zhang Qian, he saw silk fabrics, the products of the south-western Chinese province Sichuan, in the market place of Daxia (probably Afghanistan or north of it). He was told that these fabrics were re-exported by Indian merchants to the hinterlands of Central Asia. This was the famous 'Chinese discovery of India' in the first century BC.

▼ Part of the Southern maritime Silk Road. As a phrase, the Silk Road has come to symbolize international trade and cultural contacts and Eurasian terrestrial and maritime explorations beginning 3000 years ago.

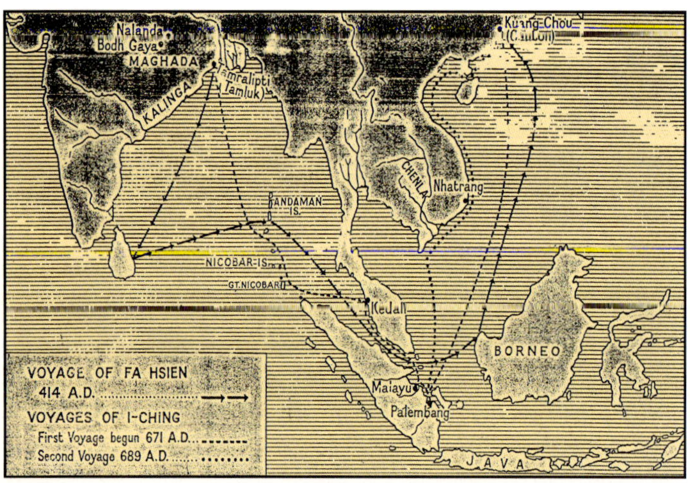

The same sources describe a distant country called 'Daqin' (denoting the Roman empire) that appeared to be connected with

India in two ways: the first was India's maritime trade links with 'Daqin', and the second, as recent research has shown, was the confusion with its identity. The ancient Chinese confused Europe with India. For instance, one ancient Chinese account mentioned that 'Daqin' was a country which produced elephant teeth and rhinocerous horns! However, we know that these commodities are not European, but Indian. Hence China's trade with 'Daqin' in ancient times must have touched India. And so when their records suggest that 'Daqin' was keenly interested in Chinese silk, it actually indicates a triangular route with the Chinese export reaching India, and then Europe via India. In AD 166, the Han court recorded the arrival of an embassy, probably sent by the Roman emperor, Marcus Aurelius Antonius. The deputation arrived by sea, landing close to what is now the Guangdong province in southern China, and then proceeded to the Han capital, Luoyang, overland where it presented the Chinese emperor with ivory, rhinoceros horn (a precious ingredient for Chinese medicine) and the shell of hawksbill turtles, all products of India.

Silk was in popular demand in the Roman empire and was a favourite of the Egyptian queen, Cleopatra. India, which was much closer to its centre of production, not only re-exported it to Europe, but also soon attempted to produce its own silk fibre and fabric. Professor Ji Xianlin, doyen of Indologists in China, theorizes that the word *kauseyan* mentioned in the *Arthasastra* denotes Indian silk, and hence conjectures that a sentence in the *Arthasastra*

▶ Chinese reconstruction of the Silk Road, painted in the eighth century on the southern wall of Cave 217, Mogao Grottoes, Dunhuang, Gansu, China.

▲ Chinese silks probably found their way to Europe via India, and among those who benefited from this was the Egyptian queen Cleopatra who, it is believed, was particularly partial to the fabric.

('Kauseyan cinapattasca cinabhumijah') is to be taken in the context of an Indian workshop with bundles of Indian and Chinese silk stacked together as early as the fourth century BC.

A Chinese historian has picked up an account of a sea route linking Guangzhou (Canton) with Sri Lanka from as early as the reign of Han Emperor Wu– and included it in a chapter of the *Han Shu* (the official annals of the Han dynasty). According to it, Chinese merchants could stay and trade at Huangzhi (also spelled Huang-chih) in what was probably a prosperous coastal Indian state in the couple of centuries both before and after Christ. Scholars are still undecided whether Huangzhi was located around Kancheepuram in Tamil Nadu, or in undivided Bengal, or in Orissa. The king of Huangzhi, states the record, had dispatched pearls, rhino horns (even a rhino) and other products to trade with Chinese rulers. Of course, he and his aristocrats were recipients of Chinese silk that the Han envoys carried with them to swap against foreign goods and to pay for their travelling expenses.

The starting point for the Silk Road was Luoyang in today's Henan province in eastern China. With a 3000–year-old history, and as the imperial capital of the Eastern Han dynasty (AD 25–220), Luoyang was a hub of international trade and cultural intercourse. Among the distinguished foreign visitors to Luoyang were two Indian Buddhist monks, Kasyapa Matenga and Dharmaraksa/ Dharmaratna who arrived there on horseback (riding white steeds) in the first century. Emperor Ming (AD 57–75) on whose invitation the two Indians had come, commemorated their arrival by building the Monastery of White Horses to inaugurate Buddhist evangelism in China.

During the period of Topa Wei (386–534), particularly after the imperial city of Luoyang became the capital in 493, there was a new high in booming trade with Buddhism flourishing. Luoyang had a very large number of shrines, each magnificent and lavishly decorated with treasures from abroad. Bodhidharma, a former prince from south India who turned immortal in China and became the patriarch of Chan/Zen Buddhism, was astonished by the marvels he saw in Luoyang in the second decade of the sixth century. These included a nine-storey high pagoda with a huge golden vase on top that was said to be visible from a distance of 50 km. It is said that when the pagoda caught fire in 534, a fire blazed in the sky for three months, and when it was finally razed to the ground, people at sea saw it reappear in the sky, proof of the linkage between Luoyang, Buddhism, and sea trade.

The Wei rulers enjoyed cruises on the imperial lake of Luoyang in boats shaped like birds' heads, similar to those depicted in Ajanta frescos and in sculptures of the Sanchi stupa. The Wei aristocrats prided themselves on their possessions — crystal bowls, agate

▼ Seated Sakyamuni, AD 509. Though 'silk' became the symbol for the Eurasian trade, its cultural contacts were no less significant, particularly in the case of the Sino-Indian segment of traffic.

cups, beryl bowls, jade pendants — all imports from India. They used Indian perfume which they turned into incense and sealed inside small brocade bags. When the Empress Dowager of Wei sent Monk Huisheng to India on pilgrimage in the winter of 518, she gave him 500 such bags to be distributed as gifts. The tradition of sealing Indian perfume in brocade bags has been in vogue in China ever since, symbolic of affection and love. Indian perfumes were so popular for their medicinal value that an Indian monk named Heluojie was said to have arrested an epidemic in Luoyang with the help of charms and scented water in AD 287.

The magnificent Buddhist resurgence in Luoyang during the sixth century was matched by what happened in Nanjing, south of the Yangtse river at the same time. China was then divided into the Northern and Southern dynasties, with Nanjing as the imperial city in south China. The Liang Emperor Wu (AD 503–549) was a rare Chinese ruler who had almost transformed himself into a Buddhist monk, and enjoyed the reputation of a Bodhisattva emperor. In his zeal to use every penny from the state treasury towards the creation of a Buddhist temple, he ordered a state ceremony to receive a sandalwood Buddha statue from Magadha (modern Bihar).

Shortly after the emperor was starved to death by a rebel, a Cambodian merchant ship from western India anchored at Nanjing with a precious cargo that was said to include a 20kg mirror made of beryl. It was rumoured that the mirror could turn coloured things invisible. Whatever the merit of such a fantastic invention, it is believed the Chinese ruler wanted to buy the marvellous mirror but his treasury could not produce the money, a billion coins, demanded by the Cambodian merchant.

The overland Silk Road was responsible for the creation of the term 'Serindia' for Central Asia. The first syllable is short for the ancient Greek and Latin terms 'Seres' or 'Serica' which describe China as a Country of Silk. Serindia thus reads Seres-India or Serica-India, or Sino-India according to modern parlance. As the term suggests, Central Asia was a confluence of Chinese and Indian cultures, besides being the overland gateway to China from where Chinese silk and other goods had to pass to reach Europe and India.

For India, Central Asia was as much a channel for the inflow of Chinese silk as that of the outflow of Indian goods (particularly jewels and perfume), culture, and art. From Kashgar to Dunhuang, this expanse of Serindia became midstream for Buddhist culture which ultimately inundated the hinterlands of China. Evidence of this flow is the spread of Buddhist cave art from Ajanta to Bamian (Afghanistan), then to Kizil in Kuca and to Turpan (Turfan), then Dunhuang and further afield to places in the Gansu province (Binglingsi, Majishan, etc.) to Longmen (at Luoyang) and Yungang

▼ Cave painting, Ajanta, showing maritime activities. Indian ships frequented the Pacific Ocean and the Chinese coasts, while large 'jewel-taking' Chinese ships were common in the Indian Ocean.

(at Datong, near the Mongolian border), forming a necklace of Buddhist art in Eurasia. Today, Chinese archaeologists are digging in Xinjiang where they have discovered a medieval Islamic cultural arena that buried ancient Buddhist relics underneath.

An enormous treasure of Buddhist texts of bark, leaf, silk or paper inscribed with ancient Indian, Central Asian and Chinese scripts has been discovered over the past hundred years that can throw light on the entire course of the movement of Buddhism from India to China via Central Asia — along the Silk Road. In this context, since Buddhadharma was more important than silk, it is equally relevant to give the Silk Road another name: Dharmaratna Marg (the road of the jewels of Buddhist truth).

Using the Silk Road as a guide, we can see the spread of silk and its production know-how from western China to Central Asia, and further to Europe and South Asia. A counter-flow was simultaneously formed, of cotton fabrics as well as cotton textile technology, from India to Central Asia and then to interior China. Historians believed that China started her cotton textile base at Songjiang in Jiangsu province on the eastern coast around the twelfth to thirteenth centuries, but relics of cotton fabrics from earlier times have been found along the Silk Road. It was the Silk Road that helped the imperial palaces of China get Indian presents of superior cotton fabrics. The Liang Emperor Wu was supposedly very fond of a hat and a quilt made of Indian cotton, discarding the hat only after using it for three years, and the quilt only after sleeping under it for two years. Chenghiz Khan (1206–70), and also Kublai Khan (1260–94) who was founder of China's Yuan dynasty, treasured their Indian cotton robes so much, they would continue to wear them even after they had been repeatedly patched. Kublai Khan especially sent a mission to Malabar in 1285 to bring back 10 Indian cotton garments. Obviously, therefore, while there was a Silk Road from China to India, there was also a Cotton Road from India to China.

As for sea routes, Indian ships frequented the Pacific Ocean and Chinese coasts in the first millennium after Christ, and there were Chinese ships (generally very large) in the Indian Ocean from the seventh to the seventeenth centuries. These were the 'jewel-taking ships' with which the merchants of Quilon and other south Indian ports did regular business. The Kerala ports, particularly Cochin and Quilon, lay on the main route between the far east and the far west. They saw a great number of famous travellers, such as Sulaiman (in the ninth century) and Marco Polo and Ibn Battuta (in the fourteenth century), on their way back from China to the western hemisphere. Marco Polo virtually retraced the contours of the enlarged triangle of the ancient Silk Road between Beijing, Kerala, and Venice. Interestingly, a sixteenth century Portuguese traveller, Hector de la Casa, called Quilon Koulang China. Mis'arbin Muhalhil, an Arab traveller well before the thirteenth century, reported that the king of Quilon was appointed from China. As today, trade and commerce could evidently blur national and ethnic boundaries. That Kerala enjoyed intimate trade relations with China can be seen from such accounts through the ages.

While there may be fanciful fables, there are also authentic accounts in Chinese literature of Chinese ships that would anchor at various ports along the entire western Indian coast for trade, to change into smaller ships to sail to the Red Sea. Chinese merchants sold silk, tea, porcelain, and other goods to India, and took from

▼ Xuan Zang returning from India to China accompanied by a white elephant gifted by King Harsha. Accounts by Chinese travellers provide important links in the commercial and cultural history between the two civilizations.

▲ Xuan Zang's pilgrimage to India, Cave 2, Eastern Thousand Buddha Grottoes, Western Xia, China. Such paintings testify to the importance India exercised in the trans-continental traffic of the time.

India pepper, perfume, jewels, even horses (mostly Indian imports from West Asia). A major event along the maritime Silk Road was a series of seven Chinese naval expeditions into the Indian Ocean led by Admiral Zheng He (or Cheng Ho) between 1405 and 1433. The fleet consisted of a giant flagship and a dozen smaller ships with several thousand sailors and other personnel on board. The admiral and his officials conducted diplomatic and trading activities with thirty-seven countries and regions along the Indian Ocean rim up to Hormuz in the Persian Gulf. Zheng He's entourage visited several Indian ports on a number of occasions, especially Bengal, Cochin, Calicut, Quilon, and Chola, and left valuable accounts about these places. Zheng He also contacted the Nair ruler of Calicut on behalf of the Ming emperor, and left behind a stone inscription.

The Silk Road has played an important role in building cultural and economic affinity between India and China. For over a century, silk fabrics and tea have been the pillars of Indian industry, commerce, and foreign trade. Interestingly, as Chinese cotton goods are cornering more and more international markets, making it unprofitable for the USA, Japan, and other developed countries to produce them any longer, China itself is a beneficiary of the Indian cotton industry. China also learnt from India how to make sugar from cane, how to decorate costumes and living spaces with beads, how to weave gold and silver threads into fabrics, how to enrich Chinese cuisine with black pepper, and how to make medicines from aromatic woods and tropical herbs. On the other hand, India learnt paper making and the use of the compass, in addition to sericulture and the silk industry, from China, and gained from such Chinese inventions as tea, gun-powder, and printing. Xuan Zang observed in the seventh century that Indians knew nothing of dates, chestnuts, and persimmons. Chestnuts and persimmons, along with tangerines, were probably introduced to India from China over the Silk Road. The list of migration of Indian plants to China is much longer and includes black pepper, lotus, pineapple, walnut, spinach, jackfruit, mango, sandalwood, turmeric, jasmine, to mention only the more common species. The Chinese not only got them from India but also borrowed their Indian names: in the case of sugar cane (Chinese name *zhe* from Sanskrit *ikus*), cotton (Chinese *gubei* from Sanskrit *karpasa*), sandalwood (Chinese *zhantan* from *chandan*), spinach (*boling* from *paling*), black pepper (*molizhi* from *mirachi*), and jasmine (*moli* from *mallika*). Indians, on the other hand, owe their cup of tea *(chai)*, peanut *(cheena-badam)*, cinnamon *(dalchini)* and their names to the Chinese. These and other symbols have immortalized the historical Silk Road for all times to come.

Commerce in South India in the Early Medieval Period

R. Champakalakshmi

South India witnessed two major periods of intense commercial activity before the establishment of the Vijayanagar empire in the fourteenth century when large-scale Western trading ventures began and ultimately led to European domination of South Asian commerce. These two periods, namely the early Historical and early Medieval, represent distinct patterns of trade, organizational structures, and institutions supporting commercial activities.

In the early Historical period (300 BC–AD 300), also known as the Sangam Age, commerce was mostly oriented towards sea trade and maritime contacts with Arab and Mediterranean countries, and with the South East Asian nations. Commercial enterprises in south India date from the mid-first millennium BC and developed significantly during the centuries immediately preceding and following the Christian era. However, the absence of a market principle, the lack of profit motive in the internal exchange (that operated on barter), and the prevalence of different levels of exchange show that organized commerce was not intrinsically linked with the local economies of the peninsular regions. Commerce was a major resource potential for the ruling elite (Chera, Chola, Pandya) which patronized poets and bards and kin groups through control over the movement of luxury/prestige goods in and out of major ports like Puhar (Kaverippumpattinam), the scene of the well-known Tamil epic, *Silappatikaram*. Hoards of Roman coins, indigenous merchant issues of punch-marked coins, and the Chera, Chola, and Pandya dynastic issues point to a fairly high degree of monetization in inter-regional commerce and the direct participation of the ruling elite in such exchange. The decline of maritime trade by third century AD thus had direct impact on the political fortunes of the rulers, leading to a political and economic vacuum in the following centuries till the rise of the Pallavas of Kancheepuram and the Pandyas of Madurai in the seventh century, and the Cholas of Thanjavur in ninth century AD.

▲ Chola gold coin from the reign of Kulottunga I (AD 1070-1120) weighing 3.988 gms, 3.8 cms diametre. On the obverse is a tiger surmounted by a sun, chouri bearer and crescent.

▲ Panels of a ninth century memorial stone in southern India, illustrates ships with banks of oars which would have carried India's seaborne trade with the rest of Asia.

In contrast, the commerce of the early Medieval period was the result of steady growth of agricultural activities, agrarian expansion and organization through institutional means like the *brahmadeya* and the temple as well as political patronage. Its principal features were a systematic development of markets and exchange centres serving peasant or agrarian regions called the *nadu/kurram* from the eighth century onwards, and networks emerging for both internal and external trade in the form of local market centres *(nagaram)* and itinerant trading organizations, supra-local in character, carrying merchandise both within the region and outside. The itinerant merchants were organized as corporate trading communities, popularly called guilds, with their own codes for interacting with local traders. Their operations covered not only the peninsula but also distant lands, their movement being facilitated by Chola rulers, whose maritime expeditions to the Malay region and Sumatra as well as embassies to China were intended to establish a trading presence for Tamil merchants in these countries. Sri Lanka, due to its geographical proximity to south India and location as an Indian Ocean island, was crucial as an entrepot in linking West Asian regions to South and South East Asian countries.

Under the aegis of the Pallavas and Pandyas, the *brahmadeya* and the temple became harbingers of advanced farming methods, such as improved irrigation technology and seasonal regulation of the cultivation process with the managerial skills of the Brahmins and the landowning Velalas. Such settlements within the peasant regions attracted trade and acquired marketing facilities in gradual phases under later Chola rule (AD 950–1279). Agricultural growth and the availability of a surplus became necessary preconditions for the important role that commerce and overseas trade played in the development of commodity production and exchange. In the pre-Chola period, commerce was principally oriented to the commercial needs of royal centres and points of inter-regional exchange, as for example Kancheepuram and Madurai as royal centres, and Mamallapuram and Korkai as ports of exchange as well as interior nodes at river crossings, the delta of the Kaveri, and meeting points of different eco-zones. No regular markets existed for the agrarian regions. The pattern, however, changed in the early Chola period (AD 850–985) as regular marketing facilities became a pressing need for every *nadu/kurram*, and this led to a spurt in commercial activity that wove the Tamil region into a larger network of inter-regional and overseas trade and to the evolution of a full-time trading community *(nagarattar)*. The *nagaram* emerged as a marketing centre and the *nagarattar*, members of the *nagaram*, came to refer to all Tamil merchants as a generic term

▼ Chola gold coins from the reign of Rajendra (AD 1012–44), weighing 4.07 gms, 1.9 cms diametre. On the obverse are figures. Monetized trade provided the impetus for organized commerce, though it came into standard use only in the fourteenth century. It was the Vijaynagar period that ushered in currency systems in which foreign and native coinages found constant use.

by which the Chettiyar community of the Nattukkottai region are known to this day.

The *nagaram* organization assumed the character of a local body maintaining local markets (*angadi* and *perangadi*), supervising the flow of goods, providing a regular link between the *nadus* and itinerant traders, bringing into existence a unified economic exchange and also acting as an agent of the Chola state synthesis along with the *brahmadeya*. Interestingly, most *nagarams* were named after the titles of Chola rulers, e.g. Mudikondacholapuram and Mummudicholapuram. In Thanjavur, there were two *nagarams* and four *angadis*. The proliferation of the *nagaram* kept pace with the expansion of Chola power. Its distribution shows remarkable increase during the eleventh and twelfth centuries, not only within Tamil country but also beyond its cultural frontiers, appearing in south Karnataka and the Andhra region over which Chola power extended in the eleventh century. The *nagaram* thus established crucial links in inter-regional commerce, the Tamils in the conquered regions holding positions of influence apart from merchants and artisans residing as far as Belgaum in Karnataka and Visakhapatnam in Andhra. Royal or political support was of great importance to the prosperity of the *nagaram*.

Under the Cholas, a further diversification of trading activities took place due to specialization in marketing and trade. Specialists like Sankarappadi *nagaram* and Sattum *parisatta nagaram* were suppliers of ghee and/or oil and textiles in specific localities and are referred to in local temple inscriptions. Seafaring merchants known as the Paraga *nagaram* are seen along trans-peninsular routes like the Kongu region (Coimbatore, Erode, and Salem districts). The Vaniya *nagaram* was a larger, supra-local organization of oil-mongers similar to the Teliki of Vijayawada in Andhra in the eleventh and twelfth centuries AD. Arab trade in horses was conducted principally through the western ports and the Kudirai Chettis of Kerala procured and transported them to the Tamil region and often acquired residential quarters in the Chola heartland and in the commercially important Pudukkottai region linking Chola land with Tondi on the eastern coast. Tondi and Kayalpattinam later became Pandyan ports for major imports like horses and aromatics.

The impetus to organized commerce came not only from revival of peninsular trade but from the revival and expansion of the South Asian trade from the tenth century AD involving South Asian and South East Asian kingdoms and China. The Ayyavole Five Hundred guild originated in Karnataka (Aihole in Hungund *taluk*, Bijapur district) in the eighth and ninth centuries and moved into the Tamil region of Pudukkottai as early as the ninth century. No direct

▼ Nataraj or dancing Shiva, Chola bronze, Tanjore. The measure of the wealth commanded in commercial centres often manifested in temples built to honour the gods, and to advance artisanal activities. Mercantile guilds commemorated the establishment of trading centres with Hindu temples and their attendant deities. Bronze, particularly, was a speciality of the Chola age.

parallels can be seen with the medieval European guilds, the Hang of China in the Sung and Yuan times, or the Karimi of Egypt under the Caliphate, yet in their inscriptional records they are described as *samayam*, meaning a convention or organization born out of agreement or contract, with a code of conduct called *bananju dharma* or convention of rules and regulations for traders *(banajiga)*. Conspicuous references to the Ayyavole or Ainnurruvar (in the Tamil region), Valanjiyar (in Sri Lanka) and Nanadesi indicate that this was a large organization with several interchangeable names, each term representing an adjective describing their character as belonging to a particular region and as militant. The term Five Hundred became a conventional numerical term to denote a forum for commerce, and at least forty-six different groups have been identified at various centres and in different contexts. The heterogenous composition of this corporate organization shows that its members came from different castes and religious affiliations, including Brahmins and Jains.

The spatial and chronological distribution of the Ainnurruvar inscriptions show the largest concentration in the Pudukkottai region and along the major trade routes linking Tamil country with Karnataka, Kerala, and Andhra, and overseas in Sri Lanka, the Malaysian peninsula, and Sumatra. Mutual benefit rather than just political control over trade appeared to be the motivating force behind Chola interest in fostering merchant activity in various regions. According to the *Chulavamsa*, a Sri Lankan horse dealer who acted as an agent for the Cholas was able to bring information on the turmoil in Sri Lanka, based on which an invasion was ordered. Northern Sri Lanka remained under Chola sway till 1070 and facilitated the movement of itinerant trade. Under the Cholas, trade missions were sent to China, and the port of Nagappattinam developed. Tamil traders established trading networks and built temples in Takua Pa (the Malay peninsula), Pagan (Burma), and in Canton and Chu'an Chou (Zayton) in China. Although Chinese annals label all trade missions as tribute missions from the south Indian and South East Asian countries, it is evident that under the Cholas, itinerant traders established their presence in all major centres of Asian commerce, especially in the east.

Other merchant organizations like the Manigramam and Anjuvannam are also known from the ninth century onwards. The Manigramam was a Tamil merchant organization operating within specific regions, a descendant of the early traders called Vanikagrama. It re-emerged as an organized trading group under the early Cholas in Uraiyur and Kodumbalur. Its members retained affiliations with their agricultural background and branched out into the trading profession through controlling the local exchange nexus and participating in overseas trade in their collective capacity. The Manigramam moved to the Pudukkottai region at the invitation of Pandya rulers.

Another body of merchants, the Anjuvannam (Anjuman) represented an organization of foreign merchants (Jews, Arabs, Muslims and Christians) and began commercial activities on the west coast (Kerala) in the eighth and ninth centuries. By the eleventh century it had spread to other coastal areas of south India. The merchants acquired settlements on the west coast. They were often accompanied by missionaries or were themselves agents of proselytization, especially among the Jewish and Christian organizations. Records of grants to such organizations carry signatures in Arabic, Hebrew and Pahlavi. They were given rights over the customs *(ulgu)* and weightment charges *(tulakkuli)*, and their religious institutions also derived revenue from trade. The Anjuvannam organization survived well into the fifteenth century in south Kanara, as in the case of the Hanjamana representing Persian traders.

In the thirteenth and fourteenth centuries there was phenomenal increase in the activities of the itinerant traders, the Five Hundred, with a tendency to expand its sphere of influence while relying less on royal support and patronage. At this stage the guild acted jointly with other large supra-local organizations in making gifts to temples, and in exercising joint authority to levy and grant cesses and tolls to the local temples on merchandise passing through the region. In a predominantly agrarian society,

The Guardian of Wealth

It is Lakshmi, the goddess of wealth, who is propitiated by most Indians, and an annual festival, Diwali, is dedicated to please her. Kuber, on the other hand, is ignored, for he is only the guardian of wealth, the treasurer of the gods. Since he cannot multiply money, most Indians are ignorant about this mythical being's appearance. Which may be just as well too, for Kuber could not stand up to too much scrutiny. His dwarf-like, pot-bellied figure belies his status as the god of Yakshas or savage beings. One of the brothers of the demon king Ravana, Kuber has his palace in the Himalayas from where he watches over the earth's storehouse of gold, silver, pearls, precious stones and other treasures.

Kuber's vehicle is Pushpak, the flying chariot, and he is sometimes depicted with three, instead of two, legs, especially when in the seated posture. He may be shown with two to four hands, and his attributes are a bag of money, a bowl, a mace and a vase. As befits the celestial treasurer, his body is often covered with ornaments and large jewels, missing in this picture.

▲ Inscriptions and plaques of south Indian rulers. These bear testimony to developed literary and commercial skills of rulers and merchants of the south. Fragment of an inscription of Rajasimha Pallava *(top)* from Kancheepuram, seventh century, in Grantha script. Donation plaque of Chalukya ruler, Pulakesin, *(middle)* Kopparam, seventh century, in Kannada script. Ponduru donation plaque *(above)* bearing the royal emblem, the boar, tenth century in Telugu, script.

merchant bodies had to seek legitimization through association with the Chittirameli, an organization of agriculturists. Dominant agricultural organizations, jointly mentioned in the guild's inscriptions, evidently had commercial transactions with the Ayyavole and exchanged their produce for exotic and non-agricultural commodities from distant lands brought to south India by merchants. Both organizations adopted impressive eulogies and emblems. In all such records, the Chittirameli is given pride of place for the itinerant merchants had no authority to levy or grant tolls and cesses independently. In the assignment of brokerage and monopolies to individuals and groups of traders on specific items of trade, the Five Hundred acted jointly with the local *nadu, nagaram,* and Chittirameli. The growing needs of urban settlements enhanced the influence of the agricultural classes, for only powerful peasant groups could mobilize grain and other products for supply to itinerant traders at centres of collection and distribution.

Close links developed between crafts and artisanal groups like weavers and the Ayyavole or Ainnurruvar for the production and marketing of textiles. Some weavers even took to trade by joining the Ayyavole. The Chilai Chettis from the Tamil region (Kancheepuram and Dharmapuri) are referred to in inscriptions, and the largest craft organization set up by the fourteenth century was that of weavers whose Mahanadu organization had its headquarters in Kancheepuram, south India's most ancient textile centre. Kancheepuram was a centre for different weaver communities such as the Saliya (Valankai caste) and the Kaikkola (Itankai caste), the former ranking higher in the social hierarchy and patronized by the Cholas as weavers of royal garments. Craft production was more intensive in the Kongu region and increased during the twelfth to fourteenth centuries. Large-scale artisanal activity and participation in civic duties meant that special privileges were conferred on artisans under the Cholas and Pandyas. Merchants granted certain privileges to the Right and Left Hand castes, pointing to the interdependence of these two sections of the commercial world, especially in areas like the Kongu region where merchants assumed control or were given control and management of temples by royal family. All emergent social and economic groups in south India sought legitimization through the temple organization as producers of various consumer goods for the temple or as service groups assigned land for cultivation in return for the supply of goods. Merchants were a powerful and economically influential force, and the volume of their grants to temples was next in value only to that of royalty and the landed Velalas.

▼ Necklace and earings, Gold, south India, second century BC. Merchants of south India traversed long distances carrying amongst other items, jewellery, which was also used to adorn temple deities. The tradition of this craft in south India had ancient roots as is apparent from this picture.

Impressive lists of countries traversed by merchants are found in the standard eulogy covering regions like Persia, north India, Nepal, the Malay peninsula, and Cambodia. Long lists of commodities are mentioned in the guild's inscriptions, notable among which are lists in Shikarpur (Shimoga district, Karnataka) and Piranmalai (Ramanathapuram district, Tamil Nadu). The Shikarpur inscription says that merchants 'travelled by land routes, water routes, covering six continents, with superior elephants, well bred horses, large sapphires, moonstones, pearls, rubies, diamonds, lapis-lazuli, onyx, topaz, carbuncles, myrobalan, sandal, camphor, musk and saffron ... selling [them] wholesale or hawking [them] about on their shoulders'. Trading helped to fill the royal treasury with gold and so the royal family became great consumers of luxury items. Temples were equally important consumers of precious stones (temple jewels), aromatics (incense), sandal, and camphor. The *matha* attached to temples from the twelfth century on, and hospitals and educational institutions established by royal grants in temples, must have created continuing demand for herbal medicinal plants used in ayurveda.

The imports mentioned in the Piranmalai record are slightly different and include aloewood, sandalwood, silk, rose-water, camphor oil, perfume, elephants, and horses. These lists generally include both *eru sattu* (exports) and *irangu sattu* (imports). Most of the imports are from South East Asia, with the exception of horses which came from Arabia. Horses were imported through the west coast and even under Vijayanagar, when the Portuguese competed with Arabs and Persians, horses were in such great demand among rulers that they were paid for whether they reached their destination alive or dead. Silk came from China and elephants from Burma to the ports of Quilon, Kayalpattinam, Nagappattinam, and Devipattinam. Silk cultivation later became a major craft in Karnataka and silk weaving in Kancheepuram. Since south India dealt in both transit and terminal trade, it had facilities at ports like Tondi for collection, stocking, and distribution for local consumption as well as onward trade. An inscription at Tondi dated 1269, refers to a meeting of the Anjuvannam, Manigramam, Samanta Pandasalis, and others. The Samanta Pandasalis were probably stockists of commodities. Provision stores probably existed at such

▲▶ Chola temple, Dharasuram. Organized trade during this period used paddy as the basis for exchange even though monetization was prevalent. The temple acted as an institution of agrarian integration and a focus of commercial and educational activities.

centres, while fortified settlements were established as toll collecting centres. Protected mercantile towns were established at several points on trade routes and were either fortified as in Ukkirankottai in Tirunelveli district, or were protected by mercenaries, as in Kattur near Chennai under a royal charter in the eleventh century.

Among the items of trade listed in Piranmalai, agricultural products such as paddy, pulses, betelnuts and leaves, and raw materials like cotton, and salt, metals like copper, zinc, lead, and iron (steel was an Indian export) figure prominently . Tin came from South East Asia and was in heavy demand for the making of the reputed Chola bronze images of temple deities, a craft at which Chola artisans excelled. Many of the agricultural items listed were meant for intra-regional trade and local consumption in urban centres, while silk and cotton yarn were supplied to the weaving communities.

Organized commerce in the Chola and Pandya periods included barter since monetization was limited, particularly in the Tamil region up to the fourteenth century when the Vijayanagar period ushered in important changes in the degree of monetization with regular currency systems, and with foreign and native coinages finding constant use. Under the Cholas, equivalence was established on the basis of goods and exigencies of supply and demand, though paddy appears to have been the overall basis of an exchange system. Coins were used at various levels by traders, but the Chola currency was 'not based on any uniform group of coins with fixed ratios between different denominations and metals', even though they were in regular use from the late tenth century on in urban centres. Interest rates were calculated in kind, particularly paddy, and occasionally money. This became a conspicuous feature under Kulottunga I (AD 1070–1118), who issued coins of greater merit from the commercial point of view, encouraged craft production, particularly weaving, due to growing demand for south Indian textiles, and abolished tolls to facilitate trade. Prices depended on supply and demand, but Manigramam and *nagaram* merchants were often given the rights to fix prices and collect levies, as at the Kerala port of Quilon in the ninth to tenth centuries, while foreign merchants were granted settlements with their own churches (Jewish and Christian) and mosques.

Commerce in south India after the thirteenth century underwent important shifts, the hub of the trading network shifting westwards to Cairo (Fustat) and the Red Sea, the Fatimid Caliphate, Jewish and Muslim merchants taking over a large part of the trade movement with the west coast of south India. The Jewish traders of the Geniza records carried on the most flourishing trade in spices (pepper) and aromatics and procured other goods

from South East Asia through Indian merchants who continued to be more directly involved in the eastern circuit. Some leading Muslim traders received special privileges from the later Pandyas and took over control of coastal towns on the east, such as Devipattinam, where they even began to direct the eastern trade with the South East Asian countries. Fatimid coins in south India, especially in the Pandya region, have been found in hoards of considerable value. Similar hoards of Chinese coins found in the Thanjavur district point to the flow of metallic currency from China in return for south Indian goods, while evidence of south Indian coins reaching other countries is more difficult to find. Arab coins, gold dinars, had earlier been in use along with Pandya dynasty issues that spanned a period from the Sangam Age right up to the seventeenth century. New currencies came into use in northern Tamil Nadu under chieftains who became independent during the Chola decline in the thirteenth century and encouraged the movement of trade to the northern parts of Tamil Nadu by extending special concessions. Chinese trade with south India also shifted to the west coast. Traders from Kerala, acting as intermediaries, helped shift trade to eastern towns like Kancheepuram, and money as a medium of exchange acquired greater salience. In the thirteenth and fourteenth centuries, Kancheepuram became a point of convergence for trade from different regions.

Ancient and Early Medieval Indian Commerce and Trade

B. D. Chattopadhyaya

The mid-first millennium BC reveals a fascinating world in transition: after centuries of decay, organized commerce and urbanism were again becoming hallmarks of social change. This was the period when the Buddha and Mahavira lived in the middle Ganga valley. The landscape of the region and of its peripheries consisted largely of forests and villages *(grama)*, but the Buddha's extensive itinerations also took him through a number of market centres, and he often stayed near the big cities *(mahanagaras)* of his time. Champa, Rajagriha, and Vaishali in Bihar; Varanasi, Sravasti and Kausambi in Uttar Pradesh; Ujjaini in Malwa in Madhya Pradesh; Takshasila or Taxila near Islamabad in Pakistan are some of the important cities *(nagaras)* referred to in texts which tell us about the Buddha and his teachings; they are also cities which archaeologists have located and excavated. If villages produced agricultural and dairy resources, and forests supplied varieties of products like meat, honey, and ivory, *nigamas* (market places) and *nagaras* were where goods were exchanged; they were also points that connected one area with another.

It is these early Buddhist texts that contain the first references to different types of traders and bankers like the *vanik*, *sreshthi*, and *sarthavaha*. A major merchant of the time, Anathapindika became fabulously wealthy through banking and organizing caravan trade for transportation of goods over long distances. He lived in the city of Sravasti near modern Gorakhpur; it is said he purchased a park that he wanted to gift the Buddha, its price paid in the number of coins required to cover its extent.

Archaeological evidence and coin hoards found in different parts of the subcontinent reveal that along with early cities, the introduction of metallic money, in silver and copper, considerably facilitated the movement and exchange of varieties of goods in the market place. The *vaniks*, *sreshthis*, and *sarthavahas* changed the pattern of exchange by taking it beyond the level of barter; trade was now of various kinds and covered a wide range of items. There

were *apanas* or shops selling food items in the market place in a city; and there was the caravan trade financed by *sreshthis* to transport luxury items for the elite over long distances. The *sarthavahas* were leaders of such caravans, and the texts mention journeys being undertaken across difficult terrain to Takshasila in the north-west from Varanasi or Sravasti.

Literature and archaeology give us some idea of the goods that formed part of these long-distance transactions: pottery, ivory, precious metals and stones, glass, textiles among them. The route networks that connected different points in north-western, northern and eastern India came to be collectively called *uttarapatha* or the northern route; this was distinct from *dakshinapatha* or the southern route which, at this time, probably reached down to Pratishthana or Paithan on the Godavari.

A simple exchange in which different goods moved from one community to another existed simultaneously with a somewhat more complex pattern of trade during the Buddha's time. Even in a simple form of exchange, there could be a wide variety of goods: salt, dried fish, honey, metal, precious stones, cowrie shells, etc. This nature of exchange between communities is beautifully portrayed in an ancient Tamil poem, *Porunarattrapadai*:

> Those selling honey and roots eatable
> Exchange them for the fish's fat and wine
> They barter sugarcane and roasted rice
> For toddy and deer-flesh. The fisherfolk
> Sing hillmen's songs, while hillmen garlands wear
> Of fragrant blooms that glow along the coast.

Organized commerce was, nevertheless, expanding into newer areas, the result of the initiatives of traders looking for profit-yielding articles of trade, and through royal conquests motivated by their revenue potential. Kautilya, who acted as chief minister and counsellor to Chandragupta, the founder of the Mauryan empire (from the close of the fourth to the beginning of the second century BC) said this of the comparative advantages of northern and southern routes:

> According to teachers, the route to the Himalayas is preferable to the southern route, for the commodities of elephants, horses, perfumes, ivory, skins, silver, and gold are of very high value. No, says Kautilya. With the exception of such commodities as blankets, skins, and horses, all these commodities plus such commodities as conch-shells, diamonds, rubies, pearls, and gold are more plentiful on the southern route.

▲ Gold coin, obverse and reverse, from the Kushan period, first century AD. Coin hoards found in different parts of the subcontinent reveal that the exchange of goods was considerably facilitated with the introduction of metallic money.

◀ Taxila in the north west region of the Indian subcontinent was a highly developed centre of learning and intense commercial activity. The city witnessed the emergence and influence of Buddhism.

Even though short-lived, the Mauryan empire, extending from Afghanistan to the southern limits of the Deccan, generated an awareness regarding the resources of different regions, and of their

▼ Torana slab from Mathura. The depiction of the cart flanked by horsemen is indicative of the transportation of goods and men over long distances. It was necessary to arrange protection for such caravans.

potential for trade. In cities like the Mauryan capital Pataliputra (modern Patna), and elsewhere, brisk trade called for measures to ensure optimum revenue for the state. The concerned bureaucracy was expected to keep a sharp eye on areas in which corrupt practices, such as those relating to weights and measures and the manufacture of coins, could become rampant. Emperor Ashoka, following the teachings of the Buddha, advised his subjects to exercise moderation in spending and saving — a practice viewed as capable of creating a congenial commercial ethos.

By the early centuries of the Christian era, Indian merchants were in contact with crucial areas of contemporary international trade. Across the north-west borders, movements of such ethnic groups as the eastern Greeks, Parthians, Sakas, and Kushanas opened up western and Central Asia on an unprecedented scale. Movements across the sea facilitated coastal trade; this received a further boost from historical changes that were taking place in the peninsula. Indian merchants participated, along the ancient *uttarapatha* and across Afghanistan and Central Asia, in the trade in silk (mentioned in Indian texts as *chinapatta* and *chinamshuka*) which connected the Chinese empire in the east and the Roman empire in the west. In the first century and beyond, the silk trade was diverted through the lower Indus region and the Gujarat coast, and the rich empire of the Kushanas (circa first to third centuries), extending from Central Asia to the Ganga valley, derived immense profit from this trade.

In the peninsula, a growing demand for certain varieties of Indian goods, in combination with the knowledge of the south-west monsoon winds, facilitated direct sailing between the Red Sea, across the Arabian Sea, and the coastal regions of India. Indian literature and several inscriptions of this period mention the *Yavanas,* a term which, in that period, referred to different categories of people from the Graeco-Roman or Hellenistic world and from West Asia. Among the patrons of religious shrines, such as the Buddhist cave monasteries constructed along the Western Ghats by rulers, merchants and others, were also the *Yavanas.* In Indian texts, *Yavanas* are mentioned as coming to Indian ports in ships laden with gold in search of spices and other valuables. [A

fascinating first century AD Greek text, *The Periplus of the Erythraean Sea,* written by an anonymous sailor, provides details about items traded in port towns along the Indian coast.] Some of the major ports then included Bharuch on the Gujarat coast, Sopara on the Konkan coast, Muziris on the Malabar coast, and Kaverippattinam on the Coromandel coast. Exports from the peninsula included pepper, ginger, cardamom, clove, and other spices; textiles of different varieties; faunal items like hide, ivory, live monkeys and peacocks; other forest items like aloe, sandal, and tea; and such significant items as beryl and pearl. [That this oceanic trade was on a significant scale, particularly for the peninsula in the early Historical period, is suggested by finds of Roman amphoras and other wares and their imitations, but more especially from hoards of Roman gold and silver coins.]

To the north of the Coromandel and Andhra coasts, Dantapura in Orissa and Tamralipti, close to the Bhagirathi estuary in lower Bengal, had also emerged as major ports by this time, particularly as points of embarkation for voyages along the coast and to south-eastern countries. Early Indian stories, like the Jatakas, have a recurring motif of Indian merchants and sailors undertaking voyages to Suvarnabhumi (literally, land of gold), Suvarnadvipa (island of gold) and other trans-oceanic countries, often becoming victims of shipwrecks . This motif can also be spotted in early works of art, sculpture, and painting, while several coins and sealings from the coastal regions also portray it.

Indian merchants formed associations or guild-like organizations for their operations, both at the local level and for long distance trading. Terms like *sreni* and *nigama* were used to refer to such associations, and they sometimes minted their own coins; while the term *srenibala* may indicate the existence of armed retainers for the safety of merchants and their goods. How organized and prosperous the guilds could be is suggested by their seals. The ancient city of Vaishali in north Bihar has yielded a large number of seals, along with those of the city administration, from the Gupta period (fourth to sixth centuries AD). Inscriptions of this period from north Bengal show that *nagara-sreshthi* and *sarthavaha,* both representing the merchant community, were closely associated with the administration of towns in that region.

By the Gupta period, the codification of transactional procedures in the commercial sphere became noticeable. The concept of *virddhi* (literally, increase), referring to returns on loan or investment, was in practice in the Buddha's time, but later developments must have induced systematic thinking on various aspects of transaction in different Smriti or Dharmasastra texts such as those attributed to Manu, Yajnavalkya, and Narada. For example, the classification of loans on the basis of security;

▲ Gold coin, obverse and reverse, from the Gupta period issued during the reign of Chandragupta II (AD 385-414).

Unorganized Bazaars

The concept of trading or bartering goods has existed for millennia in India but what is interesting is that the tradition has continued in several regions to date. While at its most basic or root level, the village *haat* or market place continues to exist, the medium of exchange, by and large, is money. However, barter is alive and flourishing in ancient and medieval market places where, on such occasions as annual *melas* (fairs), goods, cattle, or agricultural produce may be exchanged against each other. The measure of need, therefore, scores over currency.

Of course, money may be used too, and sometimes forms a simultaneous form of exchange or trade.

These fairs have continued for centuries together, and besides trading zones, form a layer of social interaction that combines religion in the nature of pilgrimage with social correspondence (matrimonial alliances and meetings are fixed) in a way of life that has held true for the Indian subcontinent for thousands of years. While a number of fairs in Rajasthan reflect this (the Pushkar and Nagaur camel fairs among them), Sonepur's cattle fair in Bihar is billed as the largest such event in the world.

differentiated computation of interest rates dependent on a large number of variables; the role of witnesses in transactions between creditors and debtors all figure in the provisions that authors of the Dharmasastras considered relevant.

It is held by some historians that Indian commerce suffered a major setback, particularly from the close of the Gupta period (end fifth to early sixth centuries AD) in the wake of overall decline in the economy. Large cities like Takshasila, Kausambi, Pataliputra, and others went into decline; and the superbly executed gold coins of the Guptas failed to create a legacy, money circulation in general having become sluggish. Available evidence does suggest that the

(previous page):

◀ Panel from Sun Temple, Konark, Orissa, AD 1240 . The giraffe in the picture indicates a trade link between India and Africa.

extensive commercial network of the earlier centuries suffered a breakdown for a few centuries, but the image of a completely ruralized, self-sufficient economy does not accord with the pattern of widespread changes evident from the eighth to ninth centuries onwards.

Initially, there was agrarian expansion on an unprecedented scale throughout the subcontinent, intensifying the mobilization of agrarian resources and the process of stratification of rural society, and thus creating more space for commercial exchange. Inscriptions of the period refer to *hatta, mandapika* (Hindi *mandi*), *pentha, pattana, pura* — all perhaps of the nature of earlier *nigama*s or market centres, but more widespread. Next, although local commerce intersected with long-distance commerce as in earlier times, there were perhaps significant regional variations now in the ways commercial enterprises were organized. The evidence from peninsular India, till at least the fourteenth century, suggests the growing importance of large merchant associations for the mobilization of goods of an astonishingly wide range, originating from disparate sources. Inscriptions refer to guilds like the Ayyavole and Manigramam, and to the goods handled by them. The presence of these guilds in countries like Thailand and Sumatra, the overseas campaigns of the early Cholas of Tamil Nadu, and references to Indian commodities and merchants in the Jewish Geniza records from Cairo, all point to the key position of the peninsula in the Indian Ocean trade that extended from Europe, West Asia, north Africa to China. The guilds were powerful enough to issue their own *prasasti*s (eulogies), guard their goods by using mercenaries and protected settlements and dealt in commodities ranging from cereals, spices and textiles to horses, elephants and precious stones.

Inscriptions from the western coast refer to Tajikas (Arabs) and probably the Parsis. By the thirteenth century, there were several Arab settlements involved in trade. In contrast to the peninsula, in areas like Gujarat and Rajasthan, control over trade was wielded by elite merchant families. Stories about the fabulous wealth they acquired in undertaking oceanic voyages from Cambay, Bharuch, and other points to Simhala, and Hormuz in West Asia, are vividly recounted in Jain texts. The Pragvata family, and especially two brothers, Vastupala and Tejahpala, were prominent figures. They were ministers to the Gujarat kings, patronized the construction of such famous shrines as the Dilwara temple of Rajasthan, and were prominent subjects of Jain narrative texts. A similar figure was their contemporary, Jagadu, whose ships sailed to Hormuz and whose pious deeds too are recorded in Jain texts. In areas like Delhi, Haryana, and Punjab, individuals from different merchant castes figure in records dating to the period of the Delhi Sultanate.

▲ Terracotta temple sculpture depicting a boat scene, Bengal. Traders undertook long sea journeys, and were often guaranteed protection for their goods.

Though the society was predominantly agrarian, the growing complexity of commerce, the heterogeneity of participants in it and the constant threat of fraudulent practices must have led to the formation of new mechanisms and institutions to safeguard commerce in pre-Sultanate and Sultanate times. Sources such as the *Lekhapaddhati* (manual for writing), compiled after the fourteenth century, reveal for the first time the use of *hundika* (*hundi* or bill of exchange) which facilitated transactions. The *Dravya-pariksha* (examination of objects), written in 1318 by Thakur Pheru, mint master of Sultans Alauddin Khalji and Mubarak Shah, suggests the meticulousness with which items connected with commerce were expected to be assessed.

The state was, as before, aware of the revenue potential of trade, an enterprise that, in fact, merited protection. This concern is excellently reflected in a mid-thirteenth century inscription of a Kakatiya king, Ganapati, from Motupalli in Andhra:

> By this glorious maharaja Ganapatideva the following edict assuring safety has been granted to traders by sea starting for and arriving from all continents, islands, foreign countries and cities.
> Formerly kings used to take away by force the whole cargo, viz., gold, elephants, horses, gems etc., carried by ships and vessels, which, after they had started from one country for another, were attacked by storms, wrecked and thrown on shore.
> But, we out of mercy for the sake of glory and merit, are granting everything besides the fixed duty to those who have incurred the great risk of sea voyage with the thought that wealth is more valuable than even life.

Wealth, generated by trade, was to ignite the imagination of society in general as well; the society's perception of the relative merits of different sources of wealth seems to be conveyed very well by the unknown poet who wrote:

> Goddess of fortune resides in commerce; only half of that fortune can be earned through agriculture; royal service yields only half [of what can be earned from agriculture], and nothing comes from begging.

Pre-Colonial Links with China, Central and West Asia

A. Rahman

In Asia, broadly three cultural zones can be identified, namely the Egyptian, Greek, Phoenician, and Babylonian, which later came to be termed the Arab area (minus the Greek), the Indian, Central Asia area, and the Chinese culture area. In their interaction, Central Asia lay at the crossroads and India played a significant role in the resultant exchange.

Paper Technology

Paper played a major role in the preservation of knowledge and in its dissemination and all accounts about its origin point towards China. According to one report, paper came into India from China via Nepal between the seventh and ninth centuries AD, where it found extensive market in centres such as Patna, Janakpur, Darbhanga, Poorneya, Govindganj, Aliganj, Gorakhpur, Tulsipur, and Bahrampur.

In Islamic countries, knowledge of the technology of manufacturing paper came in AD 751 following a battle between Arab and Chinese forces in which the Chinese were defeated. The Arabs captured skilled Chinese paper manufacturers and began to produce paper at Samarkand. From there it spread to Baghdad and other parts of the Islamic world, as well as to Kashmir, and later major production centres began in north and south India.

▼ Leather cover on a fifteenth century Quran, Central Asia. Printing was known in the Islamic culture since the seventh century but did not come into vogue till much later. In India, traces of the printing process on silk and paper was developed by Buddhist monks.

Printing

In India, we can trace the beginning of the process with the printing of images of the Buddha on silk and on paper, developed by Buddhist monks. Copies of manuscripts were made by first writing on stone and then pressing paper over it. The technique of block printing was inculcated into the printing process by the Chinese. A Chinese monk, in India from about AD 671 on, impressed images of the Buddha on silk and paper. It used the technique adopted from carved blocks for printing on cloth. Later, the technique was developed for carving whole pages on wooden blocks and making books. This development took place under the

Tang dynasty in the Sichuan province which was a major paper manufacturing centre in AD 800.

From the ninth century on, documents and scriptures were regularly being printed but it is surprising that neither in India nor in the Islamic culture area, did printing come into vogue. This, in spite of the availability of paper manuscripts being written at the time. There may have been cultural and social reasons for this lack of development, and it may also have been connected with the state's policy of limiting education and knowledge to a privileged few. In the thirteenth century, Korea adopted metal type printing, and this was followed soon after by China. In south India, the Portuguese in Goa had begun to print Tamil scripts in 1575, but there was no local interest in metal type. This lack of interest was also evident in north India, even though printed books from Europe had now begun to be available.

Hydraulic Engineering

The development of hydraulic engineering was connected with the importance of agriculture in earlier societies. Such developments were only possible under a centralized government that could undertake the construction of large canals and dams. Earlier, smaller canals served localized purposes. In reality, the large-scale development of canals and dams was the result of enlargement of earlier constructions and mud embankments of tanks and small canals.

The technology of canal and dam construction came from China from where it moved to Iran and other Islamic culture areas. Roman engineering too had its impact in this field. Following the defeat of the Roman army, the expertise of its soldiers was employed in the construction of local canals and dams.

A significant development in Iran was that of the *qanat*. Iran's sway over north-west India meant it was introduced in this region as well as in Baluchistan and Central Asia. India's contribution, in turn, was the construction of water raising devices, later adopted by the Chinese. The Persian wheel was one such device, while in the case of Fatehpur Sikri there are three level systems of raising water from ground level. A similar, if simpler, system was found in Vijayanagar in south India.

Aurangabad has the remains of a *panchakki* (watermill) built in the eighteenth century by Sufi saint, Mahmud Shah Musafir. It was attached to a *madrassa* and used for grinding corn for the students. The water for running the *panchakki* was brought through a covered canal from a spring at the top of the mountain. The canal that supplied water to the city was itself a masterpiece of engineering. The construction of canals was revived with the arrival of a Central Asian leadership in India, and a number of projects

▼ Buland Darwaza, Fatehpur Sikri. Fountains and water channels in palaces and tombs in India indicate a high degree of hydraulic engineering skills, and showed the influence of Persia, Central Asia and China, all of whom India had trading relations with.

▼ This cannon, mounted at Jaigarh Fort, above Jaipur, is believed to be among the largest in the world. While weapons were imported from other countries, the quality of Indian steel was prized even outside the country for its quality. The Mughal diaries describe the casting of cannons in detail.

(Facing page):

▲ Ear pendants, and bracelet, first century AD, Taxila.

▼ The Buddha with a jewelled crown, before he fled from court. Indian jewellery making was of a very high order, and involved an interface with other cultures.

taken up. Firoz Shah built a canal starting from the foothills, passing through various cities before joining up with the Ghaggar river. Emperor Shah Jehan's vazir, Ali Mardan Khan, built a number of canals: one of these ran from Karnal to Delhi, and another from Badshah Mahal via Saharanpur to Delhi. In south India, an elaborate canal system off the Cauvery river arose, similar to one developed earlier in Sri Lanka.

Another point of interaction between Persia, Central Asia, China and India was in the construction of fountains and water channels and *hammams* in palaces. These systems are to be found in all the countries of this region. In north India, in all probability, they were built by local craftsmen under the supervision of experts brought from Iran or Central Asia. At its most basic, these reflected the living style and aesthetics of the people in these areas. Since most palaces were located at higher levels, an elementary feature was raising all basic water supplies from ground level.

Metal Crafts

Metal crafts represented the first revolution when early societies started making objects such as agricultural tools, weapons of war, jewellery, coins and images. India's wealth in various ores, in particular copper, tin, silver, and lead, made ample use of these.

Metal technology in India dates to the Indus Valley Civilization when the casting and forging of pots, pans, bowls, cups, and dishes was in practice. The next stage of development occurred in Mongolia, in the upper Paleolithic period, with the evolution of the blade technology for shaping knives. In Turkmenistan, during the fourth and third millenniums BC, there were regular metal workshops for making various objects.

Metallurgical processes and technology of a higher order became known in India around 1000 BC, but major developments took place only around 500–400 BC. There is a reference to 'obelisks and temples of Porplegry and Syemite with hieroglyphics ... made of Indian steel'. India became renowned for making what came to be known as Damascus steel, later used in making swords. The high carbon steel was first produced near Hyderabad as early as the fourth and fifth centuries BC. The ingots produced were marketed to Persia, Syria, and West African ports. The Arabs observed the making of *wootz* and carried the technology to Spain, where Toledo became a major centre for its production. There is little information with regard to the type of foundries and furnaces used to make steel. However, the Iron Pillar at Delhi and iron beams used in the Konarak temple lend credence to the existence of very large foundries.

There were parallel developments in China where cast iron was used for making temple bells and ploughshares. China developed blast furnaces and established large factories for the manufacture of arms. By AD 1100, China was technically highly advanced, especially in the use of coke in iron smelting, canal transportation, farm implements, and in constructing bridges over gorges. China's export links with the Gulf region, Iran, and India must have stimulated developments in these areas, while it too must have imbibed technologies that helped its own development. Certainly, in India iron and alloys (like brass) came to be used for the making of guns and cannons. The *Tuzuki-Babari* and *Ain-i Akbari* describe the casting of cannons in detail.

Jewellery making in India developed techniques such as hammering, lapping, chasing, casting, and soldering. India's interface in the earlier period was widespread with Mesopotamia, Egypt, and Greece, on the one hand, and Iran and China on the other. There were colonies of foreign sculptors, architects, and wood carvers in Pataliputra and in other seats of power. Iranian refugees in India used inlay work with gold and silver. Centres of inlay work developed at Mekkah, Mosul, Damascus, Cairo, Kashmir, and in south India. This inlay work, called *koftgari* in India, had its origin in Damascus, giving the process its English name: damascening. After the sack of Damascus by Timur, the

▲ Gold wire drawer, Yeola. Highly skilled craftsmen were associated with the making of gold jewellery.

▼ Enamelled box, silver, Pratapgarh, Rajasthan, eighteenth century. The ornamentation of objects was prevalent throughout India, but during the Mughal period it gained further impetus.

artisans fled to different parts of the region, including India, carrying the techniques of silver and gold inlay with them.

A major development in India was the making of jewelled robes and silver and gold threaded cloth. The development of Takshasila jewellery can be studied in the frescos at Ajanta. Apart from using brass and bronze for the casting of statues, a blend of seven metals was also used in different parts of India, and particularly in the south. Yet another development was in the area of tin coating of copper vessels, known as *calai*, a technique probably introduced in India by the Arabs.

Carpets

Carpets developed from pile rugs, fragments of which have been found in Syria, China, Egypt, and Turkistan, their need developing out of the cold weather conditions of these regions. Major developments took place in Iran during the Sassanid period when much of Central Asia came under its dominance. However, it was under the Seljuq rulers that a rapid knotting style developed, and this soon spread to areas around the region.

Carpet design was a major art, and painters were associated with the development of motifs and their variations. During the Timurid period, geometric designs, kufic borders, and floral patterns were developed. The geometric borders may have been adopted from the Chinese.

North India had a tradition of making flat, pile-less rugs and *namdah*s (felted rugs). Carpet manufacturing took off during the Sultanate period and rapidly developed in different parts of India. It spread to the Deccan under the Bahmani and Qutub Shahi kingdoms, with major centres at Masulipatnam, Ellur, and Warangal. The use of Persian floral designs was prevalent, perhaps because of the artisans and craftsmen invited from Persia. Carpets produced during Akbar's time reveal the impact of the Safavid period, and centres were established in Agra, Fatehpur, and Lahore.

Glass, Jade, Ivory

The manufacture of glass dates back to antiquity. India produced white beads, bangles, and earrings, both opaque and transparent. Other centres of manufacture for glass were Egypt, Syria, Mesopotamia, and Phoenicia. Glass tiles were used in Buddhist stupas in Takshasila. Other objects made from glass included dishes, skull-shaped bowls, chalices, goblets, and lamps. Baghdad became a major centre for objects on which scenes of combat were etched. India's trade with China, Iran, and West Asia, and the import of craftsmen from these areas, led to the creation of new designs and major centres of production developed at Thatta and Golconda, and in the Mughal period, Bijnor and Agra.

Indian trade with other countries included ivory tusks. Ivory carving soon came to be an Indian specialty, and finds from the earliest times, for example in Mohenjodaro, include ivory objects; from Takshasila, ivory portraits of the Buddha have been found. Ivory and carved ivory objects were dispatched as gifts for rulers and nobility. The tradition of ivory carving spread from India to Greece, the Arab countries, Central Asia, and China.

Jade carving developed along the Silk Route and soon spread to other areas. Buddhist monasteries in Central Asia and eastern Turkistan created several objects from it. In India, jade carving developed under the Mauryas with Aruruvait as a major centre. The art was perfected during the Gupta period. Chinese influence in jade carving was evident from the presence of Chinese craftsmen in Indian courts.

During the sixteenth century, influenced by India and China, the art spread to Iran and Turkey. The earliest jade specimen in India is a bookstand used by Iltutmish, probably not of Indian origin. What does appear to be of Indian origin is a life-size tortoise of blue-green jade found near Allahabad. Large objects of jade were carved under the Ming dynasty in China, though they appear to be of Indian origin. The major development of jade carving in India occurred during Jehangir's reign. The difference between the Chinese and Indian methods of carving was the former's use of the treadle lathe and the latter's use of the bow lathe.

All these point to an impressive level of interaction that helped Indians produce skills and find markets outside their own, which brought to the country, in turn, discoveries and products that helped fashion a wider range of goods and techniques of manufacture.

▲ Jade box inset with precious stones, seventeenth century, Mughal. Jade was imported from China, but India developed centres for carving, particularly during the Gupta period. Carved jade was often exported back to China.

▶ Krishna and Radha, ivory, seventeenth century, from Orissa. Ivory carving was an Indian speciality that later spread to Greece, the Arab countries, Central Asia, and China.

The Commercial Spread of Science

Jawahar Dhar

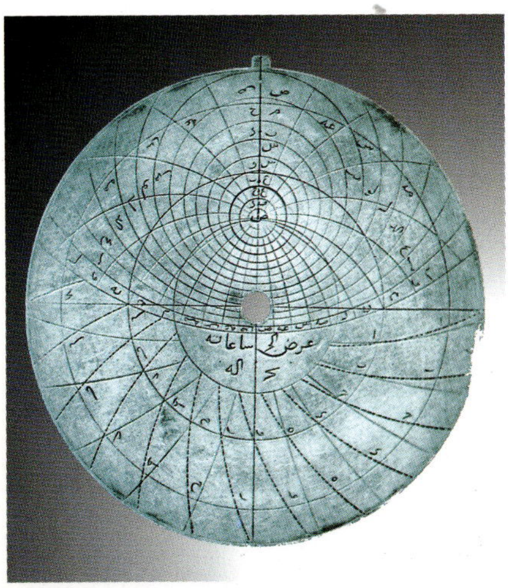

▲ Astrolabes *(top and above)* from the Red Fort Museum, Delhi. Astronomical books and astronomers were interested in marking planetary movements.

▶ *(facing page)* Astronomical observatory, Delhi. Sawai Jai Singh of Jaipur also developed such observatories in Banaras, Mathura, and Ujjain in the eighteenth century.

Scientific knowledge in ancient and medieval India and its advancement led to the establishment of intellectual, cultural and commercial bridges with other countries of the world. The earliest literature with references to scientific knowledge are the Sanskrit works from Vedic times. The four surviving Samhitas, namely, the *Rigveda,* the *Samaveda,* the *Yajurveda,* and the *Atharvaveda,* herald the beginning of astronomy and calendrical science, reveal traces of mathematical knowledge and shed light on the ancient Indian system of medical science. In the Brahmanas, many astronomical, anatomical, pathological and physiological concepts, and information about animal and plant life acquired a clearer perspective. The Upanishads, the third division of the Vedic literature, are repositories of physical concepts about the organic and the inorganic world.

Astronomy

Ancient Indian astronomers were interested in the motions of the sun and the moon, [with the aim of developing a workable calendar]. A major resurgence in Indian astronomy took place about the fifth century AD, when a new class of astronomical works, the Siddhantas, marked the beginning of a fresh era. The *Surya-siddhanta* is the most renowned of these texts which continued to be developed with additions of improved data till about the twelfth century. Aryabhata I (b. AD 476) was in the forefront of this astronomical movement and his book is a renowned mathematical-cum-astronomical work. His system of astronomy was further expounded by Bhaskara I (c. AD 600), who wrote three books on Aryabhata's work. These texts inform us of the water clock or clepsydra; the gnomon for determining cardinal points; the *cakra* for finding zenith distances and longitudes; the *turiya, dhanu,* and *kartari* which are arc instruments of different types; and the armillary sphere which is a wooden model of the celestial sphere showing the various great circles used in astronomy. The astrolabe, which was perfected by Islamic astronomers, came to India along with Arab astronomy.

Great effort was devoted by Sawai Jai Singh II (1686–1734) of Jaipur in reviving interest in astronomy during the eighteenth century. He studied the Indian, Arabic and European systems of astronomy and set up observatories in Jaipur, Ujjain, Delhi, Banaras, and Mathura.

Medicine and Surgery

The earliest examples of rational medical knowledge which form the beginning of Ayurveda (the science of life), can be traced to the *Rigveda* and the *Atharvaveda,* but our main sources of knowledge about Ayurveda are the three Samhitas. The *Caraka-samhita* is a compendium on therapeutic medicine, while in the *Susruta-samhita* surgery occupies centre stage. Arab merchants set up trading centres on the Malabar coast in the seventh century AD. They took Ayurvedic drugs along with other Indian commodities to centres in Asia, Africa and Europe. The reputation of medical and other sciences in India prompted some Arab rulers to send scholars to India and invite Indian scholars to visit them. This opened a channel of communication for the exchange of scientific ideas in different areas, including mathematics, astronomy, chemistry, medicine, and metallurgy. Ayurveda

▲▶ Anthroponaorphic figure *(above)* and harpoon *(right)* from 1500 BC. Found in copper hoards, these Harappan objects mark the advent of the copper age.

▼ The art of sword making in Damascus was at least partly the result of the high quality of Indian wootz steel which was imported here especially for this purpose. *(inset)* watering structure seen on 'Wootz' steel swords.

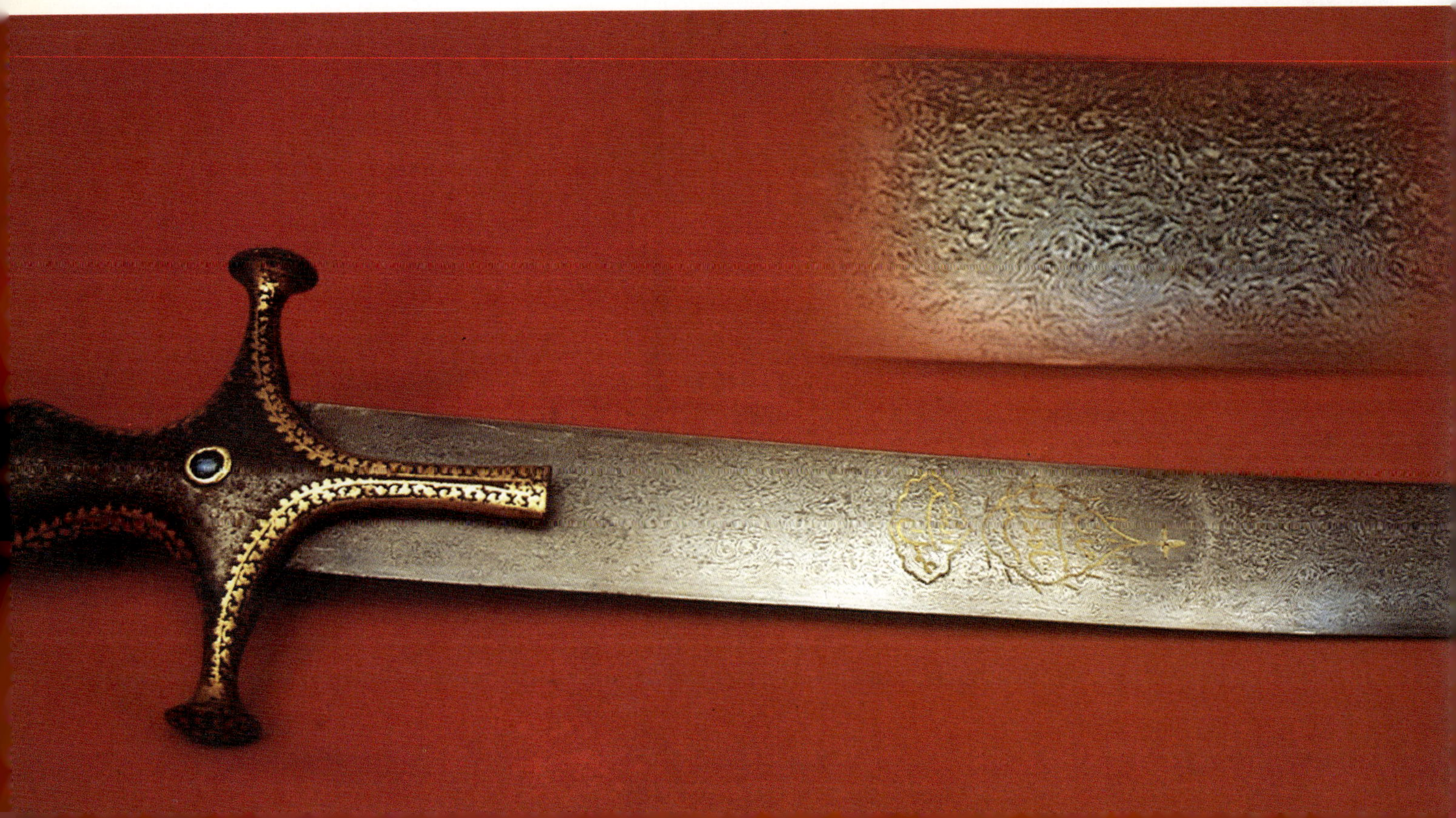

▼ Iron Pillar, Delhi. The high carbon content ensured that Indian steel was of a high quality, remained rust-proof and therefore prized internationally, a tradition that has continued into the new millennium.

became a known science in Persia, Turkey, Egypt, and the Mediterranean countries. The Ayurvedic system also spread to some other parts of the world; the discovery in Kuchi of a manuscript (the Bower Manuscript) containing seven Sanskrit texts, three of which were medical treatises, bears evidence of its having reached Central Asia; several Sanskrit treatises were translated into Tibetan during the eight century AD; Ayurvedic drugs were also introduced in Sri Lanka, Indo-China and Indonesia during the first millennium AD; Indian drugs were known in China, Japan, and Korea as well.

The Unani system of medicine, which originated in Greece and is based on the teachings of Hippocrates (460–377 BC), was introduced in India by the Arabs. When the Mongols ravaged Central Asian and Persian cities, physicians and scholars fled to India where they received the patronage of the Delhi Sultans, the Khaljis, the Tughlaqs, and the Mughals. The Unani physicians who settled in India experimented with Indian drugs through clinical trials and enriched their system with the addition of numerous native drugs.

Metallurgy

Archaeological findings at ancient sites such as Ahar (1300 BC), Atranjikhera (1025 BC), and Tadkanhalli (1000–150 BC) indicate that the Iron Age prevailed in India during the latter part of the second millennium BC. The tools and implements excavated at different places included hunting tools, agricultural implements, household objects, and building materials. The effect of carbon alloying on the strength and other properties of iron had been grasped by the beginning of the first millennium BC. The special place occupied by iron smelting technology and craftsmanship is demonstrated by the unique features of archaeological marvels like the Iron Pillar at Dhar (7 tonnes, twelfth century AD), the Iron Pillar on Kondachari hill (twelfth century AD), and the iron trident at Achaleshwar temple at Mount Abu (fourteenth century AD).

Indian steel was a highly valued commodity in international trade. This ultra-high carbon material came to be known as *wootz*, a nomenclature attributed to its corruption of *wookku*, the word used for steel in some south Indian languages. In modern technology, *wootz* may be described as high carbon steel with a carbon content ranging from 0.5 to 2.1 per cent by weight. Such steel was prepared in 'soft' and 'hard' grades, containing 0.5 to 0.8 per cent and 1.1 to 2.1 per cent carbon, respectively. The carbon content of weapons-grade *wootz* was about 1.5 per cent.

Also to India's credit goes the discovery and extraction of zinc. Excavations at Zawar in Rajasthan reveal that this metal was found around 400 BC, possibly earlier. Some scientists regard India as the

▶ Hubble bubble base, glass, seventeenth century, Mughal. Ancient literature also makes reference to glass, and by the Mughal period it had developed into a fine art.

first country to have introduced zinc to the rest of the world. There is evidence of the transfer of technology from Zawar to Bristol in England before 1730.

Glass

The people of the Indian subcontinent possessed the skills for moulding and fusing articles of faience, glazing pottery and beads, and making glass bangles and beads of various shapes and colours. Archaeological studies have shown that the techniques of this craft date back to the second millennium BC. References to *kaca* (glass) are found in ancient and medieval Indian literature, such as the *Yajurveda, Caraka-samhita, Susruta-samhita* and *Amarakosa* (seventh century AD).

Indian glass beads have been found in several countries with which India had trade connections: Java, Sumatra, the Malay peninsula, and Japan in the east, and some countries in East Africa in the west. In East Africa, the Malay peninsula, and Japan, these beads were used as a medium of exchange and have been known as 'trade-wind beads'.

Pre-Colonial Links with South East Asia

Sachchidanand Sahai

▼ Orchestra and a group of dancers infront of Balinese temple Legong Kraton. In Bali, a version of Hindu culture survives entire and unified; dance and temple belong together.

The land of gold (Suvarnabhumi) and the island of gold (Suvarnadvipa) in insular South East Asia were well-known destinations for the Indian trading community in the early centuries of the Christian era. A Jataka tale narrates the story of Prince Mahajanaka of Mithila who had resolved to carry out trade in order to accumulate wealth that would help him regain his kingdom, usurped by his uncle. His mother tried to dissuade him: 'Son, I did not come empty-handed. I have a store of pearls and jewels and diamonds sufficient for gaining the kingdom — take them and seize the throne; do not carry on trade.'

It was in vain. 'Mother,' he said, 'give that wealth to me, but I will take only half of it, and I will go to Suvarnabhumi and get great riches there, and will then seize the kingdom.' With his stock-in-trade, he boarded a ship with some merchants bound for the land of gold.

In the *Ocean of Story*, an eleventh-century work by Somadeva, when a wandering Brahmin reached a coastal city in Bengal, the merchant Prince Nidhidatta was about to sail on a trading expedition to the island of gold. The Brahmin managed to accompany him on the sea voyage. Another anecdote in the same work takes us to the port city of Tamralipti (Tamluk in Midnapore district of West Bengal). A local merchant, Guhyasena, went to the country of Kataha (Kedah in Malaysia) and began to trade in jewels. Disguised as a merchant, his wife Devasmita embarked on a ship, on the pretence of a mercantile expedition, and reached Kedah to recover her truant husband.

That these stories in the fairy tale genre are based on facts is testified to by the Chinese monk, Fa-haien. On his journey back home in October AD 411, Fa-haien embarked a large merchant vessel at Tamralipti (West Bengal), and via Sri Lanka and Java (Indonesia), reached China in 414.

In the fourth century AD, the poet Kalidasa visualizes 'the winds wafting the flowers of clove from the Dvipantara' or the Malay peninsula, to the seashores of Kalinga. Such was the flow of migrants from the Kalingan ports that all southern Indians, Tamils,

▼ Ramayana relief depicting Garuda, king of the birds, at Prambanan, Java, Indonesia. The Pallava and Chola ports were hubs for trade with South East Asian port cities.

Telugus and Malayalis, are called Kling in the Malay and Cambodian languages.

From the mouth of the Krishna, around the Amaravati region, the earliest waves of Indian migrants went to South East Asia, carrying with them images of the Buddha Dipankara in Amaravati style, along with other items of export. Considered the protector of the seas, these images appealed to sailors and early merchants. Found as far afield as Palembang (Sumatra) and Pong Tuk (Thailand), these images provide evidence of the spread of Indian trade and culture in these distant lands.

The Pallava ports around Mamallapuram and the Chola port of Kaveripattinam and Negapattam in the extreme south had a major share in this eastward thrust of Indian trade and culture. This exodus was not linked with migration, and certainly no Brahmanical priests and Buddhist monks were in a position to undertake long sea voyages on their own. On the other hand, there are indications that this eastward expansion was commercial in origin, led by a mercantile community that rose to eminence in India between circa 200 BC–AD 300.

The Roman demand for spices led Indian merchants to venture as middlemen to Malaya, Java, Sumatra, Borneo, and Cambodia. Gradually, however, a larger trade developed with Indians settled in the South East Asian port cities. Takkola (market of cardamom), Karpuradvipa (island of camphor), Narikeladvipa (island of coconut palms), and other similar Sanskrit place names shows what attracted the Indians to these regions. But above all 'it was gold that attracted India to the Eldorado of the far east'. It is not only the classical appellations of Suvarnabhumi and Suvarnadvipa that provide evidence of this. The names of rivers and streams recorded by famous geographer Ptolemy evoke 'the fabulous metal' which the sands of Indonesia still bear. Shortly before Christian era, India's supply of gold from Siberia had ceased. The Roman Emperor Vespasian (AD 69–78) had also checked the flow of gold from Rome to India. It is possible that the desire to find another source of the precious metal was one reason for the expansion of Indian trade southeastwards.

Two other factors were equally crucial. Progress in Indian shipbuilding resulted in the construction of seaworthy junks capable of transporting 600–700 passengers, and in abolishing caste barriers and the exaggerated concern for racial purity, Buddhism removed the shackles previously placed on maritime voyages by Brahmin orthodoxy.

While Indian literature abounds in stories about ships sailing to South East Asia, there is hardly any evidence available in the Indian subcontinent (with the exception of a few inscriptions) to unfold the pioneering efforts of Indian migrants. Fortunately,

▲ Attempting to wake up Kumbhakarna from deep sleep. From a Ramayana relief at the Brahma temple at Candi Lors Jongrang, Prambanan, Java.

Chinese narratives, South East Asian documents written in Sanskrit or the local languages, and monuments dedicated to Hindu and Buddhist worship in those countries, fill this lacuna.

Indian ships carried both commodities and ideas for exchange. Traders were accompanied by Brahmins, skilled technicians of rituals capable of bestowing divine Kshatriya status upon local rulers. The Brahmin ideology of dharma allowed a pluralistic society of differing traditions and beliefs. The growing knowledge of technical manuals — the Dharmasastras, the Arthasastras and the Rajyasastras — facilitated the emergence of well-organized territorial states in the region with a sharing of political and cultural ideas between the two areas.

South East Asian political centres were never a dependency of India in the remotest colonial sense. Each ethnic group of the area — Mon, Khmer, Burmese, Cham, Malayo-Polynesian, Thai — preserved its pronounced sense of identity and remained highly selective in accepting and assimilating Indian cultural elements. In consequence, the Indian social system based on the discriminative varna system, caste prejudices and untouchability remained alien to these lands. On a spiritual plane, Indian ships carried all three major belief systems, Hinduism, Buddhism and Islam, to South East Asia.

It is true that from one end of South East Asia to the other 'spectators continue to weep over the misfortunes of Rama and Sita'. But it was not only the standard, orthodox Valmiki version of the story that was taken to these lands. The more popular folk versions of the story were carried by traders and their companions who spoke Prakrit dialects or Dravidian languages. It is very probable that Gujarati Jain merchants took the fascinating story

▼ Brahma sculpture, Indonesia. The spread of Hindu influence over much of South East Asia was the work of traders rather than scholars.

of the portrait of Ravana that led to the banishment of Sita in the Indonesian and Thai versions.

Founded at the beginning of the first century AD by a Brahmin of Indian origin called Kaundinya, Funan in southern Cambodia flourished for five centuries as a major South East Asian power. Motivated by commercial concerns, a mission from Funan arrived at the court of a Kushana king in India after over a year at sea. Surprised, the Indian king exclaimed: 'What! There exist such men on the shores of the farthest seas!' The ambassador from Funan was taken on a tour of the interiors of India and was given a warm send-off with the precious gift of four Indo-Scythian horses. The entire journey took about four years (240–5). A century later, in 357, Kaundinya II brought in the second wave of Indianization in Cambodia. In the seventh century Isanapura, the political centre of the new Cambodian state, Chenla or Kambuja, patronized the building of Hindu temples, the learning of Sanskrit and Indian epics, and welcomed learned Brahmins from India. Yasodharapur or Angkor, founded in central Cambodia in the ninth century, remained a dominant power for the next 400 years. Spread over many miles, the Angkorian capital contained a large number of Hindu and Buddhist temples. Angkor Wat (eleventh century) and Bayon (thirteenth century) are considered marvels of Brahmanical and Buddhist art, respectively.

Srikshetra, around the modern city of Prome , was a stronghold of the Pyu ethnic group from the sixth to eighth centuries. That it was a preferred destination for Indians from the Orissa coast is evident from the term Srikshetra itself (a name for Puri) applied to this part of Burma.

The Mon kingdom of Pegu (Hamsavati) was founded in 825. Its capital was designated by the term Ussa (Odra/Orissa), indicating its links with India. The appellation Talaing, applied to the Mons by the Burmese, seems to indicate that at some time Telingana or the Madras region shared a particularly active relationship with the Mon country.

Located close to the confluence of the Irrawaddy and the Chindwin, at the crossroads of land routes leading to Assam and Yunnan, the temple city of Pagan flourished in Burma from 1044–1287. Traces of over 5000 monuments have been recorded here so far including a thirteenth-century copy of the temple of Bodh Gaya.

Probably commemorating Dwarka, the famous city of Krishna on the western coast of India, Dvaravati grew as an important centre of Mon civilization from the seventh to the twelfth centuries. Two silver coins bearing a Sanskrit inscription, 'the merit of the king of Dvaravati', found from Nakhon Pathom (Thailand) testify to Indian links with the kingdom. Thai historians believe that Nakhon Pathom, a Thai form of the Sanskrit expression *prathama*

▶ Steps leading to the top of Borobudur Stupa, Central Java. The spread of Brahmanical influence was the result of the religious tolerance in Indonesia.

nagara, first city, was actually founded by Sona and Uttara, two missionaries sent by Ashoka from India. [The stupa and images of Buddha from this site are an important part of the Buddhist heritage.]

Sukhothai or Sukhhodaya, the first important centre of Thai civilization in the twelfth and thirteenth centuries, patronized Theravada Buddhism influenced by Sri Lanka. A Thai prince from Sukhothai travelled in the interiors of India to explore Buddhist remains in the thirteenth century.

Founded in 1350, on an island in the Chao Praya river, 72 km from Bangkok, Ayutthaya (Ayodhya) emerged as a dominant political power in South East Asia and remained so for four centuries. The Siamese court at Ayutthaya received elements of Brahmanical culture from Cambodia after subjugating Angkor. Ayutthaya was a major port city where Indian Muslim merchants made their presence felt among the trading communities of various nations, each occupying a different quarter of the city. King Narai established trade links with Surat in the 1660s and sent an embassy to Qutb Shah, ruler of Golconda, in 1665. Coromandel weaving centres made textiles especially for the Siamese and Burmese markets. Golconda Muslims from Masulipatnam and Chulia (Tamil Muslim) merchants from Porto Novo supplied these products to Ayutthaya and carried sappanwood, hides, elephants, tin, ivory, gold, Japanese and Chinese goods back home.

▼ Beautiful human face, Bhima temple, Dieng, Indonesia. Around AD 800, a well-planned Brahmanic city existed on this 6,500 feet high plateau.

Amaravati, the capital of Champa on the Vietnamese sea coast in the province of Quang-nam, maintained close cultural links with India since the beginning of the fourth century. The temple complex of Mison around this city suggests the prevalence of the Sanskrit language and the worship of Shiva during the epoch. Cham political centres lay on the trade route between India and China. The conquest of Vijaya by the Vietnamese in 1471 marked the disappearance of the Cham kingdom.

In the mid-fifteenth century, the 'kingdom of a million elephants' in Laos received the Brahmanical and Buddhist heritage of the court of Angkor. The kingdom flourished as an outpost of Indian civilization beyond which lay the Chinese sphere of influence. The fine stupa of That Luang in Vientiane and exquisite sculptures of the Buddha suggest a flourishing Buddhism in the kingdom in the sixteenth and seventeenth centuries.

Kedah, an important settlement on the west coast of Malaysia, was in constant trade with Kaveripattinam and Tamralipti after the third century. Two inscriptions in Sanskrit discovered from Medah are written in the Pallava script, one of which records the success of a voyage undertaken by a sea captain called Buddhagupta. A short inscription in Tamil discovered from Takuapa indicates that a merchant guild from southern India was active in the Malay peninsula in the first half of the ninth century. In Indonesia, Borneo has yielded seven Sanskrit inscriptions of King Mulavarman, son of Asvavarman and grandson of Kundung. From the name of his grandfather, it appears that Mulvavarman was either a Tamil or an Indonesian.

A rich fertile island, Java (Yavadvipa) attracted Indian migrants from the early centuries of the Christian era. The Ramayana describes the island in glowing terms. Four Sanskrit inscriptions dating to 450 are the oldest evidence of Indian penetration on the island. The Sailendra dynasty patronized Buddhist art and architecture on the island of Java. In 782, a teacher from the country of Gaudi (Bengal) names Kumarghosha as consecrating an image of the Bodhisattva Manjusri in Kelurak. Other magnificent Sailendra monuments are Kalasana, temple of Tara, dated 778 by its inscription; Chandi Sari, a monastic dwelling; and Chandi Sewu, a veritable stone mandala with 250 little temples. The most dazzling, however, is the Borobudur together with its subordinate structures Chandi Mendut and Chandi Pawon built in the middle of the ninth century during the last phase of Sailendra rule.

Religious tolerance in Java allowed the flowering of Brahmanical art as well. Around AD 800, a Brahmanic city existed on the volcanic Dieng plateau in central Java, at an altitude of 6500 feet. [It was a well-planned city with sewers to drain water from the swampy plateau.] Its Shiva temples, eight of which are still standing, reveal strong affinities with the Pallava style of south India. Around the tenth century, the impressive Shiva temple complex of Prambanan with beautiful bas reliefs narrating the Ramayana, became lasting testimony to the Indian cultural legacy of central Java.

In the second half of the tenth century, the centre of the Javanese kingdom was transferred to the eastern part of the island where the Javanese version of the Ramayana, the Kakawin was composed by Yogisvara. Airlanga (1019–49) transformed Java into an important sea power, maintaining trade relations with the Klings (Indians of Kalinga), the Aryas (non-Dravidian Indians), the Golas (Gaudas of Bengal), Singhalas (Singhalese), Karnatakas (Kanarese), Cholikas (the Cholas of Coromandel), Malyala (Malabarese), Pandikiras (Pandyas and Keras) and the Dravids (Tamils). After 1049, the eastern Javanese kingdom of Kadiri dominated all the ports of the coast where Indian, Chinese and Arab merchants thrived. The bas reliefs of Chandi Jago and Panataran depicting scenes from the Krishnayana — the life of Krishna — date from this period.

▲ Kalasan, the temple of the Buddhist goddess Tara, Indonesia. A sea journey between India and Indonesia via Sri Lanka is well documented by the Chinese traveller, Fa-hsien.

The rise of Majapahit in eastern Java (1292–1403) marked the unification of the Indonesian archipelago and the growth of her northern seaboard as a centre of spice trade with the Moluccas. Among the Asian community of traders at Majapahit, India had a

▼ Shiva temple complex, Prambanan. There is a strong affinity with the Pallava temples of south India.

▶ Shiva puts a protective arm around Parvati while Ravana shakes Mount Kailasa, a sculptured panel in relief from Angkor Wat, Cambodia, twelfth century.

privileged position. In fact, in 1310, the Majapahit king Jayanagara took the title of Sri Sundarapandyadevadevesvara, a title that emphasized the spiritual relations between Java and Pandya country in the extreme south of India.

Centred around Palembang and in complete control of the straits of Sunda and Malacca from which trade between India and China passed, Srivijaya was a powerful maritime kingdom from the beginning of the eighth century. It was also a reputed centre of Mahayana Buddhism where the Chinese traveller Itsing stopped for six months in 671 on his way to India in order to study Sanskrit grammar. Srivijaya fostered close links with the Indian centres of Buddhism. The charter of Nalanda (c. 860) states that Balaputradeva, probably the first Sailendra sovereign of Srivijaya, had a monastery built in India at Nalanda. To contain its aggressive monopolistic commercial policy and to safeguard the interest of Indian traders, Rajendrachola sent a naval expedition against Srivijaya in 1025. An inscription from Tanjore dated 1030–1 claims that after having sent 'numerous ships into the midst of the rolling sea and having seized Sangramvijayottungavarman, king of Kadaram', Rajendrachola conquered a number of islands in the Indonesian archipelago. The incident did not, however, hamper future relations. From a Tamil inscription of 1088, it appears that a powerful corporation of merchants from southern India were comfortably settled around Baros on the west coast of Sumatra. In 1089–90, at the request of the king of Kidara, the Chola Kulottunga I granted a new charter to the Sri Sailendra Chudamanivarmavihara at Negapatam.

On the Malaysian coast, Malacca (1403–1511) rapidly grew as the richest seaport, visited by ships of all nations. It became, in truth, a cosmopolitan port where 'very often 84 languages have been found spoken, every one distinct'. A port official of Gujarati origin was appointed by the Sultan of Malacca to look after the affairs of traders of the region. A second port official was in charge of the Klings (Oriyas), Bengalis, Peguans, and Pasais. A third was concerned with vessels from the Malay archipelago, and a fourth with vessels from China and Indo-China. All over the archipelago, Malacca distributed Indian cloth from Pulicat and Cambay, offering Indian traders gold, spices and aromatic wood in exchange. Tamil mercantile grip over the Malaccan port city under the rule of Muzaffar Shah, Sultan of Malacca (1446–56), son of a Tamil woman, did not diminish until the Portuguese capture of the city in 1511.

As Islam advanced in Sumatra and Java, introduced from the western coast of India by Gujarati Muslim merchants in the fifteenth century, Hindu–Buddhist priests together with artists and scholars and their sacred books took shelter in the little Indonesian

▶ Relief showing fight between Ram and Ravana at Angkor Wat, Cambodia. Indian literature abounds in stories about ships sailing to the South East.

island of Bali. Bali remains to this day a stronghold of a Malayo-Polynesian version of Hinduism with the Saiva Agamas, Brahmin priests, the fourfold varna division of society without the notion of untouchability, and exquisite dance-dramas based on the Indian epics. On Indian shores, modern day Kalingans of Orissa float ritual lamp boats every year to commemorate their *Bali-yatra,* their journey to that island in the hoary past.

Craft Skills: Textiles and the Cotton 'Industry'

Lotika Varadarajan

The fabric over which India achieved particular mastery was cotton. Egypt was associated with linen, West Asia with wool, while China's identity was closely linked with silk. In spite of all the accoutrements of an industry, textile production operated within a continuum in which the major indicators were of a craft-related activity.

The cradle of cotton appears to have been the north-western part of South Asia. There were two species, *Gossypium arboream* and *Gossypium herbaceum*, their distribution shaped by the availability of a warm climate and access to water. Three samples of *G. arboreum* dated c. 1760 BC have been found in Mohenjodaro. However, the annual variety of *G. herbaceum*, dated between the sixth and seventh centuries AD, diffused over a large area, soon became the predominant species of cotton on the subcontinent.

India was not the only country associated with cotton. The crop was widely dispersed over monsoonal Asia, and it was favoured for garments throughout this region. The quality of Indian lint was far superior to those of others. Indian cotton yarn, widely spun and twisted by the spindle, enabled commercial scale production of fine count yarn. [There was no gender differentiation in the activity of cotton spinning and, as it constituted a part-time domestic occupation, was free to follow fluctuations in demand without undue social disjunction.] Yarn twisted on the *charkha*, the spinning wheel, was of coarser count and less closely twisted than that on the spindle.

▼ Hand twisting of new warp. This operation is called *piecing*.

Loom procedures helped maximize output. The development of an intricate system of multiple shafts and peddles increased the output of even a single weaver. The width of fabric could be increased by placing an additional weaver or two on the pitloom. The warp ends could be lengthened by twisting additional lengths on to existing ends on the loom, obviating the necessity of setting it up afresh. Since humidity was particularly important for fine cotton weaving, necessary levels were maintained through the intermittent sprinkling of water inside the pit.

▶ *Patola.* Ratan Chowk design.

▼ Indian cotton looms used an intricate system of multiple shafts and peddles and helped maximize the output of even a single weaver.

(facing page):

▲ *Lurik.*

▼ Mud resist to be applied by a wooden block, Rajapur-Deesa, Gujarat.

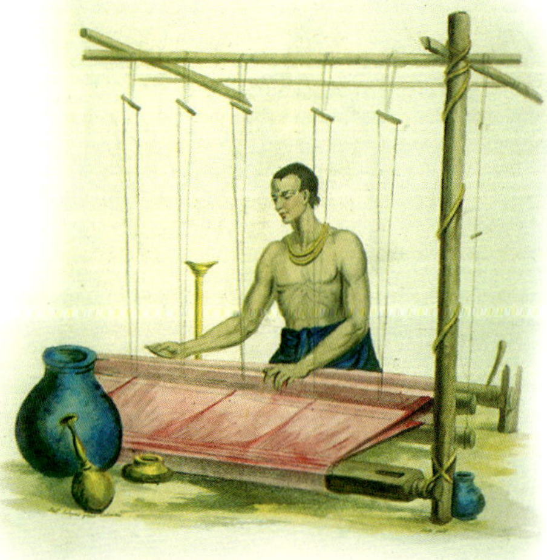

The loin loom was predominant in South East Asia and the fabrics warp faced: therefore, while stripes could be woven with facility, checked patterns posed problems. The procedures developed on the Indian counter-balance pitloom, however, facilitated the maintenance of equal tension across both warp and weft: it was possible to combine warp and weft stripes in a grid and create a symmetrically balanced check patterning. Only in China had a similar finesse been achieved, as seen in the checked silken material, *kanto.* Indian checked cotton had, however, an obvious price advantage and proved popular in Japan. In Indonesia,

the Javanese coined the term *pleket*, derived from the place name Pulicat, while the Balinese preferred the term *poleng* for Indian checked material. Black and white *poleng* was accorded special status as the chosen attire for the costumes worn by Hanuman, Bhima, Ghatotkacha, and the servants of the five Pandava brothers in all pageants based on the epics. Even Balinese women wore checked sarongs for domestic ceremonies. *Lurik*, a warp-faced fabric woven on the Indonesian back-strap loom, had a striped pattern to which the Indian checked fabric provided welcome relief. It was also accorded high symbolical value, such as the Indian *patola* called *tchinde* — silk *tchinde* was reproduced in cotton for the Indonesian market. With the entry of the Europeans, Indian checked materials became popular in Europe, particularly in the Dutch market where they were extensively used for making costumes.

The Indian advantage in yarn production and weaving was complemented by an equal technical finesse in dyeing. A cellulose fibre, cotton had a lower affinity to dye than yarn of animal origin such as wool and silk. Nor did it lend itself to textural variation in weaving, as was the case with wool. Unlike linen and silk, it did not reflect light. Dye patterning, therefore, became the most feasible method of ornamentation.

India was well endowed to surmount the inherent disadvantages of cotton in relation to dyeing. Mordants such as alum were necessary to change the chemical composition of the cellulose fibre and make it receptive to dye. Sind provided ample sources of alum. Mordant dyeing had been prevalent in India much before it became so in Egypt. Indeed, in the latter country the high cost of dyes declined only in the Coptic period (fourth to twelfth centuries). Even in Europe, dyes were exorbitant until the late medieval period, while Indian dyestuff had always been both widely available and affordable.

Dyes were sourced from forest produce, and only indigo cultivated as a dye yielding plant crop. The usage of indigo, *nila*, as a dye is referred to in 500 BC by the grammarian, Panini. The range of dyes was based on blue and black from indigo; black from iron acetate or a ferruginous earth from Kutch, Gujarat, called *khayo;* red from *Rubia cardifolia, Morinda citrifolia* or *Ventilago madraspatna;* yellow from *Curcuma longa* (turmeric), *Punica granatum* (pomegranate rind) or *Mangifera indica* (mango bark extract). The palette was greatly enlarged in the Muslim period, but several shades were not colour-fast in cotton. Such shades found ready clientele in Rajasthan where auspiciousness was associated with impermanence in colour.

Traditional dyeing usage in India comprised beating, oiling, and dunging as a preparatory stage to remove foreign bodies and

smoothen texture. Tannin, introduced at this stage, prepared the yarn to receive the mordants that were to be painted or printed on the fabric in the following stage. Mordants changed the structure of the fibre, making bonding with the madder range of colours feasible and long lasting. During the hot processes involved in madder dyeing, even penetration was facilitated by the admixture of a range of flowers and leaves such as *Grislea tomentosa* and *Memecylon edule* within the dye vat to serve as dye carriers. If blue or green were to be included in the colour range, the cloth would be appropriately resisted with mud or wax to prevent colour saturation in unwanted areas. After resist dyeing for indigo-derived blue, areas requiring green were over-painted with yellow. Other techniques of dye patterning practised in India included *ikat* and *plangi*. In *ikat*, a technique associated with Gujarat, Orissa, Andhra Pradesh, and Tamil Nadu, the yarn was tie-dyed according to pattern requirements, and then woven. In double *ikat*, popularly recognized in the *Patan patola* product, both warp and weft yarn were tie-dyed prior to weaving, and matched in the course of weaving. *Plangi*, known as *bandhani*, in this country, involved tie-dyeing of woven cloth and was practised in Gujarat and Rajasthan. A group of migrant weavers from Gujarat introduced the technique into the Madurai region where it came to be called *sungadi*. Samples of the tie-dyed fabric dating back to the eighteenth century have also been found in Bengal, probably introduced there by members of the Jain community in whose temples dedicated to the Mother Goddess in north India, *bandhani rumal*s were freely available to devotees as covering cloths.

Each group in the subcontinent exercised a limited choice in the surface adornment of cloth used in clothing. There was a sufficiently wide-ranging workforce to cater to this diverse demand and textile production stood outside the *jajmani* system. The cloth requirements of the forest-dwelling hunter–gatherer were minimal, and with the exception of those who dwelt in the Himalayan foothills inclusive of the north-east, they obtained their requirements of cloth from groups of weavers bound to them in a symbiotic relationship. An oft-quoted example is that of the Todas and their service group, the Kotas, in the Nilgiri region of south India. Resulting from consumer preferences of this clientele, a vast repertoire in design and pattern was built up over time. While little choice could be exercised at the micro level, an exuberant multiplicity existed at the macro level. The choices of the foreign customer were exercised at a macro level while the more exclusive demand created by the aristocratic Indian patron helped generate new patterns and colours at the domestic level.

▲ *Vichitrapur* sari, Orissa. Double *Ikat*.

(facing page):

▲ Costume in San'a Saudi Arabia.

▼ Hanging made for an Islamic patron in Golconda, Andhra Pradesh.

Apart from the domestic market for Indian cotton textiles, there was significant demand for the Indian product in distant climes. Africa and West and South East Asia exercised a demand for Indian cotton textiles. With the exception of Iran and Thailand, other overseas markets chose from textiles already available in India. Those items used in the Japanese tea ceremony fall into a category of their own. Each market exercised a choice within a specific range. Gujarat catered predominantly to the African and West Asian markets while Bengal and the Coromandel turned towards South East and east Asia. Merchants could, of course, create overlaps.

Wax resist painted cloth used a pen-like instrument, leading to the term *kalamkari* coined by the Persians. Called *sarassa* in the east, it has been traced to two sources: the first to the Gujarati term *saras* meaning good quality in relation to texture and durability, and the other *sarassah*, a word in old Javanese meaning variegated or scattered. When the Europeans appeared on the scene in the Indian Ocean via the Cape route, they had perforce to use Indian textiles to procure Indonesian spices for the European market. Ignoring the current terms *kalamkari* and *sarassa*, they coined their own nomenclature, terming painted, printed textiles *pintado* (Portuguese), *sits* and *chits* (Dutch), chintz (English), *toiles peintes* and *toiles imprimees* (French). Like the Persian term, these related to technique, quality or pattern rather than place of origin.

◀ Item made for Thai market in the Coromandel craft region.

▼ Indian fabric in European costume in the eighteenth century. Note different patterned chintz in female and infant clothing as also the checked material and *mulmull* used in the headgear of the woman.

Persian, Thai and European patrons and users developed their own repertoires in design and patterns were made on the basis of samples developed by them. The Persians developed a range of hangings, bath towels, and prayer mats based on their own aesthetic sensibilities. The *kalamkari* items of the Masulipatam region, Andhra Pradesh, bear this Persian design orientation even today. Cotton items made for the Thai court reveal a totally different orientation based on Khmer–Thai motifs like the *tumpal* and *kepala* (a triangular motif running along the cross border), *kanok* (flame motif), and *thep phanom* (figure of a *deva* with folded hands), within a grid pattern. Some of these motifs are found reflected in the Karuppur textiles of the nineteenth and early twentieth centuries for Tanjore royalty in Tamil Nadu. The *saudagiri* ornamentation of Gujarat constitutes a less refined repertoire within the same tradition. Europeans developed motifs such as the Tree of Life in drapery items like the coverlet and bed canopy. These were called *palampore*. Patterns in chintz were also developed for stitched garments. The habit of taking snuff created a demand for dye-patterned handkerchiefs based on the versatile Indian *rumal*. While delicate lace accessories completed sumptuous silken costumes in Europe, ephemeral *mulmul* weaves served to accentuate garments fashioned from chintz.

Indian skills, engendered, enriched, and preserved by Indian craftsmen, working within the caste system, formed the backbone of the cotton 'industry' in pre-industrial South Asia. Although it is fashionable to dismiss caste as being wholly exploitative, it is important to remember that the division between caste and class in terms of occupational status was blurred. Moreover, improverishment of artisans and the absence of empowerment is a colonial phenomenon. The market was serviced by a well-knit banking and distribution system. Roadways vied with seaways while pack-, head-, and shoulder-loads bridged ecological barriers and averted economic disjunction. The craftsman was not bound by customary usages and could cater to varied and varying demand. It is because of the strengths of the system that craft production has been able to coexist with a growing base of industrialized production up to modern times. Indeed, it was because of its ability to survive that Gandhi could draw on the *charkha* as a symbol of nationalist regeneration. Sadly, the *charkha* had by then virtually replaced the spindle. This, in turn, was symptomatic of the decline in craftsmanship. The market could no longer pay the price for high skill and the process of de-skilling had begun. One can only hope that the future will recuscitate seeds of regeneration.

Trade in Mughal India

Shireen Moosvi

It is difficult to visualize today the position India occupied in world commerce during the times of the Great Mughals. Its cotton manufactures, silk, and spices dominated East–West commerce, and large quantities of silver and gold flowed into the country. Bernier, the French traveller, noted in the 1660s that 'gold and silver, after circulating in every other quarter of the globe, came at length to be swallowed up, lost in some measure, in Hindoustan'. Indian merchants were found controlling large sectors of trade in the Red Sea, Iran, Central Asia and South East Asia. Foreign travellers were often dazzled by the wealth of Indian merchants. Sebastian Manrique in the 1630s spoke of the 'immense wealth of fortunes' of the merchants at Agra. At the great port of Surat, even the English East India Company found itself dwarfed by the local merchants Virji Vora, Zahid Beg, and, later, Mulla Ghafur.

By 1619, Virji Vora was so well established that the factors of the English East India Company were obliged to provide 'courteous usage of all English ships' to his agent, being in his constant debt, having just then taken a loan of 25,000 *mahamudis* (16 *mahamudis* = 1 rupee) from him. Virji Vora virtually monopolized the pepper trade and dealt in a wide range of commodities. His trading network was extensive; besides his headquarters at Surat, his firm had branches at Bharuch, Baroda, Ahmedabad, Burhanpur, Golconda, Agra, and in the Malabar, apart from the port towns of the Persian Gulf, Red Sea and South East Asia. His capital in time grew to an estimated eight million rupees (or at contemporary exchange value, 8,00,000 pounds sterling). He bought opium and cotton from local merchants, exchanged these for pepper in south India and the Spice Islands, and sold the pepper to the English and the Dutch, buying from them coral, quicksilver, vermilion, lead, and other

▼ Sarpech, eighteenth century, Mughal. The imperial court became synonymous with opulence, and Delhi and Agra repositories of the finest jewels of the time.

▶ Market square, Fatehpur Sikri, highlighting commercial practices akin to those in more modern times. Miniature, Akbar school.

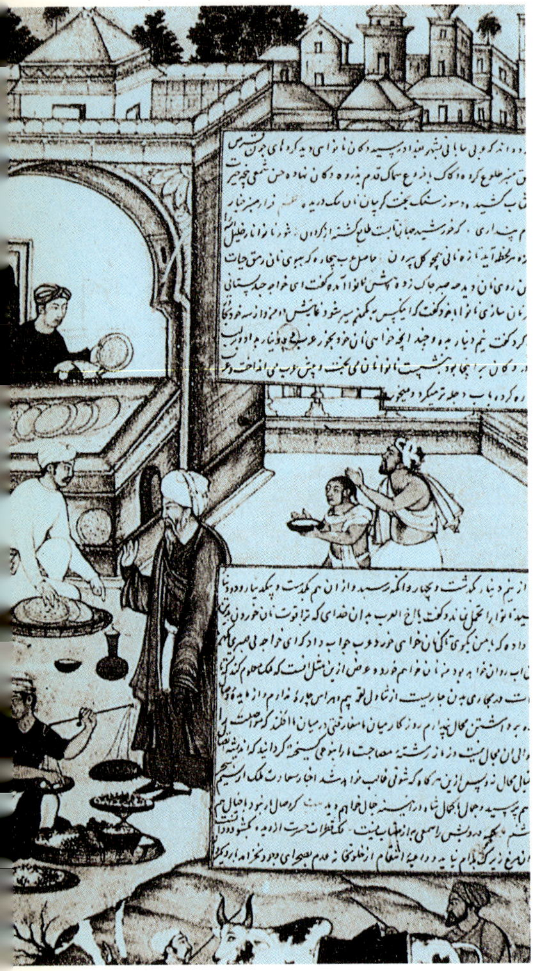

▲ Activities in a baker's shop, miniature, Akbar school. Well-established bazaars catered to the requirements of an urban population.

▶ Babur crossing the river Son in Bihar, using a bridge made with boats. His passage is monitored carefully since changes in political heads had deep repercussions on immediate trade.

commodities. In 1625, he sold to the English pepper worth 10,000 pounds sterling at a rate appreciably above the usual market rate and compelled them to sell their coral (25 chests) to him at a price below market rate. In achieving such advantageous transactions, he was aided by his intelligence network, beating the English in the present instance by ordering his agents to buy all the stock of pepper at a rate a little higher than that offered by the English. English factors ruefully complained in 1643 that Virji Vora 'knoweth that he must sell and soe beats us down till we come to his rates; and thus hath been his proceedings this many years'. Indeed, such was his domination of the market that 'no merchants in the towns dare displease him by coming to our howse to look uppon our commodities'. In 1662, he prevented Surat merchants from buying coral and copper from the English through a general diktat.

Virji Vora exploited his position as banker *(sarraf)* to assist his trade. Dependent on bullion imports to carry on their trade, the foreign companies constantly faced shortage of capital. Virji Vora exploited this handicap of the English and the Dutch by not only charging them high rates of interest on loans, but also by attaching several strings to these loans. In 1628, when the English refused to carry goods belonging to him and other Surat merchants to Persian Gulf ports, Virji Vora and Hari Vaishya, another Surat merchant, asked for immediate repayment of their loans amounting to 30,000 pounds sterling, forcing their submission. In 1632, the Dutch who were indebted to Virji Vora to the tune of 8000 pounds had a similar experience. Often Virji Vora, in being ready to lend large sums induced the foreign companies to borrow from him, even though he charged 12 per cent interest as against the usual 7 per cent per annum as happened in 1635, and again in 1636 when he exacted 3 per cent extra in lieu of the difference between the new coins *(sikka)* and the older coins *(chalni)*. The English bitterly described him as a 'costly creditor'.

Virji Vora conducted his commercial activities in an environment of 'free trade' with little use of administrative support. He was however influential enough to even get the Mughal governors of Gujarat transferred, as happened in the case of Masihuz Zaman in 1635 when Virji Vora was summoned by Mughal Emperor Shah Jahan to represent his case. Virji's firm survived him and his grandson Nanchand was considered an important merchant in the 1670s and the firm had sent large sums to the newly established French East Indian Company.

Of other Surat merchants we know less, but the operations of many of them were on no mean scale. In the last quarter of the seventeenth century, Mulla Ghafur, for example, held the centre stage of commerce: his capital was largely invested in shipping.

▲ Village merchant with goods. Traders also provided credit to peasants and artisans, which made them important links in the credit system.

▼ *Mohurs, (also facing page, below)* Mughal gold coins issued during Akbar's reign (1557-1605). Hundis, or bills of exchange, were issued for the transfer of money from one place to another.

(facing page):

▲ The killing of Bahadur Shah depicts Portuguese ships in the harbour at Diu.

Around 1700, he was said to own 20 ships, each between 300 and 800 tons, and to drive a trade equal in magnitude to that of the English East India Company.

The inland towns were populous and had large markets: Agra, Delhi, and Lahore had estimated populations of over half a million each, and Ahmedabad, Thatta, Patna, Dhaka, and Masulipatam were thought to contain 2,00,000 people each. These towns depended on supplies from the countryside for their food as well as raw materials for manufacture; and the merchants were an important cog in the wheel necessary for such transfer of resources. In the Mughal empire, land revenue was realized in cash and production was, therefore, keyed to the market. Peasants were obliged to sell the larger part of their produce immediately to meet the revenue claim that was by and large around half of the produce. They did so by carrying the crop to nearby towns, though generally the grain merchants themselves went to villages to buy the grain and other crops. How well-entrenched money transactions were in villages can be gauged by Tavernier's statement that 'in India a village must be very small indeed, if it has not a money changer, called Shroff [*sarraf*], who acts as a banker to make remittances of money and issue letters of exchange'.

Long-distance trade in bulk goods was carried out by *banjara*s or nomads who lived with their families in camps known as *tanda*s. A large *tanda* might contain as many as 600-700 persons and 12–, 15–, or even 20,000 bullocks. According to Peter Mundy (1630s): 'They never dwell in houses and they take along with them their women and children, some of them possess 100 oxen, others have more or less, and they all have a Chief, who acts as a prince.' He adds that 'they are sometimes hired by merchants, but most commonly they are the merchants themselves'.

The most important merchant caste in north India was that of the *bania*s (to which Virji Vora belonged). They controlled practically the entire inland trade and credit system. The *bania* had in each locality a shop to buy from and sell to peasants and artisans, providing credit to them when they were in need which was often the case. To the impecunious, God and the *bania* were virtually synonymous. So the great monotheist Kabir (c. 1510) sang:

> My Lord is a bania. He conducts his commerce so easily without scales and balances, he weighs the entire Universe!

Bernier describes merchants' shops in the cities as being well-ventilated buildings with residences on top and shops on the ground floor. A Mughal noble, Dargah Quli Khan observed in 1740 that in Delhi, were a person to come with a sum of one lakh rupees

for shopping, the variety of goods available was such that the sum would be readily spent and prove insufficient.

The wheels of the market were oiled by a system of brokerage *(dalali)* that foreign merchants regarded as a major convenience of Indian commerce. This practice too was the preserve of *bania*s who often employed their own capital to act for their principals and operated as commission agents on behalf of anyone who wished to employ them.

Much of the capital for trade from village to town, and between towns, was raised through the issue and discounting of bills of exchange. In major marts, such as Ahmedabad in 1761, practically all payments were made in such bills, and coins were seldom employed. *Sarraf*s were not only money-changers but also specialized in the issue and discounting of *hundi*s (bills of exchange). In order to obtain or reinforce their capacity to discount bills, *sarraf*s accepted deposits, thus becoming full-fledged bankers. They loaned money obtained through deposits to others at higher rates. In 1645, the English factors reported on the operations of these bankers in terms that could apply to modern banks and especially to the travails of banking today:

> Those that are great monied men in the towne, and live onely uppon interest receive from the sherrofs [*sarraf*s] noe more than 5/8 per cent, per month. The sherrofs they dispose of it to others [at] from 1 to 2.5 per cent, running some hazzard for same, and that is their gaines. Now when a sherrof (for lucre) hath disposed of great summes to persons of qualletie att great rates, not suddenly to be call'd in to serve his occasions, then beginn his creditours (as in other partes of the world) like sheepe one to runn over the neck of another, and quite stifle his reputacion.
>
> Thus ... hath two famous sherrofs bynn served within a moneth, one of which faileing for above three lack [3,00,000] of rupees, diverse men have lost great somes and others totally undone thereby; which hath caused men of late to be verie timerous of putting their monies into sherrof hands.

The *hundi*s, like bills of exchange in contemporary Europe, were used for safe transmission of money from one place to another as well as to raise short-term credit repayable at another place. These bore no seal or signature of witnesses but were always honoured and the payment punctually made by the drawees. Their reliability made both the Mughal administration and foreign companies use them for practically all their money transfers. There were customary links between bill markets, so that from a small place a *hundi* could directly be drawn only on a major mart nearby. Thus no *hundi* could be drawn from Bhakkar or Multan, changed there into one on Lahore; and then on Agra; and, finally, at Agra on Kanauj. The easier way, says a Mughal official, c.1700, was to obtain a 'returnable' *(jawabi) hundi* (i.e. drawn by a *sarraf* at Bhakkar on himself) and then have it discounted by a *sarraf* at Kanauj.

According to Tavernier, Agra was the main bill market of the Mughal empire with almost all important marts drawing bills directly on it. The discount rates seemed high but this was due, says Tavernier, to the fact that they were more secure: for, unlike Europe, all persons who discounted and then sold a bill in India became, in their turn, responsible for payment to the buyer if it was not honoured by the drawee.

The *sarrafs* also instituted a well-developed insurance *(bima)* system that made India the sole country outside Europe where such a system existed in the seventeenth century. In 1655, one could send cochineal from Surat to Agra, insured at a premium of 2.5 per cent, and similarly get cash from Masulipatam at 1 per cent for insurance. Even ships and their cargo could be insured; and there was an indigenous practice of bottomry called 'avog'. Even the English East India Company took the precaution of insuring its ships with the Surat *sarrafs* on voyages within the Indian Ocean, especially in troubled times.

Though the institution of joint stock companies was alien to the Indian commercial world, business partnerships were not always confined within the family or within the caste, but extended across such barriers. For example, we find a Jain merchant from Jaunpur, Banarasidas, forming a partnership with Dharmdas, a merchant from Agra. The norms of such partnerships were so firmly established that after the latter's death Banarasidas had to stay for a long period at Agra to settle accounts with the heirs of Dharmdas who showed no interest in the partnership; yet Banarasidas could not leave the city for fear that if accounts were not settled, he could be held guilty by the *qazi* (judge) or the *kotwal* (police superintendent).

Any assessment of capital in seventeenth-century India must take into account the behaviour of interest rates. The notion of a 'market rate' of interest existed, this being the rate at which bankers lent to merchants. At Surat, the interest rates on loans raised by the English East India Company or by reputable merchants fluctuated between 1 and 1.5 per cent per month from 1624 to 1650. Thereafter, there was a considerable fall: from 1651 to 1703

▲ Cotton and silk masnad, eighteenth century, Mughal. The spread of the Mughal empire, and the period of consolidation, gave rise to a level of craftsmanship that not only found logical patronage, but also sought levels of excellence.

▲ Walnuts being gathered at Farghana for export to India, *Baburnama*. Trade between Central Asia and India received a boost with the ascendancy of the Mughals in the north. Babur, the first emperor, however, continued to yearn for the gardens and orchards of his native Farghana as is evident from this scene.

the rates ranged from 0.5 to 5.8 per cent per month. At Ahmedabad, a fall of the same magnitude appears to have occurred in or by 1647; and in Agra, during the course of 1647. The rates in both these towns otherwise corresponded with those at Surat. In the Deccan, on the other hand, the interest rates were higher than in Gujarat and Agra. A great fall in commercial interest rates appears to have occurred here too, but between 1639 and 1642. Before 1642, the rates seem to have been higher than 2 per cent, whereas after 1642 the rate seems to have ranged between 0.5 and 1 per cent; though in some years at Madras it fell lower, and in the 1670s at Masulipatam it touched 2 per cent.

These rates are higher than those prevalent in Europe at the time, though in Europe too a decline in interest rates occurred around the mid-seventeenth century. The difference was, indeed, large enough for the English factors in India to argue with their principals that if money raised on loan in England was sent as bullion to India, it could be lent here at advantage. Such a situation may in fact suggest that bullion imports into India might have been concealing the real transfer of capital into India right through the seventeenth century; and this was why the declines in interest rates in Europe and India broadly synchronized around the middle of that century.

Theories that attribute stagnation to 'indigenous' commerce, or propositions that Indian merchants were mere 'peddlers' compared to the foreign companies are scarcely tenable. It was English conquest that, by throttling much of internal trade and drawing off India's resources through the notorious tribute, did so much to constrict Indian merchant capital. As European firms moved in and European-dominated banks were established, the analogous institutions within the indigenous sector were forced into a process of decline and subordination, so that some of its striking elements, such as its own systems of insurance and bottomry, became mere memories. The Indian merchant was then not so much an ally, as victim, of modern colonialism.

Section II

The Colonial Period

Overview

Business and The Raj

Sabyasachi Bhattacharya

When we talk of business and the Raj, we must remember that it was business that *became* the British Raj. In his poems, Nobel laureate Rabindranath Tagore refers to it as the trader's weighing scales becoming the ruler's sceptre in the hands of the British. This was colonialism: the transformation of a business firm called the East India Company into the Government of India in the late eighteenth and early half of the nineteenth centuries.

The East India Company was a business house with a trade monopoly guaranteed by the English sovereign that slowly took over the functions of a ruler in the subcontinent. 'The government of an exclusive company of merchants,' wrote Adam Smith in his celebrated work *The Wealth of Nations* (1776), 'is perhaps the worst of all governments for any country whatever.' Smith's reference was to the governance of parts of India by the English East India Company at the end of the eighteenth century. When you look back upon the business communities of the time, two things spring to the eye. First, the existence of numerous business communities with traditional business skills

▼ East India Company House, London. This was the heart of the trading empire of the English East India Company and oversaw the economic expansion of the company for a good hundred years.

▲ Sailing ships on the Hooghly. The waterways of the Ganga provided the scope for both inland and international trade.

▼ A trestle bridge on the rail network between Assam and Bengal. The rapid development of the railways for the movement of troops was responsible also for the acceleration in commercial activities.

and, second, the decline of their business during the East India Company regime .

Let us take an imaginary journey down the coast of India: in Bengal you would have met, in the eighteenth century, the Gandha Vaniks (spice merchants) and the Suvarna Vaniks (bullion merchants), and further down the eastern coast, the Chettiars of Coromandel (the English mispronunciation of Cholamandalam). Inland, there were the Komatis and others of the part of India now called Andhra Pradesh. At the tip of the peninsula were the Mapillahs, a product of Indo-Arab trade contact for centuries, and the Syrian Christians and Jews of Cochin — all adept at business. If you travelled up the western coast, you would come across the Parsis, not traditionally a trading community but on their way to pronounced success in trade, including overseas trade. Then there were the Bohras, traditional Indian merchants converted to Islam, and Bhatia and other Hindu business communities along the coast of Gujarat. Surat and the Gujarat coast provided access, through Rajasthan, to the prosperous markets of northern India. In Rajasthan, you would meet one of the richest business communities, the Marwaris. Further north were the Khatris and Lohnas of Punjab and Sind and several others who were middlemen in the overland trade between the Mughal capital cities of Agra, Delhi, and Lahore and western and central Asian countries. If your imaginary travels took you inland, you would have met other merchant communities engaged in internal merchandising and moneylending.

What happened to these business communities during the East India Company's regime? Though squeezed out of big business, they were by no means wiped out, taking a subordinate place under the domination of British business interests in India. In Bengal, for instance, 'native' merchants were essential as middlemen for the procurement of fine cotton cloth, silk and indigo for export to Europe. In the late eighteenth century, these independent merchants were replaced by agents and servants of English traders and the East India Company. The Company also put an end to large-scale banking businesses of the likes of Jagat Seth who was virtually state banker to the Nawab of Bengal, through its promotion of the Bank of Bengal. Smaller native bankers and shroffs or moneychangers were pushed out of the profitable foreign trade network in export-oriented industries.

The last half of the eighteenth century witnessed the establishment of the domination of British business interests, aided and abetted by the East India Company, to the detriment of native Indian enterprise. The process also involved excessive exploitation of artisans producing cotton or silk for export, and peasants producing export commodities like indigo. There is historical evidence that this foreign domination was brought about not by market forces alone but extra-economic factors: legal and

informal restrictions on the freedom of the producers and the support extended to English businessmen by the English East India Company's government.

The outcome was the subordination of Indian business communities but not their extinction, because Indian merchants and moneylenders had their use for the British. 'Native' businessmen supplied short-term credit to producers of agricultural and artisanal commodities, supplied cash with which land revenues could be paid to the British Indian government, and were petty traders who acted as brokers *(dalals)* or procurers and purchase agents *(paikars, pharias)* in internal trade. They serviced the lower deck of the colonial economy which consisted of the so-called unorganized sector, below the upper deck dominated by English-style business corporations, banks, and insurance companies.

By the turn of the century, the industrial revolution had catapulted England into the position of leading industrial power in the world. From the early decades of the nineteenth century, a new role was assigned to Indian traders and moneylenders: that of intermediaries in the marketing of imported industrial goods from England and the procurement of Indian agricultural goods like raw cotton for export to supply factories in England and other industrializing countries. In the Indian market, which took about 40 per cent of England's worldwide cotton goods exports in the 1860s, growth of industries was not 'desirable'. A doctrine spelled out specialization in agriculture for India, and industry for England, as offering the best competitive advantage to both. This remained the orthodox economic theory for decades, and as late as

▲ A ten rupee note issued on the Bank of Madras, 1861.

▼ The first office of the Chamber of Commerce in Madras.

▶ A rare photograph of the partners of one of India's oldest firms, Tata Sons and Company: J.N. Tata, R.D. Tata, Sir R.J. Tata, and Sir D.J. Tata.

1911 John Maynard Keynes wrote in *The Economic Journal* (September 1911): 'Specialization among nations' was a good thing and, though the Indian 'educated class seem to desire, with patriotic fervour, industrialization of their country', such industrialization was 'neither desirable, nor likely'.

The consequences of this thinking and the pressure of British industrial interests pervaded all aspects of Indian economic history from the middle of the nineteenth century up to the First World War. In 1860, James Wilson, founder of *The Economist*, was sent from England to lay down the financial policy of the new Government of India that replaced the East India Company in 1858. Its basic features were a tariff policy that encouraged the import of industrial goods and the export of raw materials; the development of railways and roads to encourage the process; heavy expenditure on the army and the police, and on administrative infrastructure, rather than development investments; and the facilitation of European-style business practices in India through appropriate institutional development and legislation in banking and joint-stock corporations.

British managing agencies, English banks and railway companies, shipping and industrial and commercial interests in England were the intended beneficiaries of the British Indian Government's policies. But, as often happens in history, there were

many unintended consequences of those policies in terms of Indo-British economic relations. In the interstices of British-dominated business there were spaces for Indian capital to engage profitably. In procuring opium for export to China, or raw cotton for the Manchester cotton mills, or jute for the Dundee jute mills, Indian middlemen were needed. Likewise, they were useful in opening up the interior of the country to imported industrial goods. Besides, there remained, of course, areas untouched by foreign enterprise such as petty moneylending and localized trade.

A second consequence of the impact of industrialized England on India was the creation of the possibility of technological modernization in the long run, even though there was no immediate prospect of industrialization. Bearing this in mind, Karl Marx wrote in the 1850s that the railways would eventually bring about a modern era in India. Besides modern machinery and technology such as the railways and jute mills, the relationship also imported modern corporate business organizations and banking practices and managerial know-how to India. Indian entrepreneurs became aware of these in the course of the last half of the nineteenth century. Some Indian business communities, like the Parsis in Bombay (now Mumbai), took to the new style of business like ducks to water, while others like the Marwaris in Calcutta responded more cautiously and slowly, utilizing opportunities that came their way and such modern techniques as they found profitable to adopt.

British capital investment in India did not play a significant role in nineteenth-century industrial development with the exception of jute mills, coal mines, and tea plantations, followed by some investment in tobacco, hydrogenated oil, electrical machinery, pharmaceuticals, and petrol. The bulk of British capital was invested in government bonds, railways, and in merchant companies and banks serving the export–import business. In 1948, the Reserve Bank of India Survey estimated that of all

▲ Members of the Bombay Millowners' Association with Bradbury, Herbert Greaves, Naoroji B. Saklatwala, Dwarkadas Dharamsi, Leslie Rogers, Nusservanji N. Wadia, C.J. Michael, Manmohundas Ramji, Jehangir C. Jehangir, Sir Sassoon J. David, Narondas Purshotumdas, Bomanji Dinshaw Petit, Ahmedbhoy Habibhoy, Vithuldas D. Thakersi, and Jamsetji A. Wadia in the picture.

▼ Mill labels in the 1920s reflected popular social concerns such as the spinning wheel, and picketing outside liquor shops. These labels are from the Meyer Sassoon, Sassoon Limited, and the Jacob Sassoon Mills.

foreign capital invested in India, only 28 per cent was in the manufacturing industry, whereas 37 per cent was invested in merchandising and transport, and 20 per cent in tea, coffee, and rubber plantations.

India's industrialization was left to Indian entrepreneurs. This began as early as the mid-nineteenth century in western India, mainly in the cotton textile industry. In eastern India, thanks to the stranglehold of English managing agencies, Indian enterprise entered industry rather belatedly. Industrial enterprise in southern India — notable for the migration of southern capital overseas to Burma and South East Asia — and in northern India, did not emerge till the twentieth century. The rise of the textile industry from the days of the pioneers, Cowasjee Nanabhai Davar who started the first cotton mill in 1854 in Bombay, and Sir Ranchhodlal Chhotalal in Ahmedabad, show truly innovative entrepreneurship, as does the story of the founding of the Jamshedpur steelworks by Sir J.N. Tata. In none of these cases was any assistance forthcoming from the British Indian government. Indeed, in the case of the cotton textile industry, the growth was in spite of a hostile tariff policy and excise duty on each yard of cloth produced,

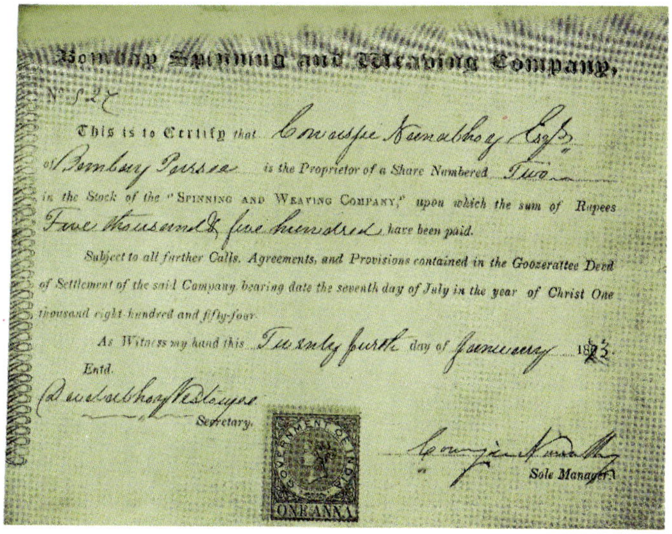

Bombay Spinning and Weaving Company,

This is to Certify that Cowasjee Nanabhoy Esqr.
of Bombay Parsee is the Proprietor of a Share Numbered Two
in the Stock of the "Spinning and Weaving Company," upon which the sum of Rupees
Five thousand & five hundred have been paid.
Subject to all further Calls, Agreements, and Provisions contained in the Goozerattee Deed of Settlement of the said Company bearing date the seventh day of July in the year of Christ One thousand eight hundred and fifty-four.
As Witness my hand this Twenty fourth day of January
Entd.
Secretary.
Sole Manager.
ONE ANNA

▲ A share certificate from 1854 recording the transfer of the Bombay Spinning and Weaving Company, to Cowasjee Davar. Such early entrepreneurship was responsible for the development of Indian industries, though it was a great deal later that they could compete favourably with the Manchester mills.

▼ An advertisement for Fiat published in *The Times of India* annual, 1921.

industry was Rs 10.2 crore in 1900–1, Rs 26.5 crore in 1925–6, and Rs 58.3 crore in 1945–6 (constant price estimate, 1938–9). In the 25 years between 1900–25, all Indian industries more than doubled their output: cotton textiles, jute, iron and steel, woollen textiles, paper, and cement. The average number of people employed in factories stood at 5.4 lakh in 1900–1, at 14.3 lakh in 1925–6, and 29.5 lakh in 1945–6.

Considering the stagnation in the previous decades, the post-World War I spurt of industry was massive. Nevertheless, in the national economy as a whole, the role of industrial manufacture continued to be marginal. I have used above Shivasubramanian's estimates; he has also estimated net domestic product trends (at constant price, 1938–9). The primary sector's share in NDP was 63.6 per cent in 1900–4, 57.4 per cent in 1920–4, and 47.6 per cent in 1940–4. The share of manufacturing, mining, the construction industry, etc. in the secondary sector was only 12.7 per cent of NDP in 1900–4, 13.4 per cent in 1920–4, and 16.7 per cent in 1940–4.

and yet the industry out-competed Manchester and found an export market for yarn and cloth in China and elsewhere. When Sir Jamsetji approached Lord George Hamilton, the Secretary of State for India in London, he was cynically informed that Lord Hamilton was prepared to eat every ounce of steel that Tata could produce. Within a few years, Tata began to roll out tons of steel. Having been rejected by the London money market when he tried to raise 1.6 m. sterling, he eventually raised it in August 1907, within a mere three weeks, from among 8000 Indian shareholders. It was a vote of confidence in national enterprise.

Yet till the First World War, industrial manufacture remained limited. British industrial competition was greatly reduced in India during the War for want of shipping, the diversion of traditional British industries to War-related purposes and the lack of capital, providing an opportunity for Indian industries to develop. This was when Manchester lost its market to Indian mills. On an average, Manchester imports into India were 262 crore yards of cloth per year in 1910–14; they fell to 181 crore in 1914–19, and to 133 crore in 1919–24. The output of the Indian cotton textile

▲ Dadabhai Naoroji believed that economic nationalism was essential for the upliftment of the Indian cause, and worked towards strengthening the links between political and business leadership.

The post-World War I period witnessed another new phenomenon: the consolidation of Indian business communities in the form of chambers of commerce and other associated forms of organization as a lobby to pressurize the government, on the one hand, and to develop links with the nationalist leadership, on the other. There were, of course, chambers of commerce right from the early nineteenth century, but these were usually initiated and dominated by English businessmen. There was the Bengal Chamber of Commerce (1834) which had its counterparts later in Bombay and Madras (now Chennai) (1836). There were also trade associations limited to a particular industry or business, e.g. the Indian Jute Mills Association of Bengal (1884) and the Bombay Millowners' Association (1875).

Soon after the formation of the Indian National Congress (1885), a Bengal National Chamber of Commerce (1887) came into existence because indigenous merchants wanted an organization of their own. There developed from the late nineteenth century on, business associations that were more specifically community based, e.g. the Bharat Chamber of Commerce (1898) of Calcutta. The growth of communal sentiments also led to the creation of Muslim Chambers of Commerce in the twentieth century. As the Indian business community grew in strength after World War I, it felt the need for a federal body to consolidate the strength of dispersed local organizations. Hence the formation of the Federation of Indian Chambers of Commerce, later known as FICCI, formed by Sir Purshotamdas Thakurdas and other business leaders in 1927. This body had precursors in the shape of the Industrial Conferences (since 1919) and the All India Association of Chambers of Commerce (1915). On the whole, a perception of some common business interests and joint action on occasions like the Tariff Commission enquiries gave these various bodies a measure of unity and influence in the public sphere.

As India moved towards Independence, the links between the business community and nationalist leadership were strengthened. Even before the Indian business class came into their own, the economic nationalism of Dadabhai Naoroji or Romesh Chandra Dutt provided a powerful critique of the British policies that were detrimental to the development of indigenous capital in India. They focused attention on, among other things, the tariff policy and the destruction and stagnation of India's industries. The *swadeshi* agitation in Bengal in 1905–7 and Mahatma Gandhi's call for the boycott of foreign goods established a direct supportive relationship between industrial interests and the nationalist cause. Although the financial contribution of nationalistically inclined businessmen to the Indian National Congress and Mahatma Gandhi was not insignificant, the ideological aspect was perhaps more important. The leaders of the mainstream nationalist movement placed the aspirations of the Indian business community high on their agenda as part of their concept of a desirable pattern of development of the national economy. This was imbued with a historical view of the colonial impact on India from the late eighteenth to the twentieth centuries. As in all other countries, in India too the construction of the nation had at its core a consciousness of history.

The Eastern Region

Kunal Bose

The story of the rise of east Indian entrepreneurship in colonial times must necessarily begin with Dwarkanath Tagore (1794–1846), Rabindranath's grandfather. The Tagore family had migrated to Calcutta, one of four major trading posts established by the East India Company, from Jessore, at the beginning of the eighteenth century. The British enclave was inviting for most Indian merchants where, besides the prospect of making money by seizing new opportunities, contracts were honoured and property rights respected. If the Parsis, the Gujarati trading communities, and the Muslim Bohras were drawn to Bombay, the Marwaris from Rajasthan and merchants from Punjab preferred the eastern coast.

Long before Dwarkanath shot into prominence as a zamindar, merchant, and industrialist, his predecessors had earned the confidence of the British in offering them insights into the Indian

▼ Nineteenth-century market place, Calcutta. The colonial capital was the result of the East India Company finding the region conducive as an entry point to India, even though it took the merging of three villages to create an appropriate urban, commercial settlement.

▲ Dwarkanath Tagore was a visionary. Educated in western ideology, he hoped to see Indians enjoying not only freedom, but also the liberty of choice in developing personal and professional relations with the British.

market. The British returned the compliment in several ways, and among the Tagores, Dwarkanath proved to be the major beneficiary of their munificence. His education and breadth of vision placed him on a par with Englishmen who, in turn, appointed him Dewan of the Board of Customs, Salt, and Opium.

Blair B. Kling, historian, with his path-breaking work on Dwarkanath, writes,

> Tagore envisioned a future India that was westernized and industrialized and whose inhabitants enjoyed without discrimination the rights and liberties of Englishmen. He would lay the foundations for this new India in his own day by promoting an all-encompassing interracial partnership of Britishers and Indians.

As he campaigned for progressive Indians to associate themselves with the British as equals in business, social, cultural, and political activities, Dwarkanath practised interracial collaboration in the running of his zamindaris and in almost all his businesses. His true mettle, however, came to light during and after the devastating commercial crisis of 1830–3 that snuffed out all the major agency houses and landed their partners in considerable debts. Kling writes that it was 'when the giants had stumbled and fallen that he [Dwarkanath] emerged as one of the leading commercial men in the period 1834–46 if not the leading one'. In those difficult times, he counted on his estates for his income and even stretched his resources to bail out several British friends.

The formation of Carr, Tagore & Company in 1834 on the basis of interracial cooperation was a trail-blazing development for the economy of the eastern region, and also for local entrepreneurs. It is following his footsteps that Motilal Seal and Ram Gopal Ghosh founded similar interracial agency houses. The outstanding success of Carr, Tagore & Co. was as much due to the enormous fund provided to it to by Dwarkanath as to his vision to establish a synergy between his estates and the agency's export business. Today, he is counted among the region's pioneers in the mining, banking, insurance, shipping, shipbuilding, plantation, and export–import businesses.

▼ Nineteenth-century Calcutta. It was here, in the heart of the city, that brokers would gather to buy and sell shares.

In a letter that Dwarkanath wrote to the governor-general, Lord William Bentinck, following the start of the agency house, he said his initiative was 'calculated to introduce

▲ Chandpal Ghat on the Hooghly, Calcutta. It was from here that the import-export trade was successfully run.

▼ The seal of the East India Company came to signify power, first as an important trading body, and later as the power that became a government.

the natives of India generally to more immediate participation in the objects of European enterprises', and that it would lead to the unfolding of the 'productive energies of the country'. Even though he, and others like him, who had put their faith in biracial business ventures, were pained to find metropolitan interests prevailing over colonial ones, nevertheless governors-general like Lord Bentinck and Lord Auckland were found to be supportive of the development of local industries. What even they could not ensure, however, was that companies in trouble failed to get any succour from the government.

By the mid-nineteenth century, educated middle-class Bengalis were forsaking interest in business to opt for jobs. However, 1855 saw Bysumber Sen, a Bengali entrepreneur, joining hands with George Acland to set up the country's first jute mill. Sir P.C. Ray, pioneer of the Indian pharmaceutical industry (founded Bengal Chemical), wrote that Marwari and other upcountry trading communities had raced past the Bengalis in trading and industrial activities by 1850.

It will be a distortion of history if the role of Rustomjee Cowasjee, a Parsi merchant, in promoting the concept of interracial business alliance almost a decade ahead of Dwarkanath, is not placed on record. Among Indian businessmen, Rustomjee ranks second only to Dwarkanath. The two virtually laid the ground rules for the Indian breakthrough in industry, as also higher levels of trade which, in the eastern part, were pursued to their immense benefit by Marwaris in particular.

Rajat K. Ray writes in his book, *Industrialisation in India*:

> The big Indian houses which came to dominate the corporate sector as monopoly concerns after 1947 showed remarkable similarity of development over time. Most of these houses began in a dependent capacity, servicing foreign interests by trade, speculation and agency business of various sorts. At some point they switched over from so-called comprador activities to industrial investment, and finally the most successful among them, having acquired large financial assets in trade and consumer industries, turned their surplus funds to hitherto untried engineering, chemical and metallurgical industries of an advanced type ... The popular distinction between comprador and national bourgeoisie was somewhat blurred. Nor is it easy ... to relate the political attitude of Indian businessman to their economic role so precisely.

The businesses controlled by many of the leading managing agency houses fell into the laps of the likes of the Goenkas, Khaitans,

▲ A Bengali merchant perusing documents. Calcutta emerged as the business hub during the colonial period.

▼ Inside a jute spinning mill. Initially controlled by the British, Indian businessmen faced several disadvantages when they attempted to enter the arena.

Bangurs, Mehtas, Thapars, Bajorias, and Jalans — businessmen who had worked closely with the British over many decades — following Independence. But the spirit of cooperation soured on occasion when the British felt that local businessmen were straying into their exclusive preserve. The industrialist Ghanshyam Das Birla (1894–1983), for example, invited the wrath of Scotsmen and Englishmen when, soon after setting up Birla Brothers Pvt. Ltd as an agency house at an investment of Rs 28 lakh, he went on to set up a jute mill. He knew the industry well, but all hell broke loose when the foreigners found out what he was up to. There was no trick they did not try to stop G.D. in his tracks: the rupee sterling exchange rate was changed to make machine imports much more expensive, the acquisition of land for the factory was delayed, and the project cost doubled.

The financial strain on the group caused considerable concern to the Calcutta-based Jugalkishor, eldest of the four Birla brothers. Andrew Yule, the English managing agency with large interests in jute, was leading the campaign against the Birla venture. G.D. was left with no alternative but to attempt to make peace with the chief executive of Andrew Yule who, however, did not relent in his campaign. According to S.S. Kanoria, former FICCI President, his father Radhakissen Kanoria, a close business associate of the Birlas,

The Impact of Colonial Hegemony

The colonial impact on business in eastern India was clearly visible in the early decades of the nineteenth century. The subordination of the Indian business class by the more influential business interests of the ruling race (mainly in the form of British managing agencies, called agency houses till the late nineteenth century) has been sometimes represented as a 'partnership' between the rulers and the ruled. However, it was nothing of the kind. Whenever British and 'native' Indian interests came into conflict, the true character of the partnership was revealed: a partnership between unequals where the the Indian business class was allowed to operate in the lower levels of the colonial economy, e.g. the unorganized money market and rural money lending, the internal trade in agricultural products for export, the business of marketing imported industrial products, etc.

By the early twentieth century, as the Indian business class began to challenge the traditional preserves of British business houses – jute and tea, shipping, banking, import-export business, etc.–the awareness of colonial hegemony spread amongst businessmen. At the same time, the *swadeshi* ideal propagated during the agitation against the partition of Bengal in 1905 had an impact among Bengali intellectuals. They, in turn, made an effort to introduce modern science and technology to open new industries, e.g. Sir P.C. Roy's enterprise to establish the chemical and pharmaceutical industry in Bengal. The overall result was to bring about an alliance, often tacit and indirect, between the leaders of the nationalist movement and Indian business interests.

The Bengali business enterprise was unable to exploit business opportunities which others exploited successfully. What accounted for the lack of enterprise among the Bengalis from the early nineteenth century on is a debatable issue. One reason may have been that, after the establishment of the East India Company's permanent settlement with zamindars in 1793, Bengali wealth was attracted away from business to investment in zamindari. Increasingly, the unearned increments to the zamindars' income and the social prestige of that status proved to be more attractive. The culture and mindset of the zamindar was devoid of the qualities which business enterprise demanded. It has also been suggested that the hold of nationalist politics over the Bengali *bhadralok* mind discouraged collaborative relationships with English business interests.

Calcutta was, in many ways, a more colonial metropolis than Bombay. Till the 1920s, industrial capital in Bengal was almost entirely in British hands, offering a contrast to the Bombay region where indigenous capital participation was vigorous right from1860s on. Thus, Calcutta's large share of paid up capital of joint stock companies in India up to the early decades of the twentieth century is more an index of British capitalistic hold than a measure of the strength of Indian business classes. In the inter-war period, for the first time Indian, particularly Marwari, capital began a takeover of industrial establishments, and later the tea plantations originally founded by British entrepreneurs. The entry of indigenous capital in the industrial area followed even later in Bengal than in Madras Presidency. This uneven pace of growth of indigenous industrial ventures in different parts of India gave shape to the patterns that emerged in the post-1947 period.

Towards the end of British rule, a series of events severely affected Bengal's economy. Business was more directly affected in Bengal than in any other part of the country by World War II; the War reached the borders of eastern India and caused depletion of resources, particularly food grains. The word 'black market' entered the Indian vocabulary. The famine of 1943 took a high toll of mortalities: usually believed to be nearly 3 million lives. The partition of 1947 cut off Calcutta from its hinterland in eastern Bengal and caused other economic dislocations. The huge influx of refugees caused a heavy burden on the state, and the poor economic conditions in East Bengal (Bangladesh) has seen a constant flow from the other side of the border, leading to pressures on employment opportunities and other resources in the state.

told him that the misbehaviour of the Andrew Yule chief strengthened G.D.'s resolve to make a success of Birla Jute Mills. Jugalkishor stood by G.D. — not surprisingly, since G.D. never ceased creating wealth, even though he remained nationalist to the core. The huge profits earned by the jute mills during the First World War and dividends of over 100 per cent declared by many

▼ Indian industrialists with Queen Elizabeth and Prince Philip. In the picture with the British royal couple are the Maharaja of Burdwan, Sir Biren Mookerjee, Sir Badridas Goenka, Padmaja Naidu, B.M. Birla, S. Gupta, Sachin Chowdhry and B.P. Singh Roy.

jute mills drew more local investment in the industry. Sir Sarupchand Hukamchand, a member of the Jain trading family of Marwar, who set up a jute mill around the same time as G.D., had already made a fortune in banking and trade in various commodities, including cotton and jute. Surajmull Nagarmull (a Jalan and Bajoria families combine) also established a jute mill. Writes Amiya Kumar Bagchi in his seminal work, *Private Investment in India (1900–39):*

> During the [First World] War Indians also seem to have captured a large part of the capital of jute mills; the explanation cannot be that Europeans were keen to sell their shares in the companies concerned, for jute shares continued to carry very high dividends well up to 1926. One plausible explanation is that during the war a large proportion of the British businessmen of Calcutta were either out in the front lines or engaged in other war work.

The Calcutta Stock Exchange, the oldest in the country, was formally inaugurated on 15 June 1908. Calcutta, however, had a tradition of stockbroking dating back to the eighteenth century when transactions were in securities of the East India Company. *The Englishman*, the forerunner of *The Statesman*, would publish quotations of East India Company loans as well as the shares of the Bank of Bengal, Agra Bank, Bengal Bonded Warehouse, and of some steamer companies.

▶ An old picture of the Bengal Chamber of Commerce, Royal Exchange, Calcutta.

For a long time, the brokers conducted trading in an open public place under a *neem* tree in the heart of the city. As the brokers made their fortunes, they wanted to move into a pukka building and felt the need for a set of rules and ethical code so that stockbroking could be recognized as an organized profession in the then capital of British India.

Official records show that there was a boom in jute shares in the 1870s, followed by tea shares in the 1880s and coal shares in the 1890s. But as the boom in coal shares petered out in 1909, the stockmarket fell into a crisis with many stockbrokers failing to meet their commitments. Dr B.B. Ghosh writes in the *History of the Calcutta Stock Exchange:* 'The crisis became so acute that at one point there was even a talk of winding up the Exchange. Fortunately, it remained only at the level of thinking, thanks to the stewardship of the then committee of the Exchange.'

Indians played as important a role as Europeans in promoting stocktrading in Calcutta. Of the two early leading lights of the Exchange, one was an Indian: Babu Buldeodass Duduawala. The first committee of the Exchange had nine members, five Europeans and four Indians. The 1918 committee comprised four Europeans, four Marwaris, and four Bengalis. In the first two decades of the Exchange, the Indians who had a domineering presence included Mugneeram Bangur, Sugan Chand Bagree, Kedarnath Khandelwal, Goralall Seal, and S.G. Boral. Khandelwal became the first Indian President of the Exchange in 1931 and occupied the office till 1936.

Some foreign observers point out that had the imperial government encouraged the growth of steel industry in India for

▲ Sir Rajendranath Mookerjee, an Anglian in social mores, followed up the TISCO venture with his own Indian Iron & Steel Co. in 1918, though on a more modest scale.

▼ A panoramic view of the Tata Iron and Steel Company, Jamshedpur. Pioneered by Sir Jamsetji Tata, it began production in 1912 against heavy odds. However, it continues to remain among the premium industrial ventures in eastern India.

feeding the elaborate railway network that was created in the nineteenth century, India 'would by 1914 have been one of the largest industrial producers in the world'. But for steel industry to develop, a strong policy of protection, including the assured offtake of steel rails by the railways, was necessary. Jamsetji Tata, who pioneered the steel industry in India, did not unfortunately live to see the Tata Iron and Steel Co. begin production in 1912.

Rajat Ray points out that the 'Tatas, unlike some big nationalist houses in the private sector, enjoyed excellent race relations'. For the first many years of TISCO, the supervisory staff was mostly foreign. During the First World War, the Tatas turned TISCO into a captive source of steel for the government, though it could have earned huge profits by selling steel in the open market at very high premia. According to economic historians, the loss of a fairly large portion of the Indian steel market to Continental producers influenced the government decision to offer protection to TISCO. In 1931, N.B. Saklatvala, chairman of TISCO, told shareholders that 'if protection has not paid you dividends, it has at least preserved your property'. TISCO continues to remain eastern India's most successful industrial venture.

Sir Rajendranath Mookerjee, regarded as a champion of English social life and cultural values, floated the Indian Iron & Steel Co. in 1918, but on a much smaller scale than TISCO. The Singhanias' JK group, which pioneered the development of the aluminium industry in the country, set up an integrated refinery, smelter, and rolling mills at Asansol.

Indian houses like the Birlas, Dalmia–Jain, and Surajmull Nagarmull took full advantage of the protective import duty on

▶ B.M. Birla takes his grandson Chandrakant on a ride in a favourite old car that was handmade for him in 1928.

▼ Inside the plant of Hindustan Motors Ltd, Calcutta, where car bodies receive a final coat of colour. Set up in technical collaboration with Morris Motors and Studebaker, for several decades the plant catered to India's automotive requirements. Today, fresh collaborations have brought in technologies more compatible with the 1990s.

sugar imposed since the mid-1930s to build sugar factories in eastern India. Sugar, by then, had also become a highly profitable industry. By the time the Second World War began, the Birlas had five factories with a daily cane crushing capacity of 5400 tonnes, and Dalmia–Jain two factories of a combined capacity of 3300 tonnes. Indian capital (represented by Birlas, Dalmia–Jain, Thapars, and Bajorias) was also drawn into the paper industry when it started generating large surpluses beginning in 1936.

Birlas, the principal representative of national capitalism, started producing textile machinery at the Calcutta factory of TEXMACO in the early 1940s, as a path-breaking venture. The scope for import substitution in this sector was huge. The Birla-promoted Hindustan Motors plant at Uttarpara in West Bengal, as also Premier Automobiles in Maharashtra, were the result of inspiration provided by Sir M. Visveswaraiya. To put the record straight, Visveswaraiya wanted Tatas, who had already made a mark in the steel industry, to produce (assemble) cars. But after some initial enthusiasm, the Tatas did not follow up Visveswaraiya's suggestion. The vision and gift of G.D. and B.M. Birla, and also of Walchand and Hirachand, must be judged against the background of the foreign car producers and their captive market interests, which attempted everything possible to derail the

▲ Among India's leading industrialists, Sir Badridas Goenka and his family found that takeovers or buying companies under the control of foreign agency houses made sound financial sense.

initiative of the two local houses. Hindustan Motors finally formed technical alliances with Morris Motors of the UK, and Studebaker Corporation of the US, on favourable terms.

Those close to him say that once G.D. had a new business idea, he would move with electrifying speed to give it concrete shape. Ram Niwas Jaju's biography of the industrialist provides one such example:

> Once in 1942, G.D. suddenly thought of starting a bank. Over a cup of tea in the evening, he broached this issue casually to a friend. When the friend corroborated G.D.'s view, he immediately wrote to a reliable friend in Bombay asking him to suggest a suitable person for his bank. The name of the late B.T. Thakur, then general manager of the Central Bank at Karachi, was suggested. Within a week G.D. invited him to an interview and the bank started its initial work in January 1943. What seemed a dim idea in October 1942 took shape in the United Commercial Bank in May 1943. This bank provided a solid base for Birla Brothers who were involved in swift industrial development.

With Independence in 1947, many local houses found they had the financial clout to start buying companies under the control of foreign agency houses. Sir Badridas Goenka and his son, Keshav Prasad Goenka, perfected the art of gaining control of companies through the takeover route. Peter Pugh writes in his book, *Williamson Magor Stuck to Tea*, that the most significant development for the group has been the partnership with Birju (B.M.) Khaitan, 'the Indian introduced to the group in the late 1940s by Pat Williamson'. Basant Kumar Birla, youngest of G.D.'s three sons, made his mark in the British-dominated tea industry when, in 1945, at the conclusion of a meeting at Birla House in New Delhi, he said: 'If no one else is interested in tea and aviation, then I want to try my hand in these industries.' On his return to Calcutta, the young Birla (24) formed Jay Shree Tea Ltd. What he did not know at that point, and even later in 1946 when he was about to acquire the Sholayar group in Madras state, was that G.D. thought that 'a tea garden was *zamindari* land ownership and not an industry', and that the Birlas should not be in that business. In fact, he had to be persuaded to let B.K. buy Sholayar. Earlier, he had bought Lohagarh Tea Estate in Assam, a small property by Birla standards. B.K. says that when he acquired Towkob Tea Estate at an auction, this again met with G.D.'s disapproval. But B.K.'s steady growth in the tea industry had been significant in the Indian context. The Goenkas too made a conscious decision quite early that the group would be a major player in tea. Today, many companies and gardens may still bear English names but are managed by concerns that owe their origins to the spirit of entrepreneurship that characterized trade in India under a colonial regime.

The Western Region

Dwijendra Tripathi

With the fall of the Maratha Confederacy in 1818, western India witnessed the eclipse of the last vestiges of Indian sovereignty. The political subjugation of the subcontinent was now complete. The British conquest of western India, therefore, marked the beginning, in a comprehensive sense, of the colonial era in Indian history.

At the time of British occupation, the northern part of western India (or present Gujarat) had a vigorous, vibrant business life, thanks to its locational advantages. It had a long coastline and boasted some of the finest ports in the country, a rich hinterland fed its economy, and major trade routes linked it with the rest of the country. Goods from northern, western, and even central Asia would gather in the Gujarat ports before being shipped onwards to Western countries, or into the hinterlands. A large number of urban centres such as Ahmedabad, Surat, Bharuch, and Cambay arose, offering lucrative business opportunities. The southern part of the region (the western districts of present Maharashtra), offered by, comparison, fewer incentives.

▼ Street scene, Bombay. Created from swampy marshlands, Bombay became the financial capital of the country on account of its rapid industrialization. It is a position it continues to hold today.

There, however, were signs of change: Surat, once the country's premier port, had passed its prime, adversely affecting its commercial significance. Cambay and Bharuch as trade centres had declined even before Surat. Ahmedabad was holding its own, but it too could not escape the brunt of the oppressive Maratha regime that the British supplanted in 1818. There is no doubt that the influence of business and businessmen was on the wane. There was a time when persons like Shantidas Zaveri in Ahmedabad or Virji Vora in Surat set the tone of society. With the disintegration of the Mughal Empire, the place of these merchant princes was taken by traders and moneylenders who operated in a limited area and on a modest scale. The petty rulers and chieftains that arose out of the ruins of the mighty Mughals depended on their money and granted them royal patronage in return, but the social relevance of the merchants had been eroded. No wonder then that the Gujarati business community rejoiced at the establishment of

British rule in the region, even if it meant being subservient to an alien economic interest.

In contrast, the southern part of western India had remained relatively backward in business development. There were fewer and smaller urban centres, and though some like Pune were noted for their cultural environment or political significance, large centres of trade were conspicuous by their absence.

Around the end of the second decade of the nineteenth century, Bombay was still a mere shadow of the present day metropolis, but it already had a population of over 1,60,000, twice that of Ahmedabad, Gujarat's largest urban centre, and was growing fast. Immigration from adjoining regions was the principal factor behind the rise in population, and among the immigrants were merchants from Gujarat — particularly Parsis from Surat and adjoining areas, and Kutchhi Bhatias from west Gujarat. Later, other social groups such as the Vaishnava *bania*s and the Jains too found immigration to Bombay a worthwhile proposition.

Bombay, in the meantime, had already developed a variegated business class, its foundation laid in the latter half of the eighteenth century by such British agency houses as Forbes & Co., Bruce Faucett & Co., Lecie & Co., and Schotten & Co., which grew into formidable concerns. Since the agency business could bring only limited returns, enterprising British merchants diversified into a variety of fields such as banking, trading, shipping, and insurance. Supporting them were a large number of Indian middlemen who, in due course, built their own firms.

▼ Seventeenth-century East India Company factory, Surat. Gujarati businessmen had initially welcomed foreign traders because it helped restore the eroded position of the trader in society.

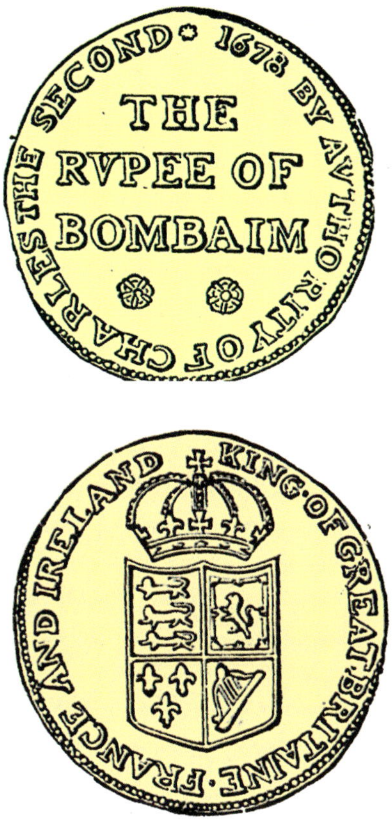

▲ Seventeenth-century Bombay rupee. Bombay developed a vigorous sea trade and was part of an extensive international shipping route that saw the import and export of goods on a large scale.

The establishment of the Bombay Chamber of Commerce in 1836 underscored the growing importance of business in the life of the city. The founders were seven Englishmen and three Parsis, reflecting the relative position of these communities in the composition of the business class. The early membership consisting of 15 British and 10 Parsi firms also indicated the dominance of these groups in Bombay's business.

For practically all large firms, opium trade with China proved the most lucrative business in the first half of the nineteenth century. During the first three decades, this was carried on clandestinely, circumventing restrictions that the Bombay government had clamped on private trade in opium. After these restrictions were abolished in 1831, opium emerged as the principal item of export from Bombay. Charles Forbes of Forbes & Co. was perhaps the only businessman to openly denounce 'this disgraceful and abominable trade', though it did not restrain him from undertaking it as a business proposition.

A brief account of the business career of Jamsetjee Jeejeebhoy will illustrate the mechanics and organization of Bombay trade. The son of a poor Parsi weaver from Navsari, a town near Surat, he migrated to Bombay where his maternal uncle had a small business selling bottles. He developed close links with several Bombay merchants and, as his commission business flourished, he made several trips to China in the first decade of the nineteenth century on behalf of some Parsi merchants. He exported cotton to England as an agent of a London firm and sold cassia and silk in Bombay for a prominent Chinese merchant. He also procured pearls for his Chinese principal and shipped them to Canton. Within a decade and a half of his migration to Bombay, he had become wealthy and developed a network of business associates in other ports such as Daman and Karachi to exploit the lucrative opium trade. When restrictions on opium trade were eased in 1831, the bulk of opium produced in the Malwa region found its way out of India through Bombay. Jamsetjee took advantage of the new situation, establishing close business links with Jardine Matheson & Co. This Canton-based British firm was perhaps the most powerful trader in the drug in east Asia, and the largest exporter of Chinese tea to Britain. In addition to opium, Jamsetjee also exported cotton, not only from Bombay but occasionally also from Calcutta and Madras. General trading and moneylending were his other sources of profits, and investment in real estate a passion.

Ahmedabad was the other major business centre in western India and the principal merchants there had similar interests. Commerce and trade recovered quickly after the end of the disastrous Maratha rule, and though silk and textile goods continued to be exported, it was trade in cotton and opium that

▼ Ranchhodlal Chhotalal belonged to the group that came to be identified as the Ahmedabad industrialists because they confined their operations to a single industry, and to their own city. The cultivation of cotton and the establishment of spinning mills was their chosen sphere of activity.

helped Ahmedabad regain its glory. Ahmedabad merchants, located closer to Daman and Karachi from where the bulk of the Malwa drug was exported before 1831, were in a better position to profit by the illegal traffic. No wonder then that much before the restrictions on opium exports from Bombay were relaxed, 'almost all the Ahmedabad merchants had agents or branches of their houses established in Malwa for the purchase of opium'. Among those who shipped opium through Jamsetjee Jeejeebhoy were prominent Jain merchants from Ahmedabad such as Vakhatchand Khushalchand, Hathising Kesarising, and Karamchand Premchand. A greatgrandson of the illustrious Shantidas Zaveri and a forerunner of the present day Lalbhai family, Vakhatchand was the *nagarseth* of Ahmedabad. Hathising was related to the family by marriage and presided over a large banking business, and Karamchand, also a banker, was an ancestor of the famous Sarabhai family of our times.

Although most merchants in the region belonged to castes and groups traditionally identified with the business profession — Parsis, Jains, Vaishanava *bania*s — others were not altogether absent from the mercantile life of western India during the first half of the nineteenth century. The Travadis of Surat, a family of *nagar* Brahmins, had been the principal bankers of the English East India Company at least up to the first decade of the nineteenth century, and were still active in the business life of their city well until the end of the second decade. Dhackjee Dadajee and Jaggannath Shankarsett, both claiming Brahmin lineage but belonging to *gotras* normally considered lower in the Brahmin hierarchy, were prominent in the Bombay business community. Muslims, among the biggest shipowners of Surat in its heyday, were still noticeable in this field. Mohammad Ali Rogay was counted among the well-known shipowner captains of Bombay and remained a close associate of Jamsetjee Jeejeebhoy until the end of his life.

Meanwhile, the business climate in the subcontinent was changing. The colonial masters were launching, or at least contemplating, a series of infrastructural changes of far-reaching consequence — roads, railways, postal services, a unified currency, a codified system of law — to link together the various parts of the country. The size of the market was being enlarged in the process. The one single event, however, that radically altered the business environment in western India, was the abolition of all restrictions on the export of textile machinery from Great Britain in 1843. It was now possible for ambitious Indians to set up textile mills using the technology that had made that country the industrial workshop of the world.

▶ The 1854 agreement between the shareholders of the Bombay Spinning and Weaving Company, and Cowasjee Davar *(inset)*. The export of cotton from India to America in the 1860s proved to be among the earliest hurdles these industrialists had to face, though the situation improved greatly a decade later.

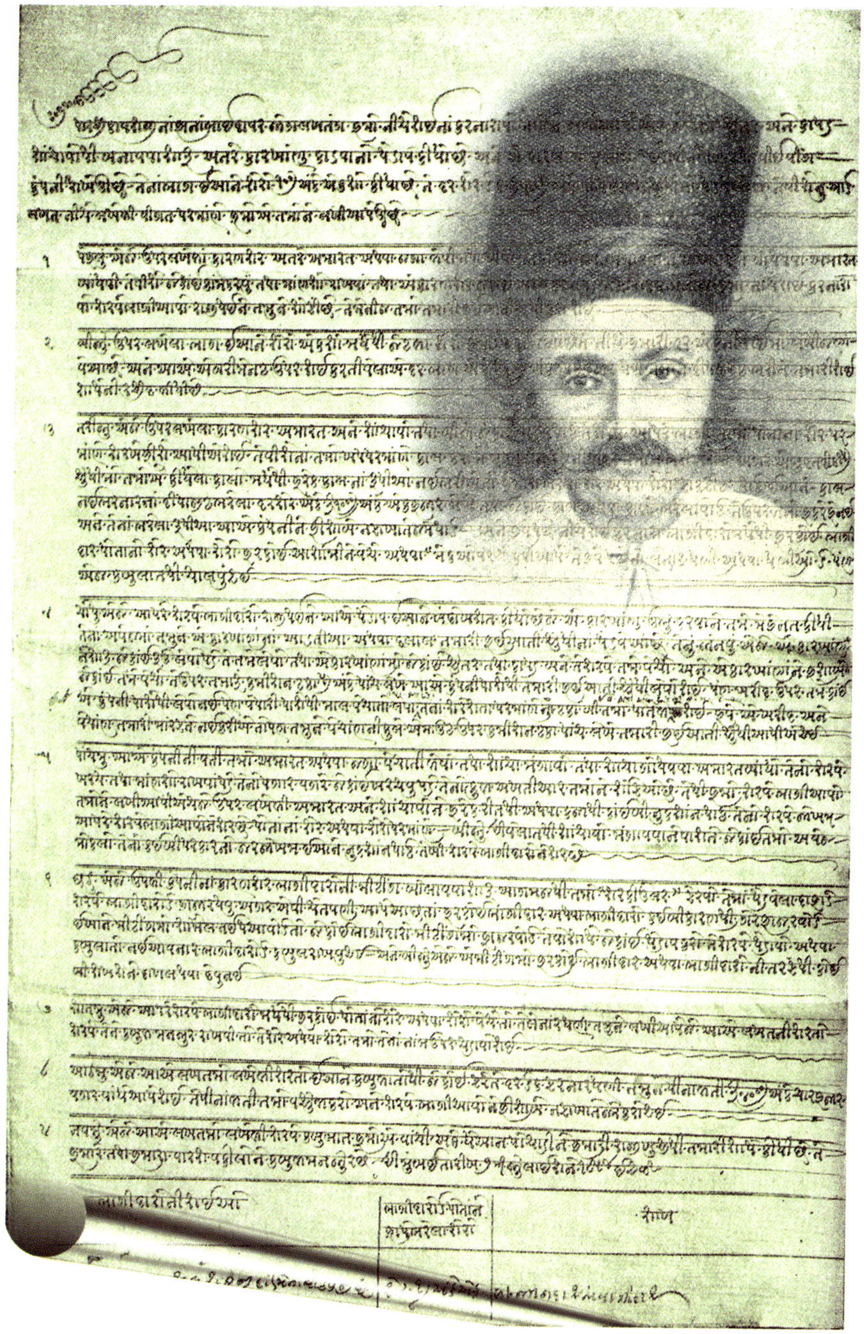

▼ Sir Jamsetjee Jeejebhoy was the son of a Parsi weaver from Gujarat who was able to seize opportunity in the export and import trade. His business revolved around Chinese tea, opium, and cotton, and he became one of the most prominent businessmen in nineteenth century Bombay.

Surprisingly, a group of Surat merchants was first to explore this possibility. With the help of some English officials, these merchants tried to set up a spinning mill as early as 1847, but unsure of its success, gave up the idea. Around the same time, a similar initiative in Ahmedabad made little headway because the promoter, Ranchhodlal Chhotalal, a highly placed civil servant, had no capital of his own and could not persuade other merchants to risk their resources in a venture the future of which nobody could guarantee. Excessive caution on the part of Gujarat merchants also stalled a cotton mill project at Bharuch mounted by an expatriate, James London, though he did manage to launch the Bharuch

Cotton Mill in 1854. Only a few months later, a prominent Parsi merchant set up a textile factory in Bombay, claiming credit for being the first Indian to promote an industrial venture in the country.

The name of the merchant was Cowasjee Nanabhai Davar and that of his mill, Bombay Spinning and Weaving Co. By 1860, Bombay had nine mills, all but two promoted by Parsi merchants. Ranchhodlal too, in the meantime, had succeeded in persuading the Ahmedabad merchants to prop up his project, although his Ahmedabad Spinning and Weaving Co., registered in 1858, was yet to start production. Then an entirely unforeseen event halted the progress of the nascent cotton industry in India: the civil war in America disrupted the export of cotton from that country, the principal source of supply for British mills. The price of cotton in Britain and Europe skyrocketed and Bombay's exporters made full use of this opportunity to make unprecedented profits. Anything that resembled cotton wool, sometimes even the material retrieved from old mattresses and pillows, found a market overseas. Promoting cotton mills at home would hardly have been a prudent business proposition under these conditions.

▲ Cotton bales, ready for dispatch. The cotton trade drew the attention of traders in western India who saw in the business an opportunity better than the moneylending which was their traditional practice. In time, it was to provide the region with much of its revenue.

The unprecedented optimism and excitement of the War years yielded to equally unprecedented gloom and depression following it, triggered by the worst kind of speculation that Bombay had ever seen, promoted by, to quote a premier daily of the time, 'men who ought never to have left the desk of a mere clerk'. New entrants to the world of business, many 'for the most part hitherto nameless', indulged in forward trading in shares at prices fixed far above their normal value. Premchand Roychand was unquestionably the most powerful of such 'hitherto nameless' persons. A migrant from Surat and originally a broker of no great consequence, he strode the Bombay market like a colossus during those years of absolute madness. The bubble burst the moment hostilities in America ended. With the inevitable crash in cotton prices, the chimera of prosperity vanished and took along with it the prestigious business house of Byramjee Hormusjee Cama, the largest shippers, which failed for a colossal sum of three million pounds sterling, followed by an unending succession of failures.

Those who preferred to make money through the normal trade channels or emerged from the ordeal unscathed but richer, were reluctant to invest in industrial ventures as long as the trauma of 1865 lasted. No new cotton company came into being at Bombay or Ahmedabad for the next six years, and then only one was added in 1871. Progress, however, was rapid once confidence returned. Within a space of barely eighteen months, from July 1873 to 1874, as many new mills were set up in Bombay, and then nearly two companies on an average came into existence every year until 1889.

By this time, the total number of factories in Bombay had risen to fifty-five, and industry had reached a plateau.

Most new ventures were floated by persons of relatively conservative social background, belonging to middle or still lower echelons of the mercantile community. Unlike the early pioneers who were among the leaders of the Bombay business world, it seems that the demonstration effect of the pioneering initiatives of the 1850s eventually percolated down the line to induce even the more cautious segments of the Bombay business community to branch out into the industrial field. The Kutchhi Bhatias were typical of the late entrants. A large number of them had been active in Bombay trade since the early years of the nineteenth century and had amassed considerable fortune. They, however, entered the textile industry only after its profitability had been firmly established. Morarji Gokuldas led the way in 1871. Others who followed in quick succession were Khatau Makanji, Dwarkadas Vasanji, Damodar Thackersey, Thackersey Mulji, and Mulji Jaitha. By 1880, there were six mills controlled by the Bhatias; more would be added in the coming decade.

Ahmedabad was to develop into a rival centre of textile production but the sequence of events here happened in the reverse. As moneyed interests stayed aloof, industry moved forward at a snail's pace and as late as 1876, there were only three textile mills in this premier business centre: two controlled by Ranchhodlal and the third in the hands of a Kanbi whose family had been a supplier of provisions to the British army in India.

▼ View of Bombay from the sea, 1773. The coast of Gujarat had been at the hub of trading networks; now Bombay was establishing its presence as a rival centre.

▼ Among the early pioneers in the textile industry in Bombay was Sir Damodar Thackersey who came from a background given to more conservative pursuits.

The Ahmedabad *seth*s took almost two decades to realize that cotton manufacturing was far more profitable than trading and moneylending. Mansukbhai Bhagubhai, a premier Jain merchant, was the first to enter the industry, followed by Karamchand Premchand. The Vaishnava *bania*s waited for another decade before taking to manufacturing. However, once the Jain and Vaishnava *bania*s entered the scene, they left all others far behind, capturing over 75 per cent of the total capacity of Ahmedabad's mills, now twenty-five by the turn of the century.

Safely entrenched in a city that had remained a thriving centre of trade since the early fifteenth century, Ahmedabad industrialists chose to insulate themselves from the risk inherent in engaging in new pursuits, and so their operations remained largely confined to a single industry and to their own city. Ahmedabad produced a galaxy of illustrious industrialists — Ranchhodlal Chhotalal, Mansukhbhai Bhagubhai, and Trikamlal Bhogilal in the nineteenth century, and Mangaldas Girdhardas, Ambalal Sarabhai, and Kasturbhai Lalbhai closer to our own times — but none of them ever contemplated setting up industrial units outside Gujarat, and they virtually made no attempt to diversify into other product lines. In contrast, the mercantile elite of Bombay was more flexible and outward looking. First in the country to launch factory production of cotton textiles, once the industry was well established, these merchants began to set up cotton mills at locations beyond the narrow confines of their city, or explore industrial possibilities other than textiles. Jamsetji Nusserwanji Tata, for instance, sold the mill he had set up in Bombay and turned his attention to other areas that, in his judgement, were more suitable for cotton production. By 1874, when he floated his Empress Mills at Nagpur, Tata had already established a reputation for taking unconventional decisions. Even the more cautious Bhatia Morarji Gokuldas promoted a cotton mill at Sholapur so that the company would benefit from its proximity to the cotton growing area and the availability of cheap labour.

Tata did promote a cotton mill in Bombay in 1886 and acquired another in Ahmedabad shortly before his death in 1904, but cotton textiles had ceased to be of interest to him by the mid-1880s. Other unconventional ideas now held far greater attraction for him, among them the first luxury hotel in Bombay which materialized when the foundation of the Taj Mahal Hotel was laid in 1898. His dream of launching steel production in India must have seemed impossible to anyone familiar with past attempts in this direction, and the prevailing situation in India. But Jamsetji persevered in the face of ludicrous prospecting regulations, an unhelpful government, financial stringency, and paucity of technical hands. Regrettably, he did not live to see the consummation of his dream

▶ The foundation for the Taj Mahal Hotel in Bombay was laid in 1898. Sir Jamsetji hoped to establish a luxury hotel that would be unrivalled in South and South East Asia, and where Indians would not be denied entrance or facilities usually available only to Europeans. A century later, it is one of the leading hotels of the world.

▼ Sir Jamsetji Nusserwanji Tata headed the formidable house of Tatas that saw a more prominent role for Indian industrialists in the development of the nation. However, that did not deflect him from seeking technical association with Western counterparts to establish modern industries and services on Indian soil.

project, but if the Tata Iron and Steel Company (TISCO) Limited finally became a reality in 1907, it was due to his vision and dogged determination. From the far off United States where he had gone in search of technicians, he continued to send elaborate instructions to his son Dorabji back home about every aspect of the projected city (in Bihar). Jamsetji's other formidable initiative aimed at supplying electric power to Bombay's mills, then dependent on costly coal, from a hydroelectric system to be set up in the Western Ghats, was no less imaginative or demanding.

If the industrial elite of Bombay was quicker to grasp the value of industrial enterprise or demonstrated more aggressive and imaginative traits in business matters than its counterpart in Ahmedabad, it was because the business climate of the then relatively young city was not overburdened by the baggage of a long commercial tradition. By the mid-nineteenth century, Bombay had become the most important international port in the country and the home of a large number of expatriate enterprises. Some of the agency houses that had laid the foundation of Bombay's business in the latter half of the previous century, were still going strong. Scores of other firms emerged on the scene during the latter half of the nineteenth century of which Killick Nixon & Co., Turner Morrison & Co., and Greaves Cotton & Co. were among the most powerful. Most of these were understandably British, but a few such as Volkant Brothers were

▲ Kasturbhai Lalbhai, an industrial magnate from Ahmedabad, was associated with the business of cotton and textiles in the nineteenth century, an area the family has taken to new heights at the close of the twentieth century.

▼ Mafatlal Gagalbhai started off with a mill in Ahmedabad. Rapid growth led to more plants in Gujarat, Bombay, and finally, Uganda. The group is well known in India for its business and social work.

promoted by Europeans, and some American companies like Standard Oil and Singer Sewing Machines had set up sales agencies.

Most British firms were engaged in general trading, banking, import–export, civil engineering, shipping and railway construction, and manufacturing held little interest for them, eliminating any conflict with the Indian mercantile community. The demonstration effect of a relatively more aggressive and risk-taking attitude that characterized the business behaviour of most expatriates could not have failed to rub off on their Indian counterparts.

This explains why only a few cotton mills were floated in Bombay after the 1890s. Even during the height of the *swadeshi* movement in the first decade of the twentieth century that gave a great boost to the indigenous production of cotton goods, the number of new flotations remained limited, although the capacity of the existing factories underwent considerable expansion. Ambitious, enterprising Bombayites were now looking for greener pastures, including some who had made their debut in industry in Ahmedabad but later made Bombay the principal theatre of their activities. Mafatlal Gagalbhai is a case in point. A peddler of textile goods during his early life, he set up his first mill in Ahmedabad and acquired two others in Gujarat, one in Surat and the other in Nadiad, before shifting to Bombay soon after the First World War. His Bombay operations started with the acquisition of an existing cotton mill and continued to expand with further acquisitions, including a textile-processing unit. He set up one of his flagship enterprises, Mafatlal Fine Spinning and Manufacturing Co., at Navsari in 1930, and a number of ginneries in Gujarat to supply good quality cotton to his own and others' mills. He extended this line of business out of India, setting up as many as forty ginneries in Uganda in collaboration with Indian settlers.

What, however, set Mafatlal apart from most of his contemporaries in western India was his move to challenge the British monopoly on jute manufacturing in India. Calcutta was the centre of jute production in the country, most of the mills were in the hands of the British, and the Indian Jute Mills Association (IJMA) was a sort of cartel that made the entry of any Indian impossible. To many, Mafatlal's decision must have appeared foolhardy. He floated the Gagalbhai Jute Mills at Calcutta in 1930 which soon established a reputation for the quality of its products. IJMA tried to thwart him in many ways but he refused to be cowed down by its machinations. Mafatlal breached another European preserve, that of shipping, by promoting the Ratnagar Steam Navigation Co. to operate on the Konkan coast, but soon agreed to merge it with the Scindia Steamship Navigation Co. formed

▲ Laxmanrao Kirloskar with his wife, Radhabai, 1914. The Kirloskar family chose to develop mechanized farming implements before adding diesel engines, centrifugal pumps and a host of other enterprises to their inventory. They were among the first to realize the importance of foreign collaborations to help upgrade domestic industry. His son S.L. Kirloskar virtually carried coal to Newcastle by exporting his top quality diesel engines to Germany.

earlier by some Bombay businessmen of nationalist persuasion. Mafatlal also had minority interests in two sugar firms near Bombay and cotton companies at Ahmedabad and Dewas (now in Madhya Pradesh). Shortly before his death in 1944, he had acquired a Mysore-based concern engaged in manufacturing and marketing plywood doors and boards.

In many ways, Mafatlal's operation symbolized, like that of the house of Tatas, a transition from nineteenth-century business, dominated by trade and textiles, to the twentieth century which brought to the fore a new breed of entrepreneurs willing and capable of grappling with daring experiments. Laxmanrao Kashirao Kirloskar was one of them. Born in a Maharashtrian Brahmin family to a father holding a petty position in the civil service, he would have been the least likely candidate for a business career. But for an incident not uncommon in those days, he would in all probability have ended his life as a teacher of mechanical drawing. At the Victoria Jubilee Technical Institute, where he was working, he was passed over for promotion in favour of someone who, he believed, was preferred purely because of racial affinity to the ruling masters. Resigning in protest, he experimented with a series of business propositions requiring little capital. None of these was particularly successful. Eventually, he started producing agricultural implements in Belgaum (now in Karnataka) in 1909, but soon moved to a site near Kolhapur provided by his friend, the Raja of Aundh. This is where the industrial township of Kirloskarwadi, the nerve centre of Laxmanrao's operations, would later develop.

Kirloskar's was the first attempt in the country to produce modern equipment for Indian farmers. Beginning with an improved plough and other relatively simple devices, he gradually expanded into more sophisticated product lines such as diesel engines and centrifugal pumps for irrigation purposes. Responding to the rising demand for indigenous products, stimulated by the exigencies of the War, Kirloskars took to the manufacture of machine tools. For this purpose a new company, Mysore Kirloskar Ltd, was set up at Harihar, India's first factory in this product line that would, in due course, develop into the largest in the private sector. The post-War years witnessed further diversification when the Kirloskar Electric Co. was set up at Bangalore in 1946 to produce electric motors, transformers, and generators needed by Indian factories. Kirloskars' interests were no longer confined to products useful only to farmers. This was emphatically underscored by the establishment of Kirloskar Oil Engines in 1946. The company would produce, among other things, internal combustion engines of the industrial and marine types. These two companies entered into technical collaboration with well-known British firms.

▲▼ Walchand Hirachand *(above)* and with his wife *(below)* inspecting Premier Automobile Limited's Kurla plant in the late 1940s. The Hirachand empire spanned everything from contract construction to agribusiness, but his most ambitious project was a shipping company which hurtled him headlong into conflict with British interests.

Kirloskars was among the very few business houses to realize so early that foreign collaboration was perhaps the only realistic route to upgrading technology in Indian industry.

In setting up and managing these enterprises, Laxmanrao was supported by his sons and their cousins, all of them highly trained in various branches of engineering. Few of his contemporaries in Indian business understood the value of education for industrial transition more than Laxmanrao, and few planned for leadership succession as consciously.

The years that witnessed the consolidation of Kirloskar's business coincided with the Gandhian era in the history of India's freedom movement. The business elite sympathized with the demand for freedom and had great admiration for Gandhi but followed a discreet policy of equidistance between the government of the day and the Indian National Congress. In contrast to traders and merchants who were more forthcoming in their support to Gandhi and the nationalist cause, seldom if ever did the industrial class align itself openly with the freedom struggle. One industrialist who swam against the tide was Walchand Hirachand. Belonging to a Sholapur-based family of traders and moneylenders, Walchand chose to move away from the narrow confines of his family business. Contracting for railway construction was far removed from the conventional lines of his father's business, but Walchand fared well in a field in which European firms had near monopoly. By the end of the First World War, both his profits and reputation were such that the prestigious house of Tatas invited him to join in partnership to form the Tata Construction Co. in 1920. Even though he held only minority interest in the firm, his was the most dominant voice in its management. Naturally, therefore, when Tatas decided to withdraw from construction in 1932, he acquired the company along with its subsidiaries. Renamed Premier Construction, it became his flagship concern.

The group, in the meantime, had moved into agribusiness, centred around the Ravalgaon sugar farm. In 1923 Walchand had purchased a vast piece of land in a village of this name in Nasik district to grow cash crops like sugarcane, cotton, and groundnut. This came in handy when tariff protection was granted to the Indian sugar industry in 1932. Utilizing the

▲ Karamshi Jetabhai Somaiya founded the Somaiya Group in the 1930s with sugar mills in Maharashtra. He introduced mechanized farming to increase his yield to 60 tons of cane per acre, then among the highest in the world.

▼ Pirojsha B. Godrej. Pirojsha seen here as a young man in a *pheta*, consolidated the Godrej enterprise. This group is very famous for the quality and durability of its products.

raw material produced on the farm, Walchand's sugar factory, located on the site, reaped rich dividends under the supervision of his brothers, Lalchand and Gulabchand, and diversified into sugar candy, confectionery, wax, cardboard, paper, alcohol, and *vanaspati*. By the end of the Second World War, Ravalgaon had emerged as a highly diversified agribusiness firm, and a sprawling industrial township named Walchand Nagar.

Despite his success, Walchand would have remained a mere footnote in the history of Indian business but for his daring initiative to launch a shipping company. This meant headlong collision with British shipping interests. He prevailed upon Narottam Morarjee, Lallubhai Samaldas, and Kilachand Devchand to join him and the trio, between them, assumed 75 per cent of the risk in the managing agency firm. Walchand held only 25 per cent interest but his position in the management of the Scindia Steamship Navigation Co., registered as a public limited concern in 1919, was so dominant that his name became synonymous with the company in popular imagination.

The British interests had not permitted any indigenous initiative to breach their monopoly. Lord Inchape, the head of the British India Navigation Co., unleashed a relentless offensive against the new concern, using every weapon in his armoury to buy off the company and its directors. Walchand proved more than his match in every respect except that his nascent enterprise was too weak to withstand a ruthless rate war, Inchape's final solution. He had to accept an agreement in 1923, clamping many unfair restrictions on Scindia's operations. Walchand looked upon the agreement as a 'slave bond' and a revised agreement ten years later granted only a few more concessions. In the face of continuing unfair competition coupled with an unsympathetic government, Scindia as a business enterprise maintained only a precarious existence. For Walchand, however, it was more than a mere business concern. It was a symbol of his firm conviction, as he put it forthrightly during one of his several encounters with Lord Inchape, that Indians 'had the right to run our own steamers on the coast of our own motherland'. While others in his profession were prudently discreet about their dealings with the alien government, he made no secret of his hostility towards it: 'I positively do not want the British in India,' he once told a prominent British author.

Other bold initiatives remained either stillborn or made little headway before Independence. His plan to erect a modern shipyard at Vishakhapatnam remained suspended until after the War, and was later taken over by the government of free India. His Hindustan Aircraft Company, set up in 1940, was taken over by the colonial government under its War powers. During the War he had acquired an air transport company, but it remained virtually in limbo while

▲ An advertisement for TISCO from *The Times of India* annual, 1935. Initially met with extreme suspicion, the plant proved to be a great boon for the British government in India in the War years.

the War lasted and was nationalized soon after India became free. Even Premier Automobiles Ltd, launched in collaboration with Dharmesey Mulraj Khatau and Tulsidas Kilachand in 1944, which would make great strides after freedom, could not start production before 1947.

It was not unrealistic for Indian industrialists to dream big in the closing decades of British rule in India. This was convincingly demonstrated by Tatas. TISCO started production by 1911 and the Tata Hydro-electric Power Supply Co. took shape with the registration of its first unit in 1910. The remaining two would be added by the end of the First World War to complete the system, making it capable of meeting the entire power needs of the Bombay region. Tatas also set up a cement company in 1912, the first successful venture in this field, and then added another shortly after the outbreak of the War.

The War years witnessed the consolidation of TISCO. British steel manufacturers, world leaders then, looked upon the Tata venture with suspicion, and their Indian distributors conducted a campaign of derisive propaganda against Tata steel. During the war, however, it was TISCO that satisfied most of the government's need while imports remained disrupted. 'I can hardly imagine,' a grateful Viceroy conceded unhesitatingly after the War, 'what we should have done during these four years if the Tata company had not been able to give us steel rails.' Having earned respect, the firm found itself in trouble soon after the War when India once again became the 'dumping ground' for cheaper goods from Europe. The company's profits plummeted sharply and its cash balances touched rock bottom. A huge loan from the Imperial Bank of India, for which Dorabji Tata pledged his personal jewellery as security, and another from the Maharaja of Gwalior saved the company from immediate embarrassment, but the only lasting remedy for TISCO's ordeal was tariff protection. It is a measure of the general goodwill that Tatas and its flagship enterprise had earned by this time that all sections, including the nationalist elements, in the Central Legislative Assembly, unitedly pressed for the grant of protection to the Indian steel industry to which the Indian Tariff Board eventually conceded. This helped TISCO stabilize its position, expand its capacity, and modernize its production facilities to such a degree that by 1934 it was fully geared to meet almost 75 per cent of India's total demand for steel. Handsome profits earned during the Second World War strengthened the company further.

Realizing that its core competencies lay in industries with high entry barriers, Tatas phased out most of its 'War babies': those enterprises set up during the buoyant business conditions of the First World War with an eye on short-term gain but without

▼ J.R.D. Tata was among India's most charismatic industrialists, and launched Tata Airlines in 1932 with a flight from Karachi to Bombay in 1932. Later nationalized and renamed Air India, JRD retraced the first flight path in 1962 when he flew solo along the route as part of the thirtieth anniversary celebrations.

advance planning. Its cement concerns were merged with the Associated Cement Company that came into existence in 1936 with the amalgamation of practically all cement firms in the country. Inter-War adjustments affected even the hydroelectric system. Dorabji sold 50 per cent of the Tata holdings to an American syndicate in 1930, much to the chagrin of rivals like the stalwart Ghanshyam Das Birla, and friends like Purshotamdas Thakurdas, a close associate and director in many Tata enterprises. Consequently, the hydroelectric system was placed under a joint management and remained so until 1951 when it would revert to the parent agency.

Painful though all this must have been, it did not whittle down Tatas' propensity for sailing in uncharted waters. In 1932, it launched Tata Airlines, heralding the air age in India. This resulted from an initiative of J.R.D. Tata, the son of Jamsetji's cousin and partner, whose personal passion for flying even the usually cautious Dorabji could not curb. In 1936, the Indian Standard Metal Co. was set up to produce non-ferrous alloys and castings. Three years later, Tata Chemicals came into being at Mithapur, then a part of the princely state of Baroda. By this time J.R.D. had taken over the command of the group. The venture, according to a competent observer, was 'the biggest chemical works in the country' to produce industrial chemicals for which India was then totally dependent on imports. In 1945, Tatas launched its biggest enterprise to date, the Tata Engineering and Locomotive Company (TELCO). A year later, the tiny Tata Airlines went public and became Air India, another company for international service was launched on the eve of Independence, and Tata Aircrafts was planned to manufacture aircraft. The airlines and aircraft ventures were yet to make headway when the government of free India decided to nationalize these industries, but TELCO would develop in due course into a giant producer of commercial vehicles.

Behind the glare of industrial giants were a number of smaller groups that were yet to carve a niche for themselves in India's business life when the colonial era

ended. Perhaps the most important among them were the Wadias and Godrejs. Both were Bombay-based and both traced their beginnings back to the last quarter of the nineteenth century. Belonging to a reputed family of shipbuilders, Nowrosjee Nusserwanjee Wadia began his business career in 1879 by establishing dye works, but took to textile manufacturing in 1895. His descendents expanded this line and acquired the agency for the Bombay Dyeing and Manufacturing Co. which in due course would grow into its flagship concern. Likewise, the Godrej family had made its industrial debut as early as 1887 with the manufacture of iron safes and would later diversify into toiletries. Other groups like Larsen & Toubro, Mahindra & Mahindra and Bajaj that would achieve great heights in free India were still laying their foundations when the colonial masters departed.

The burgeoning dominance of industrial houses in the business life of western India did not mean a total decline in the power of trading interests. Indeed, some industrialists retained their trading activities throughout, while those like Purshotamdas Thakurdas, the 'cotton king' of Bombay, were traders who commanded greater prestige and influence than even the industrialists of their time. There is no doubt, however, that during the last hundred years of British rule, there was a visible shift from trade to industry at the contours of Indian business, and this happened both because, and in spite, of colonialism.

▲ Nowrosjee Nusserwanjee Wadia moved from dyeing to textile manufacturing in the late nineteenth century, a task completed by his heirs who have created the popular Bombay Dyeing brand of textiles.

▼ Interior of what was then N. Wadia and Son's Textile Mills, Bombay.

The Southern Region

Raman Mahadevan

Tamil Nadu's industries are virtually bywords in India's industrial lexicon with Tirupur's hosiery apparel, Sivakasi's matches and firecrackers, Madras's automobile and autoparts as well as leather goods, and Coimbatore's engineering and textile goods. Ranked among the country's top industrial regions, Tamil Nadu has come a long way in narrowing and reducing the initial historical gap between it and the more advanced regions, and early starters such as Bengal and Bombay. A direct correlationship between the past and present may be tenuous, yet it would be unrealistic to ignore the weight and influence of an inherited industrial ethic that had fairly deep roots in the Tamil region. There is a tendency to perpetuate the notion that pre-1950, the region was industrially peripheral and largely rural. The inveterate and irrepressible Homi Modi's jocular remark in the 1940s that the only industry Madras (now known as Chennai) could

▼ Merchant building, Madras, nineteenth century. That Madras's only industry was curry powder was something often said in jest, but reflected a lay perception as well; it is true, however, that industrialization had a slow start in this southern metropolis.

▲▼ A.L.A.R. Arunachalam Chettiar *(above)* and Dewan Bahadur P. Somasundaram Chettiar *(below)* were among those who shifted from banking and trade operations to modern industry, or more specifically the textile industry. They also continued to extend institutional credit.

be proud of was curry powder, represented the lay and popular perception of a region too distant for comprehension.

Commercially and industrially, pre-Independence Madras lagged far behind Bombay and Bengal, the two nodal centres of industrial investment and entrepreneurship, the result of the uneven nature of colonial spread and development in India. This had implications for the growth of an indigenous entrepreneurial class.

Though the East India Company had acquired control by 1800 over a large part of what eventually came to be known as Madras Presidency, the process of economic integration was protracted and slow. Unlike Calcutta and Bombay, Madras did not assume the role of a nodal commercial and industrial centre. This is best reflected in the absence of a full-fledged harbour until as late as the turn of the century. Inadequate infrastructural conditions were a major constraining influence in retarding the early development of industries in Madras. Tendering his evidence before the Indian Industrial Commission in 1916, P. Theagaraja Chettiar attributed the region's industrial backwardness to the lack of facilities for the generation of power, the absence of coalfields and minerals, and the chronic problem of transportation and communication. Rail and road networks developed slowly, and in patches, and consequently delayed the full integration of markets. However, from the mid-nineteenth century, as part of the process of commercialization, the region was gradually drawn into a cash crop commodity producing grid. These conditions paved the way for the expansion of credit and trade networks, and provided the necessary space for the proliferation and growth of European mercantile interests on the one hand, and of indigenous moneylenders and middlemen traders, on the other.

Among prominent European agencies or trading houses which straddled the commercial scene were Parrys, Binnys, Best & Co., Arbuthnots, Harveys, and Stanes. Typically, these agency houses were engaged in a variety of commercial activities ranging from banking, insurance, and general shipping to import and export trade.

The expatriate firms, by virtue of their access to capital and overseas markets, were among the pioneers in initiating modern industries in Madras. Parry & Co. can be counted among the first firms to move into modern manufacturing when it promoted sugar refineries in the 1840s for processing palmyra jaggery into sugar. Textiles, however, formed the mainstay of modern industry in the region. Even in 1947, textiles accounted for a substantial 46 per cent of the total capital investment and 60 per cent of the total labour employed in modern industry. The vegetable oil industry

▲ M.C.T. Chidambaram Chettiar, banker, Madras. The Chettiars were able to use their credit and finance facilities to wrest control over industries.

▼ Interior of a textile mill in Coimbatore in the 1940s. Modern machinery has ensured that the textile mills in this industrial town gave it a technological advantage that attracts buyers directly from around the world even today.

ranked next and accounted for 17.6 per cent of the capital and 7 per cent of the labour employed.

Enthused by the success of Bombay textile mills, the initiative for the establishment of the first textile mills in Madras also came from entrepreneurs in Bombay. The Southern India Spinning and Weaving Co. Ltd and the Madras United Spinning and Weaving Co. Ltd were promoted by Hormusjee Jehangir and Soonderdas Moolji in 1874 and 1875, respectively. Subsequent initiative came from established European trading agencies such as Binnys, Harveys, and Stanes. Binnys' Buckingham and Carnatic Mills, set up in 1876 and 1881, were among the first composite mills in south India, and managed to secure a firm footing in the domestic market successfully establishing an all-India marketing network. The growth of Harveys was also phenomenal. Starting as a cotton-exporting firm in 1879, the firm of A. & F. Harvey had, by 1892, established a chain of three mills, and added another in 1925. The Madura Group of Mills, as it came to be known, was a formidable force in the yarn market of south India. Stanes was comparatively less overpowering, having moved from coffee plantation to textiles, promoting the Coimbatore Spinning and Weaving Co. Ltd in 1888.

The process of the formation of indigenous industrial capital in the Madras region was uneven and protracted. At one end of the spectrum were sections of Nattukottai Chettys, a traditional

▶ An advertisement for Radha Krishna Mills reproduced from a Tamil newspaper. A strict check on costs and rigid controls made the industry in southern textiles, 'Madras checks', extremely competitive.

▼ Karamuthu Thyagaraja Chetty was the uncrowned textile king of south India in the 1940s. He started his career in 1921 promoting the Sri Meenakshi Mills, and soon added several others to his booty, raising capital entirely through Chetty bankers.

business community akin to the Marwaris who, as purveyors of credit in the colonies of South East Asia, managed to sustain a relatively high rate of accumulation. On the other, Komati Chettys, Muslim traders, Nadars, Vellalas, Kamma Naidus, Devangas, Sengunthars, and Kalladaikurichi Brahmins had to operate within a relatively more restricted and circumscribed area of investment. Much of this capital was tied up in the field of indigenous banking and trade.

Though among the largest, most prominent sections of indigenous entrepreneurs of south India, the pre-1930 scale of operation of the Nattukottai Chettys was relatively marginal. Starting from around the mid-nineteenth century, there was a steady and significant outflow of Chetty capital from Madras to Burma, Malaya, Sri Lanka, and the Indo-China region. The heightened demand for credit and profitable economic opportunities in these regions tended to draw Chetty capital away from south India.

The Industrialization of the Princely South

Till the 1920s, unlike Bombay or Calcutta, Madras was not a major centre for foreign or domestic industrial investment. Notwithstanding the very old tradition of Tamil Nadu's indigenous business communities' participation in internal as well as external trade and banking, their entry into the industrial arena was delayed. Nor was tough capital as active in the industrial field as it was in Calcutta. Thus Madras Presidency remained industrially backward. However, the expansion of internal credit and trade network in agricultural commodities from the last decades of the nineteenth century on provided opportunity for the growth of indigenous capital. Apart from the more well-known Nattukottai and Komati Chetty communities, others who participated in this expansion process included the Naidus of Coimbatore, the Vellalas, the Nadars, the Tamil Brahmins, etc., even though they had no tradition in conducting business. As far as the policy of the government of Madras Presidency is concerned, it followed the straight and narrow path of *laissez faire* strictly; the only exception was the encouragement of some small industries, particularly textiles, to absorb marginal technological changes in the early decades of the twentieth century.

The early modern history of business and industry in the parts of India now known as Andhra Pradesh, Karnataka, and Kerala has received little scholarly attention. This part of the history of the princely states of Hyderabad, Mysore, Travancore, and Cochin suggests a pattern slightly different from that of the British-ruled Presidency of Madras. Within the constraints of a colonial economic pattern in the subcontinent, some of the princely states tried to promote business and industry through state sponsorship and encouragement. For instance, Hyderabad State offered not only protection to indigenous industry but also finance through the Industrial Trust Fund (1929). More modern technologies came with industries set up by entrepreneurs from outside Hyderabad, and included cement, rayon, cigarette hume pipes; local middle-scale enterprises in an intermediate level of technology also developed under Hyderabad State's protection, e.g. soap, paper, oilseed products, sugar, glass; and, of course, at a lower level, artisanal industries like handloom, carpet tanning etc. continued on traditional lines.

Hyderabad's history of a combination of private and state initiative was replicated in Mysore (inspired by the Sir M. Visveswaraiya) and Travancore (where the initial presence of a strong business class, particularly the Syrian Chrisitians, Ezhavas, and Tamil immigrants, also helped). Mysore's iron and steel works, Travancore's coir, cashew, and coconut oil processing mills in the early twentieth century laid the basis for future development. That is not to say that an industrial revolution occurred in the southern princely states, but it was certainly true that it was demonstrated that industrial development was possible outside of regions directly administered by the British Indian government.

The other significant lesson of the southern experience was the initiative shown by the traditional dealers in money capital, most prominently the Chettiars of Tamil Nadu, in transforming themselves into industrialists. This happened late but it displayed a flair for the innovative transformation of tradition.

By the turn of the century, a section of the Chettys, though still primarily engaged in banking and trade, began investing a small portion of its capital in modern industry. The Malabar Spinning and Weaving Co. Ltd was among the first indigenously promoted mills in south India. Established in 1888 at Calicut, its capital was principally subscribed by the A.L.A.R. Chetty family and the Desamangalam Namboodiri family of Travancore. Around the turn of the century, the mill came under the management of P. Somasundaram Chetty who, in association with the A.L.A.R. family, founded the Kaleeswarar Mills in Coimbatore in 1906. Both Malabar and Kaleeswarar Mills represented cases of direct

investment in industry. In the wake of the heightened demand for yarn from the local handloom industry, investment in textiles was perceived as an attractive proposition. The Chettys also acquired control over industries as creditors and financiers of industrial units. In a situation characterized by the dominance of European capital over the money market, and the lack of cheap institutional credit for Indian industry, the financial strength of the entrepreneurs was crucial, and it was here the Chettys were able to score over the others.

The sudden contraction of foreign trade during the War years and the consequent slackening of foreign competition had the effect of creating a protected domestic market. There was tremendous growth of internal commerce and trade in the region. The huge profits that accrued to traders during these years enabled them to invest in industry soon after the War. A number of these ventures came to be floated by relatively obscure middle and small capital companies, but in the wake of the recession most of them failed to take off. The bulk of the investment continued to flow into textiles. The rise of Coimbatore as a textile centre can be traced to this period. There was a mushrooming of ginning units in villages around Coimbatore, and many of these were set up by farmers-cum-traders from the Kamma and Gounder communities.

The major thrust in the promotion of Coimbatore cotton mills came from three Kamma Naidu families, namely those of V. Rangaswami Naidu, P.S.G. Naidu, and G. Kuppuswamy Naidu. All of them were substantial landowners, and from around the turn of the century had turned from cotton cultivation to cotton trading. During the War years, they made handsome profits, partly through speculation and partly through forward trading. This enabled two of the groups to move into industry in the immediate post-War period. Thus the P.S.G. Naidu group established the Ranga Vilas Spinning and Weaving Mills in 1921. Almost the entire share capital of Rs 3.3 lakh was raised within the community. The utilization of caste and kinship networks for mobilizing scarce capital and the exercise of tight control by individual families promoting the enterprises were to become hallmarks of business organization in this region. Following close on the heels of the P.S.G. Group, V. Rangaswamy Naidu established Radhakrishna Mills Ltd in 1923. On the other hand, though among the earliest of the Naidus to move into cotton trading, G. Kuppuswamy Naidu's entry into the cotton industry was delayed owing to the heavy losses incurred in forward trading and speculative dealings. It was only in the late 1920s that Kuppuswamy took the first major initiative to invest in the organized mill industry. In 1932, he promoted the Rajalakshmi Mills and, in the following year, converted the Lakshmi Mills, a ginning factory, into a full-fledged spinning mill.

▶ Machining of heavy castings in the heavy machinery division of the PSG Institute, Coimbatore. The PSG group has taken rapid strides in the heavy machine tools segment.

(previous page):

▲▼ Coimbatore today enjoys a prominent position as a textile centre due to the thrust provided by the Kamma Naidus, among them G. Kuppuswamy Naidu *(above)*, and P.S.G. Rangaswamy Naidu *(below)*. Cotton cultivators and traders who made substantial profits through speculation during the war, they turned to ginning and milling industries around the same time that it began to attract Chetty capital.

The immediate post-War period also saw the entry of some Chetty capital into textiles. Karamuthu Thyagaraja Chetty, who was to emerge in the 1940s as a leading textile magnate, made his beginning in 1921, promoting the Sri Meenakshi Mills in Madurai. The paid up capital of Rs 15 lakh was raised almost entirely by a group of Chetty bankers and traders. The ARARSM Spinning Mill, established in 1920 in Madras, and Mahalakshmi Mills,

▼ T.V. Sundaram Iyengar founded TVS and Sons, one of the major corporate houses of the south. From automobile dealership in imported vehicles to a major manufacturer of automobile parts, and of consumer goods, the transition is one of the success stories of the region.

established in 1925 in Madurai, were also products of Chetty enterprise.

The 1930s, in many ways, represent a turning point in the industrial history of the region. There was a distinct deepening and broadening of the industrialization process following the swing of capital from agriculture to industry. Industrial investment, particularly in textiles, also gained buoyancy as a consequence of a set of favourable conditions specific to the region. These included close proximity to the domestic market in the shape of the handloom industry, proximity to raw materials, a large supply of labour at relatively low wages, and the relative inexpensiveness of machinery and capital goods during the years of depression. The availability of electric power following the commissioning of the Pykara hydroelectric project in 1933 also considerably aided the spread of industrialization, especially in the Coimbatore region.

The upshot was a significant flow of indigenous capital into the textile industry. Between 1928 and 1946–7, as many as 27 mills came to be promoted in the Coimbatore region, 4 mills were set up in the adjoining Salem region, and another 6 were located elsewhere in the Tamil region. Of these, only two were the outcome of European enterprise (Pierce Leslie & Co. and W.A. Beardsell).

The commercialization of agriculture and the development of trade and industry had the effect of transforming the social and economic landscape of Madras, especially after the 1920s and 1930s. This was reflected in the growth of towns, the proliferation of the middle class and working class, and above all in the development of an institutional framework for sustaining diverse economic activities. The growth and development of the tertiary sector was a significant feature reflected in the proliferation of trading agencies, financial institutions, transport companies, and stockbroking firms. There were clear indications of an underlying dynamism in many pockets of south India.

The Second World War provided the opportunity to local industrial entrepreneurs to reap enormous profits and consolidate their positions. Around this time, there were concerted efforts to diversify investments into core sectors such as cement, chemicals, and fertilizers, and the manufacture of engineering and textile machines. The constraining factor now was no longer capital, but technology.

Two notable examples of those who moved into the field were S.N.N. Sankaralinga Iyer and the Seshasayees. S.N.N. Sankaralinga Iyer belonged to a family of bankers from Kaladaikurichi in Tirunelveli, an area renowned for its wealth and enterprise. The S.N.N. family firm diversified into organized modern banking, promoting the Indo-Commercial Bank (1932). The Prudential Investment Trust followed soon after. By the early 1940s, the group

▲ The Murugappa family founded the group of the same name when it moved into the light engineering industry during the Second World War years. In the picture, Dewan Bahadur A.M. Murugappa and his wife can be seen with their sons (standing, from left to right) A.M.M. Arunachalam, A.M. Murugappa Chettiar, and A.M.M. Vellayan Chettiar.

had diversified further, investing in a range of small-scale manufacturing units. In 1945, it took the plunge into cement manufacturing following the post-War boom in construction activity. Thus came into being India Cements in 1946, to be followed by Travancore Cements.

The Seshasayees, on the other hand, started off as road transport operators in Trichy around the First World War and subsequently moved into electric power distribution. By 1940, through their control over a chain of electric supply companies, they exercised extensive influence in the field. In the early 1940s, they moved into the field of heavy chemicals when they took over the Mettur Chemical and Industrial Corporation. Under the stewardship of C.P. Ramaswamy Iyer, Travancore had embarked upon a major programme of industrialization. As part of this effort, immigrant capital was invited and offered incentives to promote industries. Taking advantage of this opportunity as well as the growing demand for fertilizers, the Seshasayees set up FACT, Fertilizers and Chemical Travancore Ltd in 1943.

Another noticeable trend in the pre-Independence period which was to have implications in the direction of industrial investment in a subsequent period was state investment in roads. The Tamil region boasted a wide and dense network of roads linking its hinterlands. For both passenger and freight traffic, road transport was perceived as a viable alternate to rail. This had the effect of pushing up the demand for imported motor vehicles, lorries, and motorcycles. Interestingly, a number of the dealerships for these imported vehicles were taken up by Brahmins, some of whom were to later emerge as important players in the auto-assembling and autoparts manufacturing sector. Apart from T.V. Sundaram Iyengar and Sons, and Simpsons, other prominent figures in this

▲ A factory shot of Standard Motors at Vandalur, near Madras. Though the factory promoted by K. Gopalakrishnan did not succeed, the seeds its presence in the region sowed have resulted in it being called the Indian Detroit because of the automobile and auto parts industries that have taken root here.

(facing page):

▲ S. Anantharamakrishnan founded the Amalgamations Group of companies based on some of the most advanced technologies of the time in light engineering. He was responsible for the Indianization of Simpsons, a wholly European company, in the 1930s as its director.

▼ The Madras Presidency also provided entrepreneurial opportunities for immigrants such as C.M. Kothari from Gujarat. In fact, the first investments in the textiles industry of the south had been initiated by Bombay-based industrialists. His illustrious son D.C. Kothari was a very popular figure in Madras and was President of FICCI in 1970.

field were Sundaram Iyer of Enfield and K. Gopalakrishnan of Standard Motors.

From automobile dealership for a range of imported motor vehicles to passenger and freight transport, the transition of the Tamil Brahmin house of TVS to a major automobile parts manufacturing group has been one of the phenomenal success stories of the corporate sector in south India. Simpsons too charted a course broadly similar to TVS. This wholly European company was partially Indianized in 1938 with the induction of S. Anantharamakrishnan as one of the directors of the group. By the 1940s, Sri Rama Vilas Service (Simpson) and TVS were two of the largest private transport operators in the south.

As for the Nattukottai Chettys, it was only in the 1940s, when their vital overseas commercial interests were threatened in the wake of the occupation of large parts of South East Asia, that they undertook serious efforts to repatriate their capital back to south India. Some of the buoyancy in industrial investment in the 1940s and 1950s was due to this. However, a substantial portion of the repatriated capital, both during the depression of the 1930s, and later in the 1940s, found its way into banking, insurance, and trade, while some of it was ploughed into plantation. This is borne out

by the investment portfolio of all major Chetty groups. Thus the Raja Sir group (Annamalai and Muthiah Chetty), unrivalled for the wealth it commanded, is an example of capital steadfastly withheld from investment in industry. Its major investments were in the banks and trading companies it controlled: Indian Bank, Bank of Chettinad, Chettinad Corporation, and South India Corporation. The token exception was the takeover of Lotus Mills in Coimbatore in the early 1940s.

The investment portfolio of M.C.T. Chidambaram Chetty, another front-ranking business, was not substantially different. The group exercised control over a number of financial institutions in the 1930s, the more prominent among them the Indian Overseas Bank and the United India Life Insurance Co. A significant departure came about in the1940s with control over the Elphinstone Mills in Bombay in partnership with Mulraj Karsandas. In 1946, it promoted the Travancore Rayons and Pudukottai Textiles. Though the A.M.M. Chetty or the Murugappa Group, another leading Nattukottai Chetty banking family, also moved into industry only during the Second World War, it opted for an uncommon route for entry. Unlike most other Chettys who invested in textiles, A.M.M. opted for light engineering. Ajax Products was promoted in 1939 with a view to tapping the growing demand for office and security equipment. Ajax was also among the pioneers for the manufacture of coated abrasives. The manufacture of bicycles, in collaboration with Tube Investment UK, was its next major venture, but this only came about in the early 1950s.

No account of the industrial history of the region would be complete without a reference to R.M. Alagappa Chetty. For almost two decades, during the 1930s and 1940s, he occupied a prominent place in the emerging corporate world of south India, even though his major investments were in Malaya. A strong advocate of industrialization, he was also one of the leading spokesmen for the corporate sector His core investments were in textiles in Cochin and Travancore. However, over-trading and speculation led to his group virtually sinking without a trace in the late 1940s, making him among the first corporate casualties in south India.

As we look back at the history of industrialization and of industrial entrepreneurship, a comparison with Bombay and Bengal is inevitable. Madras remained a poor cousin till as late as 1947 in terms of total investment in industry, but quantitative measures tend to obscure and underestimate the intensity and diversity of industrial activity and the richness of the texture of industrial entrepreneurship in south India. Yet industrial entrepreneurship in the Madras region had truly come of age by the late 1940s.

The Northern Region

G.S.L. Devra

The peace and order established by the Mughals in most parts of the subcontinent, uniformity in state regulations within the empire, royal patronage to certain craft industries, existence of royal *karkhana*s (workshops) in the imperial capitals, and maintenance of a large salaried class comprising soldiers, retainers, and others led to the growth of a well-organized and consolidated market economy. The process was aided by the expansion of urban activities resulting from the monetization of the economy. Their tax reforms must have had a favourable impact over transactions in the business world. Among the beneficiaries of their revenue systems were *vaishyas* or *bania*s, a generic name given to all those engaged in commercial pursuits irrespective of their caste affiliations. A sizeable portion of land revenue demand was left within the regional sector, boosting market activities at local and regional levels.

▼ Merchant's shop, Allahabad. Traditional Indian enterprise relied heavily on skilled labour that catered to the royal ateliers and had to be coaxed to produce goods for export to distant countries with flourishing markets where these goods were highly coveted.

The archival records of Rajasthan and its adjoining regions in the seventeenth, eighteenth, and early nineteenth centuries clearly state that the *bania*s enjoyed a distinctive position in contemporary society. A recent study has confirmed that these *banias* from the *qasbahs* or small towns of northern India, while involved in trading and banking, were keen to move into agriculture. A sample study of *qasbah* Reni or Taranagar, located in the border region of Haryana and Rajasthan, provides amazing details. These groups, while holding 79.39 per cent of the total land of the *qasbah*, were paying 55.85 per cent of the total

▶ Bazaar scene, Jaipur. This princely kingdom created a complicated but disciplined system of mercantile lifestyles when it shifted its capital from nearby Amber to Sawai Jai Singh's modern city. The maharaja coaxed businessmen and artisans to settle in the city, making it one of the greatest hubs of skilled labour and enterprise in northern India.

▼ The overlays in society became obvious over time: though the English controlled and, to a large extent, channelized 'native' trade, they were in turn influenced and shaped by the culture and mores of the indigenous people surrounding them.

collection of land revenue to the state, and they exercised considerable control over village and *qasbah* economy. They not only advanced money for agriculture, controlling the markets, running the shops and other trading centres, but also extended loans to administrators and arranged provisions for the movement of armies. They extended loans to rajas and maharajas — Nagarseth Shantidas Jhaveri of Ahmedabad provided money to several members of the imperial family. Poddar Mirzamal of Churu (Rajasthan), in partnership with Purohit Harlal of Delhi, provided a loan of Rs 4 lakh to Maharaja Surat Singh of Bikaner, and also extended a loan to Maharaja Ranjeet Singh of Punjab. The Mohtas of Bikaner were financiers for the officers of the East India Company at Mirzapur and Banaras. The Poddar firm of Churu lent money to the East India Company and helped it control the territories of Haryana, Delhi, and Punjab.

The direct participation of *banias* in the state administration was another important feature. A late-seventeenth-century Italian traveller noted that *bania*s found preference in postings in the revenue administration. In the Indian courts, they were appointed ministers and officers, and even to the high post of dewan or prime minister.

The growing popularity of long range trade routes during the seventeenth century facilitated the growth of commercial towns like Allahabad, Banaras, Agra, Delhi, Jaunpur, Lahore, Multan, Ajmer, Ahmedabad, and Burhanpur. Lahore and Agra blossomed into vast commercial emporia attracting goods, traders, and artisans. All available evidence suggests that the inter-regional flow of commodities increased substantially during the Mughal and post-Mughal periods, and merchants became influential, forming a link between the general populace and the state.

▲ A Fresco from a *haveli* in Shekhawati, Rajasthan, to which region most Marwari industrialists belong. Frescoes in these mansions often depicted the changing socio-history during the period of the Raj, such as the *Gangaur* procession in homage of Goddess Parvati, where young maidens prayed for obtaining good husbands, painted just above that of the British introduction of the railways.

(facing page):

▲▼ The Raj ushered in changes in India with regard to communication and industrialization, and these were depicted in the Shekhawati frescoes, often as 'fantastic' elements as interpreted by painters who had not seen these at first hand.

The migration of Gujarati, Haryanvi (Aggarwal), Punjabi (Khatri), and Rajasthani (Marwari) merchants to other parts of the country accelerated during the Mughal and post-Mughal periods. The Khatris and Aggarwals went to different towns in the United Provinces (now Uttar Pradesh). The Marwaris and Gujaratis not only went to Punjab and the United Provinces but also migrated to central India and beyond. The traders and bankers of Amber (Jaipur) accompanied Sawai Man Singh to the eastern parts of the country. A number of Bikaneri merchants settled in Banaras and Mirzapur, and also went to Aurangabad in the reign of Aurangzeb and after. The author of *Ardh Kathanak* (seventeenth century) refers to a section in the town of Fatehpur inhabited exclusively by Oswal traders, tracing their descent from the city of Osian, near Jodhpur. Even the *nagarseth* family of Ahmedabad migrated from Osian. These examples show that the migration of Marwaris and Gujarati merchants did not start after the establishment of the rule of the East India Company in the Eastern or United Provinces. During the eighteenth century, the Hyderabad Nizams, the Gwalior Scindias and Holkars, and the Nawabs of Awadh and Bengal invited traders and bankers from Gujarat and Rajasthan to settle in their

principalities. The treasurers of Hyderabad and Punjab were from Jodhpur. During Ranjeet Singh's rule, the Poddars of Churu, the Somanis of Rawatsar, the Pediwals and Kochars of Bikaner, and the Dagas of Panchu settled in Punjab, and some Maheshwaris, Aggarwals and Oswals settled there permanently, particularly at Amritsar.

The eighteenth century saw the emergence of regional power groups and gave new impetus and direction to the economy in certain sectors. It is noteworthy that credit dealings with the government in the case of almost all the leading bankers of northern India became a regular feature. A study of the money market of Churu on the one hand, and of Baroda on the other, operated by the Poddar and Haribhakati firms, shows that these places contributed the maximum cash through *hundi*s to the various towns. Indeed, the small towns of Rajasthan and Gujarat became centres for the head offices of so many leading firms that a historian has remarked that 'nine-tenths of the bankers and commercial men of India are natives of Maroodesh [Marwar]'.

While the British were consolidating their position in eastern and southern India, Jaipur emerged as the major northern centre for banking and trade in jewellery. Almost 50,000 businessmen operated from this town, established in 1728. While trade in old Rajasthani towns like Nagaur and Merta declined, newer centres like Jodhpur, Bikaner, and Jaipur took their place. During the early part of the nineteenth century, small towns like Churu, Rajgarh, Fatehpur, Shahpura, Bhilwara, Malpura, and Pali grew into prominent trading centres for Rajasthan and its adjoining regions,

▲ A *sonar* or goldsmith conducts his trade in the *zenana* rooms of a merchant's *haveli*. Itinerant traders often offered such services at home.

▼ Marwari traders from Calcutta maintaining accounts. With British paramountcy, new business centres were developed wherever there were cantonments: in Delhi, Hissar, Ambala, and Ludhiana, for example.

and it was from here that a number of traders and bankers migrated to different parts of the country. Even small places like Surajgarh, Jhunjhunu, Mandawa, Ramgarh, Nawalgarh, Sikar, Ratangarh, Reni, Sardarshahar, Sojat, Barmer, Chirawa, and Laxmangarh became points of origin for many of today's industrial houses.

Pali, near Jodhpur, was the centre for the eastern and western regions where, in the words of historian Colonel James Tod, the produce of India, Kashmir, and China was interchanged for that of Europe, Africa, Persia, and Arabia. Caravans from Gujarat and Kutch imported elephants, silks, sandalwood and camphor, dyes, drugs, oxide, arsenic, spices, coffee, etc. In exchange, it exported chintzes, fruit, *zira* from Multan, and sugar and opium from the Malwa and Hadoti regions.

The establishment of British paramountcy in 1818 and the subsequent organization of a modern colonial state had profound impact on the mercantile social formation in India. Those who were *saudagar*s (traders) were unable to withstand the market policies of the new conquerors and slowly withered away in the face of a new system of finance and administration. The closure of mints and the establishment of British district treasuries reinforced by money orders encashable at every post office, took away much of the remittance business of *hundi* bankers. A large number of letters available from the collections of the Poddars of Churu and the

Haribhakatis of Baroda explain that the early British administrative officers were keen to invite traders from Delhi, Haryana, Punjab, and Rajasthan. In return, the merchants proposed their conditions for the opening of shops and branch offices in Delhi, Hissar, Ambala, and Ludhiana. In 1818, the British created Bhiwani as a new market town for attracting merchants from the neighbouring regions. Several Rajasthani, Haryanavi, and Punjabi traders moved to different regions in the United Provinces. At that time the British were planning the export of indigo, tobacco, butter, and grain from the United Provinces to the north-west.

Punjabi traders were already active in the upper Sindh, but with the growth of Karachi as a commercial port, the situation changed. Karachi became the gate of foreign commerce not only for Sindh but for a large area of north-west India, Baluchistan, and Afghanistan. Under the Mirs of Sind, important items in the list of imports were China and Bengal silks, English broadcloth, common English shawls, and cotton piece goods; sugar from Bengal, China, Manila, Batavia, and Malabar; pepper, copper, ivory, and cotton yarn from Bombay; cotton from Gujarat; and dates, pearls, and slaves from the Persian Gulf. The principal item of export was wheat brought both from Punjab and Sindh at Karachi. Other items were opium (brought from Pali–Marwar), indigo and butter (from Khairpur), madder, wool, raisins, and salted fish. In 1878, when Sindh became directly connected with Punjab by rail, the volume of trade from the Karachi port rose extraordinarily.

▲ An advertisement for New Egerton Woollen Mills, later Dhariwal Mills, in the Punjab, in *The Times of India* annual, 1921. Punjab still remains a leading centre in the north for quality woollen apparel.

▶ The trade in opium could result in dramatic changes in fortune, for both British and Indian interests. In the picture, packed chests of Akbari opium can be seen being carried to wagons for loading at Ghazipur railway station.

▲ Chandni Chowk, Delhi. Initially developed by Emperor Shah Jahan, Delhi remained the principal seat of business. From small shops, north Indian businessmen conducted operations that spanned much of India and South East Asia. Chandni Chowk continues to be a hub of business to this day.

Cotton and opium (from Malwa) has played a significant role in the rise of Marwaris and Gujaratis. During the nineteenth century, the leading merchants in the opium trade were from Ahmedabad. Slowly, Marwaris displaced Parsis and other merchants in the trade. In the early 1850s, Marwaris were shipping opium to China on their own account, not as agents or intermediaries. The profit from opium trade, though risky, was a major source of accumulating capital. Cotton too made and unmade the fortunes of many families.

After 1818, Marwari migrants comprising mostly the Aggarwals of Shekhawati and the Maheshwaris of Bikaner and Jodhpur regions, established themselves in the markets of the Doab and the Gangetic valley. Here they faced stiff competition from the Aggarwals of Haryana and the Khatris of Punjab. Some Marwari firms started new businesses. Tarachand Ghanshyam Das of Ramgarh, Shekhawati, started trading in woollen shawls. Khatri, Multani, and Muslim traders shifted and concentrated more on the political and religious centres of Banaras, Allahabad, Lucknow, Agra, and Gaya. During the second half of the nineteenth century, the idea of great Marwari firms was born. Originating from Rajasthan towns, they soon spread to major towns all over north India, and some even had offices in Rangoon, Canton, and London.

After 1860, the rapid industrialization of Kanpur in the lower Gangetic valley began and attracted a number of traders from

The Historical Spread of the North Indian Entrepreneur

Ever since the late medieval times, northern India has been endowed with a number of flourishing business communities, and not only the Aggarwals and Maheshwaris of Shekhawati, Bikaner and Jodhpur, but also other *bania* castes of north India such as the the Khatris and Lohanas of Punjab and Sind. These were middlemen in the trade between the wealthy centres of Mughal power, Agra or Lahore or Delhi, and the external world. Through their hands passed the trade from the overseas European network via Surat, and also the overland trade on the West Asian network. Apart from this, the north Indian business communities also served lucrative functions in the feudal state machinery.

With the decline of Mughal power, many of the urban centres and their business declined. Punjab under Sikh rule probably experienced a temporary revival: hence the rise of Rawalpindi and Amritsar as urban centres, and the revival of prosperity in Lahore and Multan. The Khatri, Arora, Aggarwal and Khoja traders and money-dealers continued their old businesses in agricultural commodities and artisanal products well into the nineteenth century. The scope for participation in international trade was, however, greatly reduced. It also seems that there were territorial boundaries within which each business community was concentrated. Thus the Khatris, though widely dispersed throughout north India, had as their special preserve Amritsar, Jalandhar, Lahore, and Rawalpindi; the Aroras were leaders in the regions of Derajat and Multan, and up to Peshawar and Kohat; the Aggarwal *bania*s flourished in the regions around Delhi, Hissar, and Ambala.

The establishment of British political and economic hegemony, notwithstanding the nominal 'raj' of some princely states in northern India, shifted the centre of gravity on the business map of India. For a major part of the nineteenth century, the once prosperous urban centres of Delhi, Rajasthan, and Punjab remained in the backwaters from the point of view of business. Most entrepreneurial activities occurred in Bombay and Calcutta, the new colonial metropolises. The north Indian business communities displayed serendipity of a high order. An example is the diaspora of the Marwari merchants who moved on to greener pastures and assumed new roles in the new business centres of Calcutta, Bombay, and their hinterlands. As for the substantial numbers of traditional business communities that remained in northern India, trade in foodgrains, cotton, oilseeds, opium, etc., received a boost with the growth of the railways in the later part of the nineteenth century. The resultant accumulation of capital and their fund of experience in banking and trading, enabled the Khatris or Aggarwals or Maheshwaris to re-establish themselves in the changed context. No doubt the Parsi and other business houses in Bombay had a lead of several decades over Kanpur or Karachi in the industrial field, but north India entered the race to catch up with Bombay in the years immediately preceding and following World War I.

Though Kanpur remained unrivalled in north India as an industrial centre during the period, Punjab too had eight cotton mills and the Dhariwal woollen mills, numerous steam powered factories such as ginneries, iron works, etc., as well as wool and carpet weaving, and hosiery works. Although, industrially, no urban centre in Punjab advanced to the level of Kanpur, not to speak of Bombay, entrepreneurial families were to spread to other parts of India, most notably to western Uttar Pradesh and Delhi. The partition of India in 1947 was again a big blow to the business community, but the post-colonial economy opened up new opportunities which the north Indian business communities exploited to the fullest advantage.

neighbouring regions. A new generation of Khatris, Aggarwals, and Marwaris settled in this growing town, the process peaking by the turn of the century.

After the revolution of 1857 and the establishment of British rule over the vast territory of the Indian subcontinent, a period of excessive exploitation of the country's resources began. Before the outbreak of the First World War in 1914, most towns in northern India were well connected by railway to the major port towns of India. The railways and telegraph facilitated the migration of the Marwaris and others from north India to these port towns. Though

(previous page):

◀ Padma Bhushan Seth Mungturam Jaipuria (1901-1978). Born in Rajasthan, he joined his father's business when only thirteen. Possessing no formal education but with a keen business sense, he bought Swadeshi Cotton Mills, one of the largest textile mills in 1945. Later, he diversified and set-up a large number of other industries. The Jaipurias are associated with a number of educational and social institutions.

most Marwaris started their careers as clerks or agents in the old firms established by entrepreneurs of previous generations, they soon settled into independent businesses. Marwari youth opted for trade in metals, sugar, and cotton, and later tried to monopolize jute. Khatris of Punjab and the United Provinces decided on wool, while Muslims tried their luck with machine products. Dulichand Kakrania of Chirawa, Surajmull Nagarmull, and Badridas Goenka earned their names as jute merchants. Marwaris from Mirzapur moved to the new industrial city of Kanpur. There they tried their hands at grain, oilseeds, and cloth, and soon displaced Khatris from the cloth trade. Around 1857, the Singhanias of Sevaram Ramrikhdas too opted for Kanpur. Merchants from Rajasthan and Punjab bought heavily into land, often for large-scale cultivation and horticulture, in the United Provinces and also in central India and Bihar, but did not substantially enter the field in Bengal. The firms of Laxmichand Radha Kishan of Mathura and Sital Prashad Kharag Prashad of Hathras and Agra were among those that did not trace their origins to Rajasthan but were famous in their time.

At the turn of the century, western UP was a major cotton- and grain-growing area. A number of Marwari and non-Marwari Aggarwal firms in the market towns of Ferozabad, Hathras, Khurja, and Hapur dealt in cotton and grain. They built cotton gins and presses, and even started a number of spinning mills. The Raniwals, Baglas, Sekhsarias, Hathras, Goenkas, and Jatias were among the major mercantile factors in this area. Delhi and Agra were flooded with the local *bania*s and Punjabi immigrants. Though Marwaris like the Goenkas and Garodias from Nawalgarh, the Poddars from Churu–Ramgarh, and the Jaipurias from Jaipur also came to Delhi and started trading in cloth, they were outnumbered by traders from Punjab and UP.

There are references to some Marwaris working as treasurers for the provincial government at Lahore. The Dhadhas of Bikaner conducted banking in both Lahore and Amritsar. Ramratan Daga of Bikaner was given the charge of the treasury of Lahore. In 1883, the Mohtas of Bikaner opened a branch office at Karachi and ultimately went into industry and opened an iron factory and textile mill there. Under the leadership of Marwaris and Sindhis, spindles and looms grew rapidly in the Sindh province.

In the meantime, Marwaris and Punjabis had accumulated enough capital resource and business experience to move into manufacturing. Rising internal demand and dislocation of imports encouraged these entrepreneurs to launch their investments in industry. The Birlas, particularly G.D. Birla, took the lead in this direction and built a cotton mill at Delhi and another at Gwalior. The Jalans and Bajorias, who were considered conservatives, also opted for industry. The Singhanias founded their first cotton textile

▶ Anandilal Poddar's business interests were later looked after by his sons Raja Ramdeo, Ramniranjan, Dr Ramnath, and Rambilas. Dr. Ramnath Poddar, and later his son, Kanti Kumar Poddar, gave direction to national entrepreneurial policy as Presidents of FICCI and continue to be known for their social charisma and works of philanthrophy

▼ Lala Kamlapat Singhania founded the JK Organization with a first cotton textile mill at Kanpur in 1927. Several others followed in quick succession.

(previous page):

▲ Gujar Mal Modi (1902-1976) established an entire industrial township close to Delhi that catered to the requirements of its employees within an integrated settlement. Today the Modi group, Gujar Mal founded, produces over hundred products ranging from sugar to steel, soaps to tyres and chemicals.

▼ Lala Shriram is among early entrepreneurs from Delhi who saw the opportunity in what was to become the British, and later, Indian capital. The Shriram family now has interests in a wide spectrum of industrial goods not only in the region but across a national network.

mill in 1927 at Kanpur and followed it up with several others in quick time. In the inter-War years, between 80 and 100 sugar mills were built in the United Provinces, and by 1936 there was a surplus of sugar in the country. The Khaitans too joined industry, and with the Baglas started jute mills at Kanpur. The growing participation of Indian merchants in the field of industry brought them into confrontation with their European counterparts. The rift between the two groups became even more pronounced in the wake of the rising tide of nationalism. The Marwaris established their own chamber of commerce headquartered in Calcutta in 1900, but this was soon racked by dissension between the groups of buyers and sellers of cloth. On the other hand, the confrontation between European and Indian business grew every year. No wonder then that G.D. Birla, Purshotamdas Thakurdas, Lala Shriram, Dinshaw Petit, Kasturbhai Lalbhai, M.C.T. Muthiah Chettiar, M. Jamal Mohammed Saheb, Walchand Hirachand, D.P. Khaitan, A.C. Banerjee, and others formed their own Federation of Indian Chambers of Commerce and Industry in 1927. Indian business enterprise had come of age.

The Freedom Struggle and Indian Business

Aditya Mukherjee

During the course of the nearly century-long history of the Indian national movement against British colonial rule, Indian business responded variously. Some like Jamnalal Bajaj, Vadilal Lallubhai Mehta, Lalji Mehrotra, S.R. Dhadda, Lala Shankarlal, and Samuel Aaron actively participated in movements launched by the Indian National Congress, the premier vehicle of the freedom struggle, were arrested, went to jail, and suffered the hardships that freedom fighters had routinely to face. Others like Jamsetji Tata, G.D. Birla, and Ambalal Sarabhai supported the struggle by financial assistance either directly to the Indian National Congress and its leaders, or for constructive programmes such as *khadi*, anti-untouchability, and village upliftment launched by Mahatma Gandhi. While merchants, traders, and small businessmen were among the first to come out in support of the national movement in large numbers, such as in the non-cooperation movement of the 1920s, by the 1940s even big business came out in its support on a large scale. Evidence from all over India points to big business houses like the Birlas, Tatas, Dalmias, Singhanias, Thapars, Shri Rams, the Walchand group, the Kasturbhai Lalbhai group, and Ahmedabad mill owners as a whole supporting the 1942 Quit India Movement. This was not only in the form of large monetary contributions but in providing help and shelter to underground activists (including Congress Socialists like Aruna Asaf Ali, Achyut Patwardhan, Jaiprakash Narain, and Ram Manohar Lohia) and, according to intelligence reports, even through active encouragement of strikes in their own industries (sometimes lasting up to two months) with full wages being assured to workers.

▼ A nationalist, Surendranath Banerjee was one of the elected honorary members of the Bengal National Chamber of Commerce when it was established in 1887, and was responsible for sending a delegation to participate in the third session of the Indian National Congress in Madras.

Yet others contributed by providing a sophisticated critique of imperialism in the economic sphere and pressed for the Indian case in all possible fora, whether in the Legislative Assembly, the Round Table Conference, the Tariff Boards, or at international trade and monetary negotiations such as the Indo-British Trade Negotiations of 1937–9 or the Bretton Woods conference to discuss the formation of the International Monetary Fund after the Second

▲ 'At home' with Jamnalal Bajaj in 1917 (standing centre) and flanked by Laxminarayan and Gopi Vissen, are the English chief commissioner, other guests, and N.G. Gadgil (seated, left).

▼ A young Ramakrishna, son of Jamnalal Bajaj leads members of the working committee of the AICC session at Wardha in 1942. With him are Sarojini Naidu, Maulana Azad, Acharya Kripalani, Rajendra Prasad, P.C. Ghosh, Rajaji, Khan Abdul Ghaffar Khan, Jamnalal Bajaj, and G.B. Pant.

World War. The more prominent Indian businessmen who performed this role were Sir Purshotamdas Thakurdas, G.D. Birla, A.D. Shroff, Mathuradas Vissanji, Samy V. Chetty, and Jamal Mohammed Saheb.

Many businessmen supported the national cause by promoting indigenous enterprise in competition and often intense conflict with imperial economic interests. The legendary attempt to create an Indian national shipping industry by the Scindia Steamship Navigation Co., led by Walchand Hirachand against a worldwide British monopoly, and the heroic efforts of the house of Tatas in establishing the steel industry in India are some well-known examples. However, similar efforts were made in diverse areas like cotton, jute, sugar, cement and paper manufacture, tea plantations, coal mines, banking, insurance, diesel engines, machine tools, and even the manufacture of cars, trucks, and aircraft. It is this that made India more or less self-sufficient in intermediate and capital goods by the end of the Second World War. By the time of Independence, indigenous enterprise had already cornered 72-3 per cent of the domestic market and over 80 per cent of the deposits in the organized banking sector. Indian business, therefore, enabled the process of economic and political independence to move hand in hand, in contrast to several other colonial countries where continued economic domination or neo-colonialism was the rule even after achievement of formal political independence.

From the very outset there was a link between the emerging national movement and the formation of modern Indian trade associations and chambers of commerce. The first Indian chamber of commerce, the Native Merchants' Chamber of Coconada was established in 1885, the year the Indian National Congress was founded. In 1887, the Bengal

▲ G.D. Birla, flanked by Sarojini Naidu and Mahatma Gandhi, on his way to London to attend the Round Table Conference, 1931. Also in the picture is B.M. Birla. Gandhiji had come to rely heavily on Indian industrialists to draw a blueprint for the resurgence of the Indian economy.

▼ Sir Dinshaw M. Petit was closely associated not only with the development of business, but also in reinforcing Indian interests.

National Chamber of Commerce was established with prominent early nationalists like Surendranath Banerjee being elected honorary members. On Banerjee's invitation, the chamber sent delegates to the third session of the Indian National Congress held at Madras.

From 1905, the Indian National Congress started holding the Indian Industrial Conference along with its own session. Prominent nationalists like Madan Mohan Malviya and Lajpat Rai, businessmen like Dinshaw Wacha, Vithaldas Thackersey, and Lallubhai Samaldas were closely associated with the Conference. In 1915, the Indian Merchants' Chamber, Bombay, which was closely associated with the national movement, organized the first Indian Commercial Congress which was soon merged with the Indian Industrial Conference to form the Indian Industrial and Commercial Congress in 1920.

Efforts were made by the newly formed Indian Industrial and Commercial Congress and by leading businessmen like Purshotamdas Thakurdas and G.D. Birla to establish a national-level organization of Indian (as opposed to European) commercial, industrial, and financial interests. These efforts culminated in the formation of the Federation of Indian Chambers of Commerce and Industry (FICCI) in 1927. FICCI started with 24 chambers of commerce as its members, the number rising to 103 by 1947. Some of its members, such as the Indian Chamber of Commerce,

▶ Jamnalal Bajaj, Sardar Vallabhbhai Patel and Mahadev Desai at Wardha, Gujarat. A symbiosis developed between the nationalist leadership and the country's entrepreneurs to develop an environment that would provide India with adequate commercial and industrial capability when it became independent. Sadly, the relationship suffered after Independence because of the government's orthodox socialist concerns.

▼ Sir Purshotamdas Thakurdas was a close associate of Mahatma Gandhi, and one on whom he came to rely both as a businessman and as a member of FICCI, to tender advise on economic matters.

Calcutta, South India Chamber of Commerce, Madras, the UP Chamber of Commerce, Kanpur, and the Indian Merchants' Chamber, Bombay (IMC) were themselves large bodies. The IMC had 1082 members in 1944, and 2716 in 1951. As a result, pepper and ginger merchants, jute balers, hides and skins merchants, owners of textile mills, paper mills, engineering companies, insurance companies, shipping companies, collieries, tea plantation owners, to cite just a few, all found representation in FICCI.

Small wonder then that soon after its formation, FICCI was recognized by the British government as well as Indian public as representing the dominant opinion, if not the consensus view, of Indian business. It was also able to successfully subsume within it the differences between traders, industrialists, and bankers, or between small and big houses. Nor did it allow the enormous heterogeneity in the ethnic, caste, religious, and regional origins of Indian business to hamper the emergence of a common Indian business opinion. So, for the last two decades of colonial rule, when the freedom struggle was at its peak, the position taken by FICCI could be treated broadly as the position of Indian business as a whole.

FICCI was seen by Indian business leaders not only as a platform for seeking redressal of immediate grievances of Indian business from the colonial government, but also as a forum for organizing public opinion both within Indian business and outside, on larger issues that affected not only Indian business but the economy as a

▲ Sardar Vallabhbhai Patel addressing a function of the Scindia Steamship Navigation Company. Also in the picture (sitting from the right) are Jamnalal Bajaj, Walchand Hirachand and Purshotamdas Thakurdas. Later, the Scindia Steamship flag was kept flying by Sumati Morarjee, one of the first women to control an industrial enterprise.

whole. Sir Muthiah Chettiar and Sir Shri Ram asserted that FICCI's role was that of 'national guardians of trade and industry'.

In this task, FICCI was aided by the fact that some of the most astute minds of the period constituted its leadership. There were people like Purshotamdas Thakurdas, who J.R.D. Tata described as a 'lion among sheep'. He was a major economic thinker, a director of over a hundred companies and, as a member of the Royal Commission on Indian Currency and Finance, 1926, the author of a brilliant note of dissent. Purshotamdas was respected in the world of academia. He was involved in appointing professors at the prestigious Delhi School of Economics, and the famous economist and future education minister of India, V.K.R.V. Rao, started his career as a member of his research staff. Similarly, G.D. Birla was a brilliant political tactician as well as sound economic analyst. Along with Purshotamdas, he argued with the famous British economist Lord Keynes on several economic issues, and Keynes would correspond with him on matters of currency and finance. There were several others whose talents were available to FICCI and Indian business in general, such as John Mathai, future finance minister of independent India, A.D. Shroff who represented India at Bretton Woods, Ardeshir Dalal, the planning and development member of the Government of India in 1945–6, N.R. Sarkar, G.L. Mehta, M.A. Master, Sir Muthiah Chettiar, J.C. Setalvad, Sir Badridas Goenka, and A.L. Ojha, to name just a few.

The result was that India was able to evolve a comprehensive critique of imperialism in all its manifestations: whether direct appropriation through home charges, exploitation through trade, finance, currency manipulation or foreign investments, including in their sweep the now globally celebrated concept of 'unequal exchange' where transfer of surplus is seen to occur through trade between countries with widely divergent productivity levels, even when the trade occurs at free world market prices. It monitored complex national and international developments that had a

▲ Leading industrialists often established conclaves where they could gather to discuss major points of issue with respect to government policy. Among those at one such meeting are, B.M.Birla, G.M.Modi, Ramnath Poddar and Lala Shriram.

▼ Kumararajah Sir Muthiah Chettiar from Chettinad was among those at FICCI who came to comment on the unequal exchange of trade between countries under imperial governance.

bearing on imperial domination and Indian economic development, and forcefully argued the national position.

The leaders of the national movement in the twentieth century, who unlike their predecessors, the early nationalists, made little contribution to the understanding of the economics of imperialism, readily accepted the role performed by the business leaders and treated their opinions and expertise on national economic issues with respect. In 1928, Motilal Nehru had no hesitation in seeking the expertise of Purshotamdas in preparing the economic part of his presidential address to the Indian National Congress. Similarly, in 1931, Gandhiji told the Viceroy to convey his serious misgivings to the British Prime Minister at the omission from the list of those invited to the Round Table Conference, of FICCI representatives G.D. Birla, Jamal Mohammed Saheb, and Purshotamdas Thakurdas without whose help, he said, he could not negotiate on controversial economic issues.

One of the most mature reflections of economic nationalism was the preparation of a plan for the economic development of India referred to as the Bombay Plan or the Tata–Birla Plan, its signatories including Purshotamdas Thakurdas, J.R.D. Tata, G.D. Birla, Kasturbhai Lalbhai, John Mathai, A.D. Shroff, Shri Ram, and Ardeshir Dalal. Its basic assumption was independent national government, and it worked out a detailed ambitious scheme aimed at pitchforking a backward colonial economy into an independent,

▲ Business leaders in consultation with the first President of India, Dr Rajendra Prasad. Such interactions have been a tradition at FICCI which continues to play a pivotal role in commenting on policy that has an impact on its members as well as on the commercial interests of the country.

(facing page):

▲ Dr Rajendra Prasad laying the foundation of Federation House, the headquarters of FICCI in New Delhi. To his right is G.L. Bansal who was Secretary-General of FICCI for a record twenty-five years, during which he proved to be a pillar of strength for the institution.

industrialized modern capitalist economy over a short period. The plan was in many ways similar to the recommendations made by the National Planning Committee of the Indian National Congress headed by Jawaharlal Nehru, and to a considerable extent anticipated the actual planning process initiated by independent India.

The leaders of Indian business did not see their role as being confined only to providing an economic critique but also effectively intervening in politics. As Purshotamdas Thakurdas said in his presidential address to the FICCI annual gathering of 1928: 'We can no more separate our politics from our economics.' Intervention in politics meant doing so on the side of Indian nationalism. 'Indian commerce and industry are intimately associated with and are, indeed, an integral part of the national movement, growing with its growth and strengthening with its strength.' G.D. Birla in his concluding speech as President of FICCI said in 1930, 'The only solution ... lies in every Indian businessman strengthening the hands of those who are fighting for the freedom of the country.'

While Indian businessmen decided to back the freedom struggle, they showed definite preferences regarding how it ought

India Gets Its Chambers of Commerce

The year: 1925. Nationalist sentiments echoed all over the subcontinent. As Indian industry and business prepared to take on the challenges of a self-reliant and independent nation, a unique movement took shape in Calcutta, the cradle of industrialization in India. Sixty-two Indian firms joined hands under the leadership of the pioneering industrialist G.D. Birla to form the Indian Chamber of Commerce, Calcutta, and to give a voice to the aspirations of a business society fettered under foreign rule. The history of the Indian Chamber is, in fact, enmeshed in the history of India's struggle for economic freedom and growth. The ICC's success in representing the views of Indian business is particularly laudable given the odds against which it had to operate. Said G.D. Birla: 'It fought for the economic interests of the country at a time when except the Indian mercantile community there was none to fight for it and thus it assumed the self-imposed role of the guardian of Indian economic interests.'

The formation of the Indian Chamber as the precursor to the establishment of FICCI was not only important from the point of view of providing a forum for indigenous Indian industry. A look at the thoughts expressed in a committee meeting of the ICC in 1926 shows the progressive thinking of the Indian business community of the time. Anandji Haridas, senior Vice-President of the ICC commented at that meeting:

> Modern commerce is daily assuming more and more an international character. The growth of population in certain countries, the intensive production by others, the growing efficiency in rapid communications, the economic policy of the modern state – all these have combined to make trade and commerce in the modern world matters of international importance and significance. The jute grower of Bengal is affected today by the discovery of a new fibre in Java. The presence of a Russian delegation in London reacts on the tea sales of Calcutta and the banquet speech of a Japanese minister is read with strained eyes by the directors of the Tata Iron & Steel Co. Ltd It is impossible for a modern businessman to be absolutely insular in his outlook. Methods of production are changing, new legislation is portending new conditions of factory or workshop life all over the world. It is, I think, the task of a Chamber of Commerce to broaden our economic outlook and to enlighten our commercial opinion.

Calcutta's pre-eminence as the commercial capital led to the hosting of the Indian Industrial and Commercial Congress in 1926. It was this session of the Congress that led to FICCI being brought into existence in 1927. The Indian Chamber elected three of its members to sit on the Federation Committee and G.D. Birla, the then ICC President, was elected as Vice-President of FICCI. In fact, the ICC's secretary was appointed honorary secretary of the Federation and of the Indian National Committee of the International Chamber of Commerce which was established a year later. The bond between FICCI and the ICC, therefore, dates back to its very foundation. Calcutta was the proud city where the decision to form FICCI was taken and to this day continues to play an active role through a rich heritage of industrialists and businessmen who are represented on the FICCI committee.

▶ Mahatma Gandhi with Lala Shriram at the Asian Relations Conference in New Delhi, 1947. The Indian capital has been a hub for international conferences and discourses, particularly in the context of the region.

▼ Nalini Ranjan Sarkar, as FICCI President in 1934, spoke strongly against the imperial councils' attempt to pass what he termed 'bad laws'. Indian business was often faced with a dilemma when it came to the question of participating in forums such as the Round Table Conferences, but opted in favour of attending these to ensure that it could oppose any laws inimical to Indian interests.

to be waged. Indian business was not in favour of abandoning the path of legal or constitutional opposition. It feared that abandoning constitutional spaces like the Councils or Legislatures, or boycotting negotiating tables like the Round Table Conferences would lead to policies inimical to the Indian nation being passed without any effective opposition. However, Indian business support for constitutional participation is not to be understood as their being co-opted into the imperial system or surrendering to it. As FICCI President N.R. Sarkar put it in 1934,

> We shall have no hesitation in adopting any method ... to strengthen our cause ... If the leaders think that the Councils [legislatures] can give us strength to achieve our goal, they must capture them. If they believe the Councils are impediments in the path of our political progress, they must capture them and break them. In any circumstance we must prevent others from using them to pass bad laws.

▲ Jawaharlal Nehru is greeted on his arrival at Chettinad airport by, among others, Shanmukham Chetty (extreme right) who later became the Finance Minister of India .

Though Indian business preferred to keep the constitutional avenues open, it refused to participate in them unless, as Sarkar put it, 'the nation also decided' to do so. That is, it refused to negotiate with the British government or make any commitments on constitutional or even on purely economic issues without the participation or at least the approval of the Indian National Congress. It is on this basis that FICCI advised its members to boycott the Round Table Conference of 1930, stating 'No conference ... convened for the purpose of discussing the problem of Indian constitutional advance can come to a solution ... unless such a conference is attended by Mahatma Gandhi, as a free man, or has at least his approval.'

Indian business also recognized that non-constitutional mass movements or civil disobedience was necessary to move towards the national goal, and to achieve immediate concessions that would benefit business. G.D. Birla, commenting on the existing Civil Disobedience Movement, wrote to Purshotamdas in 1931, 'There could be no doubt that what we are being offered at present is entirely due to Gandhiji ... if we are to achieve what we desire, the present movement should not be allowed to slacken.' However, the business community did not want such movements to be prolonged, not only because the burden of loss to day-to-day business as a result of protracted civil disobedience became too heavy, but also because it feared that such movements, prolonged beyond a point, could unleash socially revolutionary forces that would be difficult to contain and which would threaten capitalism itself. A number of other objective reasons why Indian business did not favour prolonged mass movements were brilliantly listed in N.R. Sarkar's presidential address to FICCI in 1934, with the inevitable conclusion: 'We, the commercial community, desire to march with our countrymen. Do not exclude us by taking a route we cannot follow or prescribing methods we cannot use.' Indian business pressed for the suspension of a movement after it had gone on for some time, often mediating between the government and the Congress to hammer out an honourable compromise. In January 1931, when the Civil Disobedience Movement of 1930 had run a long course and many business leaders were getting restive, G.D. Birla warned his colleagues that in their 'anxiety for peace' they were not to surrender or 'reduce [their] demands'. With characteristic political depth, he argued:

> We should ... have two objectives in view, one is that we should jump in at the most appropriate time to try for a conciliation, and the other is that we should not do anything which might weaken the hands of those through whose efforts we have arrived at this stage.

Whatever the level of anxiety of business regarding a prolonged mass movement, it never supported the British colonial

▲ Shyama Prasad Mookerjee, Industries Supplies Minister, with L.B. Bhupatkar, 1947. With Independence, India finally gained the opportunity to conduct business in a free environment. The promise, however, was short lived, and it took several decades before the country would shed its baggage of permits and over-regulation.

government in repressing it. On the contrary, it kept up relentless pressure on the government to stop repression of the nationalist forces and maintain all civil liberties, even at times when the Congress was at the height of its non-constitutional mass phase. It also refused to respond to British Viceroy Lord Irwin's secret exhortations to it in September 1930 to publicly repudiate the Congress stand on continuing civil disobedience, despite his assurance of government protection and a guarantee against any kind of harassment for doing so.

While Indian business had its preferences, it was never in a position to impose its views on the national movement. The Indian national movement was not created, led, or in any decisive way influenced by Indian business, nor was it in a sense crucially dependent on its support. In fact, popular mass movements, unlike political parties fighting routine elections, have avenues for sustaining themselves, including financially, which do not make them dependent on any one section of society. The British Intelligence Bureau (IB), which played an important part in the maintenance of British rule in India, Gandhiji, the chief architect of the struggle to overthrow British rule in India, and businessmen themselves did not make this error in understanding the relationship between business and the Congress. The IB conducted two detailed, all-India level enquiries in the 1930s and 1940s on orders from Lord Linlithgow, the Viceroy, and came to the conclusion that the Congress was not critically dependent on business contributions either during the movements led by it or even during the election phases. It also concluded that the evidence did not 'justify any assumption that Big Business [had] secretly been using Congress as an unsuspecting instrument towards the achievement of its own ends'.

In 1918, virtually at the beginning of his political activity in India, Gandhi declared that for *satyagraha*, money was the least important input. During the Non-cooperation Movement of the 1920s, while welcoming and even appealing for support from merchants and mill owners, Gandhiji simultaneously maintained that

> whether they do so or not, the country's march to freedom cannot be made to depend on any corporation or groups of men. This is a mass manifestation. The masses are moving rapidly towards deliverance and they must move whether with the aid of the organized capital or without. This must, therefore, be a movement independent of capital and yet antagonistic to it. Only if capital came to the aid of the masses, it would redound to the credit of the capitalist and hasten the advent of the happy day.

Indian business itself never saw the Congress as a party susceptible to its influence. The Congress was seen as a multi-class, open-ended organization; in the words of J.K. Mehta, secretary,

'I cannot forget the services rendered by commercial classes, but I want you to go a step further. I want you to make the Congress your own and we would willingly surrender the reins to you. The work can be better done by you. But if you decide to assume the reins, you can do so only on one condition. You should regard yourselves as trustees and servants of the poor. Your commerce must be regulated for the benefit of the toiling millions.'

Mahatma Gandhi, at the fourth annual session of FICCI held in April 1931.

Indian Merchants' Chamber, with 'room in it for men of all shades of political opinion and economic views'. Indeed, since the mid-1920s, as the Congress got increasingly radicalized to the Left with the growing influence of Nehru and the Socialists and Communists within the Congress, business leaders saw the urgent need to evolve an adequate response to this situation. Hence, a complex, multi-pronged, and subtle strategy was evolved to try and contain the growing Left within the national movement.

I can enumerate here only some elements of this strategy. First, and most important, Indian business representatives refused to support the colonial government in passing the Public Safety Bill which was intended to contain the Communists on the grounds that it would extend the powers of the colonial government in a manner which could be used to suppress Indian nationalists. Indian business leaders were acutely aware that if Indian business was even seen to have taken the support of the colonial government, the hold of the anti-capitalist forces in the national movement would automatically increase. They were certainly not going to vacate any nationalist space for the Left to occupy.

Second, Indian business leaders were among the first in the world to evolve a reformist welfare capitalist programme as a conscious strategy to combat the threat of the Left. As G.L. Mehta, President, FICCI, said in 1943: 'A consistent ... programme of reforms' was the 'most effective remedy against violent social upheavals'. The Post-war Economic Development Committee, which drafted the Bombay Plan, consciously functioned with this perspective in view. Its attempt was to see 'how far socialist demands could be accommodated without capitalism surrendering any of its basic features'. The Bombay Plan recommendations consequently emphasized equitable distribution along with rapid growth, argued for a public sector and partial nationalization, comprehensive land reforms including abolition of the *zamindari* system, and a series of workers' welfare demands such as minimum wages, fixed maximum working hours, housing, and so on.

Third, implementing a brilliant understanding of how a class exercises its hegemony or influence over society, Indian business leaders, particularly G.D. Birla, successfully prevented efforts by a section of business to try and push their class interests by either directly entering politics themselves or by forming a class party.

Birla argued, in 1929, that businessmen were not to attempt 'to kill Bolshevism and Communism with such frail weapons' as an attack on the Left with class organizations of business, which would carry no weight with 'the masses' or with the 'middle classes'. He said, 'I have not the least doubt in my mind that a purely capitalist organization is the last body to put an effective fight

The Politics of Business

J.R.D. Tata on the question of 'business pressure' on the Congress movement or on its leaders, based on an interview by the author in 1985

Tata was able to see that mass movements like the Civil Disobedience Movement could not be unending. They needed a pause as 'people who are driving the struggle and the people suffer from it' began to tire. This enabled Tata, unlike historians, not to have to resort to the theory of 'business pressure' in order to explain why the Congress, on occasion, such as during the Gandhi-Irwin pact in 1931, called for a period of truce in the throes of a protracted mass movement.

Tata was dismissive of the view that leaders of the national movement like Gandhi, Nehru or Patel could be pressurized, leave alone 'bought up' by business interests. As for Gandhiji, he argued that he was 'such a man that he could not have been bribed. I don't mean "bribe" in the wrong sense, but politically'. He thought of Gandhi as this 'extraordinary human being' whose 'incredible force and strength' made one feel 'very small' when one talked to him. 'I feel small when I think of him.'

Anecdotes about Tata's experiences with Nehru and Patel too are illustrative. Tata had extremely good relations with Nehru and hoped to influence his thinking and help knock off some of his 'rigid' ideas regarding socialism, nationalization, the public sector, and similar economic issues. However, after several meetings, Tata was to give up this effort because, as soon as he would try to guide the conversation to any such question, 'Nehru would freeze completely... turn around and look outside the window'.

Popular perception has it that Vallabhbhai Patel was easily accessible to businessmen and even prone to their pressure. Tata narrated his own experience as a corrective to such notions. A great admirer of Patel, Tata often tried to meet him. The endeavours invariably resulted in securing an offer of an appointment at five in the morning, when he was invited to join Patel on his morning walk. On occasion, when he did take up the offer, he found Patel had given the same appointment to several other people. The meeting would, therefore, consist of all the visitors, to Patel's visible mirth, spending the next hour 'pushing one another aside in order to get in a few words of [their] own, only to be pushed aside in turn'. Hardly a situation conducive to mounting any kind of pressure on him.

▲ K.D. Jalan greeting Vallabhbhai Patel at FICCI annual session, 1949. Jalan at the age of thirty-one, was the youngest President of FICCI, under whose dynamism the interests of the business community flourished. His son, Sudhir Jalan, is taking over as President of FICCI on twenty-fourth October, 1998.

(previous page):

▲ At the 1955 National Awards Investiture Ceremony held at Rashtrapati Bhawan, New Delhi, Prime Minister Jawaharlal Nehru admires the decoration of Padma Vibhushan awarded to J.R.D. Tata.

against Communism.' Again, in 1936, Birla wrote to Walchand Hirachand, 'It looks very crude for a man with property to say that he is ... opposed to expropriation in the wider interest of the country. Are you or myself a fit person to talk?' A much superior method was to 'let those who have given up property say what you want to say'. The role of business could only be to try and 'strengthen the hands' of Right wing nationalists 'who are fighting against two faces – the Government and Socialists'. Indian business leaders employed a very subtle understanding of the different roles of a member of a class and that of its politico-ideological representatives.

Lastly, the extremely mature Indian business leadership of that period was aware that class view could be influential within the Indian national movement or in society in general, and after Independence with the popular government and the electorate, only if its class interest could be projected as being also in societal interest. Indian business leaders took great care to ensure that they were not seen as pushing their narrow class interest or putting class before nation, but were seen as speaking in the interest of the Indian nation. Further, they were aware that this projection of class interest as national interest could not be achieved through manipulation. It could be achieved only to the extent there was a genuine coalescence of the two. The task was to discover and build on such areas of overlap, and even to create such objectives, if necessary, by business agreeing to make certain sacrifices. That, despite the growing popularity and strength of the Left stream within the national movement, no programme was adopted that would involve the overthrow of capitalism, reflects the maturity with which organized Indian business conducted itself.

Section III

Enterprise in Independent India

Overview

The Political Economy of Change in the Twentieth Century

Amit Mitra

The vibrant debate on the political economy of India spans a century treading over an entire spectrum of policy approaches from the neo-Marxist to the now liberalizing and globalizing perspective. The British colonial regime began with a laissez-faire approach seeded in the lecture theatres of Halibury College for Indian civil servants. But, pummeled by the Great Depression in Europe and chastened by the collapse of global markets, colonial policy in India shifted to Keynesian interventionism in the early 1930s. The proverbial Adam Smithian private enterprise and free markets had been eclipsed by the fears of 'market failure' and by the Keynesian apprehensions of market 'uncertainty'.

Indian nationalist leaders, on the other hand, focused squarely on socialism from day one. Their views ranged from the lure of 'central planning' to the ideal of 'trusteeship of the capitalists'. Indian leaders were deeply influenced by Western scholars of the Left, and by those who favoured 'humanism' and redistributive justice over competitive markets and aggressive private enterprise. Mahatma Gandhi himself was deeply influenced by John Ruskin. Gandhi concedes in his celebrated autobiography, *My Experiments with Truth*, that he was determined to change his life in accordance with the ideals of the essays of Ruskin although in economic matters, he favoured free enterprise along with trusteeship as an ideal mix.

▼ Constituent Assembly, New Delhi, 1947. The early seeds of business were sown in the spirit of socialism for the leadership was impressed by its ideals and favoured control by the state for key industries.

Jawaharlal Nehru was deeply affected at an impressionable age at Cambridge University, by the works of another British thinker, William Morris. Morris's call to young socialists to keep the 'fact of the class was always before them' and his emphatic conclusion that socialism 'explains past history and in the present, gives us the only solid hope of the future' touched the soul of young Nehru who was also deeply impressed by the new changes taking place in the erstwhile Soviet Union. George Bernard Shaw's renditions on socialism at Cambridge too left an indelible mark on him. These powerful influences produced what Nehru later came to all 'our innate socialist urge'.

Young Subhas Chandra Bose too was impressed by the 'achievements of the socialist municipalities' of Vienna and was influenced by the works of Professor Harold Laski. Bose's considered view was that 'local self government' or 'municipal socialism' must form the bedrock of the political economy of free India. The conspicuous exception to this direction of thought was Sardar Patel, despite his year long stint at the Bar at

London. Patel's pragmatism and innate link with the peasantry and trading communities of India left him skeptical about Western socialist perspectives. One cannot help but wonder what course the recent history of the nation would have taken had Gandhi chosen Patel, instead of Nehru, to guide the destiny of the nation.

Much of this early socialistic thinking cumulated ultimately in the landmark resolution at the Karachi session of the Indian National Congress in 1931. The Karachi session recommended the 'control by the state of key industries and ownership of mineral resources'. This was extended soon to include state controls over railways, waterway, shipping and other means of public transport, and strongly recommended a strict control over all private enterprises. Thus, when Subhas Chandra Bose, as president of the Indian National Congress in the late 1930s, initiated the (shadow) National Planning Committee and appointed Jawaharlal Nehru as its chairman, there was no room left for a debate on state versus markets. The ideological balance had shifted totally in favour of the state and the role of private enterprise had been relegated to the background.

Shortly after Independence, the Industrial Policy Resolution of 1948 was released. It unambiguously recommended monopoly of the state in three major industries with another six core industries to be under the 'exclusive' charge of the state for establishing new undertakings. These included iron and steel, manufacture of telephone and telegraph, and mineral oils. Furthermore, eighteen industries were slated for central government regulation and control.

Finally came the Avadi session of the Indian National Congress in 1955, the single most important landmark of Indian political economy. The historic resolution at the Avadi session stated that 'planning should take place with a view to the establishment of a socialistic pattern of society where the principal means of production are under social ownership or control'. It went further to opine that the state will initiate and operate large-scale schemes, and provide services such as power and transport. It would also 'check and prevent evils of anarchic industrial development by the maintenance of strategic controls, prevention of private trusts and cartels ... The public sector must play a progressively greater part, more particularly in the establishment of basic industries'. Thus, the die had been cast and the Indian private sector would now have to fight innovatively, and at times ingeniously, to hold on to a narrow band of private space in India's vast economy.

The Avadi Declaration was inevitably followed by the Industrial Policy Resolution of 1956 and then, by the draconian clauses of industrial licensing by 1961. The most crippling measure against private enterprise came in 1969 with the introduction of the Monopolies and Restrictive Trade Practices (MRTP) Act. All firms above a certain asset base were restricted from free entry into almost all sectors of Indian industry. Even expanding one's own plant required permission of the government 'case-by-case'. Thus, there was no room left for profit-driven investment decisions. Allocational efficiency was not on the front-burner, nor were cost reducing strategies or, for that matter, export competitiveness. Naturally, economic growth puttered along at 3 to 3.5 per cent per annum, partly dependent on the vagaries of nature as it affected agricultural production. A population growth of over 2 per cent menacingly chased economic growth, and the quality of life in a 'socialistic pattern of society' remained dwarfed, cobbled by the incapacity to sustain social expenditure. Private enterprise maneouvered and

▼ Russian premier N. Krushchev with Prime Minister Jawaharlal Nehru. The Indian Prime Minister was deeply impressed by the changes effecting the Soviet Union and chose it as a model. Today, both countries share the global environment of equal opportunities and capitalism.

▲ Sardar Vallabhbhai Patel remained sceptical of socialist perspectives in the West: had he led the nation at the critical juncture after Independence, instead of Nehru, the history of the nation might have been different.

▲ Mahatma Gandhi, austere in his lifestyle, favoured free enterprise based on trusteeship, but the fiery Subhas Chandra Bose, like his peers, believed in municipal socialism.

meandered to simply remain functional at the cost of low economies of scale, overemployment, low productivity, poor quality, obsolete technologies, inevitable rent seeking practices and global isolation in a regime of 'import substitution.

By the early 1980s, realization dawned that decontrol and strategic global connectivities alone could bring India out of this morass. The policy changes, however, were measured and introspective, focusing primarily on delicensing of two major groups of industries, access to imports for manufacturers of exports, and a change in mindset towards acquiring higher order technologies. The result of even these halting steps towards decontrol were almost spectacular. The growth rate of the economy wrenched out of the 3 per cent record to an average of 5.5 per cent in the decade of the 1980s and there is strong evidence that productivity too improved significantly. India was at the door step of a new vision of political economy driven by markets and private enterprise.

The radical change towards the new paradigm of liberalization and globalization arrived in 1991. Beleaguered by a financial crisis and dwindling industrial confidence, the government took the final plunge. The licensing Raj was banished in one stroke. The dreaded MRTP Act was abandoned. Import restrictions all but vanished. Exchange rates were driven closer to global markets and fiscal deficit was brought under an iron grip. Thus, the 'dirigiste dogma' of half a century was finally being swept by the march of time.

What continues to remain a matter of debate for the political economy of twentieth-century India is the 'rhetoric and reality of globalization' in the backdrop of a meltdown in East Asia, the near collapse of the Russian economy, and compression of global trade and recessionary trends in some Western economies. The tigers of economic development have been caged and partially wounded, but the cautious process of liberalization and globalization of the Indian elephant stands out in the discourses of today and those in the next millennium. Indian and global theorists are at a watershed in the year 1998 in search of a fresh paradigm entitled 'social market' where markets and the state work in tandem, stimulating each other rather than at cross-purposes. The search for an optimal synthesis between the state and the markets will characterize the main debate in the first decade of the twenty-first century and India could very well turn out to be its playing field. India's drive to become the fourth largest economy in the world by 2020 hinges on the optimal synthesis of once warring ideological and systemic perspectives.

Development and Growth of Business and Industry

Nitish Sengupta

British business houses played a pioneering role in creating the modern private sector in India, first as traders and then as manufacturers; they were closely followed by Indian business houses, once again first as traders, and then as industrial promoters. Some of the domestic businessmen grew in collaboration with British capital; others in opposition to it and also to the hostile colonial government which, in general, discouraged indigenous entrepreneurship. Contrary to folklore propagated by the first-generation political leaders that private sector entrepreneurs were only interested in quick-profit yielding projects rather than in long-gestation, capital-intensive ones, a sizeable number of domestic entrepreneurs had actually ventured into just such projects. Jamshetji Tata (Tata Steel), R.N. Mukherjee (Indian Iron & Steel), and Walchand Hirachand (Hindustan Aircraft, Hindustan Shipyard, and Scindia Steamship) are some cases in point. The Birlas, JKs, Kirloskars, and several others built up vast industrial empires. Some even shared a close relationship with the freedom movement, which they supported, and its leaders, as in the case of Mahatma Gandhi's friendship with G.D. Birla and Jamnalal Bajaj.

▼ Among Indian pioneering entrepreneurs who were able to succeed despite a hostile colonial environment were the Birlas. A rare picture of the four Birla brothers together, (from left): Jugal Kishore, Rameshwar Das, Ghanshyam Das, and Braj Mohan.

Indian industry greeted Independence with enthusiasm and optimism. A new era was unravelling with unlimited opportunities for indigenous entrepreneurs in partnership with a friendly national government, but there was also the unmistakable element of the government's

▼ Pandit Jawaharlal Nehru surveys the Rihand hydro-power station after inaugurating it; he is accompanied by C.B. Gupta, chief minister of Uttar Pradesh, and industrialist Ghanshyam Das Birla. Pandit Nehru was an exponent of such projects which he referred to as the 'modern temples' of India.

restrictive role. Partly, this arose from the survival of a number of controls affecting various aspects of the economy imposed largely in response to the needs of the War economy. These controls — import and export control, for example, or foreign exchange control, or capital issues control — became permanent landmarks of the Indian economic landscape. Some of these controls came out of an important policy document produced by the colonial government in April 1945 recommending the nationalization of basic industries of national importance and also a system of industrial licensing. Jawaharlal Nehru was influenced by Britain's Fabian socialism as practised by the Labour government of 1945, and also the Soviet system of centralized planning. Naturally, the first-generation leaders sought to impose public controls over the functioning of vast areas of private business.

From the very beginning, the government of free India embarked on a vigorous policy of industrialization. It had also to deal with a temporary dislocation on account of the breaking of the economic and political unity of the country as a result of Partition, and widespread communal disturbances in parts of the subcontinent. Partition gave India 91 per cent of the total number of industrial units, 93 per cent of the total number of workers employed, and about 97 per cent of the total value of mineral production. It, however, also lost a very significant market in general, and almost the entire supply of raw materials in two of its major industries, jute and cotton. About 81 per cent of the total production of raw jute went out of India, whereas all the mills stayed in India. Similarly, although of the 394 cotton mills in undivided India only 14 went to Pakistan, nearly all the supply of long and medium staple cotton which used to come from west Punjab and Sind was now lost to India.

Government efforts in the early years had necessarily to be concentrated on extending the area of jute cultivation and medium staple cotton from abroad which imposed severe strain on the country's foreign exchange resources. The dislocation of rail and road traffic, and of inland river navigation in eastern India, had some disturbing consequences for the growth of industrial activity. Industries such as hosiery, wool, glass, and metalwork suffered from the migration of skilled workers to Pakistan, although this was perhaps more than made up by the inflow of fresh managerial and entrepreneurial skill of migrants from Pakistan.

▲ M.S. Oberoi, the grand old man of the hospitality industry, started his career as a clerk in a Shimla hotel that he eventually bought after selling his wife's jewellery. His great coup was the acquisition of The Oberoi Grand in Calcutta following a plague epidemic, to launch a chain that has a global presence.

▼ Collaborations with automobile manufacturers from around the world were initially introduced in India. However, following the clamping of regulations, fresh proposals did not fructify and it is only recently that a flood of such collaborations have been permitted by the government.

The government directed its efforts to improving the climate of industrial relations and the well-known tripartite Industrial Conference (1947) called for a three-year truce between capital and labour and set out comprehensive measures for determination of wages and conditions of labour. Other features were the granting of tax concessions to industry in the budget for 1948–49, the continuance of a cheap money policy, the setting-up of the Industrial Finance Corporation in 1948, and welfare measures like the Factories Act, 1949. On 7 April 1948, Parliament adopted an Industrial Policy Resolution laying down the broad objectives of government policy in the field of industrial development, and demarcated spheres for the public and private sectors. It stressed the need for a policy of 'mixed economy' and struck a middle course between those who advocated free enterprise and others advocating government control. The government also took steps to clarify its policy towards foreign capital in a policy statement made by the prime minister on 6 April 1949: in this, it categorically declared its intention not to discriminate between foreign and Indian capital, welcomed foreign investment in priority areas, and said it would not impose any restrictions on foreign companies that were not applicable to similar Indian enterprises. From 1949 onwards, these set the private sector on a path of growth, facilitated by government assistance to industrial units for replacement, modernization, and import of capital goods wherever required, liberalization in the depreciation allowance, and exemption of duties in the case of industries like sugar.

▲ Advertisement for the Tata-Mercedez Benz truck, released in 1955 *(top)* and Ratan Tata with the Mercedes car in India, 1996 *(above)*. Tata first collaborated with Mercedes Benz for the manufacture of trucks and only recently it has been possible for them to sign up with Benz again for permitting it to assemble its cars for sale in the Indian market.

Interestingly, the majority of British industries found it difficult to reconcile themselves to the new environment and embarked on a policy of 'wait and see', neither undertaking new investment nor ploughing back their profits, but plugging their assets. However, Indian industry stepped in to fill the vacuum by acquiring foreign enterprises and through establishment of joint ventures. It set up a large number of joint ventures with a new breed of foreign companies wanting to participate in the Indian market. The more prominent among these included Telco (Tata collaboration with Daimler Benz), Bajaj Auto (Bajaj collaboration with Piaggio), Nocil (Mafatlals with Burma Shell), Hindustan Motors (with Austin), and Escorts (with Ford). The transformation of the Birlas from a close-knit family enterprise into a number of constellations loosely united by a common family name provides an excellent case study. Aditya Birla, the most successful scion of the family, successfully combined his knowledge of *partha*, the traditional Marwari system of monitoring accounts and financial control, with modern management techniques to set up an Indian MNC that covered not only India, but Thailand, the Philippines, Malaysia, Indonesia, and a number of African countries.

In 1950, when the Constitution came into effect and the planning commission was set up, the country entered into a new era of planned economic development. The Mahalanobis model that India chose to follow emphasized the role of heavy industries and the public sector. It did envisage a role for the private sector, but that was necessarily secondary. The Industrial Policy Resolution of 1956 excluded 29 major industries from the purview of the private sector and severely restricted its role. The Industries Development & Regulation Act, 1951, introduced a system of industrial licensing, allowing the government complete control over permissions for new industrial activities or expanding ongoing activities. The Companies Act, 1956, the Capital Issues Control Act, the Essential Commodities Act, and the Import and Export Control Act, all introduced around the same time, allowed the government total power as far as regulation of industry was concerned.

At the time, industrial licensing was generally welcomed by the private sector as a happy expression of the government's declared policy of a mixed economy, as illustrated by G.D. Birla in 1949:

> Government, of course, will have to play the primary part. But it will be fatal for private enterprises to feel that it has no duty to perform or contribution to make. Even if the government makes mistakes, we have to look upon them with helpful and friendly eyes. The intentions of government are of the very best. Their industrial policy on the whole is not unsound; it is neither to the extreme right, nor to the extreme left. It stresses a middle course which, perhaps, is the best under the circumstances.

The private sector witnessed phenomenal growth under the first three of the Five Year Plans (1951–67), partly through gradual acquisition of British-owned firms and partly through the establishment of new enterprises. To start with, industrial licences were given practically for the asking. There was a conscious move to induct non-traditional enterprises into industry. Thus, for example, a jeweller's firm was given a licence for synthetic fibres. The Birla companies were persuaded to enter nearly every field in which the Tata companies were established in order to encourage a spirit of competition. Established business houses like the Mafatlals, Lalbhais, Thapars, and Modis grew rapidly, while others grew more significant. Some like the Goenka group of companies grew rapidly both through the acquisition of existing units (Duncans, Ceat Tyre, CESC) and the establishment of new ventures (such as Philip Carbon Black). The B.M. Khaitan group witnessed amazing growth, taking over erstwhile foreign enterprises like Williamson Magor, McMill, Barry, and Union Carbide. Liberal licensing not only led to many of the units producing far below their capacity but also to the 'foreclosure' of capacity by powerful business houses to prevent new entrepreneurs from entering the field, thereby letting their monopoly continue. There was little awareness of the importance of competition or of producing goods and services of acceptable international quality. The Indian economy transformed into a seller's economy, with buyers left with little or no choice. This, in turn, led to the production of substandard goods or services, and Indian industry degenerated into a state of inefficiency. Exports, in such a situation, languished.

▲▶ Opening the green fields of summer to the Indian farmer by pioneering farm mechanization, H.P. Nanda, founder Escorts, tries his hand at the wheel of one of the several tractors the company manufactures from its plant in Faridabad, the industrial township in Haryana close to Delhi. Indian farming is gaining an impetus to mechanize agricultural methods, even in remote areas.

The Industrial Licensing Policy Inquiry Committee (1969) criticized such deliberate pre-emption or foreclosure of capacity by some large houses at the cost of new enterprise. Indeed, the licensing policy during the 1950s and 1960s seemed to alternate between spells of wholesale approval of applications in a given list to reach the targeted capacity, and *en masse* rejection of all applications after the targeted capacity had been reached on paper. Despite the phenomenal growth of the private sector, its relative size in the economy continued to shrink on account of the vast size of investments in the giant public sector units. Its share in the collective share capital of the corporate sector shrank from 93 per cent in 1951–2 to around 25 per cent by the end of the 1970s. The share of the public sector grew correspondingly, both in terms of equity and assets.

The disclosure of malpractices by a few business houses during the War years created an anti-business psyche in the minds of the people at large. Unfortunately, these activities, over which the business community in general had little or no control, not only blotted out the truly impressive entrepreneurial role of other families but also served to create an unsavoury image about corporate business in India. An oft-repeated comment was that

Indian industrialists behaved more like speculators and traders than industrialists, and that they had failed to take effective action to improve the condition of the working class which found reflection in the prevailing unsatisfactory climate of industrial relations. There was also a feeling that the Indian private sector preferred family management and discouraged the growth of professional management. But professional management did make its mark during the 1970s. A case in point is the house of Tatas: from the time in 1944 when J.R.D. Tata assumed leadership, to the late 1980s when he handed over to Ratan Tata, it had become among the most professionally managed businesses. There are other examples in the private sector, though the popular impression of family domination in businesses led to what one scholar called 'the alienation of the people and the government from the business class' which, according to him, was 'one of the greatest tragedies in the economic annals of India'.

With the gradual drift of national policy towards the 'socialistic pattern of society' and towards the 'sovereignty and supremacy of the public sector', further restrictions were introduced in the late 1960s for private business in general, and large houses in particular. Starting with R.K. Hazari's studies on industrial licensing (1966–7), a series of studies like the Monopolies Inquiry Commission of 1965 and the Industrial Licensing Policy Inquiring Committee (1969) severely indicted the working of the government's industrial licensing policy. A spate of restrictions followed: the restrictive foreign investment policy of 1968–70; the Monopolies and Restrictive Trade Practices Act (1969); the abolition of managing

▲ Bharat Ram is one of the leading industrialists of the country. A past President of FICCI, he was the first Indian to be elected as the head of the International Chambers of Commerce, Paris.

▶ Interior of Oswal spinning unit in Punjab. This northern state became associated with the manufacture of woollen yarns, fabrics, and hosiery during the early decades of the twentieth century.

(previous page):

▲ Inside a jute plant in Calcutta. Post-partition economic traumas resulted when it was discovered that eastern India was left with most of the jute plants, while the jute growing areas had gone to East Pakistan (now Bangladesh).

▼ B.M. Khaitan, Chairman and Managing Director of Williamson Magor and Company Ltd. His group is the largest manufacturer of tea in the country and has recently acquired Union Carbide.

▲ Cloth being run off the JCT plant at Phagwara, Punjab. Textiles has been, for several centuries, one of India's key areas of expertise.

agency (1969); the new industrial licensing policies of 1970 and 1973 which, for all practical purposes, shut large industrial houses out from anything except capital-intensive, core sector projects; the policy of the convertibility clause on institutional term loans; nominee directors appointed by financial institutions through whom they were made to exercise management control over large segments of private sector industry; and the Foreign Exchange Regulation Act (1973) which fettered companies and individuals with unheard of restrictions.

Private industry, in turn, became disenchanted with the system, and a wave of criticism followed. While some politicians and academics criticized government policy as having fostered the growth of large business houses and furthered the concentration of economic power, leaders of private business, including

▼ Bajaj scooters ready for dispatch from the plant in Pune. Bajaj imported its initial technology through a tie-up with Vespa, Italy. One of the leading scooter manufacturers of the world, at one time the company was threatened penalization for over-production.

chambers of commerce, criticized it for crippling the country's industrial growth and creating large production gaps and a high volume of unemployment. In all this, India remained isolated from the world economy. Industrial and GDP growths slumped to very low rates, often amounting to no more than a per cent or two per annum. This at a time when other countries in Asia, especially those in the Pacific region, were sprinting towards economic prosperity. The 1970s was truly India's decade of wasted opportunities. Even as developing countries in east, South East and West Asia enhanced their GDP, per capita income and living standards, India saw a virtual investment strike that retarded the growth of industries.

There were isolated instances of significant growth, as in the case of the groups spearheaded by Aditya Birla, the Goenkas, Thapars, J.K., Kirloskar, Godrej, Mahindra, and the DCM group. New, potentially great, groups began to emerge, among them Reliance Industries which, under Dhirubhai Ambani's leadership, was destined to rise from small beginnings to dizzy heights by the mid-1980s, thereby almost setting a world record. This was achieved by a combination of several strategies, such as reliance on domestic investors rather than the institutions by making use of the instrument of convertible debentures and vastly expanding

▲▶ Core industries in India have spanned from cement, the JK plant *(above)* to paper, Ballarpur, *(facing page)*, fuelling requirements of a developing society that is self-sufficient, with little need for imports.

the shareholders' base, regular vertical integration into a complete range of both downstream and upstream products, setting up world class manufacturing facilities, mergers and demergers, efficient tax management, and gaining access to global funds through Global Depository Receipts. There were other cases of impressive technology-oriented growth by non-traditional entrepreneurs. Bajaj Auto witnessed spectacular growth akin to

▲ Prime Minister Indira Gandhi favoured strengthening the public sector undertakings, and was responsible for the nationalization of critical areas of commercial activity, including banking.

global standards following the absorption of foreign technology. Telco, after absorbing foreign technology successfully, shed the Mercedes Benz brand from its trucks. On the other hand, the vastly overgrown public sector failed to generate the promised surpluses. This led to a somewhat inane private versus public sector controversy that did no good to Indian industry.

During the late 1970s, in response to the need for greater productivity and efficiency in the industrial economy, the government was compelled to initiate a number of liberalizing measures which, however, were still somewhat half-hearted. So were the initiatives taken by the Janata Party that formed the government during 1977–9, and which came to be known more for expelling IBM and Coca-Cola from Indian shores than for any flexibility it offered to industries.

With the return of Congress to power in 1980, the stage was set for a period of recovery. The new government's primary concern was overcoming the deteriorating state of industrial development. Industrial output had recorded a growth of only 1 per cent during 1979 and 1980. Inevitably, the government's industrial policy statements were aimed at enlarging the role of the private sector, removing restrictions on output scale and introducing greater flexibility in the implementation of licences. The validity of even these half-hearted measures was demonstrated by their success: GDP grew at an average rate of 5.5 per cent during the whole of the 1980s, and 5.6 per cent during the second half, offering relief from the earlier stagnation.

The expectation of a substantial increase in export, however, failed to materialize, notwithstanding the growth of several new, import-intensive industrial units, leading to a serious drain on foreign exchange. Despite a spectacular industrial performance, this resulted in a balance of payments crisis by the end of the decade, accelerated by the political uncertainty of the period. The government that came to power in 1991 was compelled to initiate sweeping economic reforms and structural adjustment measures that included near-abolition of industrial licensing, the MRTP Act, and FERA, a drastic pruning of the list of industries reserved for the public sector, a greater reliance on private sector initiative for business development, the introduction of convertibility of the rupee on current account, a new thrust on exports, import liberalization on a large scale, and gaining access to the global capital market. India was set on an irreversible path of economic reforms that, despite political obstacles, was to lead her to a high growth trajectory.

Economic Liberalization

Sanjaya Baru

The era of liberalization has seen the coming of age of Indian business. A measure of the change in the structure and dynamics of the private corporate sector over the past two decades is that little of what economists wrote about in the 1970s is relevant today. More strikingly, very few of the names of Indian companies and industrialists that dominate the headlines in business dailies and adorn the covers of business magazines today were even heard of two decades ago. Several of the leading business houses listed in 1969–70, ranked by asset size, find no place as major players. Some have become extinct, others have been bought over, and still others broken up into smaller companies.

In itself, corporate restructuring might not appear dramatic. The birth, growth, atrophy, and death of companies is a continuous process, but it must be remembered that a similar statement could not have been made in 1980. At that time there was a greater certainty about longevity and much smaller threat of extinction. Economic liberalization and deregulation, the end of the so-called 'licence-permit raj' and India's increased outward orientation and willingness to let market forces play their role have effectively pushed corporate India into a Darwinian world where only the fittest can hope to survive.

▼ Dhirubhai Ambani, Chairman, Reliance Industries. No single person used the system to create industries that were global in concept as well as Ambani did. Post liberalization, he has created an empire that spans among the most prestigious in the country.

Licences, protection, subsidies, ceilings on asset size, and family fiefdoms are out; competition, core competency, strategic planning, entrepreneurship, and professional management are in. The change in the structure of ownership and production, the regional spread of industry, the role of first-generation entrepreneurs, the arrival of new brand names, and the like in the period 1980–97, is severalfold more dramatic than anything India witnessed in the preceding two decades of 1960–80.

By 1980, Dhirubhai Ambani had established Reliance Industries and the Vimal brand name,

▲ Aditya Birla was an outstanding business player in post-independent India who also created an industrial empire overseas. Dr Manmohan Singh credited him as being an advisor who helped the Finance Minister in framing policies for the nation.

▼ Finance Minister Dr Manmohan Singh's budget speeches were telecast live from Parliament, and watched avidly around the nation. Dr Singh is widely credited with ushering in an era of reforms, beginning 1991.

(facing page):

▲▼ Samsung cassette factory *(above)*, Jindal Steel plant *(below)*. Today, India is part of the global economy, and its production standards match those of the world's best, whatever the industry. While imports have been liberalized, the government hopes to retain its balance of payments with an appropriate boost being provided for exports.

but few then imagined the global presence he would secure for the company. By 1980, K.V.K. Raju had esablished the Nagarjuna Group in Hyderabad, but no one predicted at the time that his would be the biggest business group in Andhra Pradesh and among the top 100 in India. By 1980, non-resident Indians like Swraj Paul had begun to seek investment opportunities back home but nobody could have visualized that NRIs would become as important players in the corporate sector as they are in 1997. In 1980, few had heard of T.P.G. Nambiar or Venugopal Dhoot or the Ruias of Essar, but by 1990 they were blazing a new trail in indigenous enterprise. In 1980, the Monopolies and Restrictive Trade Practices Commission (MRTPC) and business economists were worrying about the monopolistic and oligopolistic practices of some of the 100-year-old 'big business' groups, but few would have imagined that these family empires would subdivide into lesser satraps, competing in the market place with corporate upstarts within a period of a decade and a half.

Those who believe that economic liberalization and industrial deregulation began in India only in 1991, under the leadership of the then finance minister, Dr Manmohan Singh, might find it instructive to read the contents of the Vadilal Dagli Committee on Controls and Subsidies (1979) or the P.C. Alexander Committee on Import–Export Policies and Procedures (1978). Constituted by the Janata Party government of Morarji Desai, these committees laid the foundation for economic liberalization and the dismantling of the so-called 'licence-permit raj' in India. The liberalization of industrial and trade policy in fits and starts through the 1980s was

a response both to the problem of stagnating industrial growth in the 1970s and, paradoxically, to the emergence of a new business class of first generation entrepreneurs in such prosperous regions as the Punjab, Maharashtra, Gujarat, Karnataka, Tamil Nadu, and Andhra Pradesh.

Writing about Indian industry in the early 1980s, R.K. Hazari, doyen of industrial economists and acknowledged authority on corporate India, summed up:

> An analysis of the ownership structure [in Indian industry] clearly brings out that government occupies the commanding heights of investment, but its share of output, value-added and employment are substantially smaller. Partnership and proprietory firms own nearly two-thirds of the number of factories and provide about one-quarter of the employment; these proportions are probably underestimates.

He went on to observe:

> Foreign-controlled enterprises do not have a significant share of value-added ... their share of capital investment would be even lower. The share of large Indian houses (i.e. those which come within the purview of the MRTP Act) comes to 14 per cent in value-added and 20 per cent in capital investment. The share of 'other private Indians' in total mining and manufacturing is more than one-half. Non-manufacturing contributes 30 per cent to the total. *The entrepreneurial spectrum of industry is mixed, variegated, broad and predominantly indigenous* [emphasis in original].

▲▼ The era of liberalization has also ushered in a revolution in consumer goods. Indian brands, for example, now co-exist with international ones. This has proved advantageous to the consumer who can now exercise both choice and a competitive cost advantage.

Everyone recognized that over-regulation had stifled enterprise, but Hazari drew attention to the innovative ways in which risk-takers among Indian businessmen had overcome the system. If the mill sector was controlled, the powerloom sector flourished. 'Weber's thesis of the absence of the Protestant Ethic among orientals, the lack of a will for growth and deficient entrepreneurship has been shown up as a spectacular misbelief,' wrote Hazari. 'In India, the unsung but ubiquitous Bania Ethic (derived from Jain as well as orthodox Vaishnavite Hindu sources) stretched much further back historically and over a wider population than the Protestant Ethic.'

What Hazari failed to recognize was how much more widespread the 'business ethic' in India was, going beyond the *bania*s and the Marwaris who were the original industrial capitalists, with new enterpreneurial groups emerging across the country such as the Kammas in coastal Andhra, the Chettiars in Tamil Nadu, the Marathas in Maharashtra, and the Punjabis.

The development of agrarian capitalism in western, north-western, and southern India, thanks to land reforms, public investment in irrigation and roads, and the enterprise of Indian farmers' investment in such diverse crops as sugarcane, cotton, tobacco, oilseeds, wheat, and rice, formed the backbone of the emergence of new business groups in these regions. Only a few among the older, traditional business groups emerged stronger and more competitive. Consequently, by the 1990s, the structure of Indian industry had altered dramatically. Notwithstanding four decades of *dirigiste* state-sponsored industrial development, sometimes thanks to it, new enterpreneurial groups came into

existence and went into new industries and services. The edifice of indigenous capitalism had become firmer and bigger.

The policy of economic liberalization in the 1980s, howsoever slow-paced and half-hearted, sifted the boys from the men in the Indian corporate sector. Corporate restructuring, modernization, and core competency became the name of the game. The year 1991 posed the issues more starkly and underlined the fact that though domestic competition was the starting point, the finishing line lay in the big, bad world of global competition. A question is often asked as to the impact of liberalization on the Indian corporate sector and what its response was. The answer is somewhat mixed. Some industries and corporates have done better than others, some have benefited significantly from trade and investment liberalization, others have suffered enormously. Most are coping with new challenges and trying to find a place in the sun.

▲ Brij Mohan Munjal heads Hero Honda, an Indo-Japanese two-wheeler collaboration that revolutionized mass transportation needs in urban centres.

▼ Dr Anji K. Reddy *(below)* is responsible for taking a giant leap forward in the pharmaceuticals industry with extensive R&D facilities. In Dr Reddy's laboratories, state-of-the-art analytical instrumentation *(right)* and well-established quality assurance and quality control systems help the group supply finished dosages consistently.

▲▼ With the entry of international brands like Reebok and Coca-Cola in the Indian market, competition in the stores has hotted up, but Indian brands have surprised MNCs in being able to hold their own, and at times outperform their global competitors.

◀ Sophisticated technologies and production methods have grown by leaps and bounds in the field of chemicals.

Consider Dr Anji Reddy, CEO of Dr Reddy's Laboratories, Hyderabad. Dr Reddy is a first-generation professional who was employed by the public sector pharmaceutical company, IDPL. He quit IDPL to start his own company. Dr Reddy's pharmaceutical exports to the US attracted legal action in US courts for product patent violation and became a cause celebre during the early 1990s when India was named under the US trade law Super and Special 301. While Dr Reddy won his case in the US courts, he read the writing on the wall and decided to globalize his operations. He has since set up a production base in China, outside Shanghai, becoming one of the first Indian companies to manufacture and export drugs from China. Dr Reddy raised US$ 50 million in the GDR market in 1995 and has invested heavily in medical research and healthcare. Consider Sundaram Krishna who has converted an also-ran automobile company into a global player by tying up with General Motors and becoming a global supplier of radiator caps for GM. Consider Narayana Murthy of Bangalore's Infosys or Hero's Munjal and Ranbaxy's Parvinder Singh. These are the emerging men of Indian industry who are going global.

Cities like Hyderabad and Bangalore have been home to several entrepreneurs whose businesses have grown and horizons expanded. Did liberalization provide the stimulus, were these success stories already in the pipeline and only came to prominence in the 1980s and 1990s, did the acceleration of growth in the 1980s help their fruition, or was it two decades of government support and agrarian transformation that did it? Analysts can build theories using each of these hypotheses. The upshot of it all is that the 1980s witnessed a new era in the development of Indian enterprise when a new generation of entrepreneurs had begun to come into their own in the more prosperous regions of India. When 1991 arrived, the new business class was equipped to grab the opportunities that followed.

Liberalization has also brought in its wake a fair share of challenges. Takeovers, dumping, brand wars, and the like — nothing symbolized this better than Coca-Cola's celebrated usurpation of Thums Up. Multinationals with deep pockets and the stamina for a long distance race started turning on the heat on Indian companies that worried, and continue to worry, about hostile takeovers, loss of national control, unequal playing fields, and the like. If the debate has not ended yet, nor has the process; the question whether national ownership will survive competition and liberalization remains unresolved. Indeed, should this matter at all?

Most Indians think it should. Despite a flood of foreign brands, especially in consumer goods, Indian

▲ Hari Shankar Singhania, Chairman of JK Organization, brought honour to the country when he was elected President of the International Chamber of Commerce, Paris.

▼ TVS has stormed the Indian market with a Suzuki collaboration that produces two-wheelers in every range, ideal for use in metro areas, and catering to a range of budgets. In 1992, the company launched five new models, a record in the Indian automobile industry.

brands have been able to hold their own across a range of products. If Indian companies invest more in product quality and customer service, they should be able to take on any challenger. To be able to do so, however, Indian industry must become more quality conscious, invest in human capital and R&D, and encourage professional management. One consequence of liberalization has been the growing professionalization of management. Even so, 80 per cent of the top 100 Indian companies remain family enterprises. The more the confidence that business families have shown in allowing professionals to manage their companies, the more successful they have proved to be in running their companies and in retaining control. The more insecure and divided a business family, the less likely it is to keep a good concern going.

For all such problems that liberalization has brought with it, there have been some bonanzas too. The 1980s was the decade in which the middle-class consumer and investor came into his own. The stockmarket boom, which tapered out after the financial sector scam of 1992, and the opening up of the 'middle-class' market for consumer durables, fuelled the industrial boom of the 1980s and early 1990s. Spread across India, in big cities and small towns, in the food surplus districts of north-western, western, and southern India, and the NRI-remittance rich states of western and southern India, the economic policies of the late 1980s and early 1990s

▲ VSNL computerization: India has not only caught up with the world in most fields, it has also become a leader in some of them, chiefly in the arena of information technology and telecommunications.

encouraged this urban–rural middle class to open up its purses and purchase cars, two-wheelers, household appliances, processed foods, and the like. While the jury is still out on whether this 'pent-up demand' is finally exhausted, the fact remains that the era of liberalization will be remembered not just for the unshackling of Indian enterprises and the opening up of the Indian market, but also for encouraging unabashed consumerism.

Caught in the maelstorm of globalization, domestic enterprise is trapped midstream. However, the history of indigenous business enterprise and the great Indian diaspora that has represented, in the past, that Indian entrepreneurial and professional skills are as good as the best, gives rise to the hope that with more investment at home in our people, in their education, skills, and health, in an improved and globally competitive infrastructure sector, and a willingness to take on the world, Indian business can look forward to an era of rejuvenation, growth, and diversification as it enters the next millennium.

Developments in Indian Agriculture

M.S. Swaminathan

Agriculture is the world's largest solar energy harvesting enterprise, and India, with its abundant sunlight, has the potential of becoming a leading agricultural nation. Over the past fifty years, the transformation of the Indian agricultural industry from a static to a dynamic state has begun. From the early evidence of wheat cultivation in Mohenjodaro dating back to well over 2000 BC, up to 1947, the country's annual wheat yield was a mere 6 m. tonnes. Between 1964–8, when high yielding, semi-dwarf varieties of wheat were first cultivated, wheat production increased from about 10 to 17 m. tonnes. Such progress became possible when farming communities were assisted with appropriate technologies, services, and public policies. Concurrent attention to technology, training, techno-infrastructure, and trade is vital for its sustained progress.

The increased production is the result of improvement in productivity rather than expansion of the area under cultivation. This, in turn, has helped save millions of hectares of forest land from being cleared for the cultivation of annual crops, and the

▼ Wheat fields, near Taj Mahal. India, for several centuries, depended on rainwater for agriculture but in recent decades, the Green Revolution has revolutionized farming.

▲▶ Though rural areas still depend on ancient ploughing techniques, increasingly this is being replaced with tractor mechanization to optimize production yields.

introduction of hybrid rice technology and of the tools of molecular breeding have helped to raise the yields of both rice and wheat.

This progress has been confined largely to irrigated areas. Of the 142 m. ha. cultivated land in India, 92 m. ha. (or 65 per cent) is rain-fed. Unlike irrigated agriculture, rain-fed farming is usually diverse and risk prone, and is integrated with livestock rearing. Mixed cropping and mixed farming systems are important elements of the food and livelihood strategies adopted by rural families in rain-fed areas. By current standards, 3 ha. of rain-fed land produces cereal grains equivalent to that produced on 1 ha. of irrigated land.

Historically, attention to the development of rain-fed agriculture dates back to 1880 when the first famine commission was appointed by the then British government. A significant programme on dryland agriculture research was, however, initiated only fifty years later. It was in 1933–5 that the Imperial Council of Agricultural Research (now the Indian Council of Agricultural Research or ICAR) sponsored a dry farming scheme at five centres, namely Sholapur, Bijapur, Raichur, Hagari, and Rohtak. The setting up of a Soil and Water Conservation Research and Training Institute at Dehra Dun in 1954 was, perhaps, the first initiative made in independent India to focus on problems of soil and water

▲▼ A substantial part of irrigated land in India is under the influence of rainfed agriculture, while wastelands add to the woes of cultivable production. Harnessing and conserving water, and the conversion of these wastelands hold the solution for advancing development in agribusiness which continues to remain the country's major industry.

conservation. Since then, a number of research and development initiatives have been launched to stabilize and raise the productivity of dryland crops combined with sustainable natural resource (land, rainwater) management.

Fifty years of research and development efforts have led to the evolution of useful techniques and information on agronomic practices, and the appropriate choice of crops, and their varieties and cropping systems. However, the yield gap between the research stations and farmers' fields continues to be wide, leading to some interesting conclusions:

> Most research farm programmes have been perceived, planned, implemented, supervised, and evaluated by scientists. The transfer of results followed a top-down, 'take it or leave it approach'. The scientific findings that became the so-called 'technologies' were born from small plots and short-term research and were invariably not associated with critical cost–benefit studies.
>
> Acceptance of improved technologies was largely coterminous with the period of financial support. The moment financial support was withdrawn, farmers reverted to their traditional practices or adopted only some selected components of the technologies being promoted.
>
> Acceptance of certain components of the technologies being promoted did lead to a moderate increase in productivity, but emphasis on generation of employment was lacking. Consequently, male migration in search of jobs continues to be a serious problem. In a majority of instances, the new technologies did not suit the women who manage fields in the absence of male members.
>
> The absence of a farming system perspective ignoring rural energy or fuel needs for households and forage needs for farmers' animal support systems affected the sustainability of the programmes.
>
> Watershed programmes, whether funded from internal or external resources, were labelled 'government' programmes, with minimal involvement and empowerment of farmers in planning and

▼▶ India is self-sufficient as far as grains are concerned, and a well-developed network handles all the stages from harvesting to dispatch from public granaries, known as *dhan mandis*. Scientists are studying ways of further increasing the yield per hectare of land through the equitable distribution of water, cropping systems, and use of hybrid seeds.

implementation. Despite the fact that a watershed is owned by many farm families, soil and water conservation approaches did not emphasize community sharing of water resources. The Pani Panchayats fostered in Maharashtra, for example, failed to become a mass movement.

Rain-fed agriculture, to be productive, needs to be based on the watershed as the unit of development. A watershed is not a technology but a concept that integrates conservation, management, and budgeting of rainwater through simple but discrete hydrological units. Simultaneously, a watershed supports a holistic application of technologies on soil and water conservation with improved crop varieties, farming systems, and agronomic management, taking into account both arable and non-farm land.

Although low gains in a majority of the watershed programmes continue to be a matter of concern, the success of watersheds like Rale Gaon Sidhi (Maharashtra) and Sukkomajri (near Chandigarh) have attracted nation-wide attention. With the availability of water assured, farmers may be motivated to accept profitable, sustainable, innovative farming systems.

◀ Food processing methods are fast gaining popularity. Farmers find ample ways to use simple techniques such as this machine for blanching depodded peas, ensuring the availability of frozen peas throughout the year.

▼ Tea and coffee plantations need specific soils, drainage systems, and climates, all of which India has. Despite high yields and prices, Indian tea and coffee has been slipping in the international market because its marketing stops short of being aggressive.

Water availability has also catalyzed the adoption and spread of value-added arable technologies in the entire area of the watershed, such as horticulture. A major reason for the success of projects executed by several non-governmental agencies is the cooperative effort generated among members of the watershed community.

Integrating the watershed development programme with the village development plan to be executed by the panchayat could prove an effective method of ensuring peoples' participation and the sustainable and equitable use of water. In villages where there are several watersheds, an integrated master plan for watershed management could be developed. Also, cropping systems need to be tailored to suit different rainfall-cum-soil zones:

> High rainfall areas (mean annual rainfall: 1000 mm). Soyabean will be a suitable crop. Specific efforts should be instituted to realize the full potential of the crop in high rainfall, black soil region, with two crops a year through selective mechanization and drainage of low-lying areas.
>
> Medium rainfall regions (mean annual rainfall: 750–1000 mm). Cotton could be given high emphasis in this region. Depending upon soil and the length of the growing season, a suitable intercrop could be introduced to increase the overall profitability of the system.
>
> Low rainfall regions (mean annual rainfall: 750 mm). Pulses will be ideal. Farmers should be allowed to process the pulse into *dal*. In order to improve the availability of seeds of new varieties of pulses, including hybrid *arhar* (pigeon pea), seed villages could be organized in such areas.

Besides identifying a lead crop, each panchayat-led watershed management system should have the following goals: conservation of water, enhancement of supply and management of demand; sustainable and efficient use; equitable sharing of benefits; value-addition to water by cultivating crops of high value but low water requirements.

An eco-development mission of this type will help to trigger rapid agricultural progress in such areas, thereby helping to bridge the gap between potential and actual yields.

On the basis of these principles, FICCI, SPIC, and MSSRF jointly initiated a programme for organizing Pulses Villages in the chronically drought-prone areas of Ramanathapuram and Pudukkotai districts of Tamil Nadu. Lessons from the irrigation-led green revolution initiated by V.S. Aggarwal in the coastal areas of the Sunderbans in West Bengal were used in the design of the Pulses Villages. Dedicated non-governmental organizations like Renaissance and Speech were associated with the programme.

The experience gained during the last two years (1996 and 1997) has shown that progress in the production of pulses can be achieved by spreading such a programme. The underlying principles are: cooperative effort on the part of the village community in rainwater harvesting and the storage of the rainwater in suitably designed farm ponds; establishment of community dug tube-wells; cultivation of appropriate pulse crops chosen both according to the agro-ecological conditions and market demand; cooperative processing and marketing of the pulses.

FAO, the International Food Policy Research Institute, and the World Watch Institute have made projections regarding the likely food scenarios in the years 2010, 2020, and 2030, respectively. According to IFPRI, global demands for cereals is projected to

▲▶ Fruits Residue Drier. Cattle feed from processed fruit residue.

(previous page):

▲ Mustard is one of the key crops that feeds the demand for oilseeds production.

▼ Hybrid sugarcane has yielded excellent results for the Somaiya Group's Godavari Sugar Mills at Samirwadi, Karnataka. Experimentation in production methods was instrumental in the growth of record-breaking sugarcane crops per hectare of land.

increase between now and 2020 by 41 per cent, and for meat by 63 per cent. The 'food gap', i.e. the difference between production and demand for food, could more than double in the developing world in the next twenty-five years. The World Watch Institute predicts that India may have to import over 40 m.t. of food grains, while China will need to import 200 m.t. by the year 2030.

The further intensification of food production in industrialized countries will be ecologically disastrous. On the other hand, the inability to achieve the intensification, diversification, and value addition of farming systems and farm products will be socially disastrous in developing countries like India where agriculture is the principal source of rural income and employment. It is socially, politically, and economically essential that India realizes its potential to become a major supplier of farm products in the world. How can this be achieved?

First, we must develop a symbiotic partnership between private sector industry and resource to help poor farmers in bridging the gap between potential and actual yields, and in adding economic value to the time of agricultural labour. Some of the pathways through which such partnerships for sustainable food security can be promoted are:

Contract farming rather than corporate farming. This will involve firm buy-back arrangements of crops and commodities produced for a company. Such an arrangement can also be made in the case of tree species by the paper and pulp industries.

Water harvesting, and pulses/oilseeds villages. In dry farming areas, industry–farmer partnerships will help to promote scientific water harvesting and the use of conserved water for producing crops of high value with low water requirements like pulses and oilseeds.

The Colours of Progress

India's amazing strides in the field of agriculture and related industries, and in that of processed foods, stem from the country's recognition as both producer and consumer of food products. Changed circumstances and need-based changes are also responsible for this. Even the Thar desert, for example, is turning out crops with the waters from the Indira Gandhi irrigational canal now flowing through the dry, desert sands of the region. Nor is technology delinked from it: pisiculture is now a recognized way of breeding fish for the table in a country where the catch, traditionally, was always brought in by fishermen from the sea.

At the heart of the determined effort to tide over the vagaries of the monsoon is the Green Revolution. This post-Independence movement has created sources of irrigation, imported and grafted seed varieties, intensified crop production, and helped the farmer achieve success through a more scientific approach to agriculture.

What few people know is that, simultaneously, India can be proud of at least four more such movements that have led towards the country's self-sufficiency in this field. These include the White Revolution, tapping

milk sources in cooperatives for redistribution all over India, and for turning into dairy products. India is now one of the major milk producing countries of the world. The Blue, Yellow and Red or Rainbow revolutions, in turn, are associated with fisheries, oilseed production and horticulture. In the five decades since Independence, commendable progress has been made in increasing the production of commercial crops like cotton, oilseeds and sugarcane, and in livestock products, poultry, fisheries, fruits and vegetables. Thanks to these efforts, vegetables and fruits not traditionally associated with India have now become common produce in its markets, including everything from baby corn to strawberries.

These achievements have been made possible through a combination of technological breakthroughs and applications supported by the ICAR, agricultural universities and research institutions. Agriculture does, after all, employ two-thirds of the country's labour force, contributing to a third of its GDP. The new millennium now holds the potential for a second Green Revolution with special focus on the rain-fed and dryland areas of the country, with better water management and rainwater harvesting systems.

▲ A KW-SPV grid interactive power system in use in S.N. Palayam village, Coimbatore, Tamil Nadu. Harnessing natural energy will light the way into the future.

▼ A farmer enjoys a smoke, content in the knowledge that the solar lantern will provide him power.

Urban green belt movement. A green belt movement can be fostered by industry symbiotically linking the rural producer and the urban consumer.

Seed villages. With the spread of hybrid strains even in self-pollinated crops like rice, there are opportunities for business-farm families collaborating on seed production and technology.

Horticulture and animal husbandry. Industry–producer linkages will be of particular value in perishable commodities, since these need capital and management-intensive facilities at the post-harvest stage, such as cold storages, refrigerated transportation, and processing technologies.

Agribusiness enterprises. The Small Farmer Agribusiness Programme designed by MSSRF at the instance of the Government of India, needs for its success, the active participation of industry in promoting value addition to primary products and in linking products with markets.

Decentralized production supported by key centralized services. There is need for such arrangements in the production and marketing of a wide range of processed foods, horticultural and animal products, and goods produced in micro-enterprises. The All-Women Biotechnology Park being established at Chennai by the Government of Tamil Nadu with support from the Department of Biotechnology, Government of India, is an example.

Manufacture of farm implements. This is another area where large industries can foster small-scale manufacturing units in villages.

Farmers' service centres. There is a need for such centres, particularly in dry farming areas, for custom hiring of farm machinery and implements.

Next, we must end the prevailing mismatch between production and post-harvest technologies. Value addition to primary products, as for example spices, cereals, pulses, oil-seeds, tuber crops, and vegetables should receive high priority. Wheat and rice afford opportunities for the manufacture of a wide range of processed food such as flakes, noodles, and breads. In the case of rice, every part of the biomass — straw, bran, and husk — can be used to produce a wide range of products. To realize the full potential in value addition, we should also tailor crop varieties to end uses. Breeding for the processed foods industry is yet to receive the attention it deserves.

We should also design new crops to fulfil the needs of human health as well as food processing. For example, there is considerable variability in crops like rice and wheat in the content of iron, zinc, and sulphur. There is also variability in the tannin content and activity (tannins are phenolic compounds in plants that precipitate minerals and make them unavailable for absorption in the gut). For example, in rice varieties, the content of iron, zinc, sulphur, and tannins has been found to vary from 40 to 77 ppm, 24 to 42 ppm, 1.69 to 2.79 ppm,

and 10 to 41 ppm respectively. Tannins not only reduce the nutritional value of foods with regard to iron and zinc, but also impede the digestibility of proteins. Through the use of molecular breeding techniques, it is possible to design new crop varieties to cater to the health foods industry. India has a comparative advantage in providing the global markets with health and organic foods because of its rich traditions of ecological farming.

In 1967, a programme for the development of a high-yielding *basmati* rice was initiated at the Indian Agricultural Research Institute, New Delhi. After twenty years of carefully planned breeding and selection, the world's first high yielding dwarf *basmati*, Pusa Basmati 1, was released. Pusa Basmati yields are 1.0 to 1.50 t. higher than traditional *basmati* varieties. India exports

▲ A biogas plant: Biogas is being utilized to provide critical fuel needs in a country that is finding itself increasingly pressed to find non-conventional energy solutions.

▼ A 2 MW demonstration project at Chalkewadi, Maharashtra, demonstrates how wind energy can be tapped.

▼ Grading and sorting button mushrooms. The processing industry has come of age in the country.

(facing page):

▶ A fruit juice bottling plant. With processed foods available round the year, production facilities will receive a boost, especially in the case of delicate produce that otherwise spoils fast.

0.5 to 0.6 m. t. of high quality *basmati* rice valued at around Rs 1500 crore. The share of Pusa Basmati in such export is about 35 per cent.

In filling the gap between potential and actual yields, and by adopting low external input in sustainable agriculture and aquaculture methods, India can not only meet the food needs of its growing population but also help meet the food gap in both developing and industrialized countries. In industrialized countries, whose agriculture is driven by capital, technology and subsidies should help developing nations to increase their agricultural trade. Unfortunately, the reverse appears to be happening, as exemplified by the patent taken in the United States of America for rice varieties belonging to the *basmati* category.

Basmati rice has been cultivated for centuries in north-west India and the Punjab part of Pakistan, and is a major source of agricultural export earning for both countries. Unless patenting procedures are rooted in the principles of ethics and equity, agriculture, which is the foundation for a healthy and productive life for all, will become a source of conflict, rather than of partnership for achieving freedom from hunger.

The growing problems of unemployment, poverty, feminization of agriculture, and unplanned migration of the rural landless to towns and cities resulting in the growth of urban slums can be solved only through an agricultural renaissance. The opportunities for this are great, but to avail of them, it is essential that both government and industry make a major investment in rural infrastructure, post-harvest technology, sanitary measures, and the information and skill empowerment of rural families. The future lies in precision farming based on the conservation of soil and water, and the adoption of eco-technologies. Agriculture is the only pathway that can ensure both the livelihood security of a majority of our population and the ecological security of the countryside.

Science, Technological Innovation, and Industry

R.A. Mashelkar

To be able to compete successfully, one must comprehend the meaning and nature of the basics of competition: quality, productivity, price (hence cost), response time, innovation, economies of scale, product design and differentiation, and customer satisfaction. However, the nature of entrepreneurial and managerial competence in the next century promises to go beyond these, successful not merely at anticipating the future but at inventing and shaping it. That is the logical implication of the exploding advances in science and technology, as also the veritable revolution in the means of communication and information.

▼ Dr C.V. Raman demonstrating the light effect named after him for the benefit of Pandit Jawaharlal Nehru at a laboratory in the Indian Institute of Science, Bangalore, in 1948.

It is not easy even for experts to comprehend the meaning and implications of this mighty surge of science and technology. The consumer, then, can hardly even begin to know the possibilities. Yet industry must know it, for successful businesses will have to create a future commensurate with these possibilities. Its bedrock will prove to be science and technology, and the critical element will be innovation, not only in products, processes, and services but over the entire set of structures, systems, and strategies. Already, the key words are knowledge and creativity. The most significant asset that will give a company a sustainable competitive edge will be its intellectual capital: the knowledge, creativity, and skills of its people, not as an end in itself but to set the agenda for the corporation. Michael Porter describes this strongly when he says that companies will have to create an environment where they cannibalize their own products and render their own production processes obsolete before somebody else does.

▲ The Atomic Energy Commission carried out an underground nuclear blast at Pokhran, Rajasthan, in 1974, and a series of five blasts more recently in 1998. Photographs show the crater formed after the 1974 *(top)* and 1998 *(above)* explosions.

▶ A.P.J. Abdul Kalam and R. Chidambaram of the Atomic Energy Commission addressing a press conference after the 1998 blasts, explaining the nature of the activity, and its possible use in development.

Globalization, in this context, has come to mean organizing business operations on a worldwide basis to one's maximum advantage. The whole world is now a stage for sourcing and deploying business resources: materials, technology, personnel, production facilities, and marketing operations. Global integration has become a reality. The twentieth century, described by Lester Thurow as the 'century of niche competition', is gradually giving way to what he specifies as 'head-to-head' competition as one approaches the twenty-first century. The competitive edge is, therefore, shifting from indigenous natural resources to the brainpower industries, e.g. new materials, microchips, computers, software, biotechnologies, etc. which have no natural home. Whereas niche competition created a win-win game, head-to-head competition will result in a zero-sum game. To cope with the change, an organization has to have the capacity to change its structures, processes, workflow, and information streams at will. It has to be lean, with core competencies both in specialized tasks and skills, the traditional hierarchies replaced by networks, with work and data flowing in every direction. More importantly, it will have to be a learning, sentient, and intelligent organization.

▼ A nuclear power station: India is committed to using its nuclear facilities for peaceful purposes.

▲▼ India is one of a clutch of countries that has a successful space programme. It has its own satellites in orbit, launched from its own bases, and the defence sector has developed missiles that can offer airborne protection.

India is in a state of transition today. The results over the past seven years of turmoil are encouraging. Perceptions and attitudes have changed significantly. The country is now addressing issues of trade and not aid, investment and not borrowing, response and not coercion, facilitation not control. Above all, it is now viewing science and technology as an area for investment rather than expenditure.

The country has made considerable headway in uplifting the material conditions of its people and its achievements in food and agriculture, space, atomic energy, supercomputers, computer software, and defence have been globally acknowledged. These achievements have been arrived at a fraction of the cost that developed nations require for comparable tasks, even though the distance we have to travel is still long. However, we have not been able to make a similar impact in the industrial sector yet, because industry and R&D systems have been working apparently unmindful of, and unconcerned with, each other.

Despite India's performance in several high-tech sectors, the country's competitive advantage continues to lie in the abundance of natural resources and cheap labour it commands. Industries in which we have exploited the advantage are the two-wheeler transportation segment, leather, gems and jewellery, software development and light engineering products. The potential for high comparative advantage lies in food and food processing, agricultural commodities, textiles, specialty chemicals, automotive parts, mineral-based products, and the like, though it still remains to be realized. India's comparative advantage is poor in high-tech products, petrochemicals and consumer products.

▲ The shipbuilding industry is not new to India, but has grown of a size after Independence. During the colonial era, the British discouraged Indian entrepreneurship in shipping activities because it wanted complete control over maritime activities in India.

▼ Hansa, a two-seater composite aircraft, has joined the ranks of aeroplanes developed at the Hindustan Aeronautics plant in Bangalore using indigenous technology.

A recent analysis of forty-two countries in the Asia-Pacific region ranked the countries in terms of competitiveness over a number of parameters: domestic economic strength, internationalization, government, finance, infrastructure, management, and science and technology. India came out in a poor light in all the parameters, the worst being infrastructure where it was ranked 41; in science and technology, it ranked 29, and in domestic economic strength, 22. The ranking for science and technology reflected not only the generation of new knowledge but also the ability to create new products and new wealth. In another study on national orientation, i.e. the evidence that a nation is taking directed action to achieve technological competitiveness, India was placed at the bottom, even among the emerging Asian countries that include China, Indonesia, and Malaysia.

A study by the Indian Institute of Foreign Trade on how a nation adds value to its exports considers five factors, namely natural resources, labour, scale, technology, and

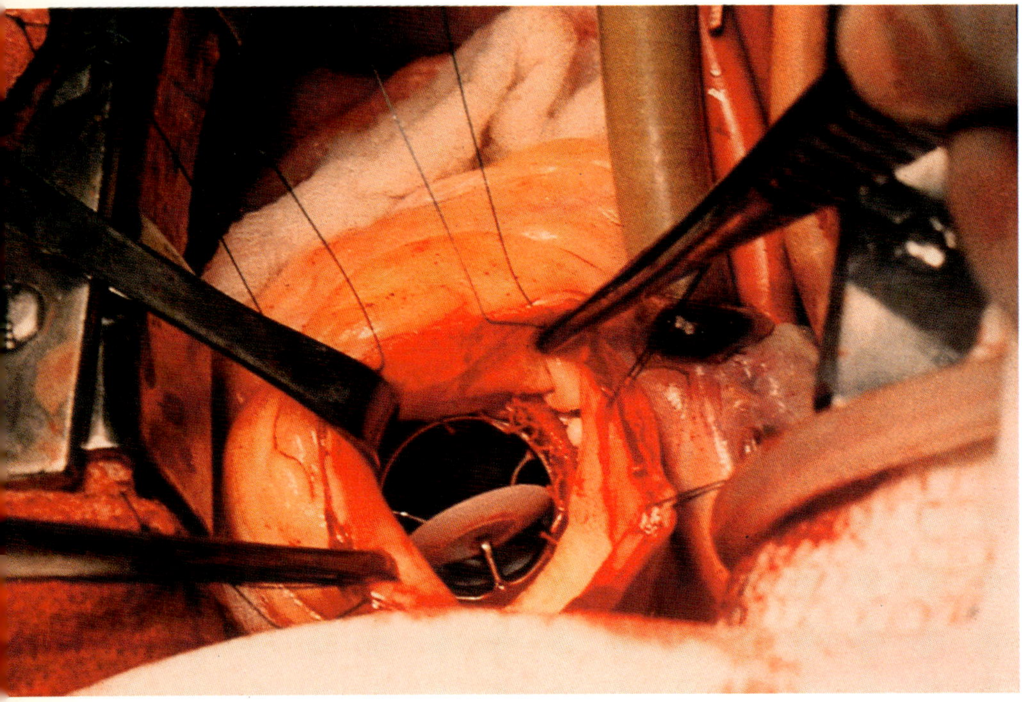

product differentiation. Almost 50 per cent of the value addition in India comes from labour-based factors and about 29 per cent from resource-based factors; technology-based factors and product differentiation together account for less than 5 per cent. The trend must be reversed to ensure that the competitive edge lies in technology and product differentiation.

Fortunately, there are reassuring success stories to show that India can, indeed, do it. Catalysts and drugs are two inspiring instances where the country has been able to register notable successes. Catalysts are low volume substances of high value and high knowledge content with a low level of investment. Drugs are high value materials with high knowledge intensity, a long gestation period (typically ten–twelue years), and very high investment.

▲ A heart valve operation being performed in India. R&D facilities and a keen mind have made Indian doctors and surgeons among the best in the world.

▼ Centron is an oral female contraceptive developed by Indian scientists to regulate population control efforts.

In a trillion dollar chemical industry dominated by a cartel-like situation, catalysts are critical elements. However, from being a perennial importer of catalysts and technology, India is emerging as an exporter of both, even to the West. One of the premier laboratories under the CSIR, namely the National Chemical Laboratory, Pune, has played a key role in this reversal. Starting with the establishment, in 1978, of a dimethylaniline plant based on an indigenous catalyst, in 1986 NCL developed the encilite catalyst for xylene isomerization which, when tried in IPCL, gave a far superior performance to a catalyst supplied by a leading multinational. In 1989, there was an entirely new technology, called the Albene technology based, again, on an innovative catalyst system. In 1991, the export of high-tech catalysts to Europe began. Today, NCL has global partnerships in industrial catalysts and catalytic processes with some of the giants in the world, e.g. General Electric, Du Pont, Nestle, FMC.

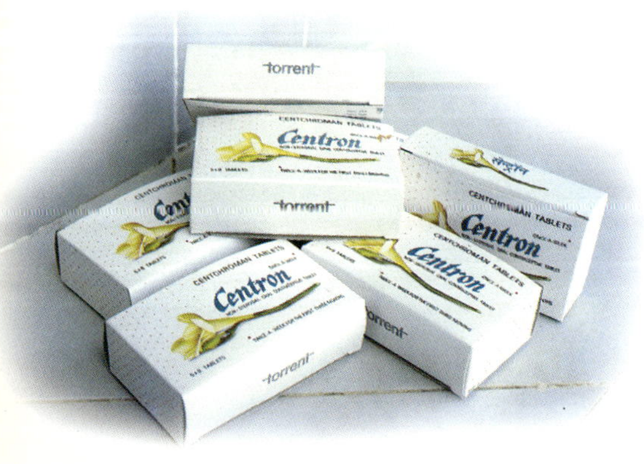

In the case of drugs, India imported formulations in the 1950s, whereas in the 1990s it has reached 90 per cent self-sufficiency in bulk drugs and has become a net exporter. This transformation came from an outstanding ability in process innovations. With India's membership of WTO, this advantage of non-acceptance of product patents in the Indian patent system will go and the country

▼ The R&D Laboratory of Ranbaxy has been able to combine research work with generic drugs from the international markets to open up new exciting opportunites for this leader in the pharmaceuticals industry.

will have to compete for the development of new innovative molecules as candidates for drugs, rather than just innovative processes.

The immediate and short-term challenges, of course, have to deal with quality, productivity cost, response time, and innovation. In the medium to long term, the challenges will lie in technology upgradation, scale of production, product design, strategic partnerships (both within India and globally), and the change of mindsets and attitudes.

▲ At the IPCL plant, the National Chemical Laboratory tested an encilite catalyst for xylene isomerization which outperformed a similar catalyst supplied by a leading multinational.

▶ Plant for manufacturing Pentaerythritol Formaldehyde and Alcohol, Kanoria Chemicals (KCl), Ankleshwar, Gujarat. The KCl complex uses environment friendly technology and has put up the first plant in India to directly generate power from effluent gas after purifying the same.

There are two other trends we should take particular note of in the manufacturing industry. The first is the ecological challenge which is not either an exotic fad or a non-trade barrier. If industry is to avoid acquiring an anti-life image, it has to make the environment a priority concern. The spate of judicial pronouncements on environmental issues is an unmistakable pointer that these obligations cannot be circumvented. In Tamil Nadu, 400 tanneries of a total of 800 were closed down since they did not use green technologies and flouted effluent disposal norms. Two CSIR laboratories, namely the Central Leather Research Institute (CLRI), Madras, and the National Environment Engineering Research Institute (NEERI), Nagpur, took up the challenge and developed a common effluent that has put more than 200 tannery treatment plants back on track. The Taj Mahal too was threatened due to the pollution by foundries around Agra. To help the foundries, CSIR laboratories like the National Metallurgical Laboratory (NML) developed technologies based on non-coke cupolas. Entire manufacturing technologies have to be reworked to conform to environmental needs. Waste management — reducing waste recycling and creating wealth out of waste — have to be built into an acceptable technology, and it may well turn out to be a paying proposition.

The other generic challenge comes from the need for miniaturization and automation. Products made with precision through automation, consuming minimal raw material, have

MOLASSES TANK

become important. New tools based on microelectronics, micro-machining, and robotics are needed. Manufacturing technologies will be driven by the urge to reduce material consumption, material substitution, reduce load on eco-systems, getting more from less, and making stronger, lighter, and cheaper products faster. Standardization will become an indispensable requirement for globalization, and Indian standards cannot afford to be different from global standards. Finally, working on a global time clock will push the change through increased pressure and increased specialization.

Such technology-driven competition will require the industry to depend more heavily on science. This has clearly been a neglected area in India. Whereas the government's role in supporting higher education, frontier science research, and high-tech R&D is undisputed, increasingly the responsibility for sustaining and nurturing them clearly has to be shared by Indian industry. They are, after all, the beneficiaries of their products. The demand from industry on the Indian knowledge system has been quite low. How can one promote an alliance between industry and knowledge workers in national laboratories that will lead to a win-win situation for both? How do the academic community and researchers find the technological niche in the knowledge-based industries? Can

▲ Quality carpets continue to be handmade in India, continuing a tradition begun centuries ago.

▼ A modern leather tannery softens calf leather, providing a boost to the export industry of completed items. Chennai and Agra are two leading centres of leather tanning.

A fluorescence-aided cell sorter in a modern facility devoted to the life sciences.

Going Global

The Council of Scientific & Industrial Research (CSIR) has been at the forefront of new developments and has won global recognition in such areas as aerospace engineering, drugs and pharmaceuticals, bioscience and biotechnology, chemicals (catalysts, polymers), petroleum (refining and petrochemicals), materials (composites), and leather (processing, chemicals, product design).

In the field of drug development and biotechnology, CSIR has proved to have outstanding capabilities in chemical synthesis as also skills that have led to the discovery of new molecules for drugs and agro-chemicals. This has gone a long way in helping to exploit the rich potential of India's biodiversity. Wide-based knowledge in the fields of molecular biology, immunology, tissue culture, recombinant DNA techniques, medicinal and aromatic plants, etc. has proved to be of a high order.

Such world-class competence has attracted a large number of foreign companies for collaboration with CSIR in these areas including some of the biggest names in the global corporate world such as Parke-Davis, Smith Kline Beecham, DuPont, American Cynamid, Abbot Laboratories, Cytomed Inc., Genecor, Zymogenetics, all from the USA. Other global tie-ups include CIBA, Switzerland, and Novodirsk, Denmark. Clients in other areas include GEC, Eastman Chemical Co., Polaroid Corporation, Mobil Oil Corporation, IBM, Boeing Corporation, UOP, Unitel, and Pratt & Whitney, all of the USA; Hitachi, Japan; and Locweld, Canada.

we effectively force cooperation among competitors for pre-competitive R&D? This is deserving of more than ordinary concern because high science and high technology are very cost intensive and the competitors have to evolve models for cooperation to compete globally.

Though successful technology-based companies do generally have R&D competence of a high order, the generation of new concepts and new ideas in technology is not the prerogative of any one particular system or group. Indeed, it is commonly realized that it is neither possible nor wise to meet one's technology requirements through in-house development alone. Technology

▲ A far cry from the traditional method of collecting honey, Dabur's honey processing plant in Himachal Pradesh is as modern as it is sterile.

sourcing from outside is an established competitive strategy; often, the possession of a core strength that can leverage other technology needs through external sources is all that is required. The excellent R&D infrastructure available in India can indeed be a valuable source for technology development in partnership and technology services for Indian industry. Indeed, leading companies outside have been more prompt in spotting and exploiting this R&D potential in India than our own. By now, several leading companies have made or plan to make India their R&D base: these include Unilever, Astra, and GE. India is fast emerging as a global R&D platform.

To pull India out of the mire of poverty, it needs a flourishing industrial economy. The life breath of modern industry is knowledge and creativity, and its lifeblood is innovation. India has the required calibre, capacity, and competence; the challenge lies in industrial and R&D systems in the country forging closer bonds for mutual benefit. Foreign companies have been quick to spot and exploit the Indian potential. It is time for Indians to network together and to transform its status from 'perpetual potential' to 'achievement'.

The scientific policy resolution of 1958 stated that it was an inherent obligation for a country like India, with its tradition of scholarship and original thinking, and its cultural heritage, to participate in the march of science, today probably mankind's greatest enterprise. It is time, as we enter the twenty-first century, to team up to this challenge and promise.

The Indian Financial System

M. Narasimham

The financial system we inherited at Independence consisted largely of the commercial banks: the Imperial Bank of India, Indian joint stock banks, and foreign banks that were referred to as 'exchange banks' in view of their role in the finance of foreign trade. Advances to industry, even as late as 1951, constituted barely a third of their credit operations. Cooperative banks, though in existence for several decades, barely touched the fringe of the agricultural sector which was meant to be their special domain and, in 1951, accounted for only 3 per cent of that sector's credit needs.

▼ Head office of the erstwhile Bank of Bengal. At the time of Independence, banks as commercial institutions were confined to the task of providing finance.

With the inauguration of planning in 1951, the objective of a promotional banking policy was the building of a geographically wide and functionally diverse financial infrastructure to meet the growing needs of a developing economy. For commercial banks, this meant an expansion of their branch network, especially in under-banked areas. Between 1951 and 1969, the number of banking offices rose from less than 6000 to a little under 9000. Deposits and advances also rose significantly in per capita terms. To meet the needs of investment finance in the private sector, a chain of specialized term lending institutions was set up at the initiative of the central and state governments. At the central level, the Industrial Finance Corporation and, at the state level, a chain of state finance and industrial development corporations

▲ Seal, Imperial Bank of India, later converted into the eponymous State Bank of India.

▼ The 1921 board of the Imperial Bank. (Seated from left): Annamalai Chettiar, R.N. Mukherjee, R.M. Watson Smyth, Norcot Warren, Sir Robert Aitken, J.F. Simpson, Sir M.B. Dadabhoy. (Standing from left): A.G. McWatters, N.M. Murray, S.A.H. Sitwell, Sir Percy Newson, A.F. Buchanan.

were established, to be followed by institutions such as the Industrial Credit and Investment Corporation of India and subsequently the Industrial Development Bank of India. The family of development finance institutions has since grown to cover housing, tourism, agriculture, foreign trade, and small industry. Investment institutions are represented by nationalized insurance corporations covering life and general business, and by the Unit Trust of India. Most of these institutions were in place by the late 1960s.

For commercial banks, the defining moments came with the conversion of the Imperial Bank of India into the State Bank of India in 1955, and the nationalization of 14 large public sector banks in 1969, followed by a second phase of nationalization of 6 banks in 1980. The objective behind nationalization was the socialization of credit to reach out to neglected sectors of agriculture and small industry and business, to expand the coverage of banking, and to mobilize resources for national development.

The phenomenal growth of banking in the decades following nationalization has few parallels anywhere in the world. In this period, the number of commercial bank branches has increased sevenfold to a little over 60,000, most of them in semi-urban and rural areas. The result has been sharp increase in the density of banking coverage as reflected in the fall in the population served

by a bank office from around 65,000 in 1969 to under 12,000 presently. That banks extended their spatial reach in this way, and particularly in rural areas where a little over half of the offices are now located, and where they have been beset by problems of inaccessibility, poor infrastructure, and other discomforts, is a tribute to their commitment to the public purpose. The widening and deepening of the financial structure have been responsible not only for enhancement of the aggregate household savings ratio but also for an increasing proportion of it being in financial and, hence, mobilizable forms. In the process, the financial intermediation and interrelations ratios have risen significantly.

For a country with a population of around 950 m., there are nearly 300 m. deposit accounts and, even allowing for multiple accounts of the same depositor, the figure is eloquent indication of the reach of the banking system and spread of the banking habit. The banking contact in the rural hinterland is becoming increasingly coterminous with the trading contact with its own implications, incidentally, for the relevance and impact of monetary policy. On the assets side, advances to agriculture and small-scale industry figure prominently in banks' credit portfolios, accounting for nearly 40 per cent of total credit and catering to around 35 m. borrowers in the so-called priority sector. We thus have a fairly developed financial infrastructure in place and one that has diversified its functioning to cater to special needs. At the end of March 1997, the aggregate deposits of banks had exceeded Rs 5,00,000 crore (or well over 40 per cent of GDP at current prices), advances were over Rs 2,75,000 crore, and investments in government and approved securities Rs 1,59,000 crore. Term lending institutions have also vastly increased their scale of

▼ Bank of Bombay building, Bombay.

▲ The first board of directors of the State Bank of India. (Sitting from left): Adam Hajee Mohammad Sait, Purshotamdas Thakurdas, F.B. Taylor, Osborne A. Smith, Sikander Hyat-Khan, Homi Mehta, Muzammilullah Khan. (Standing from left): Sundar Singh Majithia, U. Bah Oh, Lala Shriram, Badri Das Goenka, Edward Benthall, F.E. Dinshaw, F.W. Kelly, A.A. Bruce, M. Ramachandra Rao.

operations over the last couple of decades, and in March 1997 their total assets amounted to as much as Rs 3,32,000 crore of which the IDBI and NABARD accounted for Rs 48,000 and Rs 23,000 crore, respectively. State- level institutions accounted for a further Rs 11,000 crore. These are impressive figures by any reckoning.

The last couple of decades have also seen impressive growth in capital market activity. New issue activity in the private and public sectors expanded over eightfold between 1990–1 and 1994–5 to over Rs 49,600 crore, though it has since been somewhat subdued. Market capitalization in March 1996 was over Rs 4,27,000 crore. The number of institutional players has also risen, prominent among which are domestic mutual funds. Foreign institutional investors are also becoming an important segment of the market. The regulation of capital markets is vested with the Securities and Exchange Board of India. Investor protection is the *raison d'être* of such regulation even as protection of the depositors' interest is the basis for regulatory activity over banks. Scripless trading has commenced with the initiation of dematerialized trading and the institution of depositories.

The phenomenal growth of the financial system has exacted a heavy price in terms of quality of service, a deterioration in asset quality, a decline in productivity and efficiency, inevitably leading to lower profitability. By 1991, it was clear that there was need to arrest this qualitative decline even while consolidating the gains from the earlier quantitative expansion. This was the uppermost

consideration of the Committee on the Financial System (CFS) which focused particular attention on the assets side of the banks' balance sheets, their composition and quality. One of the features of the post-nationalization banking developments was the large increase in what one might call the pre-empted use of banking funds by a requirement to invest increasing proportions of bank resources in government and other approved securities at interest rates that were administered and kept relatively low. This was, in fact, a reflection of the effort to divert a growing proportion of resources to the public sector in keeping with the expanding role of public investment in economic planning. The deployment of the instruments of the cash reserve ratio and the statutory liquidity ratio thus went beyond their initial purpose in terms of monetary policy and bank safety. The combined proportion of directed investments through the use of these two ratios rose to a figure of as much as over 63 per cent at the margin by 1991, to the point of crowding out other claimants to bank resources and also affecting banks' earnings.

The impact of directed credit was also sharp on profitability as, apart from the misplaced identity between priority sectors' credit needs and concessional credit for those sectors, the unit administrative costs of servicing a large number of borrowers exacted a heavy toll on bank earnings. The credit portfolio of banks was also infected by a significant element of over 25 per cent being classified as non-performing assets. At the same time, while bank

▲ Bimal Jalan is Governor of Reserve Bank of India, which at the helm of the banking industry, closely monitors monetary policies and oversees the exchange rate of the Indian rupee.

▼ Reserve Bank of India building, New Delhi.

▲ Unit Trust of India, corporate office, Mumbai

▶ A collage of old currency notes consisting of the following: Rs 10,000 (first issued in 1938), Rs 5000 (1954), Rs 1000 (1938), Rs 100 (1944), Rs 10 (1949), Rs 5 (1949), and Rs 2 (1943). None of these series are currently in circulation; in any case, the highest currency note in existence now is of the value of Rs 500.

deposit rates were rising, the impact of directed credit was to cut into the potential income of banks. Pressures on earnings and profitability meant less ability for banks to make adequate provisions for sub-standard and doubtful assets, inadequate accretion to reserves and, in general, to under-capitalization.

There is, of course, no reason why a developmental credit policy should lead to deterioration in the quality of assets if bank operations are governed by proper appraisal methods and credit supervision, and where there is a nexus between credit and productivity in the borrower sectors. However, in the Indian experience, this did not happen. Reaching the targets became an end in itself rather than that credit be viewed in relation to the productive development of the assisted sectors. What was meant to be socially oriented credit often degenerated into irresponsible and politicized lending, a particularly unhappy example of which was the so-called loan *melas*. Loan waivers added another political dimension to banking operations and made the credit system the subject of competitive populism and hostage to electoral politics. Its impact on rural credit discipline, so carefully fostered over decades, was near fatal.

It was to the objectives of improving their financial performance, strengthening the qualitative character of their credit operations, and restoring a greater degree of functional autonomy and operational flexibility to banks that the CFS addressed its recommendations. These covered a range of issues from accounting standards, prudential norms, capital adequacy and policies relating to directed credit, directed investment, and interest rate policy. Several of these recommendations have since been implemented. Accounting standards conforming to international practices have been set, minimum capital adequacy norms prescribed, and principles for asset classification and prudential norms for income recognition and provisioning have been stipulated. These are very significant developments but cover only the 'arithmeticals' of the suggested package of reforms. Systemic, institutional, and structural reforms recommended by the committee are yet to be implemented.

A major concern with regard to our banking system is the high transaction costs that reflect high intermediation costs, and which, in turn, are related to the over-manning and low productivity of banking operations. A situation where credit interest rates are effectively determined by the wage bill in the banking industry is not conducive to operational flexibility or efficiency. The ratio of the wage bill as a percentage of assets at over 2 per cent is particularly high in public sector banks. Moves towards greater cost consciousness, efficiency, and productivity have now become imperative to the banking industry.

RESERVE BANK OF INDIA
1000
ONE THOUSAND RUPEES
RESERVE BANK OF INDIA
5000
GATEWAY OF INDIA BOMBAY
पाँच हज़ार रुपया
RESERVE BANK OF INDIA
GUARANTEED BY THE CENTRAL GOVERNMENT
I Promise to pay the bearer on demand the sum of
TEN RUPEES
at any office of issue
FOR THE RESERVE BANK OF INDIA
C D Deshmukh
GOVERNOR
Rs 10
A 15 382355
THE RESERVE BANK OF INDIA
100
ONE HUNDRED
RUPEES
GUARANTEED BY THE CENTRAL GOVERNMENT
RESERVE BANK OF INDIA
IMPERIAL BANK OF INDIA
RUPEES
TWO
THE RESERVE BANK OF INDIA
GUARANTEED BY THE CENTRAL GOVERNMENT
CALCUTTA
TEN THOUSAND RUPEES

▲ P.R. Narsimhan, Chairman and Managing Director, IFCI.

No financial system anywhere in the world is unregulated. What we had in India was an over-administered but under-regulated system. We need to replace this by a system of rule-bound, transparent, and non-discretionary regulation covering the critical aspects of a bank's functioning. At the same time, adequate internal audit and inspection systems in banks have to be set in place to ensure that these requirements are met. Such accountability is an essential counterpart to functional autonomy.

As we move into the second phase of financial sector reform, we should note not only the changes in the domestic economy but also the significant movement towards global financial integration. Domestic financial deregulation and greater internal competition should form the basis for greater contacts of the Indian financial sector with the global markets. This would help upgrade our financial technology and give us greater access to the new and emerging needs of financial engineering in India. India cannot afford financial autarky any more than industrial or trade autarky. The institution of a more open financial system and the move

IFCI building, New Delhi.

Financial Institutions

Banks or financial intermediaries accept deposits from the public at a certain rate of interest and lend to borrowers at differential rates of interest. Over the years, with the development of the financial markets, banks have begun to provide multiple services like merchant banking, credit cards, etc.

The first commercial bank in India was the Hindustan Bank, set up in Calcutta in 1770. Modern commercial banking as we know it, however, began in Calcutta in 1806. Banking, since then, has come a long way, though it received its major thrust only after Independence. The regulation of banks is directly under the Reserve Bank of India under the Banking Regulation Act, 1949.

With a globalized, liberalized economy, India today has government-owned commercial banks, private sector commercial banks, development banks, rural development banks, and foreign banks, all operating together.

Developmental financial institutions or financial intermediaries which perform the twin

▲ G.P. Gupta, Chairman and Managing Director, IDBI.

towards capital account convertibility would be consistent with the steps being taken to open up the Indian economy and enhance our ability to take competitive advantage of the increasing international opportunities for Indian trade, industry, and finance.

In a deregulated and competitive environment, and with greater flexibility in regard to foreign exchange rate management, on the one hand, and greater importance being accorded to monetary policy, on the other, one might expect enhancement of business risks in the system. In addition to the traditional concerns of banks and financial institutions with liquidity and credit risk, they now have to think in terms of market risk, income risk, and foreign exchange risk. It has become necessary, therefore, to fashion proper risk management techniques. Banking is essentially an exercise in risk management. The increase in financial risks arising out of uncertainties flowing from greater flexibility in policies, cyclical and structural changes in the macroeconomy, and exposure to international interest rate and exchange rate movements will call for suitable adoption of risk management practices and techniques.

tasks of providing medium- and long-term finance to private entrepreneurs and play a promotional role in economic development. These include the Industrial Development Bank of India set up in July 1964. The Industrial Finance Corporation of India, set up in 1948, is the first government-owned financial institution in India to be privatized. Government holding has come down to 49 per cent. The Industrial Credit and Investment Corporation of India was set up in 1955 with share capital from banks, insurance companies, and foreign institutions including the World Bank.

Today the role of banks and financial institutions is merging with both offering similar services and competing for the same clientele. The Indian financial system is strong and viable and has prudential norms in keeping with international standards.

IDBI building, Mumbai.

▲ The spread of banking in the rural areas has been particularly impressive, and there are almost 300 million deposit accounts, suggesting a savings habit that is well established among the Indian people.

(facing page):

▲ Inside view of a branch of the State Bank of India, Mumbai. Banking facilities are increasingly computerized with an emphasis on customer convenience, the new mantra in an era of liberalization. Nationalized banks have traditionally offered security and dependability but have been somewhat lacking in their approach to service.

▼ The State Bank of India building, Mumbai.

Indian banks have only recently entered the area of derivative trading in a limited way. One might expect that derivatives trading and consequently off-balance sheet items would increasingly become important. The prudential norms with regard to balance sheet items would also have to extend to off-balance sheet items, both in terms of full disclosure and capital adequacy provisions.

The contemporary trend around the world is to break down the walls between the functioning of different financial institutions. Consolidation and convergence are the new buzzwords. The distinction between commercial and investment banking is in the process of losing its significance and universal banking is once again coming into favour. We have seen the beginning of this trend with banks moving out of the narrow confines of commercial banking and engaging themselves in term finance to industry and offering other financial services such as mutual funds, housing, factoring, and security trading, either on their own or through

subsidiaries. Similarly, the development financial institutions in our country are also getting into areas earlier regarded as the preserve of the commercial banks, and are also setting up private sector banks. While these represent aspects of convergence, the move towards consolidation of financial institutions abroad has seen a growing trend towards mergers among banks and between banks and other players in the financial markets, such as near banks, housing finance institutions, and even insurance companies. In India too, there is growing recognition that the strength of a financial institution comes from both size and synergy.

The new millennium will see even greater globalization of production and markets, and the integration of financial markets and institutions. Finance is increasingly becoming a skill-intensive industry. India has the requisite skills: what we need is not so much the software of skills but the hardware of technology.

In the ultimate analysis, banking and finance are service industries and bankers, finance managers, or financial engineers must continue to strive to provide the right product at the right time, right place and right price. The resilience displayed so far by Indian banks and financial institutions offers us hope that they will rise to this task.

Stock Exchanges in India

M.G. Damani

Nothing reflects the country's troubled economic history as accurately as the equity market. The history of stock markets in independent India is largely the story of the Bombay Stock Exchange (BSE), the oldest of its kind in Asia, having been established in 1875. India inherited an extremely poor stock market at the time of Independence, the result of political upheavals. The index touched 382 (1927–8=100) in September 1946, following the end of the Second World War, slumped below 250 just before August 1947, and touched a low of 131 by July 1949, the year that the rupee saw a chilling 43.9 per cent devaluation against the US dollar. To help stabilize the situation, the BSE remained closed from 19–22 September.

At the time of Independence there were seven stock exchanges in the country. In 1956, in consultation with the BSE, the government sought to rationalize the Indian capital market with the Securities Contracts (Regulation) Act that granted the BSE permanent recognition, though the other stock exchanges were initially subject to renewal every five years.

The first three decades of Independence were characterized by an overwhelming state presence in capital markets that discouraged private enterprise. The government regulated and controlled large industries via specific price and allocation controls and general capital issues, an industrial licensing policy, and the Monopolies and Restrictive Trade Practices Act. These controls were reinforced by elaborate taxation laws that discriminated against companies with very few shareholders as well as against inter-corporate investment. This was reflected in the paltry growth of the stock market with average returns on investment of only 10 per cent per annum during the first three decades of Independence. Between 1953 and 1955, share prices appreciated before declining sharply. The slump in prices continued until 1958, mainly due to decline in foreign exchange reserves, the imposition of capital gains tax, wealth tax, and compulsory deposits by companies.

▲ The Bombay Stock Exchange at Nariman Point is the nerve centre of the investment community of the country.

India's wars with its neighbours and a change in leadership created major ripples in the stock market. The Chinese aggression in October 1962 was followed by a free fall in values, and the market was indefinitely closed on 5 November, opening again on 12 November, with transactions allowed above the closing price recorded on 3 November to provide a support point below which prices were not allowed to fall. The government introduced several stiff tax measures so that in spite of a 17.4 per cent growth in nominal GNP, market capitalization inched up by only 1 per cent.

The war with Pakistan in September 1965 had an adverse impact on the GNP and the stock market, and that in 1971 saw the market fall even though business at the BSE was conducted as usual. The strain on the economy imposed by the two crore

▲ All facilities at the stock exchanges in the country are now being increasingly computerized, and all data is regularly monitored to register even the minutest differentials.

Bangladeshi refugees was tougher to bear and continued to depress the securities prices.

A more positive impact was the favourable response of the market to the 1968–9 budget with its tax concessions to stimulate investment activity in the country. It was amidst such bullish sentiments that Morarji Desai, then finance minister, laid the foundation stone of the Stock Exchange building on 16 May 1968. Ever since, the building has become a symbol for the capital market in India. It took a knocking in May 1993 when a bomb exploded in the BSE, but though the building was damaged, the BSE emerged from that traumatic episode with flying colours not losing a single day of trading.

That, however, came later. Dark clouds loomed over the Indian economy between 1967–75, the economic woes compounded by political uncertainties. On 28 June 1969, the government prohibited forward trading in shares. This was followed by a split in the Congress and the nationalization of fourteens prominent banks. By 1970, the first phase of industrialization of independent India, the number of companies listed on the stock exchanges almost tripled, and capital grew almost nine times.

The oil price hike of 1974 came as a shock to the market. In July 1974, the government announced a package of anti-inflationary measures and promulgated an ordinance placing temporary restrictions on dividends. The BSE sent a detailed memorandum to the government suggesting that the ordinance would hamper investment in equity, encouraging the shift of savings into other non-productive assets. A deflationary situation came to prevail in the market and on 4 July1974, closing prices were announced as the floor prices for securities for business in the ensuing month, and transactions below 10 per cent of the floor price were not allowed.

From 1979 onwards, the government put a curb on state intervention, initiating measures to reduce controls and regulations in licensing, trade, prices, etc. and opening up economic sectors earlier reserved for the public sector. Following

▼ Himalaya, K.20000. This machine is used for storage of data in stock exchanges and banking institutions.

the freedom from the constraints of over-regulation and protectionism, the GDP grew by 5.5 per cent on average, and industrial production by little over 8 per cent per annum in the fourth decade. During the early 1980s, the stock market began playing a vital role in the economy due to Indira Gandhi's pragmatic economic policies that provided encouragment for the private sector; the corporate sector's performance and attractive rates of dividend; and the growing inability of development finance institutions to provide funds for the expansion and diversification of the corporate sector.

The dilution of equity by FERA (Foreign Exchange Regulation Act) companies, from 1979 onwards, attracted a large number of investors to the market. Following the share issues of FERA companies, the stock markets have moved from strength to strength, not only in terms of increases in share values but also from the point of view of their usefulness as a source of risk capital.

Between April and May 1981, share value rose daily as money flowed in from NRIs to invest in Indian shares. The bull frenzy was contained by counter measures taken by the BSE at the instance of the finance ministry. With the substantial growth in the stock markets and their operations, the number of stock exchanges

◀ New trading ring under the open outcry system was commissioned in Mumbai in May 1995 and has facilities that are comparable internationally.

increased to twenty-three; the capital raised by them increased from Rs 87.60 crore in 1960 to Rs 195.90 crore in 1980. The market capitalization of the BSE moved up from Rs 5421 crore in 1980 to Rs 21,636 crore in 1986.

The liberation of the Indian economy from decades of over-regulation, protectionism, and corruption was not an easy journey, but Rajiv Gandhi's attempt in 1985 to create an efficient, modern economy led to a boom in the stock market. Among the largest listings in 1986–7 were non-convertible debentures which rose 111 per cent to Rs 2000 crore for 299 approved issues by the Controller of Capital Issues (CCI). The highest increase was in bonus issues which rose 157 per cent to Rs 235 crore from 233 issues. This surge in confidence found reflection in the BSE Sensitive Index which began publication in January 1986. As much as 35–40 per cent of the private sector's capital needs was raised by firms in the Indian stock market. The number of private companies listed on the BSE more than doubled between 1980 and 1987, rising from 992 to 2095.

All this stood the Indian stock markets in good stead in the face of the crash in world equities, insulated by rigid controls on foreign investment and dominated by domestic influences. The bubble, however, did burst in 1987 after the government banned the conversion of non-convertible debentures, hitting the confidence of small investors hardest, leading the government to form the Securities and Exchange Board of India (SEBI).

The year 1988–9 saw a significant spurt in the capital raised from the market, and in 1989–90 it was Rs 6473 crore. The daily turnover increased from Rs 15 crore in 1979–80 to about Rs 400 crore at the end of 1991–2. The number of shareholders increased in this period from about 20 lakh to over 1.4 crore. In the booming market, companies raised Rs 5000 crore compared to Rs 165 crore in 1980.

The market crashed in the wake of the Gulf War. Margins were raised by the BSE on specified groups of shares and restrictions placed on jobbing and carry forward transactions. The BSE Sensitive Index, from a high of 1560 on 9 October 1990, slumped to 956 on 25 January 1991. But by 26 July 1991, it had peaked at 1599, signalling the nation's economic health following the announcement of the government's new industrial policy.

The year that followed proved the most volatile in the history of the stock market. An excess liquidity in the equity market worth Rs 5000 crore sent the market into a high, marking a rise of 134 per cent to touch a high of 4467. With the uncovering of the banking scam that was responsible for this, the market crashed by over 30 per cent in just a few weeks. It recovered somewhat on expectations of a sizeable flow of foreign investment and a modest decline in bank lending rates, with the index touching 3410 on 15 September 1992. This level could not, however, be sustained as companies announced poor first half results and the market witnessed a phenomenal number of rights and public issues. The demolition of the mosque at Ayodhya and events that followed intensified the bearish sentiment, and the market reached a low of 2375 on 16 December that year.

Parliament set up a joint committee to enquire into irregularities in securities and banking transactions, and a report was submitted in December 1993. The administration of the stock exchanges came under close scrutiny, with parliamentarians less than comfortable with the way in which this 'public institution' ran its affairs. A new era of unbridled diktat, regulation, guidelines and orders came into place. Developmental institutions such as IDBI, LIC, GIC, UTI, and banks set up the National Stock Exchange (NSE) to provide liquidity to the government debt market. Set up in 1992, the debt market went live in June 1994 and it started trading in equities in November 1994.

With liberalization and the paradigm shift in government economic policies, change was inevitable. Three forces spurred those changes: the first, the internationalization of India's capital markets and investment flows; the second, new technologies that increased the speed and complexity of deals; the third, the prop provided to the NSE that was funded, floated, and patronized by government-owned development financial institutions. In May 1995, the BSE's open outcry system gave way to electronic trading at the BSE, the BSE On-line Trading System (BOLT).

The ill-conceived regulatory measure of banning *badla* by SEBI was responsible for the 30 per cent decline in share values in 1995. The BSE lobbied hard for the reintroduction of *badla* to restore liquidity and controlled speculation in the market. Its new incarnation as Revised Carry-Forward was introduced in January 1996 but failed to attract interest, hamstrung by the complexity of regulations laid down by SEBI. Later, some of the impediments were removed.

The phase of excessive regulation, ban on renewals in the B1 group, tight money, and the uncertain political scene led to depression of the market in 1996. The blow to investors' sentiments dragged the BSE 30 index to a three-year low on 4 December 1996. However, with the Indian economy moving to centre stage, the BSE is set to regain its glory. In September 1997, the Department of Telecommunications gave it permission to expand BOLT nationwide. The BSE intends to become an international centre for trading in Indian equities from all major world financial centres by the year 2000.

To enhance safety, the BSE has set up a SEBI-approved Trade Guarantee Fund and Broker's Contingency Fund. An integrated, comprehensive insurance policy is in place to ensure that market intermediaries are covered for various risks other than those they face in their day-to-day business. It has set up a Bad-Delivery Cell to ensure that investors get good shares for their money, has built a database of lost, stolen, fake, and forged shares, started vetting the prospectus of companies that wish to be listed on the Exchange, revived the institution of *remisier*, and increased the amount of compensation payable from the Customer Protection Fund from Rs 1.5 lakh to Rs 2.25 lakh.

As India moves ahead to occupy its place in the world markets, the stock exchanges will continue to play their role as a conduit for ideas on management and finance, remaining an important interface between the private sector and investor.

Industry and Trade Unions

Kumar Ketkar

India has trade unions but no genuine trade union movement, a paradoxical phenomenon when seen in the context of the working class. In fact, a trade union movement along political and ideological lines was organized even before the spread of industry to various parts of the country. The trigger for trade union consciousness was provided by the railways which was the largest employer in the late nineteenth century. The railway network was built primarily to move armies to crush uprisings such as the first war of independence. Unionization among railwaymen was a reflection of the growing awareness of freedom.Trade union consciousness acquired deeper political overtones after the Russian Revolution in 1917. The message for a workers' state reached the Indian proletariat through the British Left which had a direct relationship with the communists, socialists, and Fabians in Congress.

▼ The trade union movement in India has had anti-capitalist leanings because it had its genesis in the anti-imperialist struggle. In this post-Independence picture, among those participating in the rally are S.A. Dange and Inderjit Gupta.

At this time, the trade union movement became part of the freedom movement. The All India Trade Union Congress (AITUC) which was led and directed by communists was addressed by leaders like Jawaharlal Nehru and Lala Lajpat Rai. Thus the anti-imperialist struggle also began to mean an anti-capitalist movement of sorts. It was the Congress belief that the British could not have established the Raj without the help of feudal satraps, landlords, and dominant trading community. It was because of this interpretation of 'class alliances' that the Indian National Congress took a strident stand against feudalism and capitalism.

Left consciousness became the central point of the trade union movement after the Meerut conspiracy case in 1929: the communist leaders who were arrested belonged to the textile workers' movement in Mumbai. The so-called 'anti-

▼ The trade union movement was organized well before the spread of industrialization, but took on various hues in the guise of its mentors.

establishment' mindset of the trade union movement developed during the time of the Quit India movement and dominated the thinking of working class leaders. The formation of the Mazdoor Mahajan and Indian National Trade Union Congress (INTUC) under the auspices of Gandhiji and his followers attempted to give a different tone to the workers' movement, and though they did mobilize a large membership, they failed to take on the role of ideological leadership.

Nehru's leadership set the economic model based partly on the Soviet experience and on the recommendations of Fabian

▲ Chandra Shekhar, known as the Young Turk, was a firebrand labour leader. The former Prime Minister, seen here, addressing an AITUC group. Also in the picture is George Fernandes, currently India's Defence Minister.

economists. The emphasis was on the public sector with control over such core sector industries as steel and oil, but with a substantial role chalked out for the private sector.

Dr R.K. Hazari, a renowned economist and former deputy governor of the Reserve Bank of India put the development of industry in the right perspective:

> Industrial development [in the late nineteenth century] was, to a great extent, a by-product of certain interrelated developments such as improved transport and communications, growth of foreign trade and consequent accumulation of commercial fortunes. Railway building and maintenance had effects more far-reaching than merely opening up of the interior and exposing of agriculture to the winds of commerce. It released some of the latent potentialities for industrial advance. The coal industry could grow and expand; the development of engineering firms was geared to railway needs. Railway workshops had to be founded and these workshops subsequently developed as important centres of modern mechanical engineering and nuclei of skilled labour. The development and extension of the railways posed the question of the founding of iron works under the agency of the state and when the Tatas embarked upon steel manufacture, they depended, in the initial years, to a considerable extent, upon government orders of rails. With the extension of the railway system, there arose the demand for bridge and metalled communications.

The strengthening of the British army after the first war of independence led to the construction of barracks and founding of ordnance and army clothing factories. In the interests of expanding trade, the government had to devote attention to the extension and maintenance of ports, harbours, and docks. There was considerable building activity, and the decentralization of powers to municipal administrations after 1870 and 1883–4 also generated widespread demand for water, drainage and sewerage, and iron works. The government became the largest single purchaser of iron and steel products and a big buyer of miscellaneous manufactures. The railway, military, and public works departments made the government a crucial factor in industrial development, handicapped as it was by the absence of fiscal protection and insufficient supply of entrepreneurs. Indeed, some of the paper mills, woollen, leather, iron, and engineering factories were founded in anticipation of government demand.

Dr Hazari observes, 'In a previous age, Indian industries had flourished around the thrones of the rulers and had looked to them

▼ India has experienced two modes of the trade union movement – one militant, and the other intransigent – both aimed at improving the working conditions of the labour force.

for support; and the tendency was always to expect from the government a more positive regulation of activity than has been usual in those countries where individualistic ideals have been dominant.' It is necessary to bear this in mind when analysing the rise, stagnation, and decline of the trade union movement. In the 1950s and 1960s, the tempo of 'socialistic' development was maintained. This led to two forms of trade union movement, one intransigent, the other militant, even violent.

The public sector unions could be further divided into white and blue collar unions. Large-scale mobilization of workers in units like BEL, BHEL, Indian Oil, and other public sector companies often enabled arm-twisting of public sector managements in bargaining for higher wages/bonus, better working conditions, and more rights. White collar employees in banks and insurance companies formed associations to enhance their power base as well as to expand their income opportunities. Together, these white collar employees and blue collar workers exercised tremendous control over the Left political parties and, through them, on the

▼ The honour of addressing AITUC rallies was not the preserve only of leaders who became Prime Ministers; here, Neelam Sanjeeva Reddy can be seen addressing an AITUC event. He was later to head the nation as President.

Congress. The government was frequently forced to bend before their collective power. Ironically, the unions which were brought up on an ideological diet of anti-capitalism ended up attacking public sector companies.

At the same time, blue collar workers in private sector units found their minds being controlled by forces outside their level of comprehension. This mindlessness was encouraged, even perpetuated, by the legal framework that governed industrial relations. The law permitted a multiplicity of trade unions in any one unit, and the labour machinery could rarely identify the union that represented its interests. Not only was there inter-union rivalry but also competition in militancy against the management.

No study has been able to actually account for the deaths caused by such violence. In Mumbai, when Dr Datta Samant organized a violent confrontation with the Godrej management and an existing union within the company, there was a state of virtual civil war in the sprawling Godrej campus in Vikhroli that led to the deaths of two policemen and injury of several workers. Dr Samant became the most visible and identifiable manifestation of the militancy that reigned not only in Mumbai but in many parts of industrial India. In the coal mines in Dhanbad, in industrial units in Madhya Pradesh, in factories on the outskirts of Delhi, and even in Chennai, his counterparts controlled fiefdoms within the industrial belts. In the ensuing struggle for supremacy, the unions began to take the help of the mafia, thereby bringing respectability to muscle power. In the coal mines, and also to an extent in the textile mills in Mumbai, managements too were resorting to mafia assistance to crush workers' agitations. While some unions were settling their scores on the shop floor by arriving at secret deals with the managements, the employers were seeking assistance from the unions to suit their ends, sometimes to declare closures or lockouts. A kind of symbiotic relationship was evolving between managements and unions.

It was this symbiosis that led to the stagnation of the trade union movement and its degeneration into localized struggles. Things may not have come to such a pass had there been a change in the industrial relations laws, but both

▶ S.A Dange and Siddharth Shankar Ray share views at a forum of AITUC.

unions and management, and even the government, found it more convenient to function within outdated legal parameters.

Trade unions in India basically followed five routes: a hyped political and ideological approach; subservience to some political party: INTUC to Congress, AITUC to CPI, CITU to CPM, HMS to the Socialist or Janata Party, BMS to the BJP, and so on; the lawyer–leader syndrome where labour lawyers become trade union leaders; a cult leadership pattern with Dr Datta Samant in Mumbai, Lalit Maken in New Delhi, Niyogi in Madhya Pradesh, Raghavan in Kerala, and so on; internal company or factory unions without any outside leadership.

One reason why trade unions were unable to form a common front was the lack of a common meeting ground for the different leaders and ideologies. Yet another was that wage levels and working conditions differed all over the country or, for that matter, even within one state. Workers in the textile industry in Mumbai found little in common with those in the chemicals or electronics industries. Similarly, a clerk in a school executing almost the same function as his counterpart in a bank, enjoyed totally different levels of status and pay. Unity in the private sector with its wide disparity in incomes was almost impossible.

In the government sector, however, there is apparent parity in income and working conditions as well as a definite and perceivable hierarchy. As a result, workers and employees in the government sector can be placed at a certain level within different departments. There is, therefore, a structural uniformity which is why their agitations are often coordinated and successful. An example of this is the manner in which they were able to force the government to

▲ A presentation on 'Unions in the twenty-first century'. Seen in the picture are Vineet Virmani and A.S. Kasliwal with Brendan Barber.

increase their salaries by 40 per cent over the recommendations of the Fifth Pay Commission.

Not only has liberalization produced a kind of disequilibrium between the public and private sectors, it has also created unprecedented chaos within the private sector. The complexity of its wage structure became particularly complicated after the large-scale entry of multinational companies. The multinationals, and a few large corporate companies, have given birth to a new wage island. This small class of workers and employees has distinguished itself by having an income with five digits at the lowest end of the hierarchy. It has thoroughly distorted the urban wage-earners' lifestyle. While their employees negotiate their salaries in dollar terms, most workers in medium size factories are still bargaining for the implementation of the Minimum Wage Act. Employees and workers in higher income groups are not unionized and do not wish to be, while workers in medium size factories are prevented by management from being so.

Multinationals and large-scale companies have set up smaller manufacturing units to pass on contracts to them. A considerable percentage of production is now undertaken through these contractual arrangements, and workers in these units are paid extremely low wages and work in dreadful shop floor conditions.

The working class is now distinguished by its own heirarchy, aristocracy, higher middle class, lower middle class, and a vast proletariat. There is nothing to unite it under any one banner or one slogan. The only unionized workforce that still remains powerful is in the government. It is impossible for a healthy and genuine trade union movement to be built out of such disparate and diverse manufacturing and ideological situations. Clearly, India appears to be headed for different forms of struggle for a better life for its huge workforce, particularly in the unorganized sector.

Business and the Law

R.K.P. Shankardass

At the time of Independence, two influences dominated the thinking of India's policy-makers in the government. One, of course, was the view that India had lost its freedom as a result of events which had their origin in the commercial operations of a British company, and the country must be protected against foreign business interests dominating the Indian economy; and the other was the socialist ideology of friends in the British Labour Party who had supported the Indian freedom movement. These provided the inspiration for policies and legislation to regulate or control all significant business activities and to expand the government-controlled public sector. Based on the Defence of India regulations introduced by British authorities during the War, the Foreign Exchange Regulation Act of 1947 (FERA) was already in place by April 1947 and helped establish government control over the extent to which foreign investment in India or business operations of Indian companies involving foreign exchange would be permitted. The Indian government's first Industrial Policy Resolution of April 1948 emphasized the importance to the economy of securing a continuous increase in production and its equitable distribution, and pointed out that the state must play a progressively active role in the development of industries. It laid down that the state would be exclusively responsible for the establishment of new undertakings in certain basic industries. A Planning Commission was

▼ Inspection of weights and measures in Calcutta, a picture from its colonial past. India has a system that can prove quite stringent when it comes to the protection of customer interests.

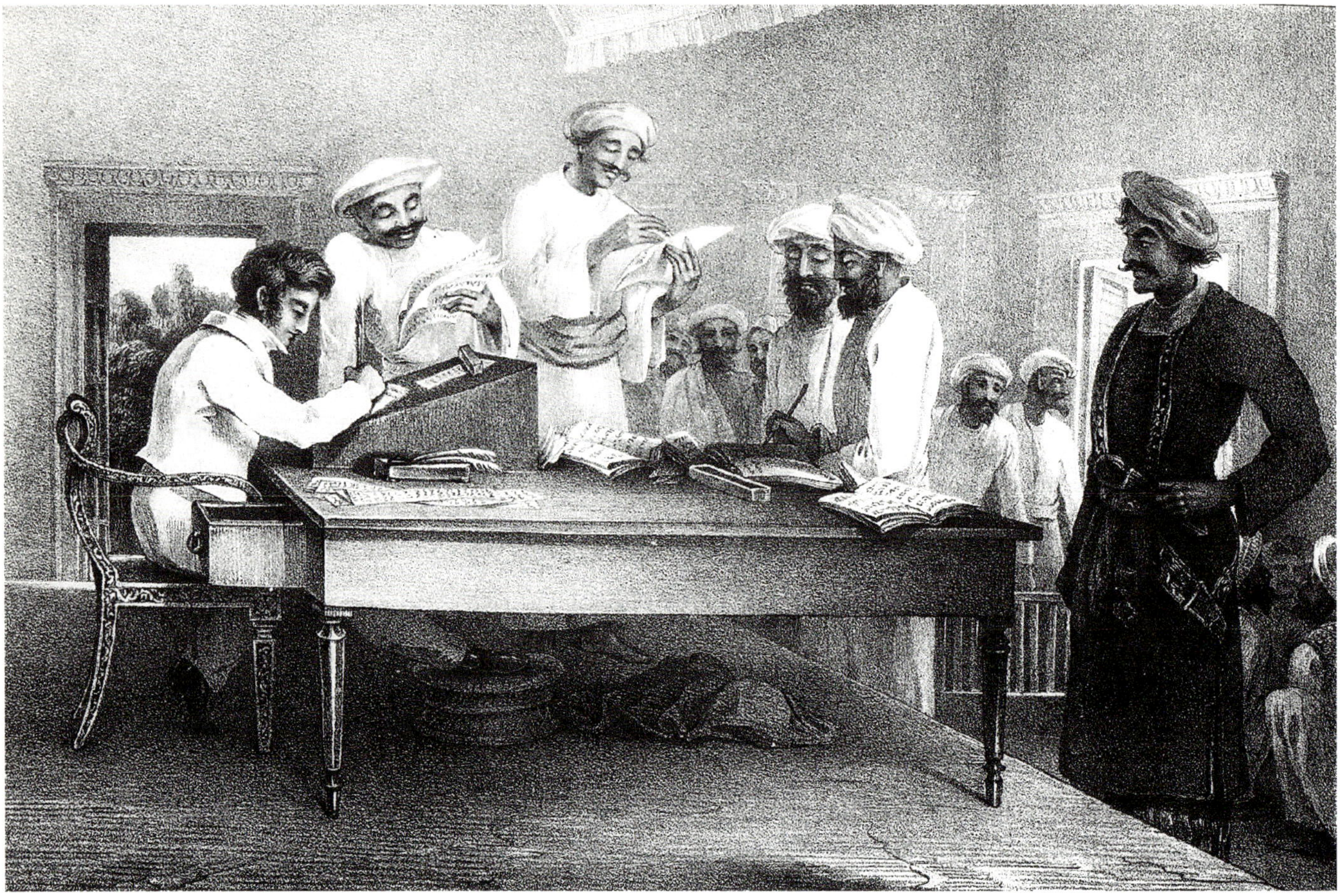

▲ Organized law was one of the gains India received under the Raj. Open courts administered to people's needs, often in distant districts, as in Meerut *(above)*. Though the Mughals and other princely kingdoms were known for their quality of justice, one uniform business law for the country was introduced under the British.

created to prepare five-year plans for the overall development of the economy.

In 1950, the new Constitution was adopted which entrenched fundamental human rights in the justice system of which Art. 14, which prohibits arbitrariness or discrimination on the part of government, and Art. 19, which guarantees the right 'to carry on any occupation, trade or business' were of the greatest significance to business organizations; at the same time, the Directive Principles of State Policy incorporated in the Constitution provided that the state shall strive to promote the welfare of the people by securing and protecting as effectively as it may a social order in which justice, social, economic and political, shall inform all the institutions of national life and ensure that the economic system does not result in the concentration of wealth and means of production to the common detriment. The Industries (Development and Regulation) Act of 1951 was then enacted for the control and regulation of all industries in India. The Act required that proposed and existing large undertakings, and any substantial expansion and manufacture of new articles be licensed.

In 1954, Parliament expressly adopted the 'socialistic pattern of society' as the objective of social and economic policy. In 1956 followed a new Industrial Policy Resolution that introduced an urgency in reducing disparities in income and wealth, prevented private monopolies and the concentration of economic power in different fields in the hands of small numbers of individuals. Accordingly, the state would progressively assume predominant and direct responsibility for setting up new industrial undertakings and developing transport facilities, as well as undertake state trading on an increasing scale. That a steadily increasing portion of the activities of the private sector should be developed along cooperative lines, and the adoption of the socialist pattern of society as national objective, as well as the need for planned and rapid development, required that all industries of basic and strategic importance, or in the nature of public utility services, should be in the public sector. The new policy provided for the category of 'scheduled industries' which would be entirely state-owned or gradually become state-owned, leaving unscheduled industries in a sector where private and public industries would co-exist.

The Companies Act of 1956, provided for an elaborate mechanism of government control and regulation of public companies running industries in the private sector and included the requirement of government approval for the appointment of all full-time directors in such companies as well as the remuneration to be paid to them. In the same year, the Securities Contracts (Regulation) Act, 1956, was passed 'to provide for the regulation of stock exchanges and of transactions in securities dealt in on them with a view to preventing undesirable speculation in them'. The provisions of these Acts, together with those of the Monopolies and Restrictive Trade Practices Act (MRTP Act), of 1969 requiring prior approvals for establishment or expansion of larger industries, were further designed to control the size and proposed expansion of important industries. In 1970, the Licensing Policy was revised extensively as a result of which large industrial houses, controlling a capital of over Rs 350 m., were almost completely regulated and confined by various restrictions, while small-scale industrialists were treated favourably, 126 items of industry being reserved for them. A heavy-handed policy laid down under FERA was used to force foreign entities to reduce their shareholdings to 40 per cent. Foreign-held equity was unloaded *en masse* at relatively low prices. This mass of legislation to regulate the private business sector supplemented by revenue laws providing for high taxation of incomes, gifts, wealth, and for levy of estate duty, not only established extensive government control but seriously inhibited business initiative, increased the powers of the bureaucracy to unacceptable levels, led to an increase in corruption and to what came to be known as the 'parallel economy'.

By the late 1970s, it was beginning to be realized that these policies were not succeeding. Unemployment had increased, rural–

urban disparities had escalated, and the rate of real investment had not changed appreciably. The growth of industrial output over the past decade had been, on an average, not more than 3 to 4 per cent per annum. The incidence of industrial sickness increased and some of the major industries were the worst affected. The pattern of industrial costs and prices tended towards distortions, and the diffusion of industrial activity from the larger urban concentrations was very slow.

In 1980, a revised Industrial Policy was announced which aimed at reviewing infrastructural gaps and inadequacies in performance. During the 1980s, efforts began to be made towards simplification of procedures both for approvals under the Companies Act (which was amended in 1988) as well as for industrial approvals including foreign collaborations; but these efforts were unable to prevent deterioration in the economic situation, in particular the adverse balance-of-payments situation and a serious decline in foreign exchange reserves partly following large withdrawals of deposits by non-resident Indians. The rate of inflation had soared to over 16 per cent and the rupee was regarded as grossly overvalued. It was not until 1991, after the almost forty-five years of India's Independence, that a new government more fully realized the need for a meaningful industrial policy. In July 1991, it boldly announced revolutionary measures to liberate the ailing economy by freeing industry from innumerable official controls. With the collapse of the socialist economies of Europe (which used to be parties to

▼ Parliament House, New Delhi. The members of this august house legislate on various national issues, including that which affects business.

significant government-to-government transactions with India), it was also realized that India's future lay in the globalization of its economy and that, in fact, there was sufficient inherent strength in the economy to absorb foreign investment on a large scale, improve technology and achieve sophistication and vastly improved exports. Sardar Manmohan Singh, then finance minister, noted in his first Budget speech of July 1991:

> After four decades of planning for industrialization, we have now reached a stage of development where we should welcome, rather than fear, foreign investment. Our entrepreneurs are second to none. Our industry has come of age. Direct foreign investment would provide access to capital, technology and markets. It would expose our industrial sector to competition from abroad in a phased manner. Cost, efficiency, and quality would begin to receive the attention they deserve. We have, therefore, decided to liberalize the policy regime for direct foreign investment.

He went on to recognize that:

> the public sector has not been able to generate internal surpluses on a large enough scale. At this critical juncture, it has therefore become necessary to take effective measures so as to make the public sector an engine of growth rather than an absorber of national savings without adequate return.

In his next Budget speech in February 1992, he reiterated:

> Concern is sometimes expressed that the policy of welcoming foreign investment will hurt Indian industry and may jeopardise our sovereignty. These fears are misplaced. We must not remain permanent captives of a fear of the East India Company, as if nothing has changed in the past 300 years! India as a nation is capable of dealing with foreign investors on its own terms. Indian industry has also come of age, and is now ready to enter a phase where it can both compete with foreign investment, and also cooperate with it. This is the trend all over the world and we cannot afford to be left out.

These pronouncements were accompanied by large-scale relaxations under FERA (leading to its extensive amendment in 1993) enabling significant foreign investment in important sectors of the economy, tax incentives for industry and individuals, and other measures freeing the economy from bureaucratic intervention. The emphasis in the MRTP Act was changed by an Amending Act of which the Statement of Objects pointed out that the basic philosophy behind the Act was never to inhibit industrial growth in any way, and that with the growing complexity of industrial structure and the need for achieving economies of scale for ensuring higher productivity and competitive advantage in the international market, the thrust of the industrial policy had shifted to controlling and regulating monopolistic, restrictive, and unfair trade practices, and that pre-entry restriction on investment decisions had not only outlived its utility but had become a hindrance to the speedy implementation of industrial projects.

The Capital Issues (Control) Act, 1947, which controlled the issue of capital, was repealed in May 1992 and the issue of capital as well as pricing of issues by companies was freed from the requirements of prior approval from the Controller of Capital Issues.

It will be seen, therefore, that after forty-five years of Independence, India finally ended its isolationist phase of economic policies (claimed to have been based on a concept of 'self-sufficiency'). The various policy-based and legal steps taken pursuant to this new policy had the effect of restoring enthusiasm and confidence among entrepreneurs, both foreign and Indian. Over the following years, the country's foreign exchange reserves began to increase significantly; annual exports increased by over 20 per cent in dollar terms. The fears that liberalization would lead to a flood of imports did not materialize. After its initial depreciation in 1991, the exchange rate for the rupee remained remarkably steady. International confidence in India appeared to have been restored as foreign investment, which was barely \$150 m. in 1991–2, rose to over \$3 bn in 1993–4. Against such a background, the country moved to a unified market-determined exchange rate system and early in 1994, the finance minister announced:

> The time has come to take the next step and move towards convertibility on the current account. Current account convertibility will substantially liberalize the access to foreign exchange for all current business transactions and also liberalize foreign exchange access for travel, education and medical expenses etc. This will virtually eliminate reliance upon illegal channels for such transactions.

Until 1991, India had appeared to be a nation that had turned its back on the rest of the world. With this turnaround in policy and a liberalized legal regime began a process that gradually changed the face of the Indian economy. The reforms, which brought about dramatic changes in the economic situation of the country, have continued despite political uncertainties (generated by coalition governments of uncertain tenure) primarily because a consensus on the need for such reforms had come to exist among virtually all the political parties. It was against this background that the finance minister of a new government was able to report three years later that the positive features of the country's performance in 1996–7 included continued high economic growth at 6.8 per cent, a strong recovery of growth in agriculture and allied sectors, rebound in foodgrains production to 191 m. t., manufacturing sector growth at 10.6 per cent and a sizeable build up in our foreign currency reserves of US\$ 19.5 bn by February 1997. He further reported that Foreign Institutional Investors (FIIs) continued to repose great confidence in India and that the net FII

▲▼ Legal luminaries, Fali Nariman and E.S. Venkataramiah *(top)* and Ramakant Khalap seen with Ashok Desai *(above)*, have played a major role in ensuring that Indian laws and business enjoy a relationship that is equitable and just.

(facing page):

▶ Supreme Court, New Delhi. The legal system in India is a mature one that ensures protection to business investments.

investment in India had reached over US$ 7 bn. Towards further globalization and freeing of the economy, he later announced substantial tariff cuts and a simplified regime of greatly reduced taxes.

A foreign observer writing on the occasion of the fiftieth anniversary of India's Independence noted that

> the results of the reforms have reshaped India: the country's estimated export earnings for 1996–7 are $33.1 bn, and the rupee is stable. Inflation is at 6.4 per cent. GDP growth for the last fiscal year marked a solid 6.8 per cent. Agricultural output, which makes up nearly 20 per cent of the country's exports, is up 5.7 per cent, and incomes of agricultural workers have been rising by more than 8 per cent a year – figures that hearten investors hoping to tap into the growing Indian consumer market. While industrial production has dropped from the remarkable 11.8 per cent it reached in 1995–6, it has maintained a respectable 6.6 per cent for 1996–97.

He further pointed out that India continued to suffer from infrastructural bottlenecks, and that the country would need some $150 bn over the next five years to upgrade its telecom, power, and transport sectors.

With the gradual establishment of the market economy, investors within India have increased from about 2 m. in 1981 to over 20 m at the present time, making it imperative for the country to develop a modernized system to handle transactions in securities and for the protection of investors. As mentioned above, the initial protection of investors was sought to be provided through the Securities Contracts (Regulation) Act, 1956, and Stock Exchange Rules in relation to listed companies. This network was supplemented in 1988 by the constitution of the Security and Exchange Board of India (SEBI) by the government as a non-statutory body to promote development of the securities market and to provide adequate investor protection. This arrangement was given statutory recognition by the Security and Exchange Board of India Act, 1992. To facilitate expeditious completion of transfers of transactions relating to securities, the Depository Act, 1996, has been enacted.

The recent financial crisis in the South East Asian economies and sharp decline in the value of their currencies has not left the Indian economy unaffected. The substantial lowering of Indian tariffs in recent years has resulted in cheap imports from these and other countries, and exposed

▼ An arbitration meeting in progress between Essar Oil Ltd vs Oil India Ltd, organized under the auspices of the Indian Council of Arbitration (ICA) promoted by FICCI.

▲ Justices J.K. Mehra, R.S. Pathak, and Rajinder Sachhar discuss an arbitration case. The legal environment in India is healthy.

Indian industry to unsustainable competition and led to a slowing down of the economy. However, there is reasonable expectation that this downturn is only temporary. India's economy owes much to the legacy of its remarkable family business companies. Despite decades of strong government controls, these companies have survived and prospered and, more recently, proved themselves ready for the world markets by successfully repositioning themselves to respond to the entry of foreign competition.

The special Indian attributes of interest to foreign and domestic investors in comparison to other developing countries, would appear to be: a mature legal system; English as the language of the government and business communities; a maturing financial market committed to modernized facilities; and a record of free repatriation of profits covering even the entire pre-liberalization period.

Of these, perhaps the most important is the existence of a mature legal system in India that ensures protection of business investments. During the period when the government's highly regulatory legislation and machinery was in force, constitutional protections, particularly those against arbitrary exercise of powers by government functionaries, were highly effective in providing relief and enabling furtherance of business operations. The exercise of powers under the MRTP Act, Income Tax Act, the Sales Tax Acts, FERA, and many other regulatory acts was often challenged in the High Courts and at times directly in the Supreme Court, and such challenges upheld in deserving cases.

The one problem area is the large arrears of cases pending in courts. However, even here, the Supreme Court is providing the lead in devising measures to reduce such arrears. This effort supplements the measures taken by way of establishing special tribunals for special categories of cases. There have already existed tribunals to deal with disputes relating to the levy of excise, customs, or income tax. The recent additions are the establishment of an Advance Ruling Authority on questions concerning income tax so as to avoid prolonged and complicated litigations, the Debt Recovery Tribunals, and fora for redressal of consumers' complaints.

▲ Anu Dutt and Lakshmi Menon (at left) are among a new breed of women corporate lawyers. India has legislation in place to protect intellectual property.

The Consumer Protection Act of 1996 provides for the establishment of a forum in each district of India and at state level with an appeal to the National Commission. The latest addition is the new Arbitration and Conciliation Act of 1996, which repeals the earlier Act of 1940 (described as outmoded and cumbersome), based on the UNCITRAL Model Law of International Commercial Arbitration. This Act supplements India's continuance as a party to the New York Convention on the Recognition and Enforcement of Foreign Arbitral Awards, the Geneva Protocol on Arbitration clauses of 1925, and the Geneva Convention on the Execution of Foreign Arbitral Awards. Thus many disputes relating to international commercial contracts can be resolved without resort to litigation in courts and, indeed, the conciliation or arbitration route is being adopted in an increasing number of cases.

India has in place legislation to protect intellectual property rights so important to the advancement of international business. While the Trade Marks Act provides for registration of trademarks and protection against infringement, the frontiers of the law of Passing Off have been significantly advanced by judgments of High Courts and the Supreme Court in recent years. A Delhi High Court judgement of 1991, after reviewing numerous cases decided by courts in different parts of the world, expressly recognized the need to protect the trans-border reputation of names and trademarks. In a recent case, the Supreme Court went further and upheld a decision granting injunction even against the owner of a registered trademark where the challenge came from an international business house which was able to establish a prior user. Courts all over India continue to follow a strict policy of protecting all such intellectual property rights. The only issue of controversy is the Patents Act and the call for its review so that it can be brought in line with international regulations. However, the controversy here is legitimate in that it involves the need to protect Indian interests for some time into the future.

To summarize, the legal environment in India for business operations is as healthy as can be expected in a country with a population of over 900 m. The rule of law is entrenched by the Constitution. The legal profession and the judiciary are committed to ensuring that this rule of law prevails, whether in relation to business transactions or otherwise.

India's Public Sector: The Road Taken

M.A. Hakeem

The public sector in India, as in most countries, denotes government activities including some of its core functions. Specifically, in the Indian context, public sector enterprises (PSEs) consist of corporate bodies where 51 per cent or more equity is held by the government, created under special acts of legislature or registered under the Companies Act, 1956. At the national level, there are 243 PSEs, their activities regulated by the Department of Public Enterprises (DPE), with an investment of Rs 1,78,628 crore. The Indian stake in the public sector is huge, considering the nationalized banks, financial institutions, insurance companies, defence enterprises and transport undertakings. Even the railways and its commercial units are repositories of massive public investment.

Two hundred years of colonial rule crushed Indian industry and exhausted resources. At the point of Independence, the national leadership was convinced that political freedom without economic independence was of little use. However, most private entrepreneurs did not have the vision, resources, capability, or even the will to undertake heavy investments in core sector industries with long gestation periods. Besides, given the ideological environment and the shortage of supplies, it was only natural for the leadership not to choose to rely on a market-led system controlled by private enterprise. It was its conviction that the state had a larger role to play in

▼ The Hindustan Machine Tools factory, a central government undertaking at Bangalore, was inaugurated by Pandit Jawaharlal Nehru in 1955. Also seen with him is Indira Gandhi.

▶ Indian Oil Corporation's recently commissioned catalytic reformer unit at Barauni Refinery, installed to produce low lead petrol.

▼ Silt ejector at the National Hydel Power Corporation's 480 MW Uri project in Jammu and Kashmir.

(facing page):

▶ The Oil and Natural Gas Commission has been leading with exploratory and production work of crude oil even in difficult and unlikely environments, such as at Bombay High off the western coast of India.

building an equitable and socialistic society that led to the government entering the arena of business. Its principal objectives in doing so were to build the base for an economic infrastructure, bring about the planned development of the country, and improve the living conditions of the people at large. In many ways, the public enterprises were used as arms for development.

Initially, the public sector was confined to core and strategic industries. Projects like the Damodar Valley Corporation and Sindri Fertilizers and Chemicals had been planned earlier, but other industries that came up in the public sector included Indian Telephone Industries, Hindustan Machine Tools, steel plants, aircraft, shipbuilding, the State Trading Corporation, Bharat Heavy Electricals, Oil and Natural Gas Commission, and a host of others. The second phase saw three main trends: a nationalization spree, takeover of sick units from the private sector, and entry of the public sector in new areas like manufacturing consumer goods, consultancy, contracting, and transportation. Foreign firms like Jessop & Co., Richardson & Cruddas, Burn & Co., and Braithwate & Co. were nationalized. Several hundred life insurance companies were absorbed in the statutory Life Insurance Corporation followed by the nationalization of general insurance in 1971. In the following year, over 200 coking coal mines were nationalized

▲▶ IFFCO fertilizer plant *(above)* and National Thermal gas plant at Dadri *(facing page)*. Public sector concerns have laid a strong foundation for industrial development, and pioneered activities, often in the country's hinterlands.

in Bharat Coking Coal and in 1973, 465 private coal mines were transferred to the Coal Mines Authority. Eight foreign oil companies were also nationalized and indigenous companies were established for exploration of oil, on land and offshore, and the refining capacity of crude was augmented. Simultaneously, a number of sick units were taken over from the private sector, including over 100 textile mills, to safeguard the interests of workers.

In February 1973, the government reiterated its direct responsibility for the future development of industries over a wide range in order to promote the cardinal objectives of growth, social justice, self-reliance, import substitution, and satisfaction of basic minimum needs. The Parliamentary Committee on Public Undertakings recommended that the public sector move into the area of consumer goods. This led to the entry of the public sector in another generation of enterprises that involved from baking bread to making medicines, weaving cloth, and running hotels.

The Industrial Policy Resolution of December 1977 reaffirmed that the public sector be used as an instrument of socializing the means of production and providing a countervailing power to the growth of large business houses. A large number of PSE units were set up around the country. The growth in the 1970s and 1980s was phenomenal, though some welfare and promotional activities were needlessly corporatized. The public sector undertook pioneering works like laying roads, providing power and potable water, constructing townships complete with basic amenities like markets, schools, hospitals, and recreation clubs.

The public sector attracted the best talent in the country and provided opportunities for the development of professional manpower. It not only provided jobs to people in different regions but invariably employed all displaced persons as well. However, the lack of professional freedom, the lure of money, and poaching by the private industry, have of late been responsible for a considerable drain of manpower from the public sector.

The public sector has succeeded, to a large extent, in meeting the objectives and laying a strong foundation for the industrial development of the country. It is widely recognized that public sector management is generally based on strong systems and

processes which is not usually the case with the private sector. At the height of its development, the public sector was less concerned with making profits and more with nation-building activities. Indeed, in the corridors of government, the making of profits was despised. In its early years, the public sector did not make (nor was expected to make) profits, since investments were made in industries which did not promise adequate return on the capital invested.

With the winds of economic liberalization sweeping through the country, it was inevitable that PSEs face competition and demands for rationalization. Post-1991, with declining revenues and budgetary gaps, the government withdrew its budgetary support to supplement the internal resources of these enterprises, and increased pressure to induce them to produce profits and, thus, dividends.

While their social and other gains were taken for granted, PSEs were criticized for not earning adequate profits, and for entering fields such as tourism (hotels) and food supplies (the manufacture of bread). As always, the critics took an aggregate view of the public sector without realizing that there are well-managed companies in the public sector as well as badly managed companies in the

▼ Vidyasagar Setu, the new bridge over the river Hooghly in Calcutta. The public sector has been entrusted with the development of infrastructure.

▶ A Bharat Heavy Engineering Ltd turbine plant. In involving itself with core industries, the public sector's objective was clearly the building of a strong foundation for industrial development. This was somewhat diluted later with public sector involvement in consumer and service industries.

private sector. This was partly the result of a global movement to privatize industry. The strident call for privatization in Britain encouraged most people to question the wisdom of continuing with huge public enterprises that were unable to post adequate returns on capital invested.

Among the reasons that different activities were commercialized in the form of business corporations one was to provide flexibility to run commercial activity. Over the years, a focused, bureaucratic, and inflexible approach led to the sapping of autonomy. Somewhere along the way, the government had lost clarity in its roles of governance, as investor, regulator, and business manager. The PSEs were allowed little autonomy to function according to market needs. As the owner, the government did not pay adequate attention to the constitution of the boards of directors and hardly empowered them. The PSEs came to be looked upon as a subsystem of the government, and all the ills of the main system percolated down to them. Indeed, one can argue that any public sector reform should really begin with the reform of the bureaucracy and government.

Bearing in mind the state of the nation, a close examination of the justifications for heavy investments in the public sector would reveal that many of those reasons are still valid. In addition, experience has shown that in spite of liberalization, certain sectors have failed to attract adequate investments either from abroad or from within. All along, the public sector has been the engine growth for the Indian economy. During the period beginning with 1991, this sector was starved of adequate investments and was neglected, contributing in no mean measure to the reduction in industrial activity during 1996–7 and 1997–8. However, while redefining the role of the PSEs and understanding their future relevance, it becomes obvious that the size and shape of the public sector over the next quarter of a century will be very different.

▲▼ Hindustan Aeronauticals Ltd, Bangalore, has played a critical role in developing aircraft for meeting India's defence requirements.

(previous page):

◀ Super thermal power project at Vindhyachal. The National Thermal Power Corporation has sought to harness natural resources to meet the requirements for power, and has proved its capabilities. However, the yawning gap between demand and supply has made it essential for the private sector to be pitchforked into the generation of power projects.

Rapid changes in the business environment coupled with other fiscal compulsions led to demands for privatization, leading to withdrawal and roll-back: the selling of equity was conveniently termed 'disinvestment' and was sometimes undertaken without even consulting the enterprises. The withdrawal from some activities and disinvestment should have led to the release of resources to be utilized in areas like the revival of sick units, retraining of labour, and investment in new infrastructure-based

industries. This did not happen. The approach paper for the eighth five year plan restricted the public sector to eight industries and enunciated no clear-cut policy. This pusillanimity led to confusion over the economic scene and demoralization among PSE employees who saw, on one hand, support systems being withdrawn, and on the other, were exposed to competition from multinationals as well as Indian companies.

The years 1996 and 1997 saw some government initiative in identifying a few PSEs for grant of financial autonomy and appointment of a disinvestment commission. The commission adopted a holistic approach and recommended measures for reform and restructuring of PSEs prior to disinvestment. While most recommendations are yet to be examined and accepted, the autonomy packages have not translated into much at the ground level. Procrastination on appointments to the boards, delays in clearance of disinvestment proposals, and hesitation in giving up control of vast commercial empires have seriously affected the companies and their performance.

There are a large number of private sector units today where ownership rests with government-owned financial institutions. These companies are not hampered by bureaucratic control, and are therefore able to perform much better. In the case of PSEs, the principles of good corporate governance have rarely received attention. Interference, on the other hand, has been justified on grounds of accountability.

In a dynamic business world, it would be absurd to think that the role of the PSEs should remain frozen. As the environment changes, so does the role that is expected of different organizations, and Indian PSEs are not exempt from this generic rule. It is necessary for the government to rethink its role, withdraw from some areas, and severely curtail its interests in some PSEs. The beginning of the new millennium should see a much leaner, customer-focused, and far more efficient public sector responding to the needs of the people. Privatization may have served as a panacea to some of the developed countries, but a country like India has to find its own solutions bearing in mind its needs. There is virtue in following a middle path.

▲◀ Computerized telecom service *(above)* and hot strip mill of SAIL's Bokaro Steel Plant *(previous page)*. The public sector attracted the best talent in the country, but more recently, inflexibility has left its role unclear, and therefore vulnerable to changes in a new business environment.

Business, Society, and Philanthropy

Pushpa Sundar

The pioneers of Indian industry during the colonial era were leaders not only in the economic but also the social field. From Cowasjee Nanabhai Davar, broker, financier, and exporter of cotton who set up the first cotton textile mill in India in 1851, to the Mahindra brothers, J.C. and K.C., who represented the new generation of educated technocrat industrialists just before Independence, they were all men of vision fired by ideals beyond the mere making of money. They were, often, also in the vanguard of social reform and provided civic leadership, apart from taking personal interest in the institutions established by them. G.D. Birla risked social ostracism from the more conservative members of his Marwari community in campaigning for reform of social practices such as child marriage, widow remarriage, outcasting on travel abroad, and temple entry for Harijans. Jamnalal Bajaj publicly deplored the unethical practices adopted by many businessmen of the time and their ostentatious and wasteful social practices. The Ahmedabad *seths* were great champions of education for girls and also played a leading role in the Ahmedabad municipality. Lala Shri Ram studied the civic problems of Delhi and sought to improve matters by involving himself in municipal administration.

▼ Jankidevi Bajaj forged a campaign against cruelty to animals, particularly bullocks, which then, as now, are used for pulling carts with heavy loads, especially in rural areas.

Till the nineteenth century, business charity in India was largely motivated by religion and, therefore, went to religious organizations or religion-sanctioned activities such as construction and maintenance of temples, *dharamshalas*, bathing ghats at pilgrim centres,

▲ Heads of various families and industries often came together to organize activities for social good. From its early days, entrepreneurship and philanthropy has been associated hand in glove, especially when it came to the emancipation of women and their education. In this picture, (from left): Motilal Lath, Bhagirath Kanoria, Prabhu Dayal Himatsingka, Sitaram Seksaria, Ramkumar Bhuwalka.

schools run by religious institutions, animal shelters, religious festivals, and feeding the poor. Secular activities supported by private charity included making provisions for drinking water, digging of wells, distress relief in times of famine or flood, and planting trees and gardens in public areas. But charity was largely ameliorative, and individually dispensed on a one-to-one basis.

Following industrialization, business charity was more substantial, more secular, and more institutionalized in organizations such as hospitals, schools, and orphanages, geographically more dispersed beyond the donor's immediate city to include nationally important institutions and causes, and was directed towards long-term change, rather than immediate relief.

Two powerful factors working for social change were the activities of Christian missionaries and the introduction of Western education. Both exposed Indian society to new ideas and produced a ferment that helped change the values and outlook of Indians. The outcome was religious and social reform directed at abolition of child marriage, widow remarriage, women's education, abolition of dowries, intermarriage between castes, Hindu–Muslim amity, and improvement of the lot of Untouchables.

Revival of pride in Indian culture manifested itself in the development of vernacular literature, the study of Sanskrit, the revival of Indian art, and research into Indian history and archaeology led to the establishment of several organizations for the purpose, including the Benaras Hindu University and Shantiniketan.

The freedom struggle provided further motivation to the wealthy to give for public causes which included support of nationalist education. Many of the pioneers saw the establishment of industries itself as a patriotic act and were fired by the vision of an economically strong, free, and modern India. They realized that freedom could only be meaningful if there were rapid progress and sustained development, and that this would need massive social investment in education, especially vocational and technical education, public health, communications, power, and water supply.

▶ A class at Shantiniketan. The experimental Vishwa Bharati University created here by Nobel laureate Rabindranath Tagore hoped to provide the best of international knowledge in the ancient Indian setting of a gurukul.

▼ Lala Shriram at an exhibition at the Lady Shriram College for women in New Delhi. The Shriram family is associated with several educational institutions in the capital.

Many of the pioneers were deeply influenced by Mahatma Gandhi who exhorted them to give for the good of society and to involve themselves in the uplift of the downtrodden. Gandhi said: 'The art of amassing riches becomes a degrading and despicable act, if it is not accompanied by the nobler art of how to spend wealth usefully. Let not possession of wealth be synonymous with degradation, vice and profligacy.' He wanted capitalists to voluntarily renounce a part of their wealth for the good of the others, and act as trustees of their wealth, administering it for the good of society. Jamnalal Bajaj, G.D. Birla, Ambalal Sarabhai, Kasturbhai Lalbhai, and many others came under his spell and contributed liberally to his schemes for the upliftment of Harijans and rural communities.

The state encouraged self-help and voluntary action to meet social needs, and to that purpose exerted subtle pressure and held out incentives in the form of titles, public recognition, access to high official circles, and even tax concessions. Income tax had been introduced in 1860, and in 1922 the government granted 50 per cent tax exemption to individuals on donations for charitable purposes. The result was a proliferation of organizations such as schools and colleges, especially for women, technical and research institutes, art galleries and museums endowed

or supported by the business community. In Mumbai, for instance, the David Sassoon Library, the Sassoon Mechanics Institute, Jehangir Art Gallery, the Sir Cowasjee Jehangir Ophthalmic Hospital, Bombay University with its grand Rajabai Tower, Elphinstone College, J.J. School of Art, Bombay Hospital, and the Tata Cancer Research Institute, all bear testimony to the vital part played by the city's business elite in Mumbai's development. The Modern High School for Girls in Calcutta; Hindu College and Shri Ram College of Commerce in Delhi; Annamalai University in Chidambaram, Birla Institute of Technology at Pilani, the Ranchhodlal Chotalal Technical Institute in Ahmedabad, and Benaras Hindu University to which many business leaders from all over India contributed, stand witness to the role played by the early business leaders in building an educational infrastructure for urban India.

Providing medical facilities was another philanthropic avenue since public health facilities were abysmally poor throughout India. Largely, it was urban India that benefited. Though there was interest in famine relief work, support for agricultural improvement to prevent famines came much later. Also, little was attempted to tackle basic problems like sanitation and housing for the poor.

Undoubtedly, the revival of Indian theatre, dance, and music, and the development of vernacular literature were possible only due to private patronage, since the state offered little support in these fields. It is also not widely known that the business community in the north did a lot to develop the Hindi language

▲▶ The Tata Memorial Hospital for Cancer Research and Treatment *(above)* and the Tata Institute of Fundamental Research *(right)* were begun by the two sons of Jamsetji Tata, widely regarded as the father of modern Indian philanthropy in the nineteenth century.

▼ K.J. Somaiya lifting a stretcher at a medical camp organized in rural India. Besides a 700-bed free hospital, the Somaiya Group runs various trusts and foundations dedicated to the promotion of learning, culture, and the upliftment of tribals.

and literature in the late nineteenth and early twentieth centuries through its patronage of authors and literary societies. The literary and linguistic movements of the 1880s and 1890s spearheaded by the Hindi Literary Society, and the Benaras Society for the Advancement of Hindi developed out of such patronage. In the south too, Chettiar philanthropy supported the Dravidian movement and the Tamil renaissance in language, literature, and the arts which was both its cause and consequence.

Among the most philanthropic of the early business leaders was Jamsetjee Jeejeebhoy. He gave so freely to every cause and individual in need that on his death in 1859, he had the unique honour of having flags flown at half mast at Government House and government offices. Nowrosjee M. Wadia set up a multi-purpose foundation for education, distress relief, and building and maintenance of hospitals in 1909, predating even the great foundations of the West like the Ford and Rockefeller Foundations. Pirojsha Godrej, at the head of the Godrej group, set up a model township in the suburbs of Mumbai where, apart from facilities for his workers, he built the Udayanchal School, and a Family Planning and Research Centre. Later, his heirs set up the Pirojsha Foundation through which they supported cultural, environmental, and educational work. The Mahindras set up, first, the Mahindra Education Trust and, later, the Mahindra Foundation.

However, perhaps the greatest visionary of the nineteenth century, and one who is widely regarded as the father of modern Indian philanthropy, was Jamsetji Tata. Generous with his money, he was against ameliorative charity on the grounds that it increased dependence, encouraged improvidence, and did nothing to tackle the root causes of poverty and destitution, or to prevent their spread. He preferred, what he called, constructive philanthropy, which would apply funds to removing the root causes of poverty, ignorance, and disease rather than merely relieving them temporarily through charity. He believed that 'what advances a nation or community is not so much to prop up its weakest and most helpless members as to lift up the best and most gifted so as to make them of the greatest service to the country'. He therefore launched the J.N.Tata Endowment Scheme in 1892 to give scholarships to

deserving students for higher studies abroad. Later, he donated many of his properties to create the Indian Institute of Science in Bangalore which, unfortunately, he did not live to see.

His work was carried on by his sons Sir Ratan and Sir Dorab who created two trusts: the Sir Ratan Tata and the Sir Dorab Tata Trusts which, between them, established the Tata Memorial Hospital for Cancer Research and Treatment, the Tata Institute of Fundamental Research, the Tata Institute of Social Sciences, and the National Centre for the Performing Arts. With the remarkable J.R.D. Tata at the helm of the group, the trusts identified uncontrolled population as the major obstacle to progress. The J.R.D. Tata Trust was set up to advance family planning, the upliftment of women, and the eradication of illiteracy, apart from contributing to other organizations devoted to these issues.

Another great philanthropist was Jamnalal Bajaj whom Gandhiji considered closest to his ideal of trusteeship. Even before he met Gandhi, Jamnalal Bajaj had set up schools and hostels in Wardha and Rajasthan, and contributed to causes elsewhere, such as Jagdish Chandra Bose's institute in Calcutta. But after meeting Gandhi, he put himself and his wealth at the disposal of Gandhi, not only for the freedom movement but also for his constructive programme of removal of untouchability, popularization of khadi and village industries, the promotion of basic education, and Hindu–Muslim unity. His desire to give away his share of the joint family business to public causes approved by Gandhi was respected by his sons who set up the Jamnalal Bajaj Seva Trust in 1942 to relieve distress and to promote spiritual, intellectual, social, and economic development, especially for the poorest, and for women. Jamnalal Bajaj is also associated with the establishment of the International Sarvodaya Centre, the Gitai Mandir and other such institutions.

▲ Tube well at village Somatne, Taluka Maval, Dist. Pune, installed at the initiative of Jankidevi Bajaj Gramvikas Sanstha, Pune, on behalf of Bajaj Auto Ltd.

▼ Continuous Counter Trench (CCT) work in village Vahangaon, (Dist. Pune) under Water Shed Development activity taken up at the initiative of Jankidevi Bajaj Gramvikas Sanstha, Pune, on behalf of Bajaj Auto Ltd.

▶ View of the Rural Sanitation Park and Rural Sanitation Training Centre at Kumarappapuram, near Wardha. This complex was developed by Jamnalal Bajaj Foundation in collaboration with Centre of Science for Villages and UNICEF.

The Birla family established its tradition of philanthropy beginning with Baldevdas, its founder. His advice to his sons was: 'Earn and give, since there is no greater sin than earning for one's own self. He who is not of help to others is worthless. Money is of no use if it does not remove the ills of others.' His eldest son, Jugalkishor, worked as a preserver of Indian culture throughout his life, preserving temples and supporting work in the fields of philosophy, sculpture, and music. Another son, Rameshwar Das, established several large institutions in Mumbai including the Maheshwari Relief Society and Bombay Hospital. But it was Braj Mohan and Ghanshyam Das who became legends in the worlds of both business and philanthropy.

Through the Birla Education Trust established by him in 1929 at Pilani, G.D. financed a vast programme of education at all levels, capping it with the establishment of the Birla Engineering College at Pilani in 1946. Later, G.D. expanded the Birla Institute of Technology into a deemed university, and his younger brother, Braj Mohan established a similar institute at Ranchi. Both commissioned beautiful temples all over India, but alongside also established modern planetariums, hospitals, and cultural academies. Braj Mohan was associated with projects for various public welfare activities ranging from health care, vocational training, cultural promotion, religious heritage conservation, research organizations and village upliftment programmes with each of his industrial undertakings.

▲ Space exhibit at Birla Planetarium, Calcutta. The Birla family believes in the tradition of 'earn and give', and a lot of its philanthropic activity is driven by creating educational opportunities so that the gains will help in the development of human resource for the country.

▼ A cardiac catheterization laboratory with an advanced swing lab system at Calcutta's B.M. Birla Heart Centre. Appropriate medical facilities in India have often been funded by industrial houses.

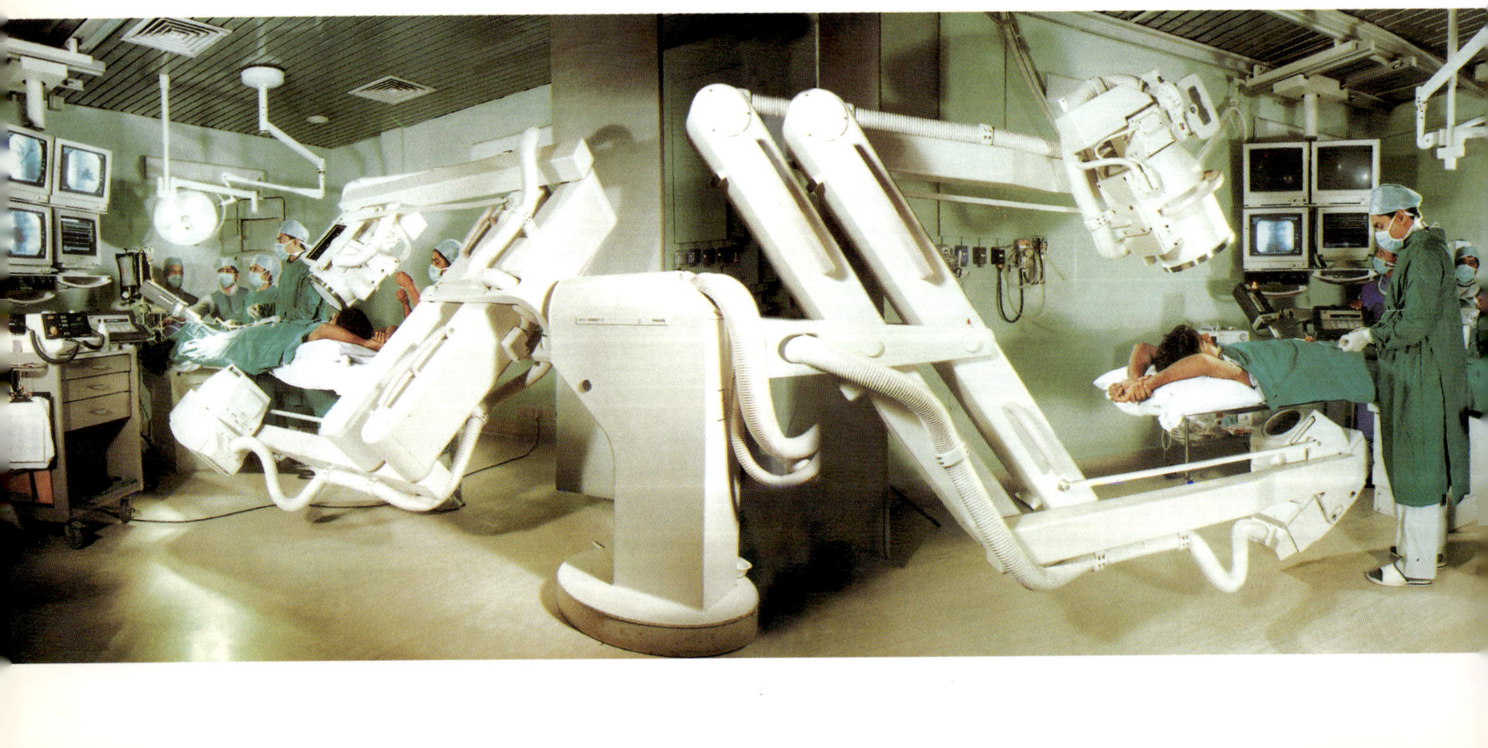

▲ Students experimenting in the laboratories of the Pilani Engineering College run by the Birla Education Trust.

▶ Chief scientific advisor – defence, Dr Abdul Kalam at the robotics laboratory of the Birla Institute of Technology, Ranchi, Bihar.

▼ K.K. Birla is the Chairman, Birla Education Trust, and associated with several academic institutions and other philanthropic activities. He is also a member of Parliament.

In Ahmedabad, the pioneer textile magnate Ranchhodlal involved himself with many a project for education and civic improvement. Ranchhodlal's grandson Chinubhai was a great patron of art and culture. Ambalal Sarabhai was deeply influenced by Gandhi and contributed generously to his work. His sister Mridulaben Sarabhai founded Jyoti Sangh, a women's welfare organization for destitute women.

Lalbhai Dalpatbhai earmarked a part of his profits for social, educational, and religious causes, and his son Kasturbhai Lalbhai became one of the most prolific institution builders in India. Ambalal Sarabhai, Kasturbhai Lalbhai, and other leading industrial magnates, individually or collectively, established a series of educational and cultural institutions such as the Physics Research Laboratory, the Ahmedabad Textile Industry's Research Association, the Indian Institute of Management, and the Lalbhai Dalpatbhai Institute of Indology.

In Delhi, Lala Shri Ram expanded the educational infrastructure of Delhi, especially in scientific and commercial education (Shri Ram College of Commerce, Lady Shri Ram College for Women, Shri Ram Institute of Industrial Research), to such a degree that he came to be known as 'College King'. The JK charities set up by Kamlapat Singhania and his sons brought literacy to the villages around Kanpur and later set up many prestigious institutions in different fields, and in different cities. Prominent JK trusts included the Lakshmipat Singhania Medical Foundation, the LS Education Foundation, and the JK Sports Foundation. These, in turn, established several educational, scientific, and research institutions

such as the JK Institute of Applied Physics and Technology at Allahabad and the JK Institute of Sociology and Human Relations in Lucknow.

Fifty kilometres from Delhi, Gujarmal Modi set up a township, Modinagar, around his various factories and embellished it with several institutions, including hospitals such as the Shri Modi Eye Hospital and Ophthalmic Research Centre, the Samaj Kalyan Vibhag, and the Adult Education Centre for women's welfare. In much of his philanthropy, he was aided by his wife, Dayawati Modi.

In the south, it was Raja Sir A.R.A.M. Annamalai who gave new direction to the charitable activities of his community, from religion-oriented charity to more secular, modern philanthropy. After establishing hospitals, schools, dispensaries and colleges, and building roads throughout Chettinad and in Madras, he founded the Meenakshi College at Chidambaram. Along with other colleges started by him, the Sanskrit College, the Music College, and the Tamil College, it became the nucleus of Annamalai University, the first university founded entirely through private means.

The Murugappa group set up the AMM Foundation for educational and medical purposes, while Ramaswamy Raja established the PAC Ramaswamy Raja Education Trust in Rajapalayam. Other notable philanthropists of the south were Sir Pitti Theagaraya Chetty, Dr Alagappa Chettiar, O.A.P.R.M.

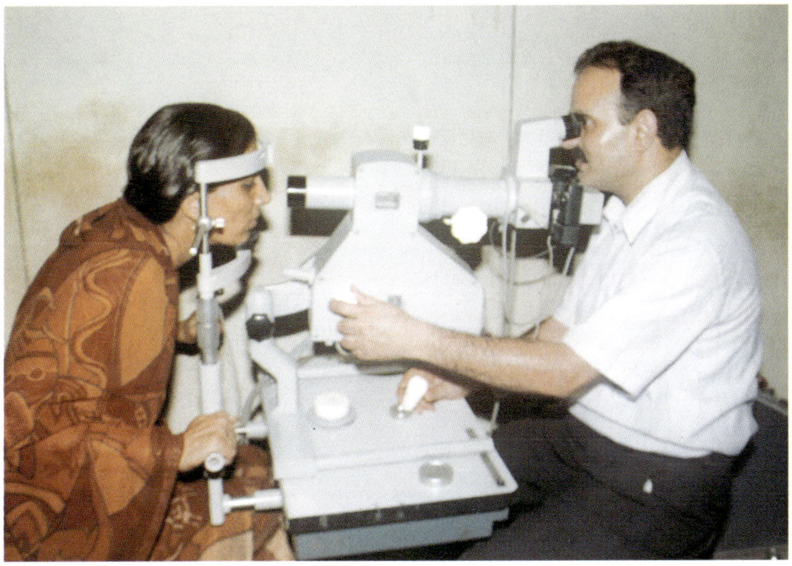

Arunachalam Chettiar, A.M. Murugappa Chettiar, and Kuppuswamy Naidu.

Following Independence, it was widely accepted that rapid industrialization held the key to the eradication of poverty and backwardness, and that the business community, therefore, had an important role to play in nation building. Before Independence, Jawaharlal Nehru expressed little sympathy for capitalists and was one of the sternest critics of Mahatma Gandhi's theory of trusteeship of the rich. He had asked, 'Is it reasonable to give unchecked power and wealth to an individual and expect him to use it entirely for the public good?' Post-1947, however, he revealed a more pragmatic streak in enlisting the cooperation of industrialists in the achievement of national goals. The government, on its part, continued to offer tax concessions to induce industry to contribute to social, educational, and charitable causes and, in 1948, extended the concessions to companies making charitable donations.

That early cooperation sowed the seeds for growth in industry and industrial production so that the period 1951–62 is often described as the golden age of Indian capitalism. It was not destined to last long. By the 1960s, the honeymoon between government and industry had ended. The government's chosen route to

▲▼ The Gujar Mal Modi Community of Opthalmic Research Centre *(above)* and the P.D. Hinduja National Hospital *(below)*. Medical facilities are expensive, which is where philanthropic foundations have been able to provide aid in establishing centres where the latest equipment and procedures become available to people.

(previous page):

▲ Dr Alagappa Chettiar was among notable philanthropists from the south where the move from religion-oriented charity to secular concerns was a more recent event, often associated with the fine arts, music, dance, and Sanskrit scholarship.

▼ Shri Ram Temple, Renukoot (UP), part of the Kanoria Chemicals premises. The building of temples reflects a tradition that goes back in time to the ancient past, since temples were seen as social centres for the spiritual upliftment of the populace.

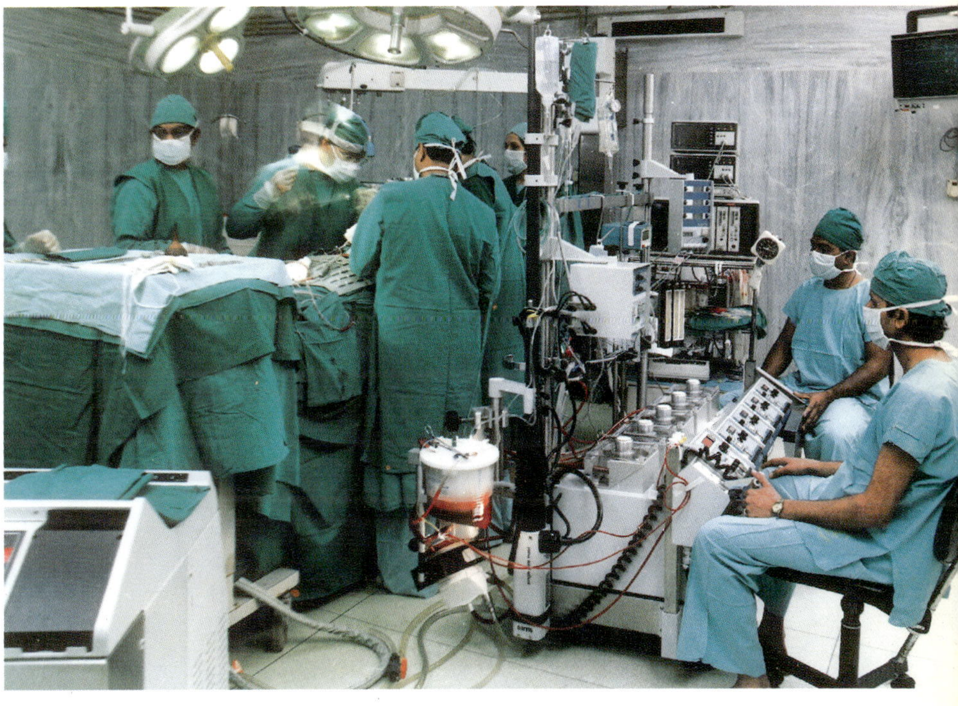

Extending Patronage to Culture

Patronage for the arts, for what is loosely described as culture but includes a vast repertoire within its ambit, has almost always had to rely on the administration. Initially, this was provided by the ruling families in various princely kingdoms where these arts flourished and were nurtured under different traditions. These eventually gave us, in India a large number of classical dance forms, of musical traditions, of what later came to be known as *gharanas* or disciplines of music and dance. Theatre, too, always had a rich tradition, with Sanskrit dramas, and those in their derivative languages, being performed on various religious and secular occasions.

With Independence, the task of patronage fell to the government, which set up various institutions for the study and preservation of art forms. However, the onus of enhancement of these forms, and their viable links with mainstream life, remained with a few individuals and with the maestros themselves. To support this task, funding was required, and the industrial sector moved in to fill this gap. Major industrialists initially treated this as another segment of their philanthropic efforts, but over time came to view this as a distinct segment that needed, besides financial assistance, also their involvement.

Not only do industrial houses sponsor cultural events, in several cases they have come to be associated with them. In Mumbai, the National Centre for Performing Arts is a major nodal head for cultural performances, whether classical or contemporary, with the Tata group looking on Indian, and partly even international, cultural interaction as crucial to life in a megapolis. At another end of the scale, Prithvi Theatre is run by the family of Prithviraj Kapoor in a bid to sustain interest in theatre. Often, sponsorships are sought to ensure that this well-managed complex is able to meet its needs.

In Delhi, the Shriram Group, and Sumitra Charat Ram in particular, have come to be associated with the Bharatiya Kala Kendra, and with the performance of the *Ramlila* ballad which has become a feature on the annual calendar of the city. At the other end of the scale are corporations like Eicher which sustain an art gallery in the capital; ITC which sponsors music soirees like the ITC Sangeet Sammelan, and books including the annual *Wills Book of Excellence* on sports; Godfrey Phillips which is associated with outdoor events such as white water rafting on the Ganga at Rishikesh; and various corporations in the south involved with the weekly musical concerts in the city halls of Chennai. In Calcutta, organizations such as Sangeet Kala Mandir, Anamika Kala Sangam and Padatik, have become a feature of the cultural life of the city. In Bangalore, Odissi dancer Protima Gauri was able to establish the first modern retreat in the nature of a dance village thanks to the efforts made by numerous corporations that funded the exercise.

As India and Indians discover more pride in their traditions, this will continue to rise, and corporations will come to be even more closely associated with cultural houses and events.

▲ A literacy drive among poor children, one among activities promoted by the Usha Martin Group's Krishi Gram Vikas Kendra. Such rural upliftment opportunities pay dividends since the issue is not short-term charity but aimed at the greater, national long-term good of the people.

development concentrated economic power with the state, while industry found itself hamstrung with industrial licensing and foreign exchange restrictions.

Part of the blame for the government's restrictive policies lay with the business community itself. Beginning with the Second World War, the misdemeanours of a section of the community resulted in hoarding, black marketeering, price manipulations, defrauding of shareholders, and fuelling administrative corruption, resulting in its collective image taking a plunge in the public eye. Still later, the younger generation which took over the mantle from the pioneers, and the new educated managerial class tended to be less religious, less frugal, and inclined to ostentatious consumption, and somewhat less inclined to take on public responsibilities. The net result was a general disinclination to give to charity or become involved in civic or community matters.

In the 1970s, the worsening economic situation and growing social problems were manifested in the Naxalite and other such movements that threatened the foundations of a stable society. The government's seeming inability to grapple with problems, and the consequent growth in the number of non-governmental organizations for development at the grass-roots level; government

▶ Various industrialists have contributed towards the Ankleshwar Industrial Development Society in Gujarat where Ashwin Dani of Asian Paints has taken the lead in establishing the Shree Gattu Vidyalaya.

pressure on business to do more for social development; a more proactive role played by chambers of commerce and industry; and finally, world trends in corporate thinking about social issues, all contributed to a slow reversal in industry's fortress mentality.

Business leaders like J.R.D. Tata, Arvind Mafatlal, Ramakrishna Bajaj, S.S. Kanoria, and, among the younger groups, people like Rohinton Aga, used every opportunity to remind their colleagues that their very survival and prosperity depended on more responsible behaviour, and on raising the standard of life of the communities in which they operated. They argued for enlightened self-interest in line with trends elsewhere in the world.

The West was seeing the steady development of the concept of social responsibility of business and ideas of managerial trusteeship: that a company is to be managed for the good not only of the owners, but also of economy and society. There was a move away from an earlier style of philanthropy with its emphasis on creating institutional infrastructure, and on making charitable contributions to social welfare organizations towards the broader concept of corporate citizenship. A corporation, so the belief ran, was answerable to many people: the shareholder, the consumer, labour, the government and the community as a whole; and being charitable was not enough if, at the same time, a business leader or his organization failed in their responsibilities in other areas such as ethical business practices, and environmentally friendly industrial practices.

The Indian government too began to use such opportunities as the annual sessions of the apex chambers to remind the business community of its responsibilities while dangling, at the same time, the carrot of tax concessions. Sections 35 CC and 35 CCA were introduced in the Income Tax Act in 1977 to make contributions to rural development and other socially oriented programmes tax deductible. (The concessions were, however, partly withdrawn in 1983 following their misuse by some companies.)

Compelled by the poor image of the business community and by economic imperatives, business chambers began initiatives to motivate members through awareness raising conferences, the institution of awards, and the offer of advice on issues such as population control, rural development, environment, and more recently, AIDS. The result was a paradigm shift on the part of business, from the creation of prestigious institutions to grass-roots community involvement directed at human resources development.

The Tatas, even as they promoted institutions like the Tata Energy Research Institute, expanded their work among communities, with TISCO taking the lead. The Arvind Mafatlal group began to bring the professional management of business to bear on the problems of rural areas through the Bharatiya Agro Industries Foundation, and the Sadguru Sewa Trust. Hindustan Lever wrested success from a failing dairy project at Etah in Uttar Pradesh to begin a highly acclaimed programme of rural development. ITC and Larsen and Toubro, both non-family managed companies, made forays into rural development, afforestation, city improvement, and culture. The Birlas and other companies, too numerous to name, began to open the medical and educational facilities they operated for their workers to surrounding communities.

Several first generation entrepreneurs too initiated programmes for community betterment, among them Escorts, Hero Honda, the Apeejay group, and the Ramco group. Even more exceptional were smaller groups like Excel Industries, Bhoruka, Lupin Laboratories, Somaiyas, and the Deepak group that, virtually from the outset,

▼ Sanjay Nagar. Pictures taken before and after a community development project, promoted by the Lalbhai group, was able to bring about radical improvement in a village in Gujarat.

▲ During the Bengal famine of 1954, Escorts manifested its concern by contributing an aeroplane to the government's relief effort. H.P. Nanda presented the aeroplane to the then Minister of Food and Agriculture, Rafi Ahmed Kidwai.

▶ Escorts Hospital, New Delhi, has brought in revolutionary heartcare facilities in India, and is now directly uplinked with USA where doctors may view operations in progress at the hospital.

made community development and spread of education integral parts of their business operations.

While the creation of prestigious institutions as memorials to members of the family, or for important personalities, continues, there is a distinct move towards funding and implementation of programmes for community betterment, either directly or through the establishment of non-governmental organizations. The Tatas, Escorts, Lupin, IPCL, Usha Martin, Excel, Arvind Mills, and several others have set up societies or trusts to undertake community programmes. Companies like the Apeejay group, the Khaitan group and Ambuja Cement prefer to contribute to independent organizations such as the Ramakrishna Mission in Calcutta, the Bombay Community Trust, and other NGOs.

Though health and education programmes continue to be the most popularly supported causes, whether in the urban or rural areas, the range of activities supported is steadily widening. A large number of business groups are involved in rural development, a role that encompasses the construction of public conveniences, drains, and roads in rural areas, social forestry and afforestation,

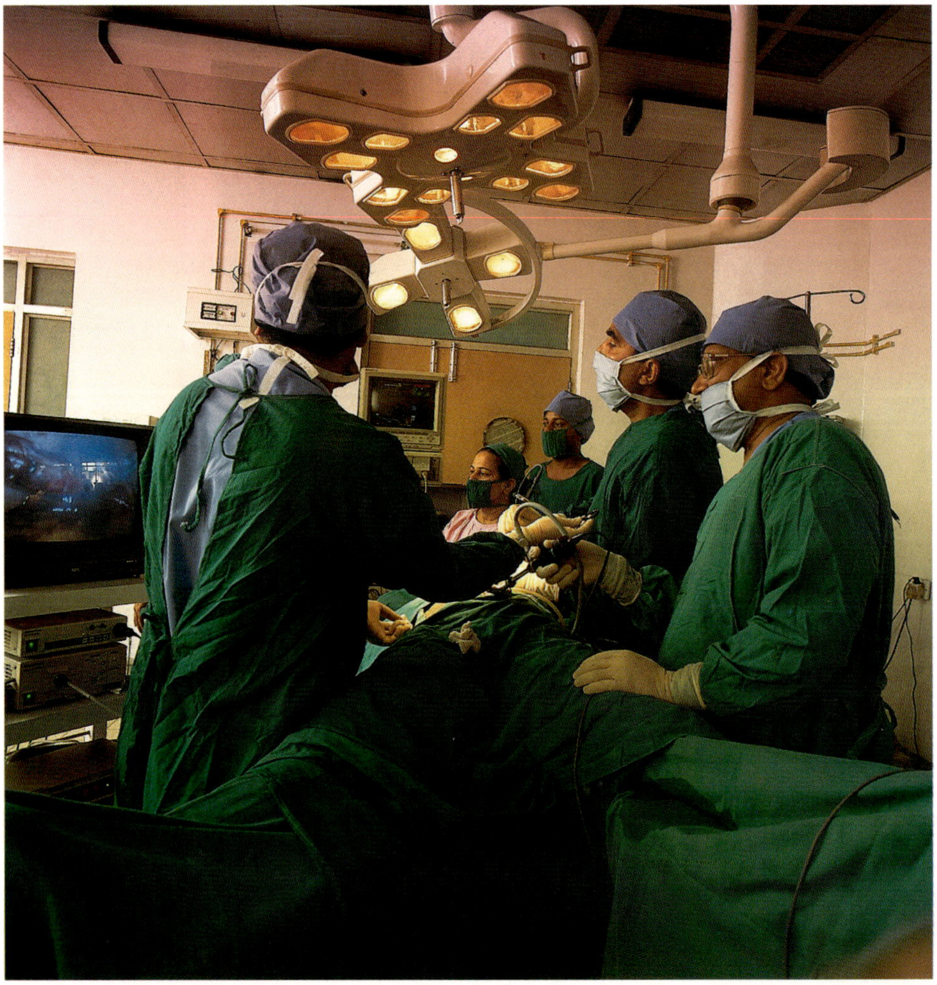

agriculture and irrigation development, provision of drinking water facilities, vocational training, and the like. But a variety of new causes such as improving the status of girl children, monument and other cultural heritage conservation, wildlife protection, and sports promotion have also become popular with companies.

Both companies and NGOs are recognizing the value of partnerships to achieve their goals. Businesses are getting together to pool their resources and expertise to achieve a common goal, as in the case of Bombay First which aims to improve civic conditions in Mumbai. There are also, albeit few, partnerships with civic authorities, as in Ahmedabad where the Arvind Lalbhai group is working on a project of slum betterment in partnership with the Ahmedabad Municipal Corporation and a non-governmental organization. Companies are also evincing interest in forming partnerships with NGOs. For instance, Essar Cellphone works with Shakti Shalini, an NGO providing shelter and counselling to women in distress, to connect with appropriate institutions for emergency assistance.

▲ Established by R.P. Mody, the Mody School, is a division of the Mody Institute of Education and Research, Lakshmangarh, Rajasthan. A well-developed residential complex, the institution is soon to become operational as a college, and has all the makings of a deemed university.

▼ Women handloom project, Lalbhai group. A number of industrial enterprises have devoted effort to creating job opportunities for women.

Though there is undoubtedly greater interest in becoming better corporate citizens, few companies take their commitment seriously enough to make an annual allocation, earmarking a defined percentage of their profits. Very few have a proper strategy and plan of work, and community betterment is yet to be integrated into mainstream operations. Companies have yet to professionalize their community betterment work, much of which suffers from ad hocism. And forming partnerships, as in the examples above, is still an exception rather than a norm. However, whatever the shortcomings, one can only hope that the business/society interface will continue to gain strength in the years ahead.

Section IV

Globalization and Challenges of the New Millennium

Overview

The Dynamics of Change in the Next Millennium

Amit Mitra

We stand at the threshold of the 'third industrial revolution' that will fundamentally restructure the way we produce, work, consume, engage in dialogue, entertain, articulate political choices, and perhaps even the way we think. At the heart of this constructive conflagration lies the genius of fresh entrepreneurship driven by a scientific and technological paradigm of a much higher order. The wonder of the opening up of cyberspace in the early 1990s through Internet is only the tip of the iceberg. Thousands of entrepreneurs, the likes of Bill Gates and Steven Jobs, will proliferate across the world discovering new 'spaces' and unimaginable frontiers.

An early glimpse at this impending revolution can already be had in India at the grass-roots level. The sight of a wireless telephone in the palm of a rustic villager calling a grain merchant for the going price is truly remarkable. This Indian villager has vaulted from a world of no phone to the unlimited world of wireless, bypassing the evolutionary stage of fixed telephone. Similarly, a semi-literate electrician in the city of Delhi brandishes his new gizmo, the electronic pager, a tiny instrument that has quadrupled his business through

its superior power of receiving and storing information 'wirelessly'. He too has leapfrogged over many conventional stages of development. At the macro-level too, a silent revolution is unfolding in the silicon valleys of India — Bangalore, and now Hyderabad. Customized software orders are booked at 5 p.m. in New York and while America sleeps, Bangalore awakes and creates advanced software packages. These are transmitted instantaneously through global satellite linkages before the sun rises over New York.

Critics from the Left, however, see glimpses of uneven development in these cataclysmic changes pointing to unmetalled village roads in the midst of wireless communication, inadequate housing, and lack of vocational training institutions in the midst of proliferating electronic pagers. Optimists, on the other hand, cheer the discontinuity as sign of a final break with the status quo of a low-level equilibrium trap characterized by puttering economic growth rates, a near-closed economy, and labyrinthine controls from the commanding heights of the state. In my considered view, as long as the entrepreneurial spirit flourishes and drives the 'third industrial revolution', the discontinuities and seeming contradictions of development will steadily even out. In fact, a large number of common men and women will force their way into the information highway giving democracy a new meaning. In this context, the arrival of Internet and cyberspace has already begun to erode the capacity of the elite to monopolize and manipulate information and with accelerating computer penetration in India, *information* could become the vehicle of mass empowerment and a weapon for battling mass deprivation. Numerous social groups that survived for centuries in the twilight zone have begun to emerge and integrate into the mainstream of the socio-politico-economic milieu. Penetration of electronic and visual media has begun to churn up social structures, revolutionizing personal choices, tastes, and worldviews.

A white collar worker in a small town of India today is literally leaping from the radio age directly to a cable-driven colour television, serviced by 35,000 registered cable operators and another 50,000 unregistered suppliers. Millions of metres of cable wires web the urban and semi-urban landscape of India today. But can one imagine the far-reaching changes that will occur when these cable wires are allowed to carry not only the television image but telephone and data transfers as well? This gigantic web will facilitate the birth of a new strata of 'home knowledge workers' and release latent 'women power'. Women and men will process ideas, conduct sales, create niche markets, operate banking services, control air booking systems, and customize software for global consumers all from the precincts of their homes, without ever entering a conventional office. As a result, the twentieth-century

◀ The farmer who occupies a low rung on the ladder of development as far as services to rural areas are concerned, but who remains a pivotal figure because of the scale of Indian agribusiness, now finds he can call markets at the touch of a button, bringing him all the benefits of wireless telephone.

▼ Skilled workers with access to pagers find that their ability to get more work has increased dramatically, even while they are out on call. Global satellite linkages are helping India create software services in, virtually, an instant.

concept of trade unions too will become obsolete and gender relations will undergo tectonic shifts. Increasingly large-sized businesses too will create cyber offices for their workers who will then navigate their way to work via Internet. Corporate headquarters will become passe.

In the area of hard core production, we see similar vibrations coming through the miniaturized computers embedded in gigantic machines. These machines have already begun to chop, lift, and restructure materials through electronic signals. Of late, a jetty to evacuate steel has begun operating in India with only 200 workers, while the old jetty doing the same job engages 1500 unskilled and semi-skilled workers. The implications of this silent shift at the ground level are far-reaching. On the one hand, they are revolutionizing the productivity per worker and productivity per unit of capital, and on the other, invoking real fears about the fate of millions of unskilled and semi-skilled workers who would be excluded from accessing the power of information technology and services. They would never visit the cybercafes already under construction in India and would never enter an intelligent office building already operating in Mumbai and Delhi, nor would they ever see the inside of an electronic control room in a new millennium factory.

Unless India collectively addresses the challenge of human capital formation at the lowest ends of the spectrum on a war footing, the proliferation of the third industrial revolution itself can be stunted and distorted, giving rise to pressures on our infant democracy. The strategy of mass 'inclusion' in the new dynamics of the market place will have to be evolved expeditiously.

While systems of production are silently undergoing radical change, India will need to address the financial matrix fuelling our economy. Today, financial institutions and banks of India offer funds on the basis of traditional collateral and asset-based securities. In the brave new world of tomorrow, lending will take place on the basis of brand names, intellectual property, and cash flow potentials. After

▼ Cyberspace is now flooded by Indian women who are looking forward to a future as 'home knowledge workers', making the concept of offices obsolete, at least as far as their requirements are concerned. For those concerned about the lack of people contact as a result of computerization, the Internet should prove less isolationist.

▲ View of 100GF PARAM 10000 at NPSF Pune. At the heart of change in the third millennium lies the 'revolution' being generated by computerization. The PARAM Supercomputer was created in India after the country had been denied the technology by the West.

all, a cellular phone company has practically no assets, nor does a TV producer or a film production company. The brand name itself will offer intrinsic value and lending will happen on the basis of 'virtual' assets. Today, 25 per cent of lending in the developed world is totally asset free. Obviously, India's financial institutions and banks will have to master the new chemistry of development finance in a radically changing world of 'cerebral commodities'.

Even economic theory is facing new challenges where economy of scale is being transcended by economy of scope, and the natural monopoly argument for allowing single companies, mostly public, to dominate the power and telecom sectors is being replaced by competition and privatization.

India, with its massive 'person power' and deeply embedded scientific, mathematical traditions, has the potential to emerge as a global economic power in the next millennium. However, the challenge lies in converting mere labour population into enriched human capital suitable for the dynamics of the information age. This will require a massive political consensus and thorough understanding of the widespread revolutionary benefits of the infotech revolution. Founded on such clarity, government policies will automatically nurture and garner gigantic entrepreneurial energies that lie latent today. The final challenge will lie in training, retaining, and reculturizing our billion people, particularly the young, towards the 'third revolution'.

The Changing Relationship of Government and Business

Ashok V. Desai

It is said of the colonial age that trade followed the flag, but centuries before that was the case, Indian business had spread to far-flung corners of the Eurasian continent leaving the flag far behind. India's cultural colonization of South East Asia was no doubt accompanied, perhaps preceded, by the development of the region by seafaring traders from our east coast. Angkor Wat and Borobudur, today sentinels of a fractured civilization, could only have been the cultural focal points in a network of cultivation, craft, and commerce. Westwards, the record is less clear; but well into the colonial age, Indian traders occupied outposts along the trade route to Tashkent and Moscow, and even at the time of Independence, Indian currency was common coin, and Indian consumer goods filled the shelves of shops, often owned by Indian businessmen, in the Arabian Gulf.

In those ages of India's business ascendancy, the relationship between Indian businessmen and their Indian rulers was remote, if not hostile. At least for the centuries of which we have written record, whether in Persian, Arabic, Portuguese, English, or Dutch, the impression is hard to avoid that businessmen were the victims of rulers, whether as sources of booty during the sack of hostile cities, or as targets of extortion at ports and toll points. Wise advice to rulers to nurture trade and business is no doubt to be found in the guides to ruling which that age brought forth. It is also no doubt true that the massive military campaigns of that age could not have been carried out without a supporting network of trade and credit that supplied the troops with everything from victuals to women. However, the trader and the rulers were thrown together by warfare which waxed and waned; there was no sustained, symbiotic relationship of mutually supporting partners.

▼ Prime Minister Indira Gandhi at the 1972 annual general meeting of FICCI with the organization's President, S.S. Kanoria and his father, Radha Kissen Kanoria. The interaction between business and government became stronger following the 1971 Indo-Pak War.

This fortuitous relationship, shaped by war, was not peculiar to India; it worked in the same way in other parts of Asia and Europe. It began to change only after Columbus, in search of India, lost his way but led the way for Europeans to all corners of the

▼ Heads of Indian government have always kept cognizance of business affairs through meetings with leading industrialists. Indira Gandhi, seen here, with B.M. Birla, Gujar Mal Modi and Ramnath Poddar.

world. With his expedition began an age of colonial expansion that made military success and commercial reach mutually dependent. Columbus, Magellan, and Vasco da Gama unknowingly began a process that brought unimaginable riches to businessmen, which made governments their protectors, partners, and often clients. Those nations which worked out the secret of this partnership conquered the world; those that did not, sank into obscurity or servitude. In our time in India, politically convenient lessons are being read into the East India Company. What the xenophobic rhetoric misses out is that the East India Company was a member of that club of traders and bankers which came to be known as the City, a two-mile stretch of stately buildings on the northern banks of the Thames in London which to this day is a financial power rivalling New York and Tokyo. It was far more powerful than now in the three centuries when it worked in concert with the Palace of Westminster which stands at its western end. The success of the East India Company in India was no less due to the King's peace it brought to Indian businessmen under its aegis than to the superior arms that made the peace possible in the Company's enclaves surrounded by the sea of violence that was the India of the eighteenth century. The migration of Indian businessmen from Mughal Surat to British Bombay (now renamed Mumbai) made the latter a commercial power. Similarly, the splendour of nineteenth-century Calcutta was as much the creation of Indian businessmen, many from as far as Punjab and Rajputana, as of British nabobs and planters. There was no partnership between the government and business; but the East India Company, being

▲ FICCI has believed in helping to formulate government policy with agenda guidelines based on nationalist considerations.
(above left): Yashwant Sinha, currently India's Finance Minister, with Sudhir Jalan, K.K. Modi and Gouri Prasad Goenka.
(above right): Commerce Minister Ramakrishna Hegde with Sudhir Jalan, R.V. Kanoria, B. Krishan and Shantilal Somaiya.

a company that got into the business of governing, created room for many indigenous businesses within its web of commercial activities. It developed the export of opium to China, but the business of procuring that opium from Malwa's peasants, of transporting it in bullock carts to Mumbai, and of shipping it to Hong Kong, was largely in Indian hands. One reason why the East India Company vanquished the most powerful Indian rulers was that it worked with Indian businessmen, whereas its adversaries only sucked their subjects dry. The unequal, often uneasy, but mutually advantageous relationship changed with the mutiny. If we get past the mythology that has been constructed around 1857 in the past fifty years, that date is significant for two developments: it marked the end of contending, foraging, pillaging traditional Indian armed gangs, and it saw the liquidation of the East India Company. Indian business was then married to the company. It was a traditional Indian marriage in which the Indian wife was by no means an equal; no doubt, she had to cook and to press her husband's ankles, but she had a position in the household. With the death of the East India Company, the wife was widowed. The relations between the successor Imperial state and Indian business were always distant, and often not cordial. In general, the nine-tenths of a century of widowhood was good neither for Indian business nor for the Indian economy.

It was better for British businessmen who got an opportunity to enter India once the East India Company closed down. The British government's concern for their interests was a major reason why Independence was so delayed; and the latent conflict between them and Indian businessmen was not far below the surface in the movement for Independence. Gandhi made a call for *swadeshi* so that poor villagers might earn a living spinning and weaving at home; but the benefit went almost entirely to the textile mills of Mumbai and Ahmedabad. It was no wonder that *swadeshi* lured

▼ Prime Minister Rajiv Gandhi addressing the US Chamber of Commerce. During Rajiv's visit, a new confidence was forged between Indian and American business. Decades earlier, in 1962, when American tycoons asked his grandfather, Jawaharlal Nehru about his government's investment policy, Panditji responded by pointedly staring out of a window.

Indian businessmen then; nor that it is being resurrected with their support in these times of hardship.

Discrimination by the colonial government between British and Indian business, and the consequent estrangement of the latter, were a factor in the defeat and departure of the British. They left because in the end, they had alienated important sections of the bureaucracy and industry, and had no influential friends except the zamindars whose support was insufficient to hold the country.

The departure of the British signified a peaceful revolution. A revolution removes one ruling class and replaces it with another. But because India's attainment of Independence was peaceful, only a handful of British civil servants were replaced — by their brown colleagues. This transfer of power provided no room for the politicians who made the British leave; they had to make room for themselves.

A role into which they could have fitted themselves was that of promoters of national industry. For a while it appeared as if the Indian government would be business' benefactor. It used exchange control to make life difficult for British businesses; and it ended the managing agency system which dealt a death-blow to the great British managing agents of Calcutta but was easily evaded by Indian businessmen who renamed themselves 'promoters'. In the 1950s it seemed as if the Indian government and Indian business were ganging up to drive out British business and share the booty.

That is not however how things worked out, for Nehru had higher ambitions: he wanted the state to go into the business of redistribution: from the rich to the poor, from consumption to savings, from private profit to social gain, from capital-intensive to labour-intensive industry, from industry to agriculture, from towns to villages. Nehru had a patrician disdain for money. After the Sino-Indian skirmish of 1962, Nehru badly needed American support, and that support required that he be receptive to American business. A lunch was set up in New York with the most powerful tycoons of America. When asked about the Indian government's policy towards foreign investment, Nehru looked out of the window and commented on the weather. The way Nehru was brought up, one did not drink before midday, and did not talk about money either before or after midday, and that was also the way of the civil service. Its members savoured the evening *chota* peg in the various Gymkhana Clubs; *dhotiwallah*s — for that is how businessmen then dressed — were not pucca enough to join them. Nor were the *topiwallah*s; but since Congressmen did not drink, they did not miss the clubs.

Together, Nehruvian politicians and civil servants began to construct the socialist state with its meticulous caste system. Within industry, public enterprises were the highest born; licensing for

▼ A delegation of industrialists on a visit to the USA organized by FICCI. Among those in the picture with G. Mehta, Ambassador, are Ramnath Poddar, Shreyans Prasad Jain, G.D. Birla, S.S. Kanoria, Madanmohan Mangaldas, Madanmohan Ruia, B.D. Garware, C.H. Bhabha, Venkataswamy Naidu, Devi Prasad Goenka, S.L. Kirloskar, Babubhai Chinai, H.V.R. Iyengar, and G.L. Bansal.

them was mere -formality. Then came small industry which was free from licensing and loaded with concessions. It was followed by large industry which bore the brunt of licensing. Within large industry were those black sheep, the business houses; they were subject to the whims of the Monopolies and Restrictive Practices Commission. At the bottom of the pile were the untouchable multinationals. Since untouchability was banned in the country, multinationals were forcibly converted into a higher caste; the Foreign Exchange Regulation Act of 1973 made them reduce their equity in their Indian subsidiaries to less than 40 per cent and conferred upon them the status of honorary Indian companies. Politicians found a living as the priesthood of this caste system.

The priesthood had an exalted occupation but not a particularly lucrative one. Of the millions of aspiring politicians, the central and state legislatures accommodated no more than 6000. Even they were paid less than subsistence wages. They were rich if the commercial value of their accommodation, of the gas and telephone connections they could give, of the jobs they could wangle in the government was reckoned; without cashing these, they were as poor as church mice.

Civil servants, on the other hand, were handsomely paid well into the 1960s. That could not continue; normal human jealousy would correct the situation, and it did. Succeeding pay commissions reduced the real income of senior civil servants until they too began to feel the pinch. Their jealousy led to restraints on corporate incomes. Slowly, the income structure lost all connection with productivity and power — and that led to the emergence of the informal economy. Evasion of controls became a thriving industry which brought prosperity to promoters, politicians, and bureaucrats.

Thus, in a sense the country has come a full circle. The East India Company governed India and had a monopoly of its trade, but its directors as well as employees were so corrupt that this monopoly was riven by suzerain states and private traders. The British government removed the monopoly of trade, and replaced the corrupt monopoly of power by one that was so honest that it was quite impervious to the needs of development. Within half a century of its departure, our indigenous rulers have brought back the East India Company — a government that still

▼ A high-level FICCI delegation was led by S.S. Kanoria to the Federal Republic of Germany in October 1971. At a meeting with Chancellor Willy Brandt, S.S. Kanoria is seen along with Indian Counsellor Yashwant Sinha (currently India's Finance Minister), Charat Ram and Ambassador Kewal Singh. Those with their backs include H.P. Nanda and B.M. Ghia. The delegation preceded a visit by Prime Minister Indira Gandhi to Germany to win Brandt's support over the Bangladesh issue.

dominates the economy, but whose power is auctioned piecemeal to all comers.

The difference between the days of the company and today is that a century and a half ago, the world economy could still be regarded as a zero-sum game. Sustained growth of productivity was unknown. The industrial revolution had touched only Britain; even there, Dickensian poverty still prevailed. A son expected to do no better than his father. In that age, robbing someone was the quickest way of getting rich, and defence of what one had was the foremost industry. Today, however, we are at the end of half a century of unprecedented growth across the world. We have examples of our own neighbouring countries which started as poor as us and have prospered beyond our dreams within a generation. Their success is the success of their business: of business afforded a nourishing environment by their governments. Today we know that we need not, cannot, should not, any longer be run by an East India Company. A better relationship between business and government is possible, and necessary.

Whether under the East India Company, the Imperial government, or our Sovereign Secular Socialist Democratic Republic, the relationship between the state and business has been a patron–client relationship in which the government exercised overwhelming influence over business. This could have been called the Indian mode of feudalism: even ten years ago it seemed impossible that this relationship would change. But then came the Manmohan–Rao reforms, the removal of industrial licensing, the dismantling of import controls, and the abolition of the Controller of Capital Issues. There was an imperceptible but unmistakable change — a change made palpable by the last two elections. Indira Gandhi used to appoint collectors who would simply inform industrialists how much they had to be paid if they wanted to stay in business. Now ex-prime ministers wait on industrialists before an election, and the first thing prime ministers do on assuming power is to meet presidents of apex industry associations. Chief ministers travel to financial capitals of the world to lure industry to their states. This may still be a patrimonial state, but the state is no longer the patron.

Politicians are the clients, but industry is not united, and the clients have no single patron.

How might this relationship develop? How should it? Surely it is of no advantage if politicians and businessmen combine only to exploit the country; the relationship should lead to faster development, to a more prosperous, peaceful, and just society. How can we move towards one? The world exhibits many varieties of state–business relationship, but no unequivocally superior model.

In Britain, the pioneer of industrialization and the world's foremost power for much of the nineteenth century, industry had little political influence. The vagaries of its electoral system ensured that its parliament was dominated by landlords. The constituencies were reorganized and franchise extended in due course; but industry as such was never a powerful influence in politics, even though the government promoted its interests abroad. Finance and trade were the sinews of Britain's economic power. Even today, when Britain's role has shrunk so greatly, London remains a financial metropolis and its financial institutions shelter quite a number of its politicians. The British doctrine of laissez-faire was not a close reflection of the global relationship between government and industry; but at home it largely reflected the reality.

The connection between government and business has been more open in the United States. Businessmen finance politicians, although increasingly severe restrictions have been placed in recent decades on the dependence of a politician on wealthy individual donors. Conversely, politicians openly espouse the cause of particular businessmen. More important, the US government has been a major buyer of military hardware, and according to the American tradition, has always bought it from private industry, leading to the emergence of what has been termed the military–industrial complex. That did not, however, prevent the US government from drastically cutting down its military purchases in the 1990s once the cold war ended. The United States is so large, political power within it is so diffused, and the mutual independence of the three arms of government — the executive, legislative, and judicial branches — is so established, that industry remains largely uninterfered with, and its influence on politics is marginal. Industrial monopolies have been ruthlessly broken up. Like the British government, the US government has promoted the interests of American industry abroad, but domestically, government and business have lived their separate lives.

Their relationship has been much closer in East and South East Asian countries. But here too, partnership would be too simple a description of the patterns. In Japan, big business was close to the Liberal Democratic Party which ruled for most of the post-War

Dedicated to the Environment

With Indian industry on the fast track of growth and committed to industrial liberalization, the pace of development is expected to accelerate further. Yet, environmental irresponsibility will not be condoned: India has a global commitment to Agenda 21, adopted at the Rio Conference, to usher progress into the twenty-first century entirely compatible with environmental aspirations. The big challenge before industry is to respond to government initiatives so that the economy picks up and the advantages of industrialization are passed on to the common man. Indian industry is aware of its responsibilities and is committed to sustainable development.

The reason for the upswing in the implementation of sustainable development practices include pressures due to mounting legislation, increasing realization that pollution prevention means good business, as also increased public awareness. With greater economic liberalization, there is a move towards the adoption of an environment managing systems, i.e. ISO 14000. Even the judiciary is playing an active role in enforcing environment friendly systems. At the extreme, there are closures of industries and efforts are on to decongest cities from polluting industries.

With the Indian economy poised for rapid growth in the coming years, it is expected that the demand for environmental technology and systems will be on the rise. The market in India for environmental business in pollution control equipment is estimated to grow at approximately 10 per cent per annum. The future looks bright in private sector due to the financial inputs and active participation of various multinational and bilateral agencies.

Though compliance level of medium- and large-scale industries is increasing rapidly, units in the small-scale sector do not have sufficient technical expertise and financial ability to control environmental pollution created by them. Problems associated with hazardous waste management need to be addressed by them. Some of the industrial units within the small-scale sector affecting the environment are electroplating, pulp and paper, secondary metal processing, tanneries, foundries, dye and dye intermediates, paints, inorganic chemicals, drugs, pesticides, dyeing and hosiery, and edible oil.

There is imminent need to pay adequate attention to proper handling and disposal of garbage and other solid wastes. Vehicular pollution is also an area of increasing concern, though pollution checks are becoming more stringent. The urban environment is increasingly becoming a matter of concern due to the health hazards it inflicts on our citizens.

period; the funding of individual politicians, usually by obscure or shady companies, has occasionally burst into the open. More important, it was the tradition for senior civil servants to be given well-paid honorific positions in business after retirement from government — a favour which no doubt reciprocated earlier favours. Below the *keiretsu*, the big business houses, were a mass of small firms which had no part in deals with the government. It was the intense competition among these small firms and their consequent low costs that made Japan the economic power that it became. Eventually these companies, which were the fount of Japan's growing prosperity, ran out of their dynamism, and therewith ended Japan's miracle.

▼ A joint venture between the public sector oil major, HPCL, and an industrial business house, Indian Rayon Group, the Mangalore Refineries and Petrochemicals Ltd was commissioned ahead of schedule in 1996. Its capacity is now being expanded from 3m. tonnes to 9m. tonnes and will be in place by 1999.

Korea constructed an even closer relationship between the government and big business. There the government used cheap credit from nationalized banks to subsidize favoured conglomerates and industries; in return, politicians and bureaucrats received bribes. When domestic savings proved inadequate, foreign credit was similarly doled out to favourites. The result was a high degree of concentration. Eventually, over-borrowing led to widespread bankruptcy and brought the rapid growth to an end.

Taiwan, on the other hand, was ruled by the followers of Chiang Kai Shek who escaped from China when it was taken over by the communists. The local people, who formed the backbone of business, routinely evaded taxes; conversely, the government sought to milk them. Here it was the lack of nexus between government and business that led to spectacular growth — growth more impressive than in Japan and Korea.

Japan, Korea, and Taiwan discouraged foreign direct investment. In contrast, China and Thailand welcomed it; China even insisted that the foreign share of equity in export business must be at least a quarter. In both countries, the ruling classes had little to do with industry. They took bribes and invested them mostly in real estate. The relationship between government and business in both countries was very similar to that in India, except that both were very open to trade and foreign investment.

An ideal relationship between business and government must entail that the government espouses the interests of national business without favouring any particular businessman, and that the relationship is in the national interest: that it leads to rapid, steady growth. No country fulfils these two criteria forever; few have fulfilled them for any length of time. We cannot build the right relationship by emulating other countries; we need to find our own way.

There are basically three problems to be solved. First, how is the influence of sectional interests on the government to be minimized? Second, how is politics to be sanitized? And finally, how can the government be made responsive to the voice of business?

Two types of societies have managed to minimize the influence of sectional interests on government. The first are the major Western countries: the United States, the United Kingdom, post-War Germany. Essentially, these countries have reduced the influence of business upon government by reducing the influence of government upon business. The more government intervenes in business, the more necessary it becomes for business in its self-interest to interfere with government. Shorn of its philosophical mystique, this is what laissez-faire is all about. A democratic government is bound to be an arena in which interests contend and come to a compromise, tidy or otherwise. The only way of keeping business interests out of contention is to make it unnecessary for them to enter the arena.

▼ Politician as poet: Prime Minister Atal Bihari Vajpayee recently released a book of his poems, *Geet Naya Gata Hoon*. Under his leadership, the country is seeking new horizons in a changing world.

Post-War Japan and Korea illustrate the other type of society where sectional interests have been kept at bay. Here, the dominant business interests — *keiretsu* in Japan and *chaebol* in Korea — are so few and evenly matched that none predominates over the state. This equilibrium is fortuitous, and cannot be reproduced. Besides, India is a more heterogeneous country: it has many business houses, more are always emerging, and the inequalities among them are such that an equilibrium of influence cannot be expected. Hence the only solution applicable here is laissez-faire: the government must minimize interference with business. This is what internal liberalization represents. It means, for instance, that small industry reservations, concessions, and privileges should be dismantled; that the myriad rates of duties should be replaced by only one rate of customs duty, one rate of excise duty, and one rate of sales tax; that barriers to the movement of goods and people, such as octroi, taxes on inter-state trade, and son-of-the-soil policies should be done away with, that property rights should be uniformly recognized and enforced, and that the standards of infrastructure — roads, ports, airports, telecommunications — across the country should be harmonized.

There is debate on how far this internal liberalization should extend to foreign enterprises on Indian soil. The Indian answer has never been a clear one; even in the days of extreme nationalism, the answer was that foreigners could take a minority share in joint ventures with Indian promoters. This answer needs to be modified because the promoter is disappearing as a factor in policy. He should have disappeared thirty years ago, when the managing agency system was abolished. But the nexus between some promoters and politicians led to their continuance, and they created an entire underground mechanism for rewarding themselves at the expense of companies. After failed experiments with state-led rescue of sick enterprises, changes in management through mergers, acquisitions and takeovers have now taken primacy. It is recognized that a company has an existence independent of the promoter; it would be conceivable to take away the promoter's right to buy, sell, or change stakes. In the circumstances, restrictions on his right to sell the stake to foreigners would only reduce its value. To do so only to protect competitors who fear competition would be even less desirable. The solution

▼ Line up of cars at the Maruti Suzuki factory in Gurgaon, Haryana. The opening of the automobile sector is a recent phenomenon, but the government tie-up with a Japanese manufacturer in the 1980s proved that such collaborations not only worked successfully, but were in fact essential if appropriate technology had to be imported to India.

▲ Chief Minister Jyoti Basu (standing, right) and R.P. Goenka (seated, right) at the sigining of a memorandum of understanding with Rolls Royce, UK, in 1995. The agreement was signed on behalf of West Bengal Industrial Development Corporation by its Chairman, Somnath Chatterjee (middle).

lies in re-recognizing promoters, separating management from ownership, and reversing the policy of insisting that promoters must have a minimum stake in a company. Promoters should have the choice of running companies or living on returns on investment in companies, and investors should be able to change underperforming promoters. Just as foreigners can make portfolio investments in Indian companies without taking over management, it should be possible for them to take over management under fixed-term contracts without investing. Once ownership and management are legally divorced, the question of foreign investment will lose its emotional edge.

Next, the question of cleaning up politics. We should be halfway towards achieving this aim if the Indian state ceases to be interventionist and to play favourites. But to complete it, it is necessary to make politicians less purchasable. Some politicians have proposed state funding of election expenses. Some business houses have proposed neutral political funding mechanisms: for instance, the Tatas set up a political fund for member companies before the 1998 elections from which parties would be funded in proportion to their seats in the previous Parliament.

Before either the government or business consider funding politicians, we need to strengthen parties as institutions that run governments. The way to do so is to move to proportional representation based on the list system, with a high threshold of vote percentage for a party to get into a legislature. Once the list system cuts down the number of parties, the first two or three can be funded by the state on a sufficient scale to allow them to build up constituency-level offices; but further funding must come from members and patrons. Instead of letting wealthy people influence politics through i n politicians, it would be better to give wealth a direct share in power by electing a part of the legislature on votes from income tax payers in proportion to the tax they pay. If those who pay taxes are given a voice in Parliament, they will be induced to pay taxes, and they will help in putting the revenue to good use. In this way, India can be made a democracy of bread-earners as well as of citizens.

The Future Lies in Services

Swaminathan S. Anklesaria Aiyar

The Federation of Indian Chambers of Commerce and Industry (FICCI) may need to call itself the Federation of Indian Chambers of Commerce and Services (FICCS) to catch up with the coming realities of the twenty-first century. Make no mistake, the future lies in services much more than in industry.

Most people who automatically equate business with manufacturing need to take note of the latest trends in India and abroad. If you study the advertisements appearing in *The Economic Times* over a week, you will find that, excluding government advertisments and tenders, up to 90 per cent of them come from services or information technology, and very few from manufacturing. This would have been unthinkable ten years ago. The trend is confirmed by economic data. Of all developing countries of the South East Asia, those that have become richest are Hong Kong and Singapore, with per capita incomes in excess of $ 22,000. Once these countries were associated with garment sweatshops and labour-intensive goods, and at that time their share of services was low. They have become super rich today only because services account for a whopping 83 per cent of Hong Kong's GDP, and 64 per cent of Singapore's.

▼ India has seen a sharp growth in the number of international trade fairs, post-liberalization, with companies, even governments and countries, wanting to participate and interact with the Indian industry.

India is transforming into a service economy. In 1995, the share of services in the GDP was 41 per cent, well above the 29 per cent share of industry (including construction). The share of services has risen steadily from 36 per cent in 1980 to 41 per cent in 1995. Since industry grew rapidly in this period, this implies that the growth in services has been even faster, as the *World Development Report 1997* has shown.

Despite this, India is actually a laggard in services which were emasculated for decades by a mistaken socialist belief that they were no more than an adjunct to manufacturing. The share of services in India's GDP remains lower than in those of its neighbours in South Asia. As against India's ratio of 41 per cent, that of Pakistan is 50 per cent, Bangladesh 52 per cent, and Sri Lanka 52 per cent. India's services-to-GDP ratio looks emasculated even in comparison with Sub-Saharan Africa (48 per cent) or Latin

▲ Combining skill with aesthetics, Indian designers and architects are capable of putting together projects, thanks to the infrastructure made available by companies like Parry's whose innovative tiles are being exported, besides having a large share of the Indian market.

America (55 per cent). It looks favourable only in comparison with low-income countries as defined in the *World Development Report* of the World Bank. Even this is because the average of low income countries is dragged down by China's astonishingly low ratio of 31 per cent, a Maoist legacy which is being rapidly jettisoned.

In high income countries, the services-to-GDP ratio was 58 per cent way back in 1980, and rose to 66 per cent by 1995. The share of industry, by contrast, declined from 37 per cent to 33 per cent. By 1995, the share of services was double that of industry, an indication of where India's future lies in the next century.

Once regarded as non-tradeable and restricted to the home market, world exports of services have been rising faster than exports of goods (10 per cent annually in 1985–95 for services against 8 per cent annually for goods). According to Dr Kalyan Raipuria (*Economic and Political Weekly*, 27 December 1997), global service exports now account for an astonishing $ 1200 bn, against $ 4800 bn for goods. No wonder then that liberalization of trade in services has become an important agenda of the World Trade Organization. The agreement on financial services in December 1997 covers 95 per cent of the world market in financial services, which adds up to $ 18,000 bn in securities, $ 38,000 bn in

▲ Rapid computerization and the availability of an organized workforce could make India a service centre for operations with regard to billing and direct mail services, not only in the case of companies in India, but also for global companies operating in different parts of the world.

international bank lending, and $ 2500 bn in worldwide insurance premia. The WTO emphasis on financial services tends to obscure the huge importance and potential of Indian service exports in other areas.

India's greatest comparative advantage lies not in manufacturing, the scope for which is quite limited, but in services. The labour content of manufacturing is dropping steadily with automated technology. In Maruti Udyog, for instance, the labour content of a car is below 2.5 per cent. In the bulk of modern industry, it is below 10 per cent. By contrast, the labour content of services can approach 100 per cent. This is where India's cheap skills give it the biggest comparative advantage. The computer, Internet, and modern telecommunications mean that service tasks can now be subcontracted across the globe.

We have already seen the shift of jobs in manufacturing from high-income to low-income countries. In the twenty-first century we should increasingly see the shift of services from high-income to low-income countries. The shift requires massive investment in communications and an overhauling of regulations to minimize impediments and make truly global operations simple. Provided we do this, we can attract billions in the form of foreign investment, earn billions more through exports, and provide employment to millions.

In one sense, we are already major exporters of services without being aware of it. Remittances from Indians abroad totalled no less than $ 11.7 bn in 1996–7, against official exports of $ 33 bn (which also include $ 1 bn of software exports). The remittances represent, in significant measure, the export of labour, a service export involving temporary migration. Part of the remittances also represent the return of flight capital, but labour exports form the core. The scope for increasing labour exports is enormous, yet little attention has been paid to this sector. We need to focus on promoting temporary migration in the form of fixed-term labour-intensive contracts. Temporary migrants send home large remittances, sometimes virtually their entire income.

Fixed-period work contracts are already standard practice in the Gulf, where contractors are allowed to bring in foreign labour under strict supervision that ensures the workers go back at the end of their contract period. In Libya, even the municipal cleaning of streets has been undertaken by foreign labour contractors. However, such contracts are not allowed in Western countries like the USA which says that people who enter the country even with a short-term visa find it easy to stay on indefinitely because of its emphasis on civil rights and privacy. Our attempt must be to focus on gradually increasing the scope for contract labour exports. The more we establish a track record of fully repatriating contract labour from the Gulf, the better placed we will be to argue for greater labour contracting in the OECD.

▼ A departmental store in New Delhi. Indians are excellent at providing services, and could run many such utilities in the future in all parts of the world.

Population growth has slowed to a trickle in OECD countries (save in countries where immigration is still substantial). In Germany, the population has been falling for years. Even as the birth rate plummets, the aged are living longer and life expectancy in the OECD may gradually rise to 85. In Germany, pensioners threaten to outnumber the labour force by the year 2025. These demographic changes are an important reason for the relentless shift from goods to services. Through most of history, living standards rose hardly at all, and population growth was the greatest factor driving consumer demand. All consumers need basic goods, so there was constantly expanding demand for such goods. However, when population growth slows to a trickle (as in the OECD), the demand for basic goods slows too, since there is a limit to the amount of coffee, tea, cloth, TVs, or cars any person will purchase. The post-War baby-boom generation has given way to the baby-bust generation, and this is changing the entire pattern of demand. As people grow richer, they demand more services. Families do less work in-house and contract out more (dining at restaurants instead of home greatly increases the demand for services). Travel, tourism, and entertainment take on an increasing share of consumption. So do medical and educational services.

▲ Consumer demand has seen a tremendous rise in outlets, such as this one in Bangalore. Most goods and facilities will become available under one roof in the future.

This has major implications for India. After years of neglecting exports, we must of course catch up, but we must also realize that we need increasingly to export services rather than goods. This includes, of course, traditional service income from tourism

▼ An art gallery in New Delhi. India's creative and intellectual initiative has not been tapped yet. Both artists as well as those who provide the link services, will find a more business-friendly environment in the future.

through hotels, travel, and trade. But we need also to focus on two non-traditional areas with enormous potential—health and education. Indeed, we need to see health and education as major industries, not just social services.

The aged constitute a market for health care. In the US, health care accounts for 14 per cent of the GDP, not far short of the 20 per cent for manufacturing. The longer Americans live, the more they spend on health, making it one of the fastest-growing segments of its economy, and this is true of all developed economies. Indeed, health care costs are now a major issue of political debate in OECD countries since their rise is squeezing budgets everywhere. Layfolk might think that doctors and hospitals constitute the bulk of health spending. In reality, the real budgetary crunch facing the OECD relates to nurses, not doctors or hospitals. Old people visit doctors and hospitals in times of crisis, but in between they need constant looking after, sometimes on a day-to-day basis. Experts like Joshua Wiener of the Brookings Institution estimate that fully half of those above 65 will need some nursing care, and most will require at least two years of nursing, the disabled much more. A paper by Wiener in the mid-1980s estimated that at the time the USA had 4.5 m. disabled elderly, and by the year 2040, would have 8m. elderly disabled. Add those from Europe and Japan, and the number in the OECD will approach 20 m. These disabled will generate an enormous number of man-years of work since, even with some mechanization, at least one man-year of work will be needed to take care of each disabled person. That means a potential 20 million

The World in a Country

It's certainly no secret that India makes the largest number of films in the world, with Hollywood a distant second, and film-based programmes capture all the TRP ratings on the small screen. It also has one of the world's largest English language readerships, making it a publishing behemoth. It has a fashion and glamour industry that's young by international standards, and only just coming to terms with a nation that refuses to be bullied into following trends, instead setting its own, and on its own terms. And all of this happens in a country that is a traveller's manna, 'the one country', Mark Twain wrote so succinctly, 'every person wants to see, and having seen once, cannot give up for all the sights of the world'.

An immense 32,68,000 sq km, India's geography is as rich as its history. Here are mountain ranges, some among the oldest in the world, others the highest; there are the icy deserts of the Tibetan plateau and the scorching ones of the Thar; ancient rivers meander through her vast expanse, some still torrential and powerful as they change their course, others lost to time and antiquity; across her plains are forests where the wildlife includes species typical only to the country, or extinct elsewhere. Here are people and cuisines, cultures and traditions that offer the perfect backdrop for a holiday; tourism provides the country among its highest foreign exchange revenues. While the infrastructure needs strengthening, the growth in business travel has ensured that the international airports are always busy with over 40 international carriers flying the route.

The Indian film industry is not only professional, and known for its excellence in the entertainment business, it also spans generations of movie-goers in the extravaganzas it has proved capable of packing on celluloid. While centred mostly in Mumbai and Chennai, it is also active in Calcutta, while studios in Noida, close to Delhi, are helping it emerge as a powerful centre for television producers. The cinema movement in India has been mostly escapist, though a strong parallel movement has resulted in extraordinary art films. Film makers of the class of Satyajit Ray have had a legendary following internationally, but more recently those such as Shekhar Kapur have been invited by prominent British and Hollywood producers to make films on Western themes and subjects. Mira Nair's films have enjoyed international viewership.

With a nation that pays homage to cinema, it is but natural that the glamour industry too has a large potential. In recent years, on the occasions when Indian women have not walked off with the Miss World and Miss Universe crowns, they have been coming within runners-up distance with their poise and confidence. Taking them there is an industry of grooming consultants and aerobics instructors, but more visible on stage is the effort of the Indian fashion designer whose work is now gaining international recognition. While traditionally Western couturists have had tailoring outfits in India, now the Indian designer is finding a place on the designer racks in crowded stores in Western shopping malls.

Part of the reason for the proliferation of the glamour and fashion industry has been the recent spurt in newspaper supplements and magazines. A record four business dailies are published in India, the highest in any country of the world. The Indian print media has had a long history in the country, with links that date back to the times of the freedom struggle. Editions of the premier newsmagazines also have international editions. Indo-Anglian writing has been thrust into the limelight, with Indian writers winning or being nominated for prestigious awards such as the Booker and the Commonwealth.

▼ Indian hotels are now ranked among the best in the world for both the quality of its services and human resources. As tourism in India grows, Indian managers will find greater opportunities to work in the hospitality industry that will come to rely on their professional skills.

jobs in looking after the disabled alone. It will make nursing of the disabled a far bigger employer than all the car factories in the world. put together. The disabled run up huge bills for nursing. The Medicaid programme in the US, aimed at poor people, was initially launched to help finance medicines and hospital fees, but by the mid-1980s, no less than 43 per cent of Medicaid was swallowed up by nursing. Wiener estimated that the proportion of Medicaid recipients using nursing was only 5 per cent, yet they spent almost as much money as the other 95 per cent who only needed medicines and hospitalization.

India needs to cash in on this demand for nursing services. One way would be to organize nurses on fixed-term contracts to go to OECD countries. There will initially be resistance to this, but India needs to forge links with medical insurance companies in OECD countries which desperately want to reduce their liabilities. Cheap labour from India and other developing countries will certainly do that. Note further that, as international transport costs drop, it can become economic for the elderly disabled from the OECD to come to India to be looked after. There will initially be resistance to this too, yet many American families are going bankrupt looking after

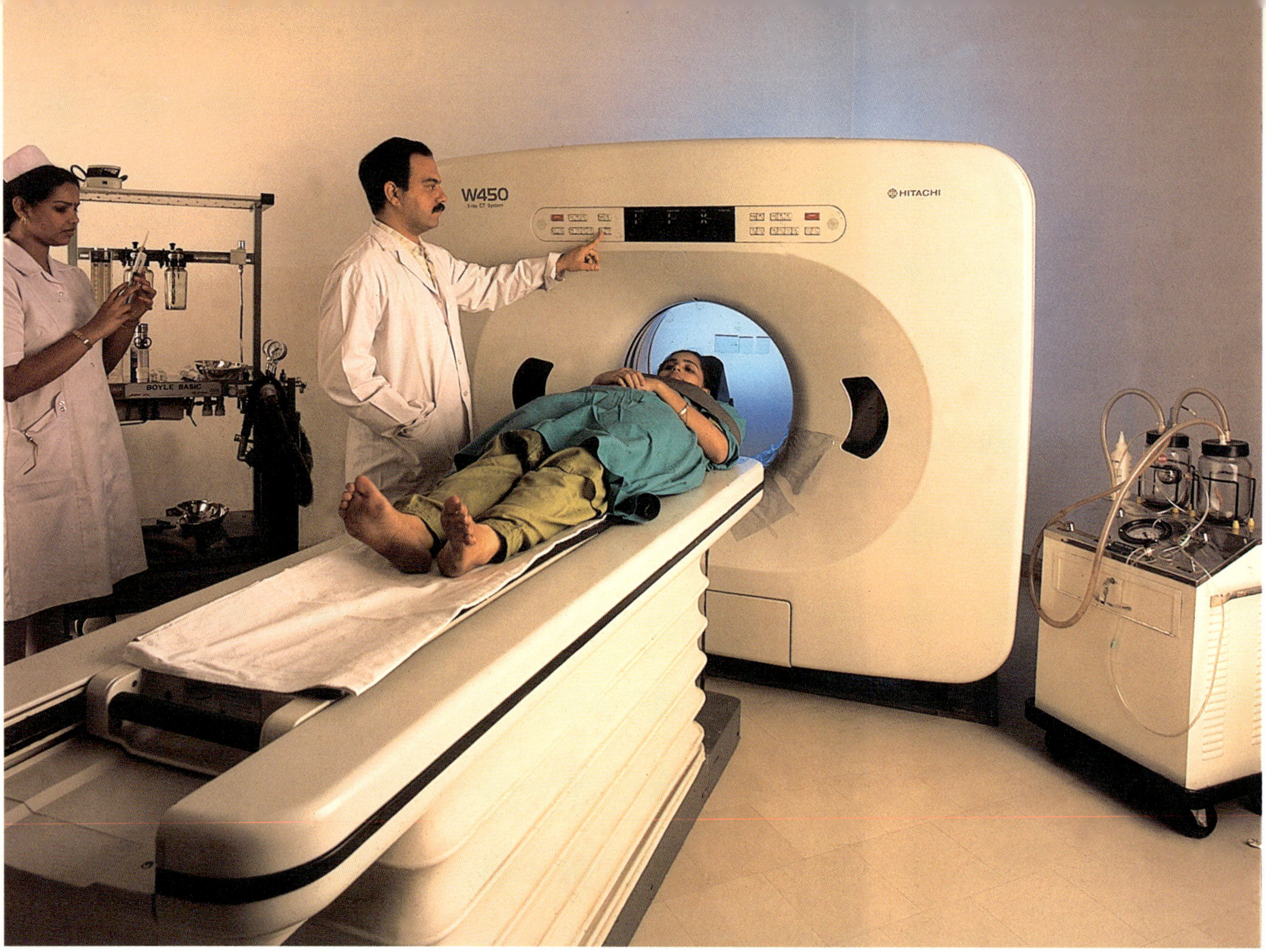

disabled members. India will need, in collaboration with foreign medical insurance companies, to set up world class facilities. The present standards of Indian hospitals and nursing homes will simply not suffice. We have top class doctors and nurses; what we lack is the overall administrative ambience.

While on the topic of health care, India also has the cheap skills suitable for large-scale R&D in pharmaceuticals. Because of our highly restrictive patents act, foreign companies do not wish to even introduce new drugs in India, leave alone use this country as an R&D base. According to a recent evaluation by McKinsey, the cost of producing generic drugs in India is 45 per cent lower than in OECD countries, and the cost of R&D is 75 per cent lower. An Indian Ph.D. researcher can be hired at one-fifth the cost of an American with similar qualifications. India also provides scope for clinical trials of drugs, which take years. Even with substantial investments to meet the GCP (Good Clinical Practices) standards of the US, clinical trials in India should be 85 per cent cheaper than in the US. For some tropical diseases like malaria and hepatitis,

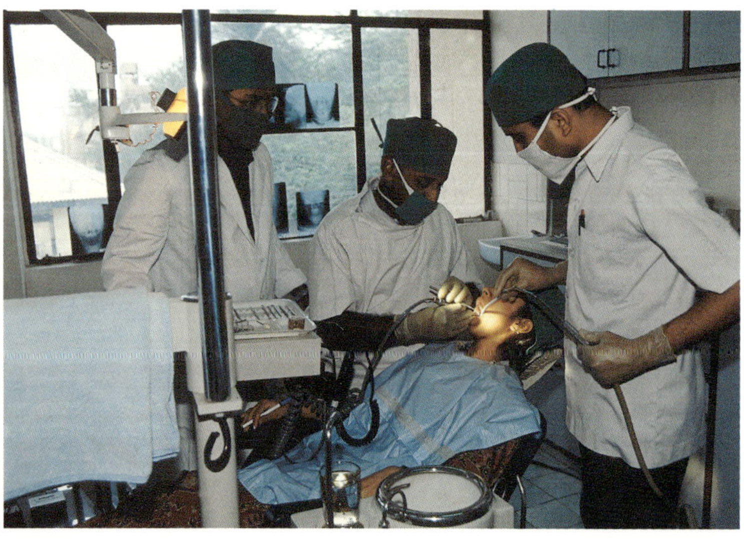

▼ VSNL building, Chandigarh. More lives have been changed over the last decade, the result of improved telecommunication services, than in all the years since Independence.

(previous page):

▲ A cat scan being performed at a modern hospital in Haryana. With populations in the West living longer and demanding more services, in times to come Indian medical facilities could be in demand.

▼ Other than opening up the country for health care facilities, India could also try and become a base for clinical trials of tropical diseases. Should this happen, the cost advantage over similar US clinics could prove a major source of foreign exchange earnings.

India is in any case the obvious place for trials. Provided we amend our patent laws and remove impediments that still plague foreign investment, this area can become a big forex earner.

Clerks may not look like obvious export material, but with modern communications, a supervisor in Chicago can supervise clerks in India better than a supervisor in India itself with traditional paper-based methods. Instead of having a babu laboriously shuffling paper, we need highly skilled clerks operating computerized networks. These super-babus can do the clerical work of the whole world sitting in India. Credit card companies handle enormous volumes of bills. Global stock markets and currency markets have a staggering volume of transactions, all of which can be handled by people sitting in India. This means, of course, competitive, world class communications, and means abandoning the costly monopoly of Videsh Sanchar Nigam Ltd. A big advantage of using super-babus would be that they would belong to the managerial cadre and so not be subject to our restrictive labour laws that inhibit foreign investment in other areas.

Yet another area of huge export potential is education. Many countries spend up to 5 per cent of their GDP on education, and the vast bulk of this is on teaching staff. Traditionally, all teaching in a country has been done locally but with modern communications, video conferencing is already well established, and a teacher in one city can teach and interact with students in other countries. The costs are still high, but are dropping fast, so cheap Indian teaching skills can be harnessed globally. Such teaching will not be suitable for primary education, which will typically be in the local language of foreign countries, but can be used for several sorts of training in the English language where India has a clear advantage. Even if India gets just 0.01 per cent of students in other countries, that will run into millions.

Apart from telecom education, India needs to set up many more centres of excellence. Our Indian Institutes of Technology and Indian Institutes of Management are already world class, and their graduates readily find employment in the global market place, but these are government-run institutes catering to Indians. To tap the global market, we need privately funded institutes with global standards, charging global fees. These can attract students from most other Asian countries, and will constitute a handsome service export.

The cost of a year's education in an American university is around \$ 30,000 today. If India can offer something similar for say \$ 10,000, that will be a bonanza by our standards, yet it will be cheap for candidates from Africa and Asia. We are currently stepping up our computer programming skills, and the teacher network for this can be used to help educate foreign students too.

The Battle of Brands

T.C.A. Srinivasa-Raghavan

During the 1990s, a new furrow has appeared on the brows of Indian businessmen: will Indian brands survive the onslaught of foreign ones? How will the consumer respond to the inevitable freeing of consumer good imports early in the next decade? Will he desert Indian products in favour of foreign ones or will he stay loyal to domestic brands?

Until 1991, when the Indian economy began to liberalize its trade policies, Indian brands – defined as brands that were owned by Indian companies and had been entirely developed here–faced no competition from foreign ones. As such they were safe.

Nothing illustrates this better than the market for soft drinks in which entirely Indian brands like Campa Cola, Thums Up, Limca, and Gold Spot ruled. There was no Coke, no Pepsi. That this had happened because Coca Cola had been ordered out in 1977 is not relevant. The fact is that for about fifteen years, there were only Indian brands in the Indian soft drinks market.

Then, as liberalization took hold, along came Pepsi to be followed a little later by Coke. The result: within a couple of years, Indian brands have all but vanished from the Indian market place, and have been replaced by Pepsi and Coke. Indeed, in some cases, even the companies that produced them have disappeared into the waiting maws of foreign competitors. Hence the worry: Is this the fate that awaits all or most Indian brands? And the answer: Not necessarily.

After an initial swing in favour of foreign brands, the Indian consumer has regained his normal rational balance. In market after market in which Indian and foreign brands compete, he has demonstrated that what he wants is value for money. Where an Indian brand is able to provide it, he has stuck to it, much to the surprise and chagrin of foreign brands. In white goods – refrigerators, washing machines, etc. – and TVs where, after some early hesitation, the consumer has rejected foreign brands in favour of Indian ones, Indian brands continue to account for well over 80 per cent of the market. Indeed, such has been the experience of foreign brands that several of them are reconsidering their strategies. India, it has become clear, is no pushover on brand wars.

The best example of the way Indian brands have held their own over foreign ones comes from the market for personal computers (PCs). This was one market where it was widely feared that the advent of foreign brands would wipe out Indian ones, but this fear has proved unfounded. Indian brands are competing fiercely with MNCs in the desktop PC market, providing a neck-and-neck race between top Indian brands and the MNCs, and the aggressive assembled products are not far behind, offering both Indian and the foreign brands fierce competition. Indian brands account for 29 per cent of the market with MNC brands like Compaq and IBM gobbling up another 24 per cent. The rest falls to unbranded, assembled PCs. The important question, of course,

in the market for PCs or for any other product, is whether Indian brands will succeed in holding their own or will eventually succumb to the greater financial muscle of the foreign brand-owners. Already, for instance, market surveys are predicting that the share of foreign brands is going to climb at the expense of first, the grey market for unbranded PCs, and then branded Indian PCs.

Could this happen with other products too? Will well-known Indian brands of soaps, edible oils, clothes, shoes, TVs, music systems, chocolates all vanish from the market place? As mentioned earlier, this is unlikely so long as Indian brands continue to give value for money. This is the critical element in brand survival because, Indian or foreign, unless the consumer is satisfied that his money is well spent, he will not stay loyal to a brand. In that sense, the Indian consumer is perhaps more savvy than his counterparts elsewhere in other emerging markets. Liberalization in India has not led to wholesale destruction of Indian brands. The key to success, Indian brand managers are realizing, is in quality and value for money. Wherever Indian companies producing branded goods have been able to provide both, there Indian brands have held. Where they have not done so, the foreign brand has taken over.

Another dimension is brand positioning, that is, the battle for the customer's mind. Often, superior Indian brands have lost ground because they have been positioned wrongly. In some cases, when they have corrected the early errors, they have managed to regain their markets.

So, do Indian firms have the savvy that is required of them to position their brands accurately in the market place? Will they be able to outdo foreign firms on the market research that is required and the patience that must accompany the exercise? The answer is that some Indian firms are qualified and some are not, but on balance it would seem that more of them have the necessary skills than not. There is, therefore, not as much cause for concern as is believed. Indian brands, provided they get their strategies right, will survive.

There is, of course, another dimension to the debate. This is the case of brands that are owned by foreign firms but are seen as entirely Indian brands, e.g. Dalda. Its owner, Hindustan Lever Ltd, is a multinational which sells many well-known international brands in India, but Dalda is uniquely Indian. Is it then an Indian or a foreign brand?

There is then the issue of upmarket and downmarket brands. When the survival or otherwise of India brands is discussed, it is generally in the context of the upmarket ones. Yet the fact is that the Indian market is deeply layered and that at every layer there can be several million consumers who make their own judgements about quality, price, and brand value. So what about the brands that occupy the lowest ends of the market, defined as market segments where consumers have incomes of less than Rs 60,000 per year? Indeed, what about those who occupy segments between this income level and around Rs 1,20,000 per year? The chances are that, barring exceptional cases, it will take foreign brands decades to make inroads into these lower layers. Therefore the brands that occupy these layers are safe for a long while to come.

▲▼ Increasingly, conveniences have begun to be offered in India, from automated banking facilities to telecommunications, bringing it at par with the global environment. Along with the wide spread of universities, and the reach of the English language, India could easily become an exporter of learning through the setting up of universities for the international market.

(facing page):

▲▼ Worldwide, entertainment is one of the fastest growing industries, a potential we have only just begun to realize. From television channels and their programming *(above)*, to the hosting of international pageants such as Miss World *(below)*, India has the talent and the resources to package entertainment on a gigantic scale.

In the process, we will upgrade our own teaching skills, and this will have a salutary effect on local teaching standards too. In education, as in all exports, being in the global market will improve domestic quality and responsiveness to consumer demand.

One of the fastest-growing service sectors the world over has been entertainment. We are just beginning to realize our export potential in this area. India has long been the largest producer of films in the world, and also a big audio producer. Traditionally, the focus has been on the domestic market, but over the years our film exports have been rising. This is due largely to the growing numbers of Indians abroad, but also in significant measure to the acceptability of Indian films in countries ranging from Indonesia to Nigeria. The tightening of intellectual property rights has come as a boon to video and music exports from India.

Before it was declared an industry, a major bottleneck in the film enterprise in India was that it was often financed by the underworld, and sometimes payments were in black money. This constituted a major barrier to the attainment of its full potential. We need the rise of Indian equivalents of Warner Brothers and Walt Disney, huge corporations quoted on stock exchanges and capable of raising billions on the capital markets. Amitabh Bachchan Corporation Ltd was India's first attempt at corporate entertainment, but it flopped. We must, however, pursue this path if we aspire to become a global entertainment power. Fortunately, corporatization is proceeding well in both advertising and TV, which potentially could be larger than even the film industry. Indian advertising companies have won international awards, and

there is scope for shifting a significant amount of global advertising to India to take advantage of cheap skills here. India should be a producer of global advertising, not just of advertisements for the domestic market.

Satellite TV is here to stay. The success of Zee TV's and Star TV's resort to dubbing English programmes in Hindi proves that we need not worry about being conquered by foreign culture. On the contrary, Indians are already beginning to change the course of the BBC and CNN, for which they have begun to do an increasing share of programming. To begin with, much of this work is for local consumption, but in the long run an increasing number of Indian producers will be able to produce for the world market. Here again, we need a more liberal atmosphere. Curbs on foreign investment must be relaxed, censorship must go, uplinking should be free of impediments. That alone will enable true globalization and help us capture a decent slice of the world TV software market.

This is an illustrative list of service exports, and by no means a comprehensive one. Here are a few more straws in the wind:

▲ Production studios are equipped with hardware and software of international quality, and with satellites beaming professionally produced Indian programmes, it is only a matter of time, and the easing of curbs, before they develop into a global market.

Varun Shipping, an Indian company, is diversifying into the training of foreign ship-cruises in matters like hospitality, food, and beverages. In principle, Indian companies can undertake such training for all other areas of tourism and hospitality.

Malaysia has contracted the service and maintenance of its Russian MiG planes to India because it can do the job much more cheaply. This principle can be extended to civilian aircraft too.

Hindustan Shipyard Ltd lost money for decades in its attempt to make ships, but has since diversified into ship repairs, and has proved much more successful. OECD countries have become use-and-throw societies because high labour costs make repairs too expensive to undertake. This has created a vacuum that we can fill, becoming world class in repairs of all sorts.

This, then, is where the future lies. I am not suggesting that manufacturing will cease to matter: on the contrary, it will grow rapidly. What I am asserting is that services will grow even faster, and that the miracle of the microchip will facilitate the transfer of service jobs to India on a scale unthinkable even a decade ago. Indian businessmen need to break away from the traditional notion that manufacturing is the beginning and end of all business. This will soon be exposed as a quaint, obsolete notion of the twentieth century.

The Challenge of the Twenty-first Century

Prem Shankar Jha

In the closing years of the twentieth century, India's future looks anything but assured. This is not because its economy is structurally weak: on the contrary, in sharp contrast to China, it has a robust, rapidly growing agricultural economy that is hungry for labour and is steadily absorbing the bulk of new job seekers coming into the market every year. Again, in contrast to China, it has a highly developed national market, a competent nationwide financial and banking system, and a clearly defined, if excruciatingly slow, legal system with well-developed laws pertaining to property and contracts. Its management class, and now the higher echelons of the working class, are conversant with English. In every way, therefore, India is well placed to take advantage of globalization.

▼ Southern Petrochemical Industries Corporation Ltd (SPIC) is involved with the manufacture of nitrogenous and phosphatic fertilizers and pesticides, and has relatively diversified into areas like petrochemicals, pharmaceuticals and services.

▲ An overview of Indian business in the twenty-first century is not easy. With globalization, there will be a greater movement of capital and labour which Indians can take advantage of.

What India does not have is a ruling elite with a clear view of what the globalized world of the twenty-first century will look like. Immersed in an isolated economy and parochial concerns, it does not realize that globalization is an epochal change that is shaking the foundations of every social belief and institution it grew up with, including that most basic institution one: the nation-state. And what it does not understand fills it with fear. It harbours the illusion that India can opt out of globalization if it so chooses. From this, it is a short road to magnifying each and every one of the disadvantages of globalization and belittling or ignoring its benefits. In the resulting indecision about the desirability of reform, India is rapidly becoming a victim of globalization instead of its beneficiary.

Every economic reform that makes the country capable of taking advantage of globalization has its downside. Devaluation is a precondition for the opening of the economy, but devaluation causes inflation, and inflation widens differences in real income. However, if growth accelerates and employment increases rapidly, aggregate money income will rise faster than prices, and the country will benefit from globalization. But if, as happened in 1997 and 1998, the rate of growth slows down, the rate of growth of employment drops sharply, and the number of job seekers at employment exchanges begins to rise rapidly, the country turns into a victim of globalization. If liberalizing imports and foreign investment strengthens the capacity to export, the country emerges a net gainer. But if it displaces domestic production without increasing exports, as happens when the currency is overvalued, or foreign investment comes in chiefly to exploit the domestic market, as happens when continuing high tariffs or import bans in some sectors push up the profitability of investment in them, the country ends up net loser. By the same token, if foreign institutional investment is evenly distributed between the primary and secondary share markets, it is less volatile and increases foreign exchange reserves and investible capital. But when it comes solely into the secondary market in search of short-term gains, it is volatile and can make the country vulnerable to sudden shifts of market sentiment. As East and South East Asia have shown, the effects can then be devastating.

▼ Automatic spindle plant in Rajasthan, part of an export-oriented spinning unit. Not enough incentive is being offered to the export-oriented units by government, even though increasing exports remains a national priority.

Even a cursory glance at India's performance shows that, post-1996, India turned from a beneficiary to a victim of globalization. The rate of growth of GDP fell from an average of 7 per cent between 1993–4 and 1996–7, to less than 1 per cent in 1997–8. (The official rate of 5.1 per cent is not comparable with the previous years because it includes a huge payment of salary arrears to central government servants which has been taken as representing a genuine increase in value added.) The rate of growth of exports fell from over 20 per cent between 1993–4 and 1995–6, to 4.4 per cent in 1996–7, and 2.6 per cent in 1997–8. The rate of growth of industrial output fell from 12.6 per cent in 1995–6, to 4.4 per cent in 1997–8. India has no reliable annual unemployment data but judging from the register of job seekers, unemployment (which declined marginally between 1992 and 1996) has begun to climb rapidly since 1997. Lastly, Foreign Direct Investment (FDI) inflows peaked in 1995–6 at an unimpressive $2.9 bn in 1996–7, and fell to $ 2.6 bn in 1997–8. The bulk of this investment is in infrastructure projects that do not directly generate exports, but have to be paid for. The FDI in manufacturing is almost exclusively to exploit the domestic market.

How did India turn so suddenly from beneficiary into victim of globalization? The answers, in brief, are:

A massive and growing fiscal deficit. Throughout the boom years of 1993–6, the consoliated fiscal deficit of the centre and states continued to rise and reached 9.2 per cent of the GDP in 1997–8. The Public Sector Borrowing Requirement (PSBR), which includes

▶ Power transmission station. Despite opening the power sector to private and international companies, the government is seen as sending out mixed signals, as in the case of the renegotiation of the Enron power project at Dabhol, Maharashtra. Today, several power projects in different states have failed to take off as a result of this.

net increase in indebtedness of the public sector, rose more rapidly as states, in particular, started using public enterprises to borrow in order to meet their fiscal deficits. The PSBR is therefore much higher and may exceed 11 per cent of GDP. The high fiscal deficit makes it impossible to bring down the growth of money supply. Thus when the economy starts to boom, the latter spirals out of control and results in sharp inflation. In 1995, the government literally killed the boom by curbing credit to the commercial sector in an attempt to bring down inflation. The fiscal crisis has been immeasurably worsened by the United Front government's acceptance, and indeed enhancement, of the recommendations for salary increases made by the Fifth Pay Commission. These have cost the central government an additional Rs 18,000 crore. They will cost the state governments Rs 35,266 crore. In all, the salary hike will increase the fiscal deficit by 3.5 per cent of GDP by April 1999.

Incomplete economic reforms. While the reform of product markets has been largely completed except in areas reserved for small-scale industry, tax and tariff rationalization, exchange rate unification, current account convertibility, and the dismantling of price, production and investment controls on domestic and, to a large extent, foreign investment, the reform of factor markets has not even begun. Today, Indian companies facing foreign investors, or competition from imports, cannot lay off workers, cannot sell their surplus land to raise interest free capital, cannot borrow money against their own shares in order to pick up rights issues in the expansion of share capital of their own firms, and cannot easily sell off marginal businesses or loss making factories in order to improve their overall financial viability. Indian entrepreneurs are thus denied the managerial freedom that alone will enable them to withstand the challenge of competition. If economic reform is not to be stalled by the growing opposition of the Indian entrepreneurial class, these shackles need to be shed as soon as possible.

Neglect of the public sector. No segment of industry has been as studiously neglected during the past seven years of economic reform. If the reformers have a mantra for the public sector, it is to let public sector enterprises sink or swim on their own merit. It may, however, find itself unable to swim, the result of finding both its hands tied behind its back. In addition to the shackles that bind the private sector, the public sector does not even have the freedom to change prices or its product mix without the permission of parent ministries.

Return of the dirigiste *mindset.* As commitment to reform has faltered in the coalition governments that have succeeded the Congress, the bureaucracy has lost its sense of direction. This has

ASEA

resulted in the return of the *dirigiste* mindset with a strong temptation to return to a regime of controls and exemptions which is the antithesis of market friendly economies. Glaring examples are:

> The shotgun renegotiation of the Enron power project at Dabhol in Maharashtra by the BJP–Shiv Sena government.
>
> The sabotaging of the Bangalore international airport project by central government bureaucrats who have overridden commitments given to the investors to close the existing airport on the grounds that national security forbids handing over control of an airport to a private foreign investor.
>
> Tacit encouragement to MTNL to start cellular phone services, thereby gravely jeopardizing the investment made by sixteen struggling private companies that have invested more than a $ 1 bn in these services.

An excess of red tape — leading to corruption, delay, and inefficiency. In conjunction with poor instrastructure, this has effectively dissuaded investment in manufacturing facilities designed to serve the world, as distinct from domestic, market. Such investment eventually displaces domestic manufacturers and therefore does not create much additional employment or output but adds to the foreign currency liabilities of the nation.

The solution to the problems lies in more, and not less, reform. India is facing the consequences of a globalized victim because it has lost its courage after venturing halfway into a market economy. The result today appears to combine the worst of both market and *dirigiste* economies.

Immediate measures to restore financial viability must include lowering of interest rates, devaluation of the rupee, raising of the retirement age of not just central but also state civil servants, and the sale of government land. The first two are simply a return to correct economic policies, but they will close at least half of the fiscal burden created by the salary hikes. For instance, correcting the serious overvaluation of the rupee, which is reflected by the two-year stagnation in exports, and allowing its value to fall to around Rs 45 to the dollar, will add Rs15,000 to Rs 20,000 crore to central revenues by way of customs duties. Since the strong rupee is being defended by high interest rates, lowering these is a prerequisite for devaluation. But lower interest rates, if complemented by other measures to stimulate investment, will also push up share prices, and bring down the cost of raising capital. This will reverse the decline in investment that began at the end of 1995 and start an economic recovery, and that will widen the tax base and further increase tax revenues .

Raising the retirement age by two years was suggested by the Fifth Pay Commission, rejected by the United Front government, but implemented by the BJP coalition. Two years will not, however, suffice: retirement age must be raised by five years, and the money paid into an autonomous pension fund. In five years, the capital of the fund will be large enough to meet all future pension and retirement benefits from its interest and dividend incomes.

The sale of urban land will stimulate investment in urban infrastructure and meet the urgent need for urban housing and commercial space. Thanks to the Urban Land Ceiling and Regulation Act of 1977 which froze sales of urban vacant land, there is deep-seated land hunger in the people. As a result, urban land prices are so high that the sale of 2000 hectares a year in and around a dozen major cities would bring bloated land prices crashing down and still yield at least Rs 10–15,000 crore a year.

However, none of these measures is a substitute for the elimination of most of the Rs 2,00,000 crore worth of subsidies, identified in a government White Paper released in April 1997.

▼ Indian Oil refinery. Contrary to popular perception, the private sector is not the complete panacea for setting the economy on the highway to growth. Government spending on infrastructure is not only essential, but also necessary because it has access to more capital.

Four-fifths of these subisides do not go to the poor and needy but to powerful, political lobbies that have wrested concessions from weak governments. The bulk of these subsidies need to be eliminated because they profoundly distort the signals from the market, to the general detriment of economic efficiency. It will also lower the fiscal deficit, and PSBR, bring down interest rates, increase investment, and restart rapid but sustainable growth. It will increase government savings and provide the funds the centre and state governments need to invest in infrastructure, and build the social capital — health, shelter, and education — without which India cannot hope to profit from globalization in the long run.

Contrary to what the World Bank and IMF have been advocating, privatization cannot fill this gap. Private investors do not have access to free capital, and so all their investment must make a profit. No matter how efficient they are, the private sector cannot do this without charging prices that will put many of these essential services beyond the reach of the poor. Even in the development of power and roadways, as the government has belatedly learned, private investment can only supplement public investment and make it more efficient. It cannot replace it.

To get the best out of private investment, Indian industry needs to study portfolio and direct investment potential. The government can retain control of the foreign exchange and financial markets by delay introducing capital account convertibility. Whenever it does so, it should simultaneously impose a tax on cross border capital movements on the lines proposed by economist James Tobin. This will keep highly speculative capital out of the market. It would also be advisable to funnel all private borrowing overseas through a few public sector banks. These measures should suffice to shield India from the ravages of speculative capital flows without giving the government and its bankers the capacity to ignore the dictates of the market altogether in using the public's deposits, as it has done in the past. To the extent that foreign investment does come in to exploit the home market, it is necessry to make sure that Indian industry is not squeezed out without being given a fair chance to survive. This needs the completion of reforms in the factor markets.

Essential reforms must include: freedom to sell industrial land to raise cost-free, risk-free capital for modernization and expansion; a nationwide contribution-based unemployment insurance scheme as a prelude to the reform of the Industrial Disputes Act 1977 that will allow employers to lay off workers; freedom to promoters to buy back shares in their own enterprises; complete elimination of formalities for the sale and purchase of companies, and units of a company. This is needed to nip the development of industrial sickness in the bud.

The New Business Maharajas

Gita Piramal

It is said that those who forget history are condemned to repeat it, that any crystal gazing into the future should start by reflecting on the past. In terms of the family business, certainly the institution is teetering on a unique cusp: local and global events are combining to force change. Nobody knows what 'change' actually means, yet across the board there is consensus that 'change' will occur. How able and capable India's business maharajas are in adapting to the unpredictable forces of change will shape their position in the coming millennium.

Without going into details of possible factors of change, it is worth comparing two quite distinct decades: the 1950s and the 1990s. Superficially, a comparison between the two might appear overly academic. Technology has radically altered the way business used to be conducted in the 1950s. Most Indians eat and live better than their ancestors — no 1990s child can relate to the traumatic famines of the 1950s — and this improvement is chiefly due to India's investments in irrigation and genetic engineering of seeds. For businessmen, better telecommunication facilities have dramatically reduced risk — a wider telephone network, computers, and a host of other management tools enable the 1990s corporate sector to judge product acceptability, measure market size, and refine customer profiles. Despite such accoutrements, today's corporate sector appears as frightened of the future as that of the 1950s.

▼ Keshub Mahindra represents the new face of Indian industry. Mahindra & Mahindra is a transportation giant where traditional practices have given way to increasing compliance with professional modes of administering companies.

As the commercial Raj cracked up in the wake of Independence, Indian entrepreneurs found vast new horizons emerging before them. In a way, the challenge of conquering virgin territory was similar to the liberalization of 1991: awed by the abrupt unshackling of controls, corporate response was muted, but as individual opportunities

▲ That the Lalbhais continue to be associated with textiles is hardly exceptional, considering the family was among the first in the nineteenth century to enter the field. What is creditworthy, however, is Arvind Lalbhai's determination to emerge as the world's largest manufacturer of denim.

▼ Lalit Mohan Thapar, Chairman and Managing Director, Ballarpur Industries, oversees a business that spans from the flagship newsprint paper to chemicals, food, and is in agribusiness.

became apparent, there was a rush towards them. The hectic pace of creating assets in the 1990s is remarkably similar to that of the 1950s.

In the 1950s, for example, J.R.D. Tata succumbed to a takeover fever in acquiring a slew of managing agency firms, some of which made strategic sense while others were just opportunistic deals. Among the new entrants to the Tata stables were Telco, Forbes Forbes & Campbell, Auto Ancillaries, Bombay Safe Deposit, Gokak Mills, and Indian Vegetable Products. In 1954, the Tatas formed a new company called Voltas to acquire the Swiss-owned Volkart Brothers, a trading company dealing in dyes and pharmaceuticals. JRD also acquired a minority interest in Macneill & Barry, one of the oldest and largest British houses in Calcutta, which secured for it a substantial indirect interest in coal. He also acquired the entire share capital of Sassoon J. David, a large investment company in Bombay. A number of new companies were started during this period, among them Tata Fisons and Lakme. JRD simultaneously busied himself in hiking Tisco's capacity and building up Tata Chemicals. In the 1990s, Ratan Tata's dynamism equals that of his uncle. Tisco's capacity continues to be hiked, Telco is introducing a wide range of new automobiles even as the rest of the group multiplies. There was little evidence of such aggressive behaviour in the decades in between; on the contrary, the Tata group in the 1970s allowed itself to be overtaken by the Birlas.

Ahmedabad and the Lalbhai family provide another example. By the 1950s, Kasturbhai Lalbhai had built one of India's largest textile empires. In the 1990s, his grandson Sanjay Lalbhai has become one of the top five producers of denim in the world. The group's business scale has expanded, the family's entrepreneurship and ability to dream remains the same.

It is this raw drive which builds assets and creates wealth for a nation. The giant — in the context of those times — industrial complexes built in the 1950s sustained India through the 1970s and 1980s. The first Mahindra jeep rolled off the assembly line at Mazagaon (Mumbai) in 1949; G.D. Birla pioneered India's entry into the synthetic fibre industry by commissioning a viscose plant at Gwalior (Madhya Pradesh) in August 1947. Today, after a long and an unfortunate gap, India is once again building industrial complexes. The Ambanis are constructing one of the world's largest refineries at Jamnagar in Gujarat. The Bajajs want to transform Bajaj Auto into a world class two-wheeler company.

In the 1990s, freshly minted groups sprang up overnight, almost as if from nowhere, repeating what

▶ Rahul Bajaj, Managing Director of Bajaj Auto Ltd, is the grandson of one of India's pioneering industrialists and Mahatma Gandhi associate, Jamnalal Bajaj. He is one of the founder fathers of the Bombay Club, a pressure group of businessmen calling for a level playing field and critical of the government's liberalization policy.

▼ C.K. Birla, at Hindustan Motors, the company that gave the country its ubiquitous Ambassador car, has turned around the company with technology partnerships with foreign manufacturers. Today the HM stable has launched the Mitsubishi Lancer passenger car for the top end of the market, and the RTV multipurpose vehicle for rural areas, addressing different segments of the Indian market.

had also happened in the 1950s. Sterlite's Anil Aggarwal once said, the only essential a businessman needs today is guts. With the stakes so high, businessmen are naturally scared, and the key question is: how many of the mega projects announced will actually metamorphose from paper licences to concrete reality? Can the business dynasties of the 1990s deliver as did those of the 1950s?

A study of the top fifty family business groups' performance in the twelve months between 1996 and 1997 provides an interesting glimpse into what the future could look like. Despite the shortness of the time-frame, there has been a dramatic shakeout in India's leading groups. Typically, it takes about five years for business to react to major changes; and the impact of the 1991 reforms on family business began to show during this period. A quick analysis reveals that 8 groups retained their position, 25 climbed up, and 17 skidded down. Of greater significance was the extremely sharp movement of so many groups. Manu Chhabria, for example, slithered down 11 rungs while Ruias leapfrogged 17. Of even greater import is that there were many more unfamiliar names than familiar ones in the list.

This highlights some thought-provoking issues, one of which is that of community affiliation. Sixteen out of the fifty groups are Marwaris. Twenty years ago, R.K. Hazari, a leading economist and bureaucrat, undertook a study of the effects of industrial licensing. In doing so, he discovered that Marwaris were India's most energetic business community. Though many names have since dropped out of his 1977 ranking, their places have been taken by new entrants, proving that Marwaris continue to be a vibrant

▲ K.K. Modi's interests span cigarettes, grooming products, and entertainment business. Widely travelled, his tenure as president of FICCI was dynamic, and covered a period of change in the Indian economy.

▶ Sudarshan Birla with his son, Siddharth Birla. With OCM, the family has proved that a significant proportion of industrial wealth in India remains embedded in textiles.

business community. Established leaders such as the Birlas, Bajajs, Goenkas, and Singhanias, who have been at the forefront of Indian industry for decades, are in the 1990s being jostled by assertive families such as the Jindals, Ruias, Dhoots, and Mittals. The 1996–7 list also suggests that while traditional business communities continue to dominate the corporate scene, there are more Sindhis, Parsis, Punjabis, Chettiars, and Brahmins on it than ever before. If there is a trend, it would point to greater broad-basing of entrepreneurship rather than less.

The list offers a possible insight into one of the biggest enigmas of business: is it more distinguished to be a greenfield businessman than a turnaround artist? It is significant that most of the big survivors (Tata, Birla, Bajaj, Godrej, Lalbhai, Mafatlal, Mahindra, and Shri Ram) have grown through the greenfield route, though all of them have at some point acquired a company or two. A significant proportion of today's wealth remains embedded in textiles despite India's heavy investments in petrochemicals, cement, and engineering over the past fifty years. The entry of the steel barons in the 1990s, however, hints that change is round the corner. RPG Enterprises is a pointer to fresh investments in the power sector as is the entry of Torrent and Ranbaxy in the pharmaceuticals business. The automotive sector has always been well represented but the presence of so many tyre companies is something of a surprise.

Impressive as these cases of success are, they equally highlight the failure of Indian family business. Sales of the Tata group, India's largest business house in 1947 and in 1997, have rocketed from around Rs 500 crore to touch Rs 40,000 crore but sales figures for

companies a little lower on the rung are nothing to write home about. It takes sales of a mere Rs 1200 crore to make it to the big league in India – peanuts in global terms. Also, over half the groups in the list have sales of under Rs 2000 crore. That is depressing. Obviously, the scale of Indian entrepreneurship today leaves much to be desired, but more serious is the quality of entrepreneurship. During the pre-Independence era, men like G.D. Birla and Walchand Hirachand displayed a rare sense of nationalist entrepreneurship. They fought for and established companies that created wealth for the country as well as for themselves. During the last years of the Raj, most British businessmen withdrew their money from their Indian operations, leaving some of India's largest companies seriously undercapitalized. Indian entrepreneurs acquired the giant orphans in the 1950s and early 1960s and laid the foundations of today's big business. The Goenkas started out by acquiring Duncans and Octavious Steel from the Armenians and the British. B.M. Khaitan, the tea king, bought a slew of estates and engineering companies. J.R.D. Tata acquired Finlay and a stable of smaller firms. The Indian takeover knights pumped in money and revitalized the colonial leftovers.

Our industrial wealth was created during Jawaharlal Nehru's prime ministership. Nehru might have though profit a dirty word, but he criss-crossed India inaugurating one industrial complex after another. G.D. Birla built Grasim and Hindalco during the years 1947–67. J.R.D. Tata doubled Tisco's capacity in 1958. Lalbhai turned a barren piece of land into a huge chemical complex called Atul. Walchand Hirachand founded Hindustan Shipyard and Premier Automobiles. In the south, the TVS group built a major engineering complex at Padi. These are a few, stray examples picked at random, but the 1950s is what India is surviving on today, and unless we replenish the store when its shelves are empty, we will be in deeper trouble than we are in already. In the 1990s, more than ever before, we need a revival of nationalist entrepreneurship.

A remarkable community camaraderie flourished in the 1950s. G.D. Birla, for example, encouraged other Indian businessmen to enter the jute business along with him. Walchand Hirachand bailed out small Indian shippers wherever and whenever he could. Kasturbhai Lalbhai helped other mill owners in Ahmedabad to improve the quality of their cotton mills. J.R.D. Tata developed satellite empires around Tisco. Such nurturing is a far cry from today's cut-throat scenario. What went wrong? Where did we take a wrong turn? Why are we so shame-faced about acknowledging

▲ Dr Parvinder Singh is Chairman and Managing Director of the innovative, research-intensive Ranbaxy Laboratories, considered by consultancy firm Arthur D. Little as among the top fifty Asian firms prepared to excel in the global market place.

▲ Jamshed Godrej heads the house of Godrej associated with the steel furniture, refrigerators, and other consumer durables. The group has come to be associated with reliability in the Indian market.

▼ A.C. Muthiah with his father M.A. Chidambaram and son Ashwin. The Chidambaram group's core interest is in the areas of chemicals and petrochemicals.

the important role nationalist entrepreneurship can play in a country's resurgence?

Perhaps one facet of the enigma is linked to the nexus between business and politics. In the 1950s, Indian entrepreneurs created assets by collaborating with the government. During Nehru's administration, businessmen helped service Nehru's 'temples'. JRD, for example, trained men for the three new public sector steel complexes that came up in the 1960s. M.S. Oberoi's training school provided chefs and staff for the Ashok Hotel. Kasturbhai Lalbhai's prodding kicked the Indian Institute of Management at Ahmedabad off the ground. This healthy nexus between business and politics came to an abrupt end in the 1960s and 1970s. Indira Gandhi laid foundation stones, not factories. Haldia Petrochemicals, for example, has been blessed with half a dozen foundation stones but even after decades of planning, has not produced a single kilo of plastic raw material. Her mania for control led to the birth of the 'licence Raj', her appetite for donations to the 'permit Raj'. Entrepreneurs were no longer permitted to base their business plans on market conditions but on the whims and fancies of the mandarins of New Delhi.

Inevitably, this led to a crippling of entrepreneurship, ensuring that the world overtook India. Other Asian countries produced better goods and provided their citizens with better standards of living. When Richard Attenborough shot the movie *Gandhi*, he did not have to go far to find a film set; far too much of India remains where it was fifty years ago. During this period India was probably the only country in the world that threatened to penalize management for overproduction. Exasperated beyond endurance by a government which refused to allow him to satisfy the demand for scooters, Rahul Bajaj once defiantly declared that he was 'ready to go to jail for excess production just as both my parents had for the freedom struggle'.

Unable to cope with the red tape, many entrepreneurs simply left India for the US and Europe. Some like Aditya Birla built new empires outside India — the world's largest palm oil factory, textile mills, carbon black plants in Egypt and Thailand, Malaysia and Indonesia. Under the British, Walchand Hirachand got permits to start Scindia Shipping in one month and ten days. Thailand's prime minister processed Birla's applications in record time. In India, bureaucrats took eleven long years to clear Birla's Mangalore refinery project, nine for Vikram Ispat, six for a polyester filament yarn plant, three for argon gas and hydrogen peroxide, and two for Indo-Gulf fertilizers.

The breakdown of confidence between business and politics during the 1960s and 1970s had serious repercussions that led to the perversion of entrepreneurship in the 1980s. Stifled and

▲ Karsanbhai Patel's is the classic rags-to-riches story: a laboratory assistant, he launched a small-scale detergent powder, Nirma, using indigenous technology, and placed it in the market at a third of the price of similar products. Cited as a marketing success, Nirma has gone on to become a classic Indian brand in only a few decades.

suffocated by byzantine laws, entrepreneurs sought to quench their hunger for expansion through whichever route opened before them. The growth kings during these years were takeover businessmen, with Manu Chhabria, R.P. Goenka and Vittal Mallya as role models. Entrepreneurs like Dhirubhai Ambani, Karsanbhai Patel of Nirma, and Venugopal Dhoot of Videocon provided yet another kind of role model. These men understood the system, knew the loopholes in the law, and exploited them.

The liberalization movement initiated by P.V. Narasimha Rao's administration is hacking away at the red tape and, to some extent, has revived the excitement of the 1950s. In the 1990s, there is again a flowering of industrial entrepreneurship. There are today new groups in fresh sectors such as the steel barons (Jindals, Mittals, Ruias, and Guptas), the pharma shoguns (Torrent and Ranbaxy), as well as a vast and throbbing substratum of innovative smaller empires in diverse fields such as pens and packaging, electric switches and computer services, biscuits, buckets, and spectacle frames. Many may turn out to be fly-by-night operators but, hopefully, the majority will become the face of tomorrow's big business.

With so much hectic activity, why is there a feeling that Indians have lost their zest for a good fight? Instead of being proactive, entrepreneurs appear content to be reactive in their response to opportunities and challenges. The reasons are not hard to find. Large capital investments require a bellyful of guts, competition is on the rise, and demand is elusive. The abyss scaring businessmen is competition: local and global. Will Indian business clear the abyss or stumble into it? Admittedly, from a punter's standpoint, it does not look too good. Few of the old guard have money, technology or world class products. Their manufacturing processes are outmoded, their factories too small. The new business groups are brash with an engaging can-do devilry, but often appear short-sighted with a taste for quick profits. Neither seems to display the patriotic, nation-building attitude India needs. That is why we need to revive the spirit of the 1950s.

India's Global Players of the Future

N. Chandra Mohan

Over the next ten years, the landscape of corporate India is set to undergo a fundamental transformation. As the winds of globalization blow through its boardrooms, family-owned conglomerates, which have so far dominated the country's business scenario, will bear the brunt of adjustment. Those that survive will include some of the best run companies in the country, but half of the top fifty business houses are unlikely to weather the competition.

Family business will still dominate corporate India, but with a difference. There will be a sharp break from the paradigms of the licence Raj. Then, it made sense to corner licences and set up suboptimal firms in a bewildering range of industries. Not any more, when streamlining and consolidation of their activities is imperative. In the brave new world, survivors have to focus on their core competencies and acquire critical mass. To do so, some family businesses will opt for the fixed investment route to acquire scale economies. Many will merge subsidiaries and acquire companies to grow bigger. With the chilling winds of competition, the flavour of the Indian corporates will be consolidation. Most will internalize the new buzzwords 'restructuring and re-engineering' to their activities. What will differentiate the front-runners from the also-rans is ultimately vision statement. Ten years down the road, successful business houses will have to look beyond the confines of India. The borderless world is a reality. After acquiring critical size, they will perforce have to think global. This implies benchmarking their practices to international standards to register their presence in the world market.

▼▶ Reliance Industries' Anil and Mukesh Ambani *(below)* and one of their plants *(facing page)*. Reliance is indisputably India's global giant and has successfully shown how, with strategic focus, it is possible to integrate operations and industries (branded textiles, petrochemicals, oil) in one single generation.

The compulsions for change are obvious enough. The Indian state cannot prevent the demonstration effects of metropolitan lifestyles abroad. Indian consumers are demanding the latest consumer goods, including jeans, colas, sneakers, cars, and other gizmos — a process of 'California-ization' as Kenichi Ohmae puts it. Indian family businesses that address such requirements will be in a win-win situation.

Consumer tastes have become progressively homogenized, thanks to TV satellites. Responding to this challenge entails producing goods of international class at competitive prices. This implies accessing the best resources of the world economy so that the consumer is satisfied. In responding to this challenge, a churning process is already under way in corporate India. This process will snowball over the next decade.

The surviving family business houses participate in a variety of industries including smokestack ones like steel, autos, and cement; traditional ones like textiles, paper, and sugar; and sunrise industries like information technology (IT) and telecom. There is no inevitable transition from smoke stack to sunrise industries. Whichever the industry, the winners represent its modern face as it confronts the challenges of the future.

Over the next decade, if there is one group that will indisputably be India's global giant, it is Reliance Industries belonging to the house of Dhirubhai Ambani. In one single generation, it has achieved a strategic focus that commands respect the world over: Reliance has integrated backwards and forwards, horizontally and vertically, from branded textiles to petrochemicals and oil. This group's dynamic exemplifies rapid growth through fixed investments rather than through mergers and acquisitions (M&As).

Reliance is investing close to Rs 2 crore an hour to complete its ambitious Rs 20,500 crore grass-roots refinery, petrochemicals and power complex at Jamnagar. Once that is completed, it will venture upstream into oil, gas, and energy. Such a relentless drive will take it outside India. By the year 2000, the group's turnover will zoom to Rs 40,000–50,000 crore, assets will be worth Rs 30,000–35,000 crore. This is world class.

Paradoxically, Reliance is the finest creation of the licence Raj. The group ruthlessly used the 'system' to grow bigger, while others diversified into motley activities and remained pygmies by international standards. Reliance devoted its energies to integration and tapped the resources of 2.6 m. shareholders. The group accessed state-of-the-art technology to realize its ambitions of being a global player.

Older business houses are also throwing up winners. Ratan Tata, head of the Rs 36,000 crore house of the Tatas, is one of those

▲ Finished acrylic at the JCT plant in Punjab. There is a transition from smoke-stack industries to sunrise industries, and those willing to confront the challenges of the future represent its modern face.

spearheading the dynamic response of the family business to globalization. The making of the Telco small car exemplifies this process. Tata wanted to build a car of international standards. Instead of designing one at Telco, he decided this could be reached through a proven world class design. The legendary Italian I.D.E.A institute founded by Franco Mantegazza, which is a 360-degree global design service, took 24–30 months to deliver a running prototype which was tested on European roads. What then emerged as the Telco small car was internationally benchmarked.

▲ From one of India's oldest business houses is emerging one of the most visible benefits of globalization: Telco's indigenously developed car named Indica. Designed in Italy, with engine modifications in France, this 'Indian' car proves that the country is capable of developing world-class products.

Its engine too incorporated significant inputs from Le Moteur Modeme based in France. Tata clearly has a global vision. He has used the best inputs in the world that money could buy to produce such a car.

Over the next ten years, Ratan Tata will streamline and consolidate the group's presence in other areas where it has strengths. Currently, Tatas has a stake in twenty-five different industries ranging from steel to knitwear. To get leaner and meaner, the focus will be on areas that can survive competition from a borderless world. Clearly, he has worked out a game-plan to remain internationally competitive.

Slowly but purposefully, Tatas is also beginning to go global in an Asian setting. For starters, plans are afoot for Indian Hotels Co. Ltd (the Taj group of hotels), to purchase properties in the region in league with Jardine Matheson of Hong Kong. Tata Exports Ltd too intends to strengthen its presence in South East Asia. It already has a wholly owned subsidiary in Hong Kong which has an office in Shanghai and operations in Nantong. Tata Exports is now tracking opportunities in Indonesia.

By contrast, Rahul Bajaj, Chairman of Bajaj Auto, appears to have dropped out from the pack. Till now, if there was one Indian family run business that had the potential to be a global player, it

▼ Manufacturers today are making extensive use of the CAD/CAM processes to create scale models of the products they wish to design and manufacture. Among those benefiting most from this technology are industries associated with automobiles, auto parts, and two-wheelers.

was Bajaj Auto. Consider its advantages: it has global scales next only to Honda of Japan. Despite being the world's lowest cost producer of two-wheelers, this advantage has not translated into an international presence for Bajaj. This is because Bajaj still operates with the 'purely local mindset of a shortage economy' (to borrow an expression from management guru, Gurcharan Das). Although he adroitly survived the licence Raj, he has fumbled in the era of liberalization. The legacy of the last forty years has prevented him from taking a great leap forward to becoming a global player. Not surprisingly, this is reflected in the steady erosion of Bajaj's domestic leadership in scooters to groups like LML.

Cars and scooters: can the auto component industry be far behind? Here again, those who will prosper over the next ten years will be those with export or global plans in mind. There is simply no other way of surviving the entry of auto majors like Ford, GM, Honda, Daewoo, and Hyundai which are setting up facilities to manufacture components in India. A shake-out is in the offing as production facilities get more fragmented. The Chennai-based TVS Group is upfront in responding to this challenge. By subjecting itself to the discipline of the world market, it plans to realize scale economies, upgrade quality, and become competitive. Sundaram Fasteners is a trailblazer of sorts as it supplies radiator caps to the original equipment manufacturer, General Motors (GM). A few years ago, it won the Supplier of the Year award from GM for being the 'best of the best' in respect of price, product, quality, and service.

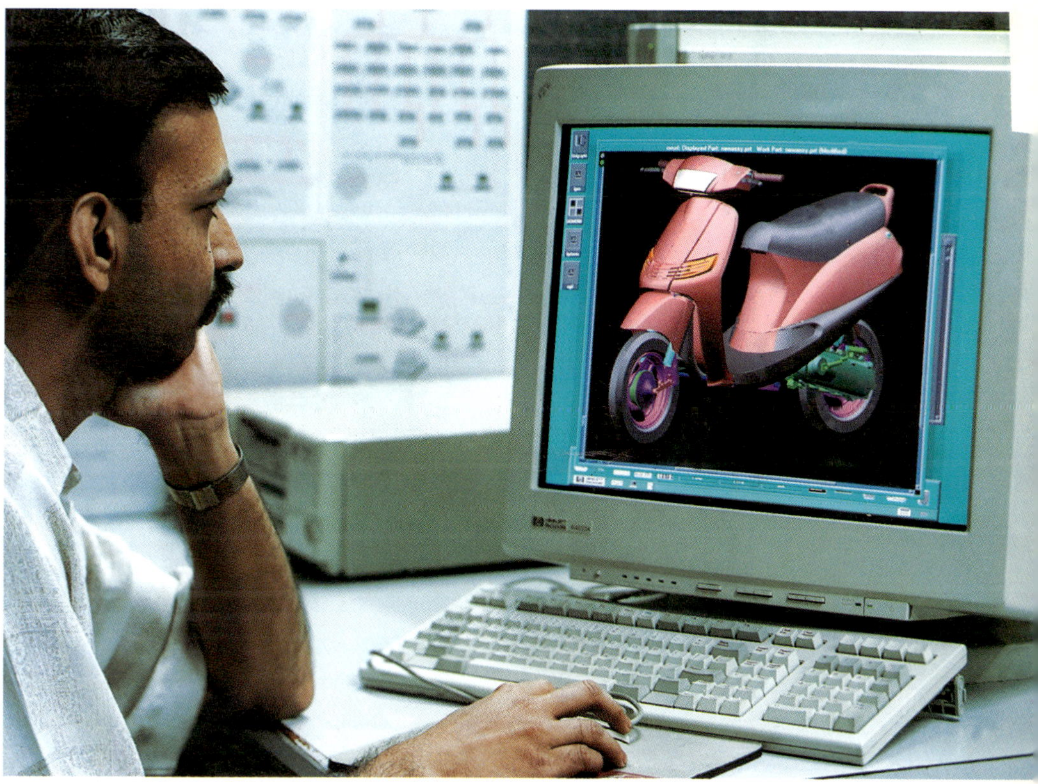

▲ Assembly line at the Daewoo plant in India. Foreign car manufacturers are finding India ideal for the manufacture of components for their use in their own and other countries.

It was one of four Asian companies chosen out of 10,000 international competitors. Other group companies like Brakes India, Wheels India, and Lucas TVS too are gearing up for similar challenges down the road.

Tata and Bajaj represent the oldest family dynasties of India. Another front-runner is the young scion of the Aditya Birla Group, Kumarmangalam Birla. The Rs 20,000 crore group is India's first truly global operation spanning 61 companies in 14 countries and employing 1,40,000 employees. Thanks to the licence Raj, its product profile comprises carbon black, aluminium, cement, textiles, fibres, fertilizers, copper, sponge iron, chemicals, refining, and telecom among many others. Hindalco, the country's largest integrated producer of aluminium illustrates Birla's commitment in this regard. This company, with its captive bauxite mines and power plant, has successfully benchmarked itself against the best practices in the world. Hindalco's cost of production thus is $1033 per tonne as against Alcoa's $1250 per tonne and Alcan's $1129 per tonne. With this sort of vision, Birla is clearly a global player.

As noted earlier, M&As is also a favoured route to expansion. An impetus to aggressive M&As is the growing incidence of sickness in corporate India. Given the marked slowdown in overall industrial growth and full-blown recessionary conditions in capital goods, steel, basic industries, drugs and pharmaceuticals, many companies are ready to go under. This provides opportunities for cash-rich corporates and family-owned groups to grow through acquisition. According to the Centre for Monitoring Indian Economy (CMIE), 297 companies were referred to BIFR last year. Moreover, in many industries, excess capacities have been built up over the past few years. The cement industry is thus experiencing a wave of mergers as big players gobble up smaller ones. Together with his grandfather B.K. Birla's group of companies, Kumarmangalam Birla's firms make him India's leading cement producer. Nevertheless, he is scouting around for more acquisitions to enable him to have world class capacities. A takeover of Shree Digvijay Cements is on the cards. Grasim, a

▼ Kumarmangalam Birla is one of the major cement barons in the country, but is scouting around for more companies to enable him to develop world-class capacities.

flagship of the A.V. Birla Group, has also acquired Dharani Cements, giving it a presence in south India.

Through M&As, India has been put on the world map in steel, thanks to go-getter L.N. Mittal, head of Ispat International NV. With far-flung operations in the US, Canada, Germany, Ireland, Mexico, Indonesia, Trinidad and Tobago, and Kazakhistan, secured through buy-outs, Mittal now produces 17 m.t. of steel which is just less than India's entire production of 20 m.t.! He represents the most global face of Indian steel industry. Mittal's secret has been to spot a business opportunity in steel anywhere in the world and zero in for the kill. His success in cost control and turning around his acquisitions is now legendary. By sitting in India, Mittal could not have realized his borderless ambitions. He had to move out to become the fourth-largest steel producer in the world. Even without further M&As, he is confident of producing 20 m. t. by the year 2000. Ten years later, his empire will be the stuff of which dreams are made.

Excess capacities in the age-old sugar industry — the last surviving bastion of the licence Raj — are also providing an impetus for global players to emerge. This industry too has been experiencing a boom-bust cycle since 1995–6. Sickness is pervasive as marginal mills find it uneconomical to operate. Sugar, thus, is ripe for M&As and capacity consolidation. Dynamic Indian players can storm the international sugar market as exporters, once the industry is. Worldwide, capacities of 10,000 tonnes crushed per day (TCD) are the norm while in India they are suboptimal at 2000 TCD. Only a handful of private sugar mills have 10,000 TCD capacities. In this scenario, the recent M&A activity on the part of Balrampur Chini Mills (15,500 TCD) owned by the Saraogis is a pointer to the future. Balrampur earlier acquired Babhnan Sugar Mills and has now taken over the 2500 TCD Tulsipur Sugar Co. With a capacity of 18,000 TCD, Balrampur now joins the big league. With such scales of production, sugar can be competitively produced in the country for export. Costs of production will automatically decline as efficient players grow larger and larger. Two million tonnes of sugar can thus be profitably offloaded on to the world market every year. This would account for 10 per cent of the world sugar trade of 22 m. t., and this is the bonanza in store if the

▲ R&D laboratory at the distillery attached to the Daurala Sugar Mills. Excess capacity in the sugar industry is providing an impetus for global players to emerge.

sugar industry is decontrolled and deregulated over the next ten years.

Global players are also emerging in India's drugs and pharmaceuticals industry. This might appear paradoxical given the country's patents regime which is out of sync with WTO requirements. In consequence, out of about 400 formulations developed worldwide in recent years that are available in the global market, only 33 are seen in India. Several global drug majors like Pfizer and Eli Lilly shun the Indian market. In this milieu, Ranbaxy, headed by Dr Parvinder Singh, has taken a novel route to go global. The company's dynamic comparative advantage lies in generics and formulations rather than developing new drugs that cost a whopping $450 m. apiece. As patents for a variety of drugs expire, Ranbaxy floods the world market with generic versions of these. It has become India's first pharmaceutical company to launch generic products under its own name and label in the US.

Spurring the company forward is Singh's vision of making it a research-based international pharmaceutical company. Ranbaxy now sells its products in over forty countries and has manufacturing operations in seven countries including China. Net global sales stand at $ 433 m. Its entry into the US marked a major step forward in its internationalization dynamic. A survey by the consultancy firm Arthur D. Little considered Ranbaxy one of the top fifty Asian firms which were best prepared to excel in the global market place.

Among the sunrise industries, India is indisputably a leading edge player in software and IT. With its educational institutions churning out 55,000 engineers annually, the software industry has become a source of global competitive advantage. Leveraging the cost advantage, exports are booming. As many as 1,00,000 software developers exist now in India. Fears are rife in the US that IT jobs are being shipped out to India on a permanent basis. This spells megabucks for those with global vision like Wipro.

This Rs 1600 crore group headed by A.H. Premji is cresting the IT boom in India. Wipro is India's largest IT company and second largest software exporter. Currently, its market capitalization of

▲ The assembly line at the HCL computers factory. Among the sunrise industries, India is definitely a leading player in software and information technology.

▼ Azim H. Premji, Chairman and Managing Director, Wipro Ltd, is among those riding the IT boom, and 50 per cent of Wipro's profits come from overseas operations.

Rs 6550 crore is larger than that of the RPG, Essar, B.K. Birla and Wadia groups put together. It has set up two subsidiaries, Wipro Nihon in Japan and Wipro Inc. in the US, to further its software business. Japan and the Pacific Rim are an important part of Wipro's business drive and it plans to devote 500 software engineers to exploit that region's potentiality. Fifty per cent of its profit comes from its overseas operations, making it a global player by any reckoning. Wipro turns out customized software rather than products like Windows or Java. A transition to the latter requires an enormous amount of capital which can perhaps become available once venture capital funding takes off in India. Over the near term, however, the company intends to move up the value chain and extend its expertise to Java, object-oriented planning and data warehousing.

Significantly, such winners, across a diverse range of industries, are emerging over the horizon with little or no support from the Indian government. The current BJP-led government even talks about 'calibrating' the process of globalization. To this day, policy regimes have deep-rooted suspicion of opening up to a borderless world. For more Indian players to emerge, the policy regime must be less wary of globalization. It must encourage liberal capital remittances abroad so that Indian corporates can access the best resources from the global economy. Setting up joint ventures or formation of wholly owned subsidiaries abroad must be encouraged. Corporates must be allowed to acquire the latest technology and assets. What sets Ambani, Tata, Mittal, Suresh Krishna, Kumarmangalam Birla, and Premji apart from the rest is that they realize they must grow bigger to realize their global ambitions, that the opening up of the Indian economy with economic reforms is irreversible, that to survive globalization they must develop their comparative advantages, and that consumers are demanding world class goods. They have already begun responding to such challenges.

▼ The Ranbaxy bulk plant at Mohali, Chandigarh. As patents for a variety of drugs expire, Ranbaxy floods the world market with generic versions of these, indicating the route drugs and pharmaceuticals industries need to take to become global players.

As noted earlier, 50 per cent of today's top fifty family businesses are set to go under if they delay adjustment to a borderless world. The sprawling fiefdoms of the Modis, Thapars, Singhanias, Mafatlals, Birlas, Ruias, to name a few, are thinly spread over a diverse range of activities. Many remain smaller league players by global standards. They are aggressively lobbying to survive competition through protection, but this cannot hold back for long the surging tide of globalization over the next ten years.

Postscript:

India's nuclear tests of 11–13 May 1998 are a watershed in its affairs as it heads into the twenty-first century. Pakistan has predictably responded with six nuclear tests which have escalated tensions in the subcontinent. Their emergence as nuclear weapon states has triggered US-led economic sanctions. What is their impact on corporate India's drive to become a global player? According to a doomsday scenario, such sanctions would devastate Indian corporates. Aid flows would dry up. Foreign investors would shun India. Trade would get choked off. Domestic firms would have to pay higher interest rates to borrow from abroad. These factors could set off a run on the rupee. India's forex reserves would then melt like butter in summer.

None of this has happened. Donors remain too divided to cut off aid. With sanctions, US$ 22 bn of foreign currency inflows into India were to dry up, but their actual impact is only US$ 1.14 bn. Foreign investors are still bullish on India. Trade has not been affected. Indian firms have not postponed borrowings because of costlier spreads. The rupee has not nosedived. Paradoxically, the US-led sanctions affect their own MNCs more than corporate India. With reduced EXIM funding and OPIC (Overseas Private Investment Corporation) guarantees, many projects of US companies in India — which are involved in software development, power generation, fast food, soft drinks, and apparel — would grind to a halt. If they withdrew from the Indian market, the doors would slam shut once and for all.

For Indian corporates, the fallout of Pokharan II has been rather favourable. Backed by a strong nationalist wind, the BJP-led government's hand has been strengthened politically to implement economic reforms, and this is also reflected in the union budget for 1998–9. The decks have been cleared for 'growth, more growth and still more growth', to borrow an expression from Prime Minister Atal Bihari Vajpayee. India Inc. is getting leaner and more competitive. After the Buddha smiled again, many long-pending projects were thus cleared in power, mining, and petroleum. The Prime Minister's Office (PMO) has directed various ministries and departments to also speed up clearances for infrastructural projects in coal, ports, and telecom. Activism on reforms is most evident in the area of Foreign Direct Investment (FDI). Although such clearances were strategic in nature to get around the threat of US-led sanctions, there is a rethink within the government in terms of presenting a more FDI-friendly face to reforms than its *swadeshi* rhetoric earlier suggested. The government will now aggressively woo rather than selectively discourage FDI along the lines of the 'microchips vs. potato chips' dichotomy. There has also been an aggressive marketing of India Inc. Apex chambers of commerce like FICCI, CII, and ASSOCHAM have chipped in to tell the rest of the world that the country is a vast business potentiality; that its domestic market comprising a middle class of 250 m. plus is too large to ignore. By leveraging the economy's strengths, such efforts resemble China's tactics in getting around US-led sanctions.

Times are thus changing for corporate India. With more FDI coming in, opportunities widen for participating in a borderless world. The challenges of globalization remain the same with or without sanctions. Corporates have to acquire critical mass in order to matter in the world. They have to focus on their core competencies. Towards this end, they have to access the best global resources. The process of adjustment is already under way. The 11–13 May events and their aftermath have provided a fillip to those ongoing transformations. Many of India's family-owned groups, that dominate India's corporate landscape, are moving out of unrelated areas of business into those where they have strengths. They are consolidating their empires with advice from consultancy firms like McKinsey and Arthur D. Little. M&As are also on the rise as corporates grow larger in scale and acquire critical mass.

The emergence of India and Pakistan as nuclear weapons states has therefore already impacted on the economic sphere. To counter US-led sanctions, the reform process is being widened, deepened, and accelerated. Corporate India can thus become a major player in the global arena. A nationalist surge is carrying this process forward, and India is now taking sure-footed and confident strides to survive globalization.

Indian Reforms: How the World Views Us

S.K. Singh

The economic reforms of 1991 were an attempt to open up the country's economy to the world, to more trade and investment through capital flows and competition. India reached out to the world with confidence in itself; the assurance of the size of its domestic market; and its track record amongst the post-colonial societies of the non-aligned and the G-77 world. During the 1980s and 1990s, development based on the expansion of exports, and liberalization and globalization have proved successful all over the world and, therefore, attractive to a large number of G-77 countries of the developing world, including China and, more recently, India. Export-based growth had earlier proved its effectiveness in the cases of Japan, Taiwan, Hong Kong, South Korea and members of the ASEAN group. This model was attractive enough even for Maoist Marxist China in 1979–80.

Of the larger economies, India was among the last to commence reforming its economy, but before doing so it studied the problems that faced it. It recognized that an overhaul of the system it had built over the past few decades would be required. Its great asset was the experimentation it had attempted during the 1980s to become more market oriented. After the inauguration of her second administration in 1980, Indira Gandhi started liberalizing the Indian economy. After her death, Rajiv Gandhi too undertook a similar exercise. Though both were limited, brief experiments at liberalization, neither being holistic, even so they were also seen as successful and growth oriented.

During 1980–4, Mrs Gandhi liberalized the rules concerning industry, placed greater accent on exports, and moved to borrow from the IMF in order to relieve resource constraints caused by the second 'oil shock'. However, she quickly found strong Left-wing political opposition, both within her own party, as also from mainstream Left parties and groups, and so denied India the last instalment of the loan that the IMF had approved. Rajiv Gandhi did succeed in borrowing from international sources in his attempt to open up India's economy. He was able to move the Indian industry towards deregulation and import liberalization. He gave

Export container being lifted. Export is an important component in the overall development of the economy. To boost exports in this era of liberalization, the government and the RBI have provided incentives to the exporters.

a fillip to the expansion of exports by providing major incentives to exporters, and in agreeing to manipulate currency rates with a view to making Indian exports less expensive and more competitive. The private sector was given priority for new industrial products and processes. While providing incentives to exporters in the private sector, he was squeamish about undertaking basic or drastic restructuring of the economy, perhaps because his prime ministership was beset with a number of political problems.

It was an act of great political courage on the part of Dr Manmohan Singh, on becoming finance minister and taking over the stewardship of the Indian economy, to undertake to restructure India's economic policies in a fundamental way. This effort effectively brought about signal changes in all sectors of our economy — trade, industry, foreign investment, financial flows, taxation, and public sector industrial and other units. Larger foreign investments too started flowing in.

Rajiv Gandhi's partial reforms had already ensured greater openness, transparency, and partial globalization and liberalization of India's economy. These served the purpose of enabling the reallocation of some resources and their efficient utilization. However, the reforms initiated by Manmohan Singh ensured a shift towards the traded goods sector, to more vigorous exporting; and from the public sector to the private sector. The country's investment climate was helped, and improved, through innovative measures in the areas of trade, industry, and foreign investment. Trade policy was simplified and streamlined, and in the process effectively modified. The same treatment was given to industrial policy and foreign investment policy. The tariffs structure was rationalized, and the process of rationalization has continued. In India's liberalized, somewhat more globalized economy, government, industry, financiers, and economists have come to recognize that trade intensity and foreign trade are both crucial for the overall growth and health of India's economy.

This first instalment of Dr Manmohan Singh's reforms saved the economy from a collapse that was threatening it due to grave fiscal and external imbalances. Dr Manmohan Singh went on to build on the inherent strengths of the Indian economy, such as the high domestic savings and investment rates, as well as its strong, mature private sector. The manufacturing sector was already large and diversified, the research and extension-based agricultural sector already self-sufficient; and the capital market of significant size. The task of the reformers was, therefore, facilitated by the country's self-confident effort at global integration.

The process of globalization was facilitated because it entailed only a certain further strengthening of a system that already existed. Contemporary Indian economic reformers have had no trouble recognizing that alongside the globalization of their economy, they need more efficient production which can result from better technology, greater investment, and the capacity to innovate. The increased foreign direct investment into India has resulted in greater investor confidence in the country.

The Indian economic reform process is built on broad consensus of all segments in the country's political spectrum. The reforms have not been as rapid as some would desire. However, the policy-makers have been anxious to chart out a new path of liberalization so that there is no infliction of avoidable pain on the lower income groups in society. The free market was left free to create a healthier economy, with the state intervening only in support of the poor. A deliberate effort has been made to take advantage of the country's situation in the international labour market, and of its other comparative advantages. India needs to produce goods and services for the home market, which is both huge and expanding, but even more importantly to ensure the expansion of exports, which alone can guarantee the economy's rapid growth. It is recognized that growth in trade and capital flows characterizes the overall health of the world economy. India seeks trade, not aid, and is happy to seek capital, not loans.

There has been a period of shifting the gears of economy in India, from a slow rate of growth to a higher one. The Indian state has come to recognize its essential role in this transition from a command economy to a market-driven one.

India's dilemma, however, is that it is involved in attempting to reach a self-sustainable growth of GNP, and GNP per capita, while at the same time it is anxious to ensure that the economic aspects of development — better education, higher literacy rates, better health services, more social consciousness, and better and more transparent governance — too are made available to the people.

It has been noted by many, in the context of our economic reform process, that the last two finance ministers (Manmohan Singh and P. Chidambaram) have worked hard to generate enthusiasm at home and abroad for these reforms, but the three prime ministers (Narasimha Rao, Deve Gowda, and I.K. Gujral) have been both reticent and somewhat defensive on this account. Our political leaders have been conscious of the need to stave off allegations of political submission or economic dependence. In a democracy as large and vast as India, with twenty-five federating units, each larger than most medium-size nation states in the world, with some election or the other taking place most of the

▼ Work at the container base welding jig at DCM Hyundai Ltd. Korea has been among those who reacted quickly to India's liberalized economy and formed strategic partnerships with Indian companies.

time, political exigencies have become a continuing process, affecting the economic thinking of the political decision-makers. The Indian political hierarchy has, therefore, had to be deliberately cautious in these matters, especially after the post-reform economic problems faced by Mexico, and more recently those faced by Thailand, South Korea, Malaysia, and Indonesia. There is a clear appreciation that the economic problems faced by Japan are of a different genre. However, the problems that affected the economies of Mexico, Malaysia, etc. could easily be replicated in India, and hence the Indian predilection for caution and prudence.

▲ The South Asian Association for Regional Cooperation (SAARC) is a pivotal body for creating a dynamic environment within the region. Trade relations within it are an important instrument of development and Kanti Kumar Podar, a past President of FICCI, represents Indian interests as President of the SAARC Chamber of Commerce and Industry.

The Indian government and economists have not yet made the effort of explaining India's hesitations to the world. The results of the 1996 elections, and India's inexperience in handling coalition politics at the federal level, combined to create several complexities for the country's policy-makers. Coincidentally, the economic setbacks and foreign exchange collapses in the Pacific-East Asian region, especially South Korea, Malaysia, Thailand, Indonesia and, to an extent Japan, created great anxiety throughout Asia.

Despite this, the United Front government in India continued to pursue the objectives of economic reforms but, at the same time, became extraordinarily cautious in formulating an overall legislative strategy to transform the legal landscape of the Indian economy. It had drafted this legislation before the economic problems of East Asia surfaced, but found itself unable to push the legislation through parliament. Just before the United Front government demitted office, Finance Minister P. Chidambaram made a public statement that his ministry had drafted several bills to cope with the country's future requirements but that these, unfortunately, could not be introduced.

As regards public sector undertakings, a three-way difference of opinion has surfaced, increasingly reflected in government statements on the subject. At the same time, all segments of opinion in the country support a much larger allocation of resources to primary education and health in the social sector. The country's dilemma, however, is with regard to scaling down subsidies for fertilizers and food. There is acceptance within Indian society that these subsidies will need to be maintained for some more time. At the same time, there is realization too that requirements of health and primary education will not brook any delay.

The world expects India to succeed in its efforts at economic liberalization and globalization. In the background of kaleidoscopic political changes in India, many nations around the world may be excused for wondering what its long-term economic strategy may be. The potential of India is enormous, given the size of its domestic market; and the quality of the talent and promise of its human resources. It is to be hoped that India will soon have infrastructure capable of sustaining rapid and massive growth of its economy in all its facets and aspects. India has always had friends, supporters, and admirers in the non-aligned, G-77 world in Asia, Africa, and Latin America. Now it has friends in Europe and the US who hope that India will be able to realize the promise it had shown during the 1950s and the 1960s. A worrisome, hopefully temporary, impediment arose in this context in May 1998. This was due to certain negative measures that were imposed by Japan and the USA restricting loans and other economic assistance to India, after India and Pakistan carried out their underground nuclear tests in May 1998. Despite this, the world hopes India will be one of the global leaders in trade, industry, science, and technology. The world expects India to attain the role of a global economic leader, and a major economy.

India and the United States

Frank Wisner

The United States' relationship with India is as old as Indian Independence, for it was not until India was free of British colonial rule that our two governments and nations could establish firm ties and build a relationship worthy of the principles, traditions, and ambitions which our peoples cherish. Over the past five decades, interactions between Americans and Indians have grown exponentially. Our governments work with each other, our scholars and students travel across the oceans, businessmen trade and invest, and tourists and travellers mingle freely across our respective continents. We are joined in international and bi-national conventions almost too numerous to count. The onset of the information technology age is reducing even more rapidly the distance between us.

▼ Cyber savvy Andhra Pradesh Chief Minister Chandrababu Naidu (extreme left) attends a presentation with former US Ambassador in India, Frank Wisner (extreme right).

Any American company with its eyes set on the global market place, interested in reducing its costs, committed to research and development, and looking for highly qualified manpower needs a position in today's India. It should expand on that position in the years ahead and make India a major platform for its future development.

I have been impressed by the fundamental good judgment of India's economic policy officials, especially those at the top ranks of the public service. I have also been struck by the good sense of India's business community which knows that India must live in a competitive world and that they can compete effectively. The time is right for Indians to have the courage of their convictions and press ahead stoutly with the economic reform agenda, doing what is necessary to develop infrastructure, to strengthen capital markets, and to give foreign and domestic private enterprises the policies and incentives they require.

Those coming to India must be prepared to accept that change will take time, for India is a democratic society. Americans and others from abroad need also to bear in mind the special sensitivities Indians have about foreign capital, given India's history. Entry strategies must be prepared with great care. India's legislators, press, and public interest groups and citizens must be taken into confidence and persuaded of the merits of a new industry and its way of doing business. Foreign enterprises must be especially careful with their environmental protection and labour management techniques. Business ethics are of the highest importance.

An American investor planning to take his place in India in the new century must gauge the size of the market carefully. It is easy to overestimate the market; it is equally wrong to underestimate its dynamics. India's market is large and its ability to consume new products is growing daily, but growth in consumption and income will not be even. It is necessary to concentrate time and attention on distribution. Product design is another key factor.

Those coming to India must decide whether or not to seek joint ventures. The answer is not easy and conditions in every industry are not the same. In some cases, joint ventures are the right choice; in others the venture partner might be the Indian public through equity offerings in India's lively stock exchanges.

India's economic geography is changing rapidly and will be very different in the new century. Tomorrow's industrial India will not be limited to the borders of Maharashtra and Gujarat. The Delhi area including Rajasthan, Punjab, Haryana and western Uttar Pradesh will bustle as will south India, especially the states of Karnataka, Tamil Nadu, and Andhra Pradesh. Over time, economic activity will also increase in the east. Early in the next century,

Calcutta should emerge as a major centre of industrial and financial activity as well as for technology research. India's states are becoming increasingly shrewd in offering inducements to investors.

India and the European Union

Michael Barrie McGeever

The EU–India partnership rests on the foundations of mutual interest and the mutually reinforcing tandem of trade and investment and economic cooperation. It has effectively synergized the opportunities arising in India since 1991 with the challenges of the EU in its movement towards the Single European Market in 1992, and now the Economic and Monetary Union by 1999.

The dynamism of EU–India economic cooperation is best demonstrated by the fact that the EU remains, by far, India's largest trade and investment partner. Currently, as India enters the global mainstream economy, the EU has responded with three multi-million ECU framework programmes to complement the effort: the Economic Cross Culture Programme to enhance mutual appreciation of economic culture, and business

▼ The European Parliament, Strasbourg, where the plenary sessions are held. The EU is India's largest trade and investment partner.

▲ At the behest of the Indo-British Partnership Initiative, former Prime Minister Narasimha Rao met the British Prime Minister John Major at 10 Downing Street. Industrialists with them in the picture include K.K. Bajoria, V.L. Dutt, R.P. Goenka and Rahul Bajaj.

ethos, the Asia-Invest to provide an impetus to mutual business networking, and the Asia-Urbs for mutual strengthening of urban institutions.

EU–India economic cooperation initiatives are set against the backdrop of the Indian economy's increasing globalization, with economic reforms and the liberalization process placing a growing emphasis on the private sector and decentralized structures. Beginning with primarily trade-related activities, EU–India economic cooperation has matured in both coverage and content, responding to rapid changes in the European and Indian economies. Over the past decade, EU–India economic cooperation has undergone a structural metamorphosis from pilot projects to larger multi-annual programmes.

These different elements of economic cooperation have led to the emergence of a coherent strategy, the priorities of which are general framework improvement, strengthening of institutional structures, and facilitation for business and sectoral initiatives.

Institutional-building, one of the cornerstones of EU–India economic cooperation, aims at the establishment of new institutions or the strengthening of linkages between institutions in India and Europe. Through this model, the EU has intervened in India in the areas of standards and quality, packaging and bar coding, intellectual property, and technology information.

Since 1987, when the first structured industrial cooperation programme was put in place, one stream of cooperation activities was focused on sectoral initiatives, shifting from merely trade promotion to integrated development, i.e. raw materials, production and process control techniques, quality and standards, market development, exports and joint ventures, and institutional linkages. The areas targeted included shellfish, mini-steel plants, office automation, medical and surgical tools, machine tools, automotive components, information technology, and infrastructure. With the rapid and progressive structural changes in the Indian economy, the EU fine-tuned its sectoral choice towards the infrastructure sector, which became the prime choice for both ongoing and future cooperation priorities. Energy, telecom, maritime transport, and civil aviation cooperation projects reflect that trend.

ASEAN and India

Kishore Mahbubani

Geography is destiny. India and South East Asia have been and will be neighbours for thousands of years. The ebb and flow of history will always link these two regions. When the twenty-first century is upon us, those living in it will look back at the past centuries and see that both colonial rule and the cold war created only a brief disruption in a close relationship of several millennia. The cultural bedrock of all South East Asian societies (with the exception of Vietnam) originates from India. The rise and fall of ancient empires and the advent and spread of Hinduism, Buddhism, and Islam have added complex layers to the multifaceted relationship between our two regions.

▼ Singapore has an ethnic population of Indians who, along with other investors, wish to extend their business relationship with India.

India has abandoned its licence Raj and embarked upon a course of economic openness. If this course succeeds and India joins ASEAN in being closely integrated with the modern, pan-global economy, this could uplift the lives of 950 m. people and their descendants. ASEAN, with the rest of East Asia, is now passing through a difficult period of economic adjustment. If, however, ASEAN pursues the right policies and undertakes the necessary structural changes, there is no doubt that the region will emerge stronger.

Long-run stability will rest eventually on the shaping of the relationship among the major powers in the region, including the US, Russia, Japan, China, and India. ASEAN has created and launched the ASEAN Regional Forum (ARF) to provide a platform for discussing sensitive regional issues. India can make a critical contribution to the accomplishment of its goals. Under the ASEAN–India dialogue, mechanisms have been set up to bring about closer cooperation in the economic, political, and security fields.

Trade has run through history as the main channel of South East Asia's relations with India. It will continue to do so. India's economic reform has sparked a dramatic improvement in trade. Within a short span of three years, ASEAN's total trade with India rose from US$ 2.9 bn in 1993 to US$ 6.5 bn in 1996. This represents an average annual growth of 41 per cent. In 1996, total cumulative investment by ASEAN nations in India stood at US$ 1.8 bn.

Other recent developments augur well. ASEAN has established itself as a major trading entity with its overall trade growing from US$ 10 bn in 1967 to over US$ 620 bn in 1995. Trade within ASEAN has also boomed. In 1995, intra-ASEAN trade reached US$ 122 bn. ASEAN's trading capacity will be further enhanced when the ASEAN Free Trade Area (AFTA) is established. By the year 2003, tariffs within ASEAN would be reduced to 0–5 per cent on virtually all products. Likewise, India is also rapidly bringing down trade tariffs and actively promoting investment in India's export sector. Five years ago, international trade accounted for just 15 per cent of India's GDP, today it accounts for 20 per cent and is still growing.

ASEAN and India have taken the initial steps to strengthen collaboration in the science and technology sector. The potential for synergy is immense. India, supported by a large pool of scientific and creative talent, has established a global reputation for research and development. ASEAN, with a large market network, can help to launch ideas and innovations from India's laboratories. The importance of pooling our resources in this sector cannot be overemphasized. Cooperation is the key to our common future.

India and Japan

Nobuhiko Kawamoto

Ever since India liberalized its economic policy, Japanese enterprises have made 280 investments in India, nearly ten times greater than the combined total prior to 1991. This is dramatic evidence of Japanese interest in Indian enterprises as major economic partners in the twenty-first century.

Among India's greatest attractions for investors are: a potentially enormous market with a middle class numbering about 150 m. at present, and increasing by 20 m. people every year; a great number of good quality engineers; a well-trained and competitive labour force; a functioning legal system to assure foreign investors that they may carry out legitimate activities with freedom and confidence; and general proficiency in the English language.

▼ A view of the recently constructed Nizammuddin Bridge in New Delhi, the result of Japanese assistance towards creating viable infrastructure in the country. Though the most obvious Indo-Japanese collaborations are in the passenger car and two-wheeler segment, the Japanese have a respectable presence in other industries as well.

To turn this potential market into reality, there remain some issues which investors feel need improvement to further enhance the investment environment. First, politics in India should become more stable. Businesspeople place great importance on political stability in the long term when they consider investments. Political instability often leads to social unrest which in turn may endanger an investor's activity. Second, as is often said, India's industrial infrastructure needs improvement. It is a especially urgent task of the government to satisfy such fundamental needs as electricity, transportation, port facilities, and communication. Though India has announced its intention of involving the private sector in infrastructural projects, each of these will entail risks and high gestation for return on investments. If the Indian government fails to provide some form of guarantees on investments, considering the actual conditions prevalent in India, there might be delays in improving the infrastructure, in consequence hindering speedy and sustainable economic growth.

India has demonstrated the success of, and shown steady economic growth since, its policy change of 1991, while some Asian countries have been in serious economic difficulties caused by financial problems in the recent past. Its further progress is very important to all those Japanese enterprises that have invested in the country or propose to do so. To that end it is, I feel, essential for us to develop personal contacts between the Indian and Japanese people at every level.

India–China–Hong Kong

James Tien

Over the years, there has been remarkable growth in trade between Hong Kong and India, with two-way trade increasing at 30 per cent per annum over the period 1993–6. This reflects the significance of the long-standing relations between the two economic entities. The business relationship between Hong Kong, mainland China, and India will be further extended in the coming century, especially with dramatic economic reforms continuing on the mainland and on the subcontinent. China and India are the two largest nations in Asia accounting for nearly 70 per cent of pan-regional GDP. Both countries' economic liberalization will provide a new diversity to their economies, adding to their huge potential and advantages as business and investment locations.

With the introduction of the economic reform programme of the early 1990s, the Indian economy began to grow rapidly. The liberalization of both trade and investment also enhanced India's integration into the global economy. The ninth Five-Year Plan (1997–2001) is expected to speed up the pace of economic reforms and allow for a more positive trade and investment regime. Hong Kong, by virtue of its sophisticated financial markets and role as a trading hub, as well as its substantial expatriate Indian population, has been able to provide a good business environment to develop opportunities between India and the mainland. By one recent estimate, Hong Kong companies have invested upwards of US$ 350 m. in India in 1996, and this is expected to edge upward in the near future, especially in the areas of infrastructure and hotels.

Reform in China has also provided new opportunities, and the mainland economy has shown remarkable development as, consistently, the fastest growing in the world, with per capita income more than quadrupling since 1978. In its 1997 *Global Economic Prospects* report prepared for the World Bank–IMF annual meeting in Hong Kong in September 1997, the World Bank named India and China as two of five countries (China, India, Indonesia, Brazil, and Russia) which would help redraw the economic map of the world in the new century. This ensures investors a good economic outlook for both mainland China and India in the long run.

The reunification of Hong Kong with the mainland means that Hong Kong companies will no longer just play the role of middlemen but serve as initiators and instruments of business activity. Hong Kong's service sector has been growing faster than anywhere else in the world over the past fifteen years and the new Special Administrative Region (SAR) has been called the world's

▲ Hong Kong is an important trading partner for India with a significant growth in business relations between them in recent times.

freest economy. It is also Asia's second leading financial centre, a major cargo centre, and a leading communications centre. With valuable international trade experience, the business sector of Hong Kong is unrivalled at exploring international trade opportunities and markets. Hong Kong is currently the seventh largest trading economy in the world.

While the uncertainties that have gripped East Asia in recent months may raise some questions about the prospects of some Asian countries, there seems little doubt that India and China (including Hong Kong) will play key roles in future regional and global economic development.

India and The Republic of Korea

Choi Dae-Hwa

In 1998, Korea claimed fourth place among investor nations in India, following America, the UK, and Mauritius. To keep up with the increasing pace of commercial ties, there has been a marked increase in the number of ministerial- and official-level bilateral talks. The faith that Korea has in the Indian market is expressed in its increasing investment in India. (The volume of trade between the two countries was around US$ 1.9 bn in 1995, US$ 2.2 bn in the following year; Korean investment is expected to be US$ 3 bn by the turn of the century, with a bilateral trade of US$ 5 bn.)

Having been on a fast track for the past three decades, the time has come for the Korean economy to pause for breath, a time when economic strategies need to be reconsidered, altered, and restructured. The current liquidity problem in the country is not a reflection of weak fundamentals, for these have supported rapid growth and still remain dynamic. The Korean economic foundation is constituted of a solid resource base, high savings ratio, strong export sectors, market orientation, low tax rates, skilled labour, and entrepreneurial dynamism.

Korean investors regard India as a huge market and fertile investment area. A few examples of continuing Korean investment may be appropriate. Kumho Tyre Co. plans a $120 m. joint venture production facility in Tamil Nadu to produce millions of tyres by the turn of the century. A leading Korean chemical company is poised to enter the Indian cosmetic market. In order to supply

▼ The author, Choi Dae-Hwa at a FICCI seminar with Sudhir Jalan and Dr Amit Mitra. Korean investors regard India as a huge market and fertile investment area.

▲ Santro, the latest small car to hit the Indian roads. Korean car manufacturers had a large presence at the last auto fair in the capital.

parts for Hyundai's 100 per cent Indian company, Hyundai Motor India Ltd, a host of Korean auto component vendors have entered into tie-ups with Indian partners with investments in these joint ventures amounting to several hundred crore rupees. This will make India a sourcing base for Hyundai's global demands. Daewoo Motors invested Rs 2400 crore when it commissioned its plant in Surajpur (UP) to manufacture auto engines, gearboxes, and body panels. Daewoo Anchor Electronics invested Rs 1800 crore and plans to bring in expertise and double its investment by the year 2000. Daewoo Power has a huge power project coming up at Korba which will require an investment of several billion dollars. LG's refrigerators and televisions have begun to storm the market. India has been identified as one of Samsung Electronics' four major strategic countries in the world. Over and above the $20 m. invested in India so far, it plans to put in another $20 m. in 1998 alone. The total investment by the year 2003 is targeted at $200 m.

Economic cooperation between Korea and India has reached a new level in the past few years. The essence of the bilateral relationship has not been overnight gains but laying of stepping stones into the next millennium for a strong and unshakeable partnership.

India and Australia

Tim Fischer

India's size, its economic potential, and geographical location make it a country of growing regional and global importance. After six years of economic reform, India has emerged as a major investment and trade location which is attracting considerable attention at a global level. Its economic reforms have been impressive. Tariffs have been slashed, the system of industrial licensing wound back, and the rupee floated. With a solid and sustained economic growth rate of 6 per cent, a growing consumer market, and the prospect of further liberalization of important economic sectors, India is rapidly becoming a key commercial destination in the Asia–Pacific region. A further welcome development which will considerably expand economic opportunities has been the Indian government's agreement in November 1997 to phase out import restrictions on a broad range of products. The agreement will enhance prospects for Australian exporters to meet the significant Indian demand for agricultural and horticultural products as well as a wide variety of other goods.

Australia has much to offer India as commercial partner in the region. It has a deregulated and highly competitive financial sector, a general tariff rate of 5 per cent, a diversified manufacturing and services sector, and efficient agricultural and mining sectors. The Australian economy has grown faster than most developed countries over the past few years and has done so with low inflation. Australian businesses now look to export and overseas investment. Trade amounts to 40 per cent of Australia's GDP and manufactures make up nearly 35 per cent of merchandise exports. Sixty per cent of Australia's exports go to Asia and over half its foreign direct investment now goes to countries in the Asia–Pacific region.

▼ Australia's Deputy Prime Minister and Minister for Trade Tim Fischer with former Commerce Minister Dr B.B. Ramaiah at the Fifth Joint Ministerial Commission, Canberra, in September 1997.

Recognizing the vast potential of the Indian market, the Australian government has made its relationship with India a priority. In late 1996, it launched a major integrated promotional presentation of Australia in India called New Horizons. The initiative featured a range of business, science, technology, education, cultural, and sporting events in six major Indian cities. Its core objectives were to raise Australia's profile in India as a trade and investment partner, to foster links between the Australian and Indian commercial sectors, and to facilitate Australia's

▲ A taste of the way Australia does business, at a meeting arranged by the Greater Mysore Chamber of Industry, Bangalore, 1996.

entry into the Indian market. During 1997, the Australian government encouraged the establishment of the Australia India Business Exchange Programme to promote understanding and contacts between young executives and to build on links forged during New Horizons.

Australian business has responded positively to the improved commercial landscape and opportunities in India. At the end of 1997, India was Australia's sixteenth largest market for merchandise exports, while Australia was India's tenth largest source of imports. Between 1991 and 1997, two-way trade doubled to reach in excess of A$ 2 bn which is anticipated to increase by the year 2000 to over A$3 bn. Australian exports to India increased by 11.5 per cent from 1991 to 1996. Coal is Australia's major export commodity to India. Australia is also the largest supplier of wool to India with a growing export quota. The most rapidly growing area of exports is in elaborately transformed manufactures (ETMs), which grew from A$ 30 m. in 1991 to A$ 195 m. in 1996.

In 1996, Australia was ranked the ninth largest country source of investment approvals for India. Australian investment in India now covers banking and financial services, manufacturing, and telecommunications. Further opportunities for investment by Australian companies are likely to arise from the massive development needs of India's mining and minerals processing, energy, telecommunications and infrastructure sectors.

There are strong opportunities for Australia to increase and diversify its investment in India, particularly in India's infrastructure development. Australian companies are already providing capital and expertise for major upgradation of India's ports, roads, and power generation facilities. In future, Australian investment in the mining sector is likely to grow. There is also significant potential for Australian companies to become involved in the expanding insurance, legal, education, telecommunications, and aviation sectors. Australia has much to offer India's continuing process of economic development and liberalization in terms of expertise and considerable experience in other regional countries.

Section V

Some Entrepreneurs: At Home and Abroad

Overview

Coming of Age

Kishore Singh

Midnight's children: it is a beautiful, and in the Indian context, an apt phrase. A civilization, thousands of years old, gained a new lease of life when it shrugged off the colonial yoke and set off to keep its tryst with destiny. It carried with it baggage that, in the five decades since, has been slow to move, given apathetic public institutions and dysfunctional bureaucratic systems. However, if ever there were a people willing to take their destinies into their own hands and rise above petty social considerations, it is the young generation of Indians who have come up to take charge of their lives, building a future for India, with India.

It has been no easy task, yet the Indian professional is an achiever who, given but a little of what the world takes for granted, has converted it into so much more. Denied opportunities under foreign rule, and faced with alarming rates of poverty, illiteracy and insufficiency, India has taken on the battle of bettering the lives of millions of people who have so much to give back, to India and the world. In small towns, girls battle the unavailability of public transport systems by pedalling to school on bicycles, or attending diploma courses and colleges on motorized two-wheelers. In urban schools, little children barely out of kindergarten are discovering the multiple opportunities of computerization. Housewives are taking courses that will provide them a vocation: the money it will bring is welcome, but even more

▼ Members of the ladies study group of Indian Chamber of Commerce, Calcutta with Prime Minister India Gandhi. Among those in the picture are Premlata Mody, Roma Bhagat, Sheela Kanoria, Sumangala Birla, Veena Singhania, Urmila Kanoria, Usha Patodia, and Sheela Davar.

important is the independence it will provide them as they take decisions, perhaps for the first time, that affect their lives.

Newspaper supplements are a healthy index of the state of a dynamic, new society in transition. Young professionals today find that choice is no longer limited to the big four career options of their parents' generation: the civil service, defence services, engineering, and medicine. Careers are being carved, international reputations established, and awards snapped up in writing, publishing, fashion, graphics; in brain and human resource industries, the arts, music, entertainment; in media, law, environmental research. And in each one of these, with niche specialization, the Indian has arrived not just on the national, but the international firmament. It is so easy to also name today, Indians commanding positions of power and responsibility in UN organizations, MNC corporations, software industries, and core industries; even where they may not head organizations, they are appointed for the sincerity, common sense and hard work they bring to their jobs.

It is these Indians who have made India the flavour of the forthcoming millennium. In a sense, the Indianization of the world has begun, as Indian intellect, its cuisine and its couture, its moral and social proprieties, have begun to make an impression around the world. Indian entrepreneurs have proved that they can run successful businesses outside India, often with greater ease. India is no longer isolated and insular; it is at once an ancient country and a modern one with a futuristic outlook; a country with multiple layers that has taken its rightful place on the world stage with an insouciance that comes from having within its folds a bank of human resource that would do any nation proud.

While the professional world is benefiting most from this, it has also given rise to a wave of entrepreneurial excitement. The new Indian sees and seizes opportunity, whether in the backlanes of small market towns in India, or when creating software packages in the Silicon Valley; the rise of a new Indian entrepreneurial class has begun, and the only currency it needs to carry in the world market is its intellectual merit. This new breed of entrepreneurs is now increasingly establishing its presence in the national and global market places. The families that have

▲ Modern Indian women have assumed more complex and varied roles than ever before – managing homes even as they train and work as pilots.

contributed to the Indian economy despite, first, foreign rule and, later, overpowering socialistic concerns of government, are now seeing a new generation of heirs change the way companies look at human resource, technology, and family-owned, top-heavy establishments. Educated in the global way of doing business and running industries, this crop of owner-managers welcomes intervention from professionals in the way businesses are run. Heirarchies are being shaken, new systems set in place, the best the world has to offer is being tapped by way of technology upgradation.

Women, too, are making a major difference at the workplace. No longer are professions gender biased. From flying fighter aircraft to running hotels, from inheriting businesses to establishing them, from being women to becoming colleagues, women in India are making their mark. The new generation now at school may never face discrimination in professional opportunities: it will grow up to work, as professionals or as entrepreneurs, not as men or women. And increasingly the world will lean towards them: men and women. For even as the millennium slips past us, we have proved that when it comes to work, there is none better than the Indians.

Modern India and the Emerging Businesswoman

Anuradha K. Rajivan

Whether women are better than men I cannot say — but I can say they are certainly no worse.

Golda Meir

I love the idea of men and women being equal ... In the old days things didn't function without women. Today a guy can live without a woman.

Mario Puzo

Picture this: a woman in a business of her own for the explicit purpose of earning a profit; taking hiring and firing, investment and borrowing, procurement and sales, technology choice, strategic, and a hundred other decisions; working not as a helper with her husband or father, but for herself. Fifty years ago a woman heading a substantial business was a rarity and would attract considerable attention and discussion. Sumati Morarjee of Scindia Shipping and Sharayu Daftary of Bharat Radiators experienced this in their times. Today, women in the echelons of business continue to generate the interest of a rare species. Though there are definitely more women entrepreneurs around, it is still not a widespread phenomenon.

▼ Protima Gauri Bedi was a socialite who found her true calling as an Odissi dancer late in life. She got industrialists to provide her support for setting up a dance school on the outskirts of Bangalore in the Indian *guru-shishya* tradition.

Social attitudes influence choices that both men and women make. In contrast to the USA, in India enterprise itself has had a narrow base, the dominant attitude being to prefer salaried jobs in large established companies or government. There are negative attitudes towards entrepreneurship, unless it is an inheritance. Starting out on one's own is even associated with the failure to get a job.

A part of the phenomenon of women taking to occupations outside their homes in all spheres is their growing numbers in business enterprises. In contrast to the past, there are decreasing inhibitions about taking charge, seeking out and holding leadership positions, making money, and being financially independent. A desire for control over money and assets is a clearly emerging trend. It is not as if women in India have not worked

▲▼ Bina Modi *(above)* may have come from a conservative background, but she has managed to find the support within her family to open one of New Delhi's trendiest restaurants, Ego *(below)*.

outside the home; this has always been common among those in the lower economic strata. Even among the more inhibited middle and upper classes, during the days preceding India's Independence and immediately after 1947, women in public life were not uncommon, displaying remarkable qualities of 'social enterprise'. However, commercial enterprise was frowned upon — social attitudes held by both men and women circumscribed choice and worked against taking charge of creating and retaining wealth. Not that women were considered incapable of handling leadership positions. Rather, among the upper and middle classes, the dominant view prescribed that women should confine themselves to 'elevating' occupations; teaching, social service, or even art, craft or music was acceptable, making money and the creation of wealth were not. Then there were the inheritance laws of a patriarchal society, the complications of dowry, and a social position that considered women as part of her marital family rather than her natal. These interfered with a clear convergence of financial interest between daughter and father, the way it did not with son and father.

Since women play a pivotal role in families, family support is crucial without which their participation in economic activity is hindered. The primary responsibility of childcare and household work is placed squarely at their door, and equal sharing is an exception rather than a rule. In fact, domestic work is a central issue for all working women, including entrepreneurs. Women are learning to cope in a variety of ways — with some family support, paid outside help, careful time management, and a sharp compromise on leisure. Often, it is enterprise rather than regular, salaried work that women have preferred because it offers greater flexibility in handling work at home and at the office.

Women have had to walk the tightrope between desire for personal success and pressure to not better their husbands. That this is not an exclusively Indian phenomenon is evident from a study on women's enterprise in Sweden edited by Caroline Turner:

> A married woman who wants to set up her own business will usually inform her husband in detail about her plans, that she will have to work long hours ... if he is willing ... there will be no trouble ... it is also a difficult thing for a man to accept that his wife earns more money than he does.

A similar study in India edited by V.S. Mahajan draws the same conclusions: '[The] occupational backgrounds of the families and educational attainments of the husbands have a direct bearing on the development of women's entrepreneurship. [It is expecterd that] the woman entrepreneur ... [enters] business in such a manner ... that their husbands' [sic] prestige is not affected in any manner.' Access to finance tends to be a problem with women starters. Businesswomen complain that banks do not consider them good

▲ Shobana Bhartia, President of FLO, and Madhu Kanoria, who held the same post earlier, with former Commerce Minister P. Chidambaram in India's liberalization years.

borrowers. Financial institutions often insist on a male signatory, not quite trusting the capacity of women to repay. This has irked many and hindered those with no close male relatives willing to stand guarantee for them. Years of conditioning have gone into giving women the appearance of underconfidence when it comes to, for example, negotiating with banks.

It is against such a background that women are carving out a niche for themselves in the world of business. This is also reflected in the composition of associations like the FICCI Ladies Organization (FLO) which is increasingly composed of businesswomen themselves.

Given the recent pattern of girls outperforming boys in schools in India, reflecting a trend already much discussed in the UK, Europe, and the US, women are increasingly likely to improve their opportunities in the job market during the next two decades. An increasing number of role models are contributing to their expanding horizons and expectations. Social legitimacy for women's work is rapidly gaining ground, and more families are now rallying around their right to carve a career for themselves. This has contributed to the start of more egalitarian relationships between spouses among the younger generation, with greater options available to women, but the reallocation of work at home is still in its infancy. How men and families respond to rising expectations among women will influence future relationships between the sexes. This, in turn, is influenced by how parents bring up their boys and girls. This will be a crucial issue over the next two decades. Will the relationships be more fractious, or will they be mutually supportive? With stronger family bonds, it might well be that Indian men and women show the rest of the world the way to cope with twin ambitions and incomes.

What follows are snapshots of a few businesswomen who have taken to substantial business enterprises after 1980. These women are not only successful, they are stockholders as well as decision-makers.

Eggs and Chicks

Definitely a new breed inheritor–daughter, Anuradha Desai, Chairperson and Managing Director of the Pune-based Venkateswara Hatcheries Ltd, runs a Rs 4800 m. turnover poultry business. What strikes an observer is the easy blend of tradition and modernity in her demeanour. Indian clothes, *kumkum,* and

▲▼ Anuradha Desai of Venkateswara Hatcheries runs one of the country's most modern poultry business with automated processes. Her dream is to see India move up the ladder from number five to number one in global poultry production.

the *mangalsutra* are combined with a sharp business instinct and hard work. Born in 1962 in a Telugu family, she had an arranged marriage with a Maharashtrian boy chosen by her parents. With no plans to join the business of her father, the late B.V. Rao, she nevertheless agreed to a three-month summer stint in the company after her graduation in 1984, in accordance with her parents' wishes. That was it; she was hooked. The three months stretched to over a year during which she was made to start right at the bottom: cleaning coops, washing sheds, and feeding the birds. B.V. Rao insisted that she work in every department. She was soon running Ventri, the group's division manufacturing vaccines and other drugs for poultry.

Anuradha's entry into business was in compliance with her parents' wishes. There was no complication about a daughter joining and taking charge, even though they had two sons. Nor was it the result of a marriage gone sour, with the parents compensating their child by letting her run a part of the business. Anuradha's chartered accountant husband, Jitendra Desai, is today the group's financial director; her two younger brothers work with the company. Any family discord? There was some when B.V. Rao married a second time after his wife's death in 1992 resulting in the three children being sidelined, but there was a reconciliation before his death. Soon after, in January 1996, the board had little hesitation in appointing Anuradha its CMD.

Venkateswara Hatcheries is today a hi-tech, multi-million enterprise. While hatcheries are the group's flagship, it is also associated with a wide range of related activities such as world class poultry health products, disinfectants, and vaccines. Backward integration through automated feeding systems, pelletized feed, and hi-tech hatcheries is combined with forward integration covering poultry processing, converting broilers into pre-portioned chicken, ready-to-eat chicken products like nuggets, samosas and burgers, egg products like whole egg powder, yolk powder, albumen powder, lysozyme, and egg shell flakes. All processing is automated and meets the standards of the USDA and EU.

Question her about possible negatives such as eggs having too much cholesterol, and she counters, 'All that is highly exaggerated. The consumers need to be educated. You tell me, is there a food safer and cleaner, and a source of protein cheaper than an egg?'

Future plans? India ranks fifth in world egg production and twenty-second in chicken and meat production. Anuradha would like to see India rank No. 1, at least in poultry. Little wonder that she plans to make Venkateswara Hatcheries into a Rs 10 bn group. It is strictly eggs and chicks for this businesswoman.

▲ Kiran Mazumdar was embarrassed that her father was a brewmaster, but took a course herself in Australia, and with no business background, went on to set up Biocon Biochemicals to produce enzymes.

Brewing Designer Genes

With a brewmaster father who worked for the UB group and a housewife mother, no one really expected Kiran Mazumdar to launch into enterprise. Born in 1953 in a Gujarati family, brought up in Bangalore, Kiran was at a loose end after her B.Sc. All she knew was that she was not academically inclined, and that her parents were putting no pressure on her to get married. That was when her father came up with an unusual suggestion: Why not study brewing?

It was the early 1970s. Kiran did not think brewing beer was very respectable. Conservatively, she even hid her father's profession from her friends. Now how could she, a girl, study brewing? But an offer to do a brewmaster's course in Australia and a scholarship from the Bangalore City Women's Association determined the course of her life. She accepted. That was the first step towards eventually becoming the Managing Director of Biocon India Ltd. Kiran, the only woman in the course, topped a class of ten students. She returned to India only to find that there were no jobs for women in brewing! At best, women were 'allowed' to work in laboratories, but never as brewmasters. A chance meeting with an Irishman from Biocon Biochemicals resulted in his offering her a job with the company in Ireland. He had heard about Kiran through a classmate in Australia. Two weeks later she was on her way to Ireland. At Biocon Biochemicals, she was put through intensive training in all aspects of the European brewing business. People addressed each other by their first names, no one bothered about her nationality; the atmosphere suited her perfectly. 'It was a great way of working,' she recalls.

Returning once more to India, this time armed with self-confidence, Kiran set up her own company in 1978, Biocon India (Pvt.) Ltd, in Bangalore, with 70 per cent Indian and 30 per cent foreign holding from Biocon Biochemicals. She had no family business background, no business school training, only a large measure of entrepreneurial spirit. Had she been better trained in business management, she might have spent time evaluating risks rather than jumping into the fray, and there might have been no Biocon group in India.

It was the pre-liberalization era. Starting a business implied inevitable trips to Udyog Bhavan and the DGTD, but she found help in the most unexpected situations. A major problem was finance. 'Women are considered high risk cases,' she was told; an experience common to first-generation entrepreneurs. The bank wanted her father's guarantee even for an agreed working capital limit, though she had guaranteed exports. Now, of course, the

▼ Priya Paul found herself a hotelier when her father died suddenly, but she accepted the mantle and went on to rebuild the ventures as modern, boutique hotels, using their strategic locations to her advantage.

tables have turned. With a turnover of Rs 350 m., today it is Kiran who is wooed by institutional lenders!

Starting as a modest manufacturer of papain and isinglass, the Biocon group has grown into an important producer of microbial enzymes for the domestic and international markets. Little wonder that Kiran is considered a trailblazer in the field. Since enzymes are eco-friendly products in comparison with harsher chemicals, she expects to play an increasingly dominant role in the coming years. To the food industry's traditional applications for brewing and distilling and the manufacture of bread and cheese have been added cocoa, tea, and coffee. Fibres for the fashion industry include cotton, cellulose, jute, and viscose. Pharmaceutical applications aim to produce consistent and stable formulations. Biocon India claims to be the first enzyme company to be given the ISO 9001 accreditation.

A woman often has to work against the odds, says Kiran. 'Even if she brings in more money than the man, she is still not treated as the primary breadwinner.' She adds, 'Too many people are ready to criticize working women.' Well-wishers often ask her when she plans to settle. 'They really want to know when I'm getting married,' she smiles. 'It just hasn't happened so far, that's all.'

Kiran's future business plans? An increasing focus on the development of products for the pharmaceutical and food industries, concentrating on fermentation, genetic engineering and chemistry. Eventually, of course, Kiran plans to straddle all emerging areas in the biotechnology industry.

Boutique Hotels

An example of the younger breed of inheritors, Priya Paul is very much a woman of the 1990s. Part of the Apeejay Surrendra group with diversified interests in steel, engineering, shipping, trade, tea, confectionery, real estate, construction, and hotels, she handles the group's Park Hotels with a Rs 530 m. turnover.

Born in Calcutta in 1966, of Sindhi–Punjabi Bania parentage, the eldest of the four children of Surrendra and Shirin Paul, Priya started as marketing manager in Park Hotels under her father in 1988. Having grown up in a joint family with a business background, it was natural for her to spend vacation time in her father's hotel business. There was no resistance to a daughter entering the family business even though she had two brothers, indicating changing trends among parents as well. After her father's death in 1990, her mother took over Apeejay Surrendra. Their hotel business needed a revamp programme, and Priya was thrust into the centre of this. She not only took complete charge, but also initiated a major renovation plan to reposition Park Hotels in a

special niche as boutique hotels. 'We were not large enough to compete head-on with the others, but our property locations were excellent.' The idea of boutique hotels is fairly common overseas but relatively new in India. Small enough for personalized service, with no compromise on luxury, an attention to detail, stylish, and pleasant was Priya's concept, which was rewarded by the inclusion of their New Delhi venture in the exclusive club called the Small Luxury Hotels of the World. Two other hotels are located in Calcutta and Vishakapatnam.

The repositioning and revamp came at a cost, a whopping Rs 350 m. which to her credit was funded entirely from internal accruals. She had considered going public a couple of years ago, 'but with the subsequent crash in the stock market, it had to be given up', she explains. What about returns on investment? There was an increase in occupancy in the beginning, but the trend is mixed after 1993–4. The fate of the hospitality industry is inextricably linked with economic swings, yet she is building in New Bombay and exploring avenues in Bangalore and Chennai for extension, confident of her competitive capability. After all, eventually, whatever happens in the short term, one cannot go too wrong in India within the hotel and real estate business.

▲ Lobby of the Park Hotel in New Delhi, now listed in the prestigious Small Luxury Hotels of the world's guide to exclusive properties.

▲ Dilnawaz Shroff used her insatiable curiosity to learn, and then gave positive shape to that knowledge to set up a financial constancy that has a Rs 800 m. turnover today.

Telephone Operator to Founder Director

From telephone operator to founder director of the E'l Dorado group of finance companies is an unusual path to traverse. Dilnawaz Shroff did it with sheer grit and a determination to succeed.

Born in 1960, she lost her father at the tender age of 10. Her mother, though illiterate, was tough and ensured that Dilnawaz and her younger brother continued their studies. Even before her mother died, Dilnawaz had begun to think of herself as head of the family. Immediately after graduation in 1978, she needed to earn and took up the first job she could get: that of telephone operator with a merchant banking firm. But Dilnawaz was destined for greater things. With her insatiable curiosity, she would constantly pose questions about how the firm was run. She was often seen pestering colleagues to post her elsewhere within the company. In a couple of years she rose to become the confidential executive assistant to the CMD. This gave her the exposure and confidence to eventually strike out on her own.

In 1986, triggered by a burning ambition to reach the top, she and a male colleague left the firm together, invested Rs 700 each ('It seemed like a lot of money then!'), and so was born the E'l Dorado group for financial consultancy in Mumbai. Today, it has a turnover of Rs 800 m.

Recalling the group's growing pains, Dilnawaz explains how they started from a tiny cabin with crates draped in bedsheets as furniture. Job seekers turned away saying, 'Oh no! You'll fold up tomorrow.' Today the group offers a variety of financial services that includes merchant banking, stockbroking, portfolio management, and investment in securities and real estate. The group has membership of the Bombay Stock Exchange, the National Stock Exchange, and the Over The Counter Exchange in India. With five offices in Mumbai itself, and branches in New Delhi, Bangalore, Goa, and Guwahati, the group also plans to open others in India and overseas. Expansion plans include foreign exchange operations, exports, and publishing. This last is a foray into a non-finance area; writing is something Dilnawaz enjoys.

Dilnawaz recognizes that she was fortunate to enter the field during a boom, contributing to her early success, but sheer dedication and capacity for hard work were no less important. The E'l Dorado group now has ten constituents, each a private limited company. Whatever their legal status, the two originators continue to this day to consider themselves partners.

Married in 1983, with a 5-year-old son, her husband has been supportive of her ambitions, contributing his share to childcare and adjusting schedules so that neither work nor child suffers.

▼ Sminu Jindal is the only woman in the Jindal family to take to business, and since she is in charge of a cold-rolling unit for stainless steel coils, is fussy about pollution and safety standards, reflecting the concerns of her generation.

Dilnawaz believes that the glass ceiling does not apply to women entrepreneurs, though it may in salaried employment. Banks and financial institutions are becoming more open to lending to women, though some still insist on archaic procedures like the husband's signature. 'I am an optimist and stubborn, I am a survivor,' she says, capturing the essence of her strategy in a single sentence.

Steely Sminu

Granddaughter of O.P. Jindal, daughter of his eldest son, Prithviraj Jindal, Sminu Jindal is the only woman to take to business in the Rs 27,000 m. turnover house of the Jindals. 'There was never any question of my doing anything else,' she insists. 'I used to like going around with my father. After Class XII, I worked as a management trainee for some time.'

Born in 1973, educated in Delhi, in 1994 she took over as CEO of Swastik Foils Ltd, a division of SAW Pipes (submerged arc welded steel pipes). With a turnover of Rs 250 m. and a 200-strong staff, nearly all male, Sminu is in charge of the cold-rolling unit for stainless steel coils. We expect to touch Rs 1 bn by the year 2000,' she says with confidence. On finance, 'my grandfather used to be conservative. Between my father and his brothers, internal generation was the only source. Until seven years ago, we did not tap outside sources.' Now listed in the stockmarket and tapping institutional sources, Jindal the proprietorship has been transformed into Jindal the organization.

Reflecting the concerns of her generation, Sminu is fussy about pollution and safety standards. All acidic rinsing water is recycled in an effluent treatment plant. Visitors are requested to use safety gear such as helmets. Sminu has endeavoured to introduce a sense of team spirit through regular departmental meetings. Started as tea-sipping, biscuit-crunching sessions, they made the atmosphere uncomfortable for those unused to bonhomie at work until the ice was finally broken. Another typical Sminu touch is giving a half day birthday holiday to anyone on the SFL team. Employee welfare has stretched well beyond what is statutorily required. Her management style reflects her youthful enthusiasm, a desire to be liked, a concern for others, and an endeavour to make work fun.

Still single, though her younger sister is married, she says, 'Right now work is very important to me ... hey! I'm only 24.' She grins and continues, 'For a businesswoman, unless there is adjustment at home, marriage can be difficult.' What Sminu does not voluntarily talk about is her operating out of a wheelchair. When asked, she explains matter-of-factly, 'Oh, I'm a paraplegic,' the result 'of a road accident when I was 11 years old'. There is no self-

consciousness, no attempt to project or camouflage her disability. Sminu and her younger sister were both in the accident. 'After a while my sister started walking, I did not.' Though she makes light of it, this remarkable woman has taken much in her stride. The progressive attitude of her parents has undoubtedly helped. For example, when she got admission to the Sri Ram College of Commerce, New Delhi, Sminu was nervous about the ragging. 'I begged my father to let me skip the ragging period but he didn't agree. He just said, "Go and face it". I did.' Clearly a woman of steel in more ways than one.

Commitment Can Pay

Founders of Kali for Women, India's first feminist publishing house, Urvashi Butalia and Ritu Menon have made their commitment to women's issues into a paying proposition. Started in 1984 in New Delhi, working out of Ritu's Panchsheel Park garage with just Rs 1000, their survival prospects were rated low. How could one make money out of such a narrow subject area with its limited readership? They were advised not to test their commitment to a cause against the relentless discipline of the market. As it turned out, Ritu and Urvashi have had the last laugh, proving their critics wrong.

With a Masters each in English, it was education rather than business that the two women shared. Born in 1948, Ritu had worked with Vikas and Orient Longman in India, and Doubleday in the US. Urvashi, four years younger, had worked with the Oxford University Press in Delhi and London, and also with Zed Books, London. 'Publishing being a small world, we had heard about each other.' Correspondence between the two confirmed their common, strong concern for women's causes. Starting their own publishing house was almost a natural corollary.

Now located in Delhi's upmarket locality of Hauz Khas, the neat, elegant office is different from the overcrowded Daryaganj premises of many of Delhi's publishers. Today Kali is known for its slickly produced, quality books — the result of intelligence, personal attention, unconventional titles, carefully chosen manuscripts, combined with low overheads. In fact, Kali has given large publishing houses a run for their money, and has also resulted in some of them starting a separate 'women's studies' list.

Unlike larger publishers whose principal concern is volume, with special attention paid only to a potentially high sales author, 'we pay close attention to all our authors. In fact, most of the time we pick up ideas and commission authors whom we know about. Only about one per cent of the manuscripts we accept are unsolicited,' explains Ritu, as Urvashi nods in agreement. They have some strict rules about what they will and won't publish. A great

▲▼ Ritu Menon *(above)* and Urvashi Butalia *(below)*, have used the feminist plank to set up a publishing company, Kali for Women, trading their careers as professionals to entrepreneurs.

▲ Catalogue jacket of Kali for Women.

majority of their authors are women, though they do accept some men for non-fiction writing. Kali's fiction, however, is only by women. Why this policy against men? Urvashi clarifies, 'They can always get their work published elsewhere. Besides, we don't accept any woman either. Shobha De, for example, would not be considered by Kali. Apart from content, she could also get other publishers.' The prerequisite is that the writing should reflect a woman's point of view. Urvashi and Ritu have a distinct preference for authors from less developed countries, and especially the subcontinent. Very soon Kali plans to bring out more celebratory work, fun writing, and non-sexist children's stories, as feminine concerns have changed over the years.

'The final test, of course, is that the book has to work in the market. But here, one book of ours is really like three books for a regular publisher.' If this appears perplexing, they explain, 'You see, first we get the original market. Then there is the export market. Finally, we have reprints.' It has turned out to be a successful strategy: by being careful at the manuscript selection stage itself, they have been able to maximize sales in the long run.

Future plans look at 'growing and developing in the same direction, but exploring many areas within it', says Urvashi. 'Ditto,' echoes Ritu.

Sweet Business

An inheritor–daughter, Coimbatore-based Rajshree Pathy came into the family business by accident when her father died unexpectedly in 1990. Born in 1958, daughter of G. Varadaraj, she is from one of the Kamma Naidu families that moved to Coimbatore from Andhra Pradesh in search of black soil for their cotton business over 200 years ago. Married at the early age of 18 to an inheritor–son of a Coimbatore business family, Rajshree had no plans of joining her father, least of all taking over completely, but when the unexpected happened she quickly came to terms with the changed circumstances and decided to step into her father's shoes. 'I knew I had to do it. I had no time to cry. There was no thinking it over,' she says simply.

Today, as Chairperson of the Rajshree Group of Companies, she is not only in total command of her Rs 850 m. sugar business as Managing Director of Rajshree Sugars and Chemicals Ltd, but along with sister Jaishree, she also oversees the operations of the Rs 3000 m. turnover group with interests in textiles, spinning, auto ancillaries, finance, and travel.

At the outset it was tough. People expected the business to be sold, clearly underestimating Rajshree's capabilities. A drought year added to her troubles when the new sugar factory ran into

▲ Rajshree Pathy's inheritance was the legacy of business that ran in the veins of the Kamma Naidu family, but circumstances led her to accept her father's business where, besides sugar, she oversees operations in textiles, spinning, auto ancillaries, finance, and travel, along with her sister, Jaishree.

huge losses and the cane farmers could not be paid on time. She went around in the villages talking to the farmers. Now, with the hard days behind it, RSCL has grown into a dividend paying listed company. The Rajshree–Jaishree duo is poised to take the group beyond national boundaries. With the vagaries of the monsoon, rising cane prices, fluctuating sugar prices, dual pricing policy of sugar and sugar imports, there is never a dull moment in the sugar industry. There is no point complaining, Rajshree asserts, 'We have to use the liberalized regime to move ahead. The industrial sector is in a period of transition. If we don't modernize, we'll be overtaken.'

RSCL was, in fact, the first to install high pressure boilers in its technologically advanced manufacturing complex. The company is identifying related chemicals as a separate profit centre. With steam and bagasse generated as a by-product of sugar, the co-generation of power is also being undertaken.

The family has always combined philanthropy with its business activities. Conscious of her responsibility as a good corporate citizen, Rajshree tries to return some of what she has received from the community. She says, 'Social reform is a must with economic reform. The corporate sector must be sensitive to this — in an underdeveloped country it is shameful to focus only on bottom lines.' Ethics, quality, environmental matters — all these concern her. 'Even though our project costs are a little on the high side, I feel you should not compromise on quality and ethics.'

There is a strong creative urge in her that surfaces when she talks of new projects. 'I'm really a projects person, I don't get a charge out of day-to-day operations. I'm happiest setting up new projects.' The creative urge surfaces again when she talks of art. 'I'm into art appreciation, talking to artists, collecting pieces.' An art foundation for emerging artists in Coimbatore is on the cards. She plans to make funds available to support upcoming artists so that their work can be exhibited in India and overseas. Rajshree's Coimbatore home bears testimony to her love for art, craft, and beauty.

When Rajshree entered the sugar business, it was an exclusive male bastion. 'There was no advantage being a woman.' Having established herself, she no longer feels the need to prove anything to anyone. Acknowledging that gender bias exists in every country, '... success, not anger, is the only solution', she says with quiet confidence.

Her vision for the future is to expand, go international, grow with a social commitment and, more importantly, live life intensely.

Businesswomen at the Helm

Kanika Goswami

It is a man's world; or is it? It no longer even raises a perfunctory eyebrow to see a woman heading an organization. We no longer require Vedic sages to dictate to us that the Gods dwell where a woman is respected. Whether there are Gods dwelling around us today or not, women have certainly ensured that they receive the respect they deserve. As the rest of the world wakes up to this fact, it is a leading group of a handful of women in India who are bringing this awareness to women with somewhat fewer opportunities. It sometimes takes just one successful woman to inspire several others and to raise the general level of self-esteem. 'It is my confidence that has carried me through my toughest times,' says Vinita Singhania, who needed all the strength God could give her when, in 1988, her husband Shripat Singhania passed away, leaving her with two young sons to bring up. She was only 35 then, but bore her loss with admirable fortitude. 'You have to earn respect, your confidence can carry you through the toughest times,' she says. 'Self-realization, brought to me by religious discourses gave me the courage to go on, to believe in myself, to know that I am as good if not better than a man,' Vinita smiles. She took over her husband's office as Director of JK Corporation in 1990, gradually learned the art of organization and, in almost no time, was heading the Rs 4000 m. cement division of the organization, Lakshmi Cement.

Competing with her is V.L. Indira Dutt, Executive Director of KCP Limited, manufacturing high strength Portland cement used for railway sleepers and oil wells. KCP also produces machinery for sugar, cement, chemical plants, and heavy steel castings. In a joint venture with FCB of France, as Director of FCB KCP Limited, she is also engaged in the building, commissioning, and servicing of sugar plants, her latest venture being a 500 TCD sugar plant in Vietnam. If she seems to be in quite a heavy industry for a woman to handle, Indira Dutt's self-confidence is evident in the unique way in which she looks at the world: 'Women are the better half of the population,' she says, and 'society and the world at large can gain from our productivity.'

▼ Ritu Kumar is truly India's global fashion maker and designer. Working with traditional embroideries and weaves, she has not only given a new lease of life to the artisans but also has an international following with Western women opting for her Indian outfits.

(previous page):

▲ V.L. Indira Dutt is truly a woman in a man's, world, heading an organization that manufactures Portland cement for railway sleepers and oil wells, and produces machinery for sugar, cement and chemical plants, and heavy steel castings.

▼ Vinita Singhania took over the reins of Lakshmi Cement on the death of her husband and proved that a housewife could enter the of business late in life and yet make a success of it.

In another field which, ironically, was intended for women but far from represented by them on the corporate front, Simone Naval Tata entered more 'by accident than by intent': 'I felt I could contribute in a small way, as a woman who could understand a woman's needs and aspirations.' Simone , who was born in Geneva and married to Naval Tata, was appointed Director of Lakme Ltd in 1962 when the concept of 'the bold and the beautiful' woman had not even taken root. For the next thirty-three years, she served as Managing Director and, for some years, Chairperson, of Lakme Ltd, till her retirement from the post in 1995. She still continues to hold the Directorship of Tata Industries Ltd and Chairpersonship of Lakme Ltd, Lakme Lever Ltd, Lakme Exports Ltd, and Lakme Brands Ltd. She was awarded the Udyog Ratan Award in 1988 for her contribution to industry.

A similar family scene was that of Shobana Bhartia, Editorial and Executive Director of the Hindustan Times and Chairperson of the Press Trust of India (among other things). Shobana is a typical example of a very successful woman taking adequate care of home and children and being a very well-informed and powerful media 'baroness' of the country, being the daughter of K.K. Birla and the wife of S.S. Bhartia (of Vam Organics). She is, today, a successful businesswoman in her own right who ventured into the Hindustan Times group because she 'always had an interest in publishing'. To succeed, a great deal of hard work was required. 'After all,' she says, 'in every field you have to work hard to succeed.' The base gave her an opportunity to develop her strengths in her chosen field. However, coming from a conservative though illustrious family, to rub shoulders with media personnel and rise to such heights in such a competitive field was no mean achievement.

Ritu Kumar was deeply interested in and involved with Indian history and culture, in particular textile crafts of the country, especially those that were dying due to lack of patronage. Ritu says feelingly,

> As a matter of fact, the field had been neglected and the situation aggravated during colonization by the British. The effects of industrialization on these crafts was devastating, in fact there was a systematic cutting down on their production by filling the markets with material from the Western world which placed these hand-crafted textiles into the lowest section of the market. The mindset of the royalty and the then fashionable elite of the country was such that there was a preference for the French and English manufactured clothes.

Ritu set about bringing a radical change in the thinking of the people who mattered. It led not to a mere show of *swadeshi* but victory for a woman with a mission that counted; of showing the world that India had a splendid heritage of crafts and textiles that even centuries of colonization were unable to erase. Today Ritu's,

▼ Preetha Reddy's chosen field of specialization is medicine, though it may be more appropriate to qualify that further as the management of medicine, given her role in Apollo Hospitals where she is Managing Director.

a premier design label in women's wear and the first Indian designer store to open in London, is more an expression of Indian heritage than just couture.

In an allied field, that of herbal cosmetics, an Indian princess has achieved worldwide recognition. Shahnaz Husain, born in the family of Chief Justice N.U. Beg, claims descent from royal Mughal lineage. Shahnaz's dream was to see the Indian flag flying high in the cosmetic capitals of the world; after all, it too had its secret herbal preparations that had been used by generations of Indian women to enhance their beauty. She set about her task with tenacity. With an initial capital investment of Rs 35,000, borrowed from her father, Shahnaz set about creating her herbal empire. Married at 15 and a mother at 16, nothing dampened her relentless drive towards success. She trained at foreign institutes of cosmetology like Helena Rubinstein, Lancome, Christian Valmy, and Arnould-Taylor. Back home, she pioneered the concept of herbal care and cure, revolutionizing the concept of beauty in India. Thanks to Shahnaz, Indian beauty therapies gained popularity and acceptance. Single-handedly, she made an industry out of grandma's home remedies for a glowing skin, bright eyes, and lustrous hair. 'I knew that the "back-to-nature" trend would overtake the world, and I have tremendous faith in the healing power of nature,' she says. Armed with such confidence, Shahnaz has reached a position where she is undisputed queen of the herbal beauty concept throughout the world.

From beauty to health is but a stone's throw, and here Preetha Reddy fits the bill as the 'cure' woman. Managing Director of Apollo Hospitals, Preetha comes across as a hauntingly sweet and soft-spoken lady. But beware of the exterior for it hides an iron will and strong determination to change the healthcare scenario in the country. 'We are four sisters,' smiles Preetha, 'so when my father was setting up Apollo Hospitals, he had only his daughters to help him.' In 1983, when Apollo was set up, Preetha was already married. 'Health care services in India had no status as an industry before we started; we had to change an entire mindset towards the concept.' It took hard work, tremendous opposition, and firm determination on Dr Reddy's and his daughter's part to achieve what Apollo is known for at this point of time: quality health care services. 'Elsewhere in the world, the best medical assistance is available to people while in India all we have are overpriced nursing homes

▲ Sarparveen Kaur trained professionally in bee-keeping and then turned her interest into a business, as producer and exporter of Honey Bee, utilizing a natural resource that is plentiful in India.

or government hospitals.' Apollo Hospitals changed the scenario bringing in quality health care, albeit at a price, readily available to everyone. Preetha Reddy, who is proving more than a son to her father, surely leaves him no room to regret the lack of one.

Not quite the woman behind a successful man, Sarparveen Kaur is the commercial brain behind Honey Bee, producers and exporters of honey in various flavours and textures. A defence officer's daughter, Sarparveen met and married Peter Satwant Singh, with a doctorate in mathematics, in 1973. It was when she went to live with him in his ancestral home at Phillore, in Jalandhar district, that her business instincts came to the fore. Along with her husband, she trained at Punjab Agricultural University in bee-keeping and then began the arduous task of persuading farmers to maintain beehives to encourage honey production. 'It could have been difficult,' she reminiscences, 'but I had faith in myself, and so did my husband — that, and respect.'

That brings us to another important aspect: how do families, especially husbands and their families, react to a woman's aspirations and ambitions, and then success? Most successful businesswomen of our times maintain that they have had complete support from their spouses and in-laws. Family provides the basic support structure that builds one's confidence, the most important ingredient for success. 'My family has been with me totally,' smiles Sarparveen. 'I did not have to rush around for a support system for my children. I knew they had a family around them, even if I was travelling abroad for months.' This, in itself, is a great advantage, for children continue to remain an area of concern for

most working women. 'My husband and in-laws encouraged me,' say Sarparveen, and other entrepreneurs like her, when asked for the 'mantra' of their success. In the same breath, Shahnaz Husain is glad that at least initially she could work from home, though in later years she was able to devote far less time to her children, 'but I had my husband's full support and that is why I could carry on'.

In the case of Vinita Singhania, it was brother-in-law Harishankar Singhania 'who encouraged me to move out of the house, initially as light work to keep me busy,' she says, 'but later I picked up the job very well.' It was the unlimited support she received from the company's senior employees that enabled her to develop her strengths; they are people she feels indebted to for standing by her in what was her time of need — and growth.

There are those who swear by the 'will to succeed' like Shobana Bhartia, though she concedes that 'it is more difficult for women because they cannot completely discard their responsibilities at home. A woman has to work harder than a man because she has to manage more than just her work,' she says. 'A woman's creative strength must come from within herself — her own courage of conviction, steely determination, and tenacity of purpose,' feels Indira Dutt. It is not merely a man's world they are fighting, but also the world of a woman's fears: of failure, of insecurities, and a mode of thinking conditioned to look upon women as weak or inferior.

A noteworthy point is a basic trait in a woman's nature that emerges in her many endeavours, whether producing beauty products or cement or providing health care, and that is the instinct for caring, and for nurturing people and relationships. That is why the entire JK Corporation runs to do Vinita Singhania's bidding, and not just because she is the boss. That is also what enabled Shahnaz to hold an audience captive at the CIDESCO World Congress in New York in 1980, as the Indian representative and President for the day, and to achieve the many laurels that followed the rare honour. It is this unmistakable touch of caring that has helped Indian women overcome personal and professional hurdles, even as a Ritu Kumar grappled with restoring India's lost prestige in handicrafts and textiles, or a Simone Tata bringing in a personal touch to the Lakme range which still has not lost its magic, even in the face of invasion by foreign brands. The feminine touch comes across as a healing one in the case of Preetha Reddy striving to make quality health care 'easily accessible' to all those who need it. It is what makes Indira Dutt, Director of the Velagapudi Foundation that promotes education among the economically weaker sections, and also a major trustee in Arogya Nilayam Charitable Trust, a women's organization that conducts free medical healing for the poor, tick. The caring side of this tough businesswoman also

encourages her to work as Vice-President of the Spastics Society of Tamil Nadu and the National Association for the Blind, dedicated to the cause of the physically, and otherwise, disadvantaged fellow beings.

Eventually, however, it is their hard work that has taken these women along a road rarely travelled. They, and many others, are the inspiration for an entire generation of women who have the confidence but need the guidance to step out of their homes to seek opportunities in the world outside. 'Focus yourself and move on,' advises Preetha, and Ritu Kumar agrees, when she points out:

> It is important to be honest and committed to the cause of one's chosen career. With the changing mood of Indian media and business, there is always the possibility (and attraction) of getting to the goal in the shortest given time, thereby perhaps cutting corners and compromising both on quality and content of one's chosen work. A balance needs to be struck between working towards and meeting the challenges of the twentieth century, and at the same time keeping to the values and the conviction of doing one's work well.

Ritu Kumar's philosophy can indeed be summed up in just one word: dedication. More sound advice from Simone Tata: 'I would recommend any new entrant to concentrate on her areas of strength and delegate the rest to strong and capable professionals. And remember, education is a never ending process.' But in addition to professional abilities, one needs personal strength. 'Learn to respect yourself, the others will respect you. I've worked in the fields with the farmers and earned it,' muses Sarparveen. Shahnaz Husain, 'a child of tomorrow', endorses this. 'I never rest [on my laurels]. I never stop trying, so I never fail.'

▲ Shahnaz Husain chose the ayurveda route to beauty, drawing on the country's ancient research and resources in this field. Her products are now sold at counters around the world.

(previous page):

▲▼ Simone Tata *(above)* entered the beauty business with Lakme *(below)* when she married Naval Tata. She believes only a woman has full understanding of another woman's needs.

The New Face of Indian Industry

Suresh Achar

If India's long history is about its multifarious people, places, cultures, and religions, it is equally about its industry: the enterprise that moved goods and services from across the country to the furthermost reaches of the world. The early leaders of the country's trade and commerce were visionaries, people who could see beyond the prosaic to create a world vastly different from the existing one. Today, on the eve of a new millennium, India's new business messiahs continue to be driven by that vision which encompasses not just their own narrow concerns, and those of their companies, but also those of the country and its economic future.

Reaching out, Reaching up

At 31, Kumarmangalam Birla heads India's second largest business house. Inheritor of the Aditya Birla Group's business empire, the Group's global turnover for 1997-98 was Rs 200 bn with fixed assets of nearly Rs 180 bn and a 1,40,000 strong workforce spanning over sixteen countries. He is the youngest ever business leader in India of such a vast empire.

A chartered accountant by qualification, he is also an MBA from the London Business School. While actively involved in the group's business since 1990, it was in 1995, with the sudden passing away of his father, the legendary Aditya Birla, that Kumarmangalam Birla was appointed Chairman. Barely 27-years-old then, he did and continues to admirably shoulder the responsibility of steering the group successfully into the new millennium, giving it more strategic focus and streamlining and consolidating its operations. He has pulled out of unrelated diversification projects such as its proposed foray into steel, sugar, paper, glass fibre and PTA, worth over US$ 2 bn.

His sight firmly fixated on the future, Kumarmangalam provides the blueprint of the group's strategy.

> We will continue to retain and build on our leadership in our existing businesses and expand our global presence. Our focus is on consolidation. We have redefined our criteria for investment. For all new investments, we ask: 'Do we have a sustainable competitive advantage here? Can we become a dominant player? Can we create shareholder value?

▼ Ingot Casting Machine at Hindalco Plant, Renusagar. Within the Aditya Birla Group, globalization is not a new phenomenon, though Kumarmangalam Birla's drive towards relentless productivity is.

▼ Mukul Kasliwal of S. Kumar used his MBA not just to revitalize his interest in his business, but also in his country. He believes his schooling has been in the actual conditions of tough business.

Under his dynamic leadership, four companies have been acquired in the last four months: the Atholville Pulp Mill in Canada, signalling the group's first overseas acquisition; Dharani Cements, Chennai; and Shri Digvijay Cement Company, Gujarat and India Foils, Calcutta. He adds, 'To stay ahead, we place a premium on the customer, on people's orientation, on building systems into every aspect of the management process.'

He believes implicitly in the trusteeship concept of management. This entails being committed not only to one's shareholders but to meaningful, welfare-driven initiatives that make a qualitative difference to the lives of marginalized people, a part of the Indian tradition of business.

Globalization to him is not a new phenomenon. With an already strong global hold, being the first to venture into setting up production bases in the then vibrant and free markets of South East Asia, the group is well attuned to the culture of competition. 'Ours is a driven, learning and growing organization that is global by vision, but Indian by heart,' smiles Kumarmangalam.

Importantly, under him, there has been a steady stream of new concepts, innovations in work practices and relentless productivity improvements across his thirty-eight performing companies. Single-mindedly, the group is working towards withstanding the vicissitudes of an economy in slump.

A sterling, spontaneous person, he comes across as a man of remarkable humility and depth. Not surprisingly, *Business World* named him 'CEO of the Next Millennium'. Proud to be an Indian, Kumarmangalam says,

> Relative to many other economies our brain power is immense as are our other resources. We need to exponentially leverage these so that India can take its rightful position as a force to reckon with in the international economic scenario. I believe together as a nation we can make it happen.

Re-energizing the Corporation

An heir to the S. Kumar's brand name, Mukul Kasliwal is no typical owner-inheritor. Having done his 'on cloud nine' MBA in America, Mukul Kasliwal came back feeling as if he had been 'born again'. He recounts:

> I did very well in B-School and that gave me very great levels of satisfaction. Enriched with knowledge, energy, and lots of positive thoughts, I came back feeling that I could actually contribute; that I could take hold of my own destiny, and shape events and situations, even organizations, in the way that I thought they should be.

A sense of confidence, a positive feeling about himself, and a firm belief that the only way to revitalize the country was to revitalize the corporation, convinced Mukul that 'incentives were at the heart of every decision-making process; that the survival instinct drives human beings, and that if you are in a position to change a certain situation, why not?' He also came with a 'wariness', the feeling that there was a lot that needed to be done in the area of image and reputation as far as the country and its industry were concerned. As he puts it, 'We needed to spruce up our image' and 'somehow impact upon the system, so that changes could not only be carried out, but would also be welcomed as catalysts of better things.'

While bemoaning the fact that the system in India tends to take away much of one's time, preventing any real value addition, Mukul is confident that a scientific approach to change, based upon empirical testing and result analysis, could yield dividends. Alongside his personal concern for his country and its development, Mukul began to play a key role in the family business. The results, he says, 'were surprising, even to myself', for they were far better than his expectations, and because the response from the people directly concerned with the changes was very positive. The 'period of internship', as he calls it, was rewarding for it taught him patience, gave him a more mature approach towards dealing with problems. He is now poised to take the company into new directions, away from traditional business interests.

Today, Mukul Kasliwal is ready to take on the challenges of the future. His schooling, after all, has been in the actual conditions of tough business. 'The only thing which matters is a win-win situation — for everyone concerned.'

Connecting Everywhere

▼ Sunil Bharti Mittal represents the new face of IT in India. A driven man, he aspires to drive the company and the country to the cutting edge of information technology.

Telecom is the new face of Indian industry and Sunil Mittal of Bharti Telecom its most appropriate mascot. Telecommunication, he believes, is the key to business, and in the next century he wants to help meet the urgent communication needs of the country. According to him, if India is to join the comity of nations that are economically strong and growth oriented, then effective communication systems are a prerequisite.

From a mere telephone instruments manufacturing company till as late as 1993, in a short period of five years Bharti Telecom has become a major player in multi-fields like push button

▶ The telecom industry has changed rapidly in India, in the short space of five years.

telephones, radio pagers, transmission equipments, and specialized silicone-coated telecom ducts. Besides, the company has emerged as a viable alternative for businessmen in the capital (and in Himachal Pradesh and Madhya Pradesh) with its Airtel Cellular communication service. Besides providing basic telephone services in Madhya Pradesh, Bharti Telecom now offers V-sat services in partnership with British Telecom, and telecom services to the island of Seychelles in conjunction with Emtel of Mauritius. Given technology partnerships with world leaders Ericsson, Motorola, Alcatel, Siemens, and Lucent, Mittal has seen a steep rise in his company's turnover from a mere Rs 300 m. in 1993 to Rs 5000 m. in 1998, a commendable performance indeed.

A man who describes himself as a 'simple businessman', Mittal has a vision for himself and his group: to be best in its chosen areas and to possess international levels of productivity and services, a

▼ At Tube Investments, A. Vellayan chose to opt out of certain businesses so that in the others he would remain and grow into a leader.

value base for satisfied and loyal customers that would provide the edifice for the next century that his group requires. Mittal knows that time waits for no one, so he works at a frenetic pace setting standards of performance within his group which, by example, inspire a large and diverse workforce to achieve levels of excellence and growth.

Tubular Growth

Tube Investments of India Ltd (TI), the flagship company of the Murugappa group based in the south is a multi-product company which has achieved significant growth over the years. The group turnover for the year ended 1997–8 was Rs 29,000 m. and the turnover for TI for the same year was Rs 6000 m. TI's main businesses are bicycles, steel strips, steel tubes and metal sections.

In 1994–5, TI successfully tapped the GDR market with an issue of US$ 50 million. The proceeds of this issue were used to literally double the capacities in the steel tube, steel strip, bicycle and metal sections businesses. In each of these businesses, TI is either the leader or number two player in the country. As Vellayan explained:

> Post-liberalization, we decided to concentrate on a few major businesses. In doing so, we have consciously got out of certain businesses. The guiding parameter for remaining in the areas that we are in is whether we can be the No. 1 or No. 2 player in the country in our chosen fields of business, and also whether we are able to compete effectively in the export market.

What Vellayan does not put into words is his belief that the only way to survive is to plan for the future in a manner which provides a business portfolio that possesses the intrinsic ability to create value. That, for Vellayan, is the true barometer of success:

> To set in place a vigorous planning and review process which will drive out performance to match the best in the international markets, and to ensure that exports become a focus area to such an extent that 15 per cent of our total group sales turnover should come from it.

A man of few words, Vellayan is clear about his vision for the group, that 'in its chosen field of activity, it should occupy one of the top two national positions'. What he may like to add is that the group must at all times ensure adequate returns to its investors who have placed their trust in TI, and in the process create a company so strong in its essentials that its very presence becomes a strong entry barrier to MNCs, and simultaneously create an organization capable of responding to the world market.

Planning the Road Ahead

That tyres are an essential commodity which motoring India needs is a truism well brought out by Apollo Tyres, the flagship company

▼ At TI, Vellayan has helped create an international work environment that he hopes will give it a global edge, ensuring its competitiveness with MNCs.

belonging to Onkar S. Kanwar. From a Rs 7000 m. turnover just five years ago to Rs 14,000 m. at present seems to bear this out, but the road has not always been easy. As Kanwar says, 'We achieved this growth through continuous expansion at all our production units,' upgradation of technology through in-house research and product development, diversification and cost reduction.

Commenting on the challenge of national and international competition, Kanwar adds, 'As a long-term strategy, we are in the process of re-engineering so as to make both organizational and individual impact, be it on a plant, a product, the market or the employee.' The company focus has remained heavy vehicle tyres which consumes 75 per cent of the country's tyre output and accounts for 80 per cent of the market.

▼ Gujarat Ambuja Cements Plant. Narotam Sekhsaria's philosophy – 'I can' – has percolated down to all levels and been imbibed by the second longest cement producing company in India in its pursuit of excellence.

Confident that liberalization and global competition will have little adverse impact on him or his company, Kanwar points to his strategy of focusing on exports at a time when the domestic market was extremely sluggish. His strength? 'My outstanding marketing and customer service proficiency with the largest distributor network in the segment' is something that any international competitor will find hard to replicate.

Cementing the Future

The importance of cement in modern life need not be laboured. Thus it can also be considered an indicator of the shape of an economy because building activities the world over mark the first sign of commercial depression or recovery. Narotam Sekhsaria's Gujarat Ambuja Cements consists of three cement plants at Ambujanagar in Gujarat, one split location, an integrated cement plant at Darlaghat in Himachal Pradesh, and a grinding facility at Ropar, Punjab. Sekhsaria, evidently, is neither worried about overcapacities nor underutilization. His recent move to acquire the Modi Cements plant at Raipur as a BIFR case has merely added to his overall capacity, making him the second largest producer of cement in the country.

Deeply committed to self-sufficiency as a major strategy for survival, Sekhsaria has created Gujarat Ambuja's own infrastructure by building 82 MW in-house power generation capacity and three jetties, and ownership of five ships. Thus he says, 'GACL, since its inception, has always worked with a global mindset, or maximum possible cost-cutting through creation of its own infrastructure and devising innovative ways to cut costs.'

An optimist, Sekhsaria appears unfazed by the process of liberalization or the fact that the Indian market is globalizing so rapidly. As he puts it:

> The Indian economy is going through hard times, but we also find these times full of challenges and opportunities. At the micro level, infrastructure inadequacies are a bottleneck for cement plants, but at the macro level these contain a vast potential of enhanced demand for the cement industry.

Totally committed to retaining customer loyalty through customer satisfaction, Sekhsaria is clear that the environment and the country must always get top priority. Looking ahead when the Indian cement industry will emerge as the world's largest, Sekhsaria is pinning his future on the belief 'I Can'. As he explains, 'Give a man orders and he'll do a task reasonably well. But let him set his own targets, give him freedom and authority and his task becomes a personal mission.' He has resolved many intricate problems and achieved many difficult objectives by following this policy and making his company comparable in efficiency and

▲ Uday Kotak runs a financial service that is comparably young, yet has a major presence because of his clear sighted perception of the market and the business.

quality to world standards. It is abundantly clear that Sekhsaria's own mission is the 'pursuit of excellence, empowerment of employees at all levels and consumer and investor satisfaction'. He adds, 'In respect of the uncertainties of the future, we take one day at a time. As and when we encounter obstacles, we will face them and work out the best solution under the circumstances.' It is a philosophy that has served him and his company well till now, and should do so in the coming millennium.

Brokering a Future

Financial services was not a particularly reputable field in the 1980s when Uday Kotak entered it. Looked upon with deep suspicion, it was nevertheless the one segment that Kotak thought held great promise of growth and future development. It was also very different. And so it was that the Kotak Mahindra group was created. Kotak admits,

> Our group is relatively young, founded only in the mid-1980s. Yet the last five years have seen us registering tremendous growth in almost all the areas that we have entered. We are not only the pioneers in e-commerce on the Internet, but we have prestigious tie-ups with leading world players like Ford Credit and Goldman Sachs. Today you have Kotak Mahindra operations in around thirty cities across the country besides international operations in select cities like Dubai, London, New York, and Mauritius. As a result, we are clear leaders in every one of our two dozen financial businesses.

Kotak emphasizes that liberalization of the Indian economy and globalization of the market place deeply affect diversified financial players like theirs. But going forward from their present position, he believes that success in the financial services segment will depend largely upon capital, the quality of his people and the organization, their market reputation, their ability to innovate and take risks, besides the processes and information technology levels that they would manage to establish and use in their business.

Addressing the question of his personal perception for his organization, Kotak was clear that despite the number of years of its existence, it continues to be 'a learning organization which will grasp every opportunity to deliver ethically transparent and profitable quality to its customers. It will also offer exciting career opportunities to its people and superior long-term value to its shareholders'. This commendable plan-process meshes well with his own reading of the future for financial services when he says:

> As the world continues to integrate, the demand for top quality financial services will grow exponentially. At the same time competitive pressures will enjoin consolidation among the service providers. As we are building to emerge as the leaders in this field, we expect to build on our existing expertise in mergers and acquisitions and corporate advisory services.

▲ Shashi Ruia of Essar with his brother (seated) and sons (standing). In a short span of two decades he has provided the quality of leadership and vision so essential to a business enterprise.

An Inexhaustible Appetite

Ten years is not a long time when it comes to business growth. It is even shorter when one is referring to a small Rs 1500 m. Chennai-based shipping company catapulting itself into the big league and emerging as the fourth largest industrial conglomerate in the subcontinent with a turnover of over Rs 30,000 m. Besides steel, power, refineries, shipping, telecom, were all profitably encompassed by the Ruias in creating the Essar empire. The group is now able and willing to challenge the hitherto exclusive preserve of international companies in oil exploration, marine construction, and offshore engineering. The Essar group will continue to invest in high technology, high growth, infrastructure and related businesses with investments secured by long-term contracts.

Shashi Ruia is confident, and with good reason. As he puts it, 'Consolidation — that will be the growth driver at Essar.' The strategy is bound to bear good results, considering that the Ruias have expanded as much as they safely can. Now is the time to take stock and prepare for the fresh challenges of a new century, and they have intrinsic advantages which will make Shashi Ruia's task that much easier. A strategic and prime locational advantage for Essar Steel will ensure that the company can leverage cost benefits in terms of freight savings, and an emphasis upon customized production processes can ensure the delivery of a superior range of products directly to the customers' line, emphasizing customer loyalty. A master of the art of backward and forward integration, Shashi Ruia has proved that he knows his business. A diversified range of activities might tend to show little synergy between them, but one cannot deny that all forays are in the essential core sector which in turn has propelled the group to its present position on the industrial map of India.

Driving the Market

Think Mahindra and Mahindra (M&M), and tractors and jeeps immediately comes to one's mind. The saga of this multifarious group began with the brothers Jagdish Chandra and Kailash Chandra, and now carries on under the overall chairmanship of Keshub Mahindra, and the dynamic and youthful energy of Anand Mahindra.

▲ Anand Mahindra oversees operations at Mahindra & Mahindra – in India, a byword for the manufacture of jeeps. M&M has also taken the tractor division to greater heights with a technical collaboration with Ford.

▼ Ajay Piramal inherited the textile business from his brother and knew that he would diversify into the sunrise business (pharmaceuticals) while ensuring a long-term and healthy strategy for the existing business.

Anand Mahindra is an unlikely candidate for the position he occupies. A major in film-making from Harvard, he is heir-apparent to a manufacturing company whose *raison d'être* has been the making and selling of cars, tractors, and utility vehicles. Proving that appearances, like degrees, can be deceptive, he has held the reins at M&M for over seven years, first as Deputy Managing Director and more recently as Managing Director. He has, as a leading business magazine recently put it, 'led by example', and helped transform M&M from an underperforming, overstaffed, low profit automaker into an industry leader in every sense of the term.

The task has not been easy, but Anand states confidently, 'Today the trajectory itself is not visible. There is a need for people who can create a vision for the future — then, and only then, do you start worrying about how to go about achieving it.' Perhaps it has helped Anand that he has leveraged the advantage of a host of international tie-ups that not only brought with them brand equity but helped the Mahindra group focus and emerge as a competitive entity. These tie-ups include Ford Motors for car manufacturing, and an electronic data interchange service provided by Singapore Network Service.

Though its presence in the urban market is low, M&M is a market leader when it comes to tractors (27 per cent share) and utility vehicles (56 per cent share). Its approach towards technology is simple, aimed at developing whatever it can.

The energetic performance of the group is also reflected in its stock market position. It was one of the companies that outperformed the market in the bear phase and its stock price has jumped 27 times over the past six years. Obviously, Anand is ideally suited to craft the M&M film which has as its basis a successful script.

M&A as a Business Strategy

Ajay Piramal, the Indian takeover tycoon that corporate India swears by, is a swift hunter. There is no one to match his speed once Piramal has identified his target, and he identifies targets better than most.

Ajay G. Piramal, Chairman of the Rs 15,000m. Piramal Enterprises is a man with diverse interests and varied activities. He believes staunchly in his own corporate motto of 'partnerships

▼ Sanjay Lalbhai is clearly focused: on being a leading producer of denim, and of running his business with the help of industry professionals.

that prosper', and in a short span of five or six years, has ensured that his attempts to expand and diversify through the fast track of mergers and acquisitions have lived up to that philosophy. New to the field of pharmaceuticals, he has emerged as one of the five largest pharma players nationally. As Piramal says, 'The big picture is what is important.' Apparently the picture is now large enough to satisfy even Piramal himself, but to weigh Piramal on the basis of his ability to take over and run companies is to do grave injustice to the non-aggressive, affable, and mild-tempered tycoon. Though his decisions are often fast, even instantaneous, they are based on a clear idea of what he wants to do. His insistence on tying up with some of the biggest names in the world — in textiles, his various joint ventures or strategic alliances with various Italian houses such as Manifattura di Valle Brembana S.p.A., Manufacttura Castiglioni, and Legler Industria Tessile S.p.A., besides his direct tie-ups with world leaders such as TDK of Japan in the hard ferrite business, Cromwell Tools of the UK for his cutting tools business, and the American Saw Manufacturing Company of the USA in his saw business — is indicative of the ambitions of a corporate leader who wants only the best in his search for further growth and development.

When he inherited the business from his eldest brother Ashok, Piramal was clear that there was very little growth potential in a group that had an 'overwhelming 77 per cent dependence on textiles, 7 per cent in cutting tools, and 6 per cent in auto ancillaries, besides 1.6 per cent in hard ferrites and 6.5 per cent in glassware, and the balance in a texturing unit'. As he adds,

> We had two priorities. The first was to diversify into a sunrise industry (pharmaceuticals) with long-term future growth and strong entry barriers, and the second, to develop and implement a strategy to ensure a healthy and long-term growth for the existing business.

That he has managed to achieve both is a tribute to the fact that Piramal is a thinking leader.

Building a Globocorp

Sanjay Lalbhai of the Lalbhai Group is not a man in a hurry, nor does he choose to imprint his image upon his companies to the exclusion of anything else. But he is determined to emerge as the world's largest denim manufacturer over the next couple of years, and the rivets are already in place, thanks to a series of strategic decisions he took at a time when the textiles segment was very challenging.

Lalbhai is a planning and methodical individual; he is also courageous and given to taking hard decisions. Arvind Mills

▲ Rope dyeing process at the new product development centre that helps Sanjay Lalbhai monitor global trends and develop newer denim products.

deliberately moved away from powerlooms, the mainstay of the industry, as far back as 1985. The 'setting free' had begun and it was now for the company to build upon its new found freedom. This started with a level of professionalization that brought his managers freedom of action, responsibility, and innovation. In turn, Lalbhai received their loyalty and built a dedicated team.

With the exception of Arvind Mills which is under the direct control of Arvind himself and Atul under Sunil Lalbhai, Lalbhai has always insisted on hiring professionals to manage the group's companies. The Lalbhais believe that succession needs to be based on competence and not birth, a refreshing change from traditional thinking in the corridors of corporate India. As a logical extension, Lalbhai has ensured that the CEOs of his various companies have the freedom to exercise their own creativity and innovation while running the units. He feels that it is no point appointing a CEO only to bind him to oneself, and has chosen empowerment as an ethical, economic, and businesslike alternative.

While admitting that it takes a lot of effort to ensure that his organization is in sync with domestic and global trends, the focus is clear: to emphasize his core strength in denim exports while exploring the potential of a rapidly awakening domestic market. Lalbhai is equally clear that even the largest denim manufacturer in the world cannot depend upon or survive through a single cost-focus strategy, that diverse markets demand diverse plans. You can count on that flexibility on the path beyond the year 2000.

The Reliance Factor

Investors have always been the key to success in the Reliance behemoth, the one corporate entity that realized early that the way to grow was to carry the investor along by building 'bridges of trust'. This is testified to by an investor family of over 2.5 m., the largest in the country.

▼ The 1,20,000 tonne per annum MEG plant at Hazira: as India's first megacorps company, Reliance is showing that the time scale required for industrialization is shrinking around the world – and in India.

Figures apart, the growth of Reliance is the story of a huge company that has galloped to become the largest in the country. Despite its megacorp status Reliance, under the stewardship of Mukesh Ambani, is clear about its destiny. As Mukesh Ambani is wont to emphasize, India is a huge market with large, untapped potential for growth and development in the entire range of Reliance products. Given the economies of scale the company enjoys, it is easy to see how Mukesh Ambani is in a position to drive change by adjusting the company's vision.

Mukesh learnt the ropes along with his younger brother Anil, and today the Ambani brothers are fitting partners to their father Dhirubhai Ambani's efforts to make the company India's first true megacorp. Business aside, Mukesh is clear about the direction the country has to take to emerge as a superpower and advocates swift growth. 'Most experts seem to have settled for a 7 per cent annual growth rate in our GDP,' he says,

> but at this rate India will have to wait 68 years to achieve a GDP which is comparable with the developed world. Does anyone believe that with television exposing the remotest village to modern life, you can have patience, peace and stability? Either we perform or we perish.

As to how this is to be achieved, Mukesh opines:

> There is only one course, to summon the will of all sections of our society and make this dream a reality. We have to discard poverty of ambitions and lethargy of action. We have to make [the idea of] India an economic superpower, a mission of all Indians, and arouse a sense of national pride.

Brewing Success

Say beer or whisky, think UB. That is the type of association that Vijay Mallya has managed to achieve for his company, the Rs 2.5 m. United Breweries (UB) group. For most Indians, Vijay Mallya the brewer totally dominates the liquor market while leading an enviable lifestyle where his precious horses figure prominently in the odds at the Bangalore Turf Club.

Behind the somewhat flamboyant facade is a business brain that matches the sharpest in the country. Mallya set up such huge capacities and flooded the market with so many choices that they served as formidable entry barriers for most new entrants. Mallya claims, 'Every group has to move with the times. At UB, as soon as things started changing with the liberalization that began in the early 1990s, we started restructuring.' This resulted in such premium brands that it set UB on the road to success, leaving competition in its wake.

Not content with launching leading brands every year, he went on to take control of the market by creating huge in-house capacities, investing in very large-scale plants. As a result, he has within his fold almost a third of the industry's total beer production capacity. As industry watchers indicate, widespread and distributed manufacturing facilities, large size, and strong brands are the three principal pillars of UB's success.

▼ Vijaya Mallya is India's liquor baron who has made globalization the cornerstone of his group's future strategy.

For Mallya the domestic market, huge though it might be, is not enough. As a hedge against domestic policy changes, he went in for distributed manufacturing facilities (around 30 distilleries) in a number of states (16), but for him exports offer the dual benefit of an even larger market, with higher premiums to be earned, a strategy that appears to have paid off to a degree. He emphasizes, 'We will have to reduce the risk to our group business by putting our eggs in various baskets. Since we understand the nuances of the liquor and beer business, it's not difficult to leverage on it for international investments.'

In parallel Mallya has put together a rescue plan for his group which should see it through the challenging times ahead. 'Our focus is clear. Get out of all those businesses which do not match with our core strengths.' The result is that UB is hiving off all loss making and diversionary divisions, while adding on others like resorts and game parks in line with the plan to internationalize the UB brand. The acquisition of additional manufacturing facilities abroad indicates that Mallya is serious about emerging not just as king of spirits, but as emperor.

The Brave New Industrialists

Kanika Goswami

The post-Independence industrial climate is vibrant with entrepreneurial ventures led by younger captains at the helm, whether those who inherited their companies and set them on new paths to growth, carved new directions within established boundaries, or even more creditably, those who set off to chase a dream and created new companies as a result. Finally, however, it is consistently good performance that sustains them.

In most cases, the scions of successful industrialists have inherited their business instincts, yet what marks them off is their radically different approach in dealings and priorities. Among the most important areas where today's industrialists, heirs, or entrepreneurs are at variance with earlier corporate philosophies is in the recognition of talent and dedication within the human resources of the organization. This has formed a major thrust in corporate ethics over the last decade or so, and is a philosophy vehemently endorsed by a younger generation of industrialists in the country.

▼ At Kanoria Chemicals, R.V. Kanoria is as concerned about the future of business as he is about society at large – no wonder environmental considerations play such a large part at his plants in Renukoot and Ankleshwar.

At Kanoria Chemicals, R.V. Kanoria says, 'The perfect industry is one that satisfies the needs of society as a whole.' The young heir could be oblivious to such concerns, but has chosen not to be. It is this concept that Ramalinga Raju, the 43-year-old Vice Chairman of the Satyam Corporate group, and Chairman of Satyam Computer Services Ltd, feels has been the primary reason for his stupendous success, charting a course of vertical growth. The group was founded in 1987; its target: excellence in the IT arena. Within a decade, it has become a totally integrated solutions provider. 'People before all else,' insists Raju, and says,

> Satyam's core competency lies in its people who work towards a unified vision ... A unique management style has been the nucleus of its success where every Satyamite is considered an 'associate'. A seamlessly integrated environment empowers people and encourages the entrepreneurial spirit, and is reflected in a conscious endeavour to add value in every aspect of service.

This departure from the traditional is also visible in the case of another young visionary, Ajay Shriram, 44-year-old Vice Chairman

▲ Ajay Shriram of DCM Shriram Consolidated is Harvard-educated and uses human resources as his main strength, turning to appropriate brain power for the right positions, saying that genius should be rewarded.

▼ Tilak Dhar of DCM, insists that the new generation entrepreneur, above all, needs to be innovative in his concepts and its application.

and Managing Director of DCM Shriram Consolidated. A product of Doon School, Dehra Dun and Sydenham College of Commerce, Mumbai, Ajay rounded off his academic qualifications with a management programme from the Harvard Business School. Today, he heads the Rs 6000 m. DSCL comprising Shriram Fertilizers and Chemicals, Shriram Cement in Kota, and Shriram Alkali and Chemicals in Bharuch. 'No one has a monopoly over brains,' he insists; 'the management has to see that the right job goes to the right person, and then motivate him to perform.' True to his word, the group has an unwritten rule that provides at least a week's training to every executive once a year, while a few are sent overseas for more comprehensive training.

Lala Shriram, it appears, also built his corporate philosophy along similar lines: 'Excellence takes birth in people; people unified by the same dream. The dream of excellence.' Ajay says, 'We are seeking motivation, accountability and responsibility with delegation. It is our job to get the individual's aspirations to match the company's; this makes for very powerful synergy.'

This concept of man above all else is something Raghupati Singhania, the youngest son of Lakshmipati Singhania, too endorses. Raghupati is director of the US$ 1.5 bn JK Organization and JK Industries (a leading producer of steel belted radial tyres). Though he has inherited sound business acumen, Raghupati's approach has been different from that of his elders. Raghupati called for radical changes, treating his team of 'dedicated professionals' as important cogs in the corporate machinery. 'To create this high performing team of dedicated human beings, we ... undertake extensive human resource development programmes for improvement in cross functional team management skills and sharpening quick response ability to market needs in particular,' he emphasizes.

This particularly innovative concept of achievers is well imbibed in the philosophy of the Kanoria group of industries, now being carried into the next millennium by S.S. Kanoria's son, R.V. Kanoria. Kanoria Chemicals and Industries Ltd boasts an entire township in Renukoot dedicated to the manufacture of heavy chemicals and pesticides and other complex chemicals at its plant in Ankleshwar, Gujarat. RV is a well-organized and open-minded 43-year-old, with an MBA from the IMEDE Business School Masters in Laussane, Switzerland, which he passed with honors, followed up with the Advanced Management Program from Wharton in USA. The latter programme is available only to industrial CEOs with fifteen years' experience, and provides an extremely high level of management skills, adding quality to the organization he runs as its Vice Chairman and Managing Director. 'Our corporate philosophy is based on a few key elements, the most

▼ Sajjan Jindal believes in encouraging individual talent, one of the reasons for JISCO'S forward-looking approach to management.

important of which is encouraging an ethos of belonging,' says RV. He attaches importance to the people who work 'with' him. 'The problem I face is with a conditioned attitude: few people give me frank feedback. The aura that comes with your parentage restrains people from talking openly,' he says wistfully. Even his father, he says, encouraged free communication within the organization; in that sense, his is not a major shift away from the parental philosophy, though, of course, RV has a much more futuristic attitude regarding the prospects and development of business in India.

It is a philosophy shared by Harshvardhan Neotia, 37-year-old alumnus of Harvard Business School, Managing Director of Ambuja Cement Eastern Ltd, Director, Ganapati Greenfields, and associated with construction projects in partnership with the state government of West Bengal. His philosophy is simple: 'Retaining people and keeping them at a highly motivated level is a growing challenge. Empowering them, giving them responsibility and authority ... seem to be the order of the day,' he says. 'Ethics and human values in a business are gaining importance. The long-term sustainability of any business will be largely dependent on the strength of moral and human values within the organization.'

Sajjan Jindal, the second of O.P. Jindal's four sons, is Vice Chairman and Managing Director of Jindal Iron and Steel Co. (JISCO), and MD of Jindal Vijaynagar Steel Co., both companies a part of the Rs 27,000 m. crore Jindal Group his father set up. At JISCO, Sajjan has been instrumental in building the country's largest galvanizing facility for mild steel HR plates and galvanized products. An engineering graduate from Bangalore University, Sajjan's philosophy borders on academic concepts aimed at improving the future of the country: 'By putting into practice management concepts of delegation and empowerment, we have succeeded in creating a very professional and forward looking organization,' he opines. 'The Jindal group's philosophy encourages individual talent. The management concept is inculcating in executives down the line a sense of belonging and group values.'

Saroj Poddar, 53-year-old Chairman of the Rs 11,000 m. Indian Shaving Products company that has brought Gillette to India, concurs with the concept but has a more functional attitude. He says,

> The need of today's business environment is total dedication and commitment. It is not necessary that all entrepreneurs be good managers too. I am of the firm opinion that day-to-day management of the organization should be left in the hands of competent professional managers. After all, delegation is the key to success.

Here is another divergence from the traditional Indian concept of management with ownership. Poddar believes that giving his

▼ Galvanizing unit, JISCO: according to the company, it is not merely the interests of profit but those of the country's as well that must be given priority.

managers a more decisive role in the company will not only contribute to its growth but also ensure dedication by way of improved value systems.

A similar concept has been maintained by Subhash Chandra, the Chairman of the US$ 280 m. Essel Group of Industries. 'We believe that a successful entrepreneur need not necessarily be a good manager,' he says. 'We, as entrepreneurs, have learned to conceptualize and develop the businesses ... and then leave them in the capable hands of professional managers.' No wonder he has experienced such stupendous success in all his ventures including

▲ Saroj K. Poddar of Indian Shaving Products believes that good entrepreneurs need not necessarily be good managers: 'delegation is the key to success'.

the Zee TV Network. At the core of his business philosophy is the need to accord dignity to his human resource. 'We need to treat human resource as another capital, like financial capital,' he muses.

In a totally different environment and industry, 52-year-old CEO of the Wipro Group, Azim Hasham Premji, attaches as much importance to his commitment to human resources as he does to organization. 'Wipro focuses on four core values, the topmost slot going to human values,' Premji says, and points out that

> at Wipro we have learnt that the future is not what happens to you, but what you make of it. Our vision for tomorrow is leadership, not only in terms of size; it is about being the best in whatever we are. Our people give us the competitive edge in achieving our vision. I am convinced that we have some of the best talent in the world.

In keeping with the importance on the human resource aspect of his business, Premji plans for the future keeping in mind that 'people come first'.

This concept of prioritizing an organization's personnel and conceding them a position of importance in the organizational machinery is new to the traditionally hierarchical corridors of business. With team work replacing the need for control from the top, it is a concept, however, most business houses place high on their list of 'must dos' for the coming years.

An equally important aspect with the new generation at the helm of business, is technological upgradation. An ideal that in the opinion of Dr K. Anji Reddy seems to be of most value. Dr Reddy's foresight not only gave birth to Dr Reddy's Laboratories, but also took it to heights of success even as the industry as a whole in the country was suffering a major setback. 'Survival in today's times depends not only on size but also on new discoveries,' says Dr Reddy, 57-year-old Chairman of the Rs 3400 m. organization. His brief is simple, if not easy: 'It is important to be focused, and to have a good starting point.' He did, when he started R&D on drugs for diabetes and cancer, research that will not only be another landmark for the laboratory but also benefit humanity in a significant manner. With a doctorate from the National Chemical Laboratory in Pune, he started his career associated with the IDPL in Hyderabad. Here he spent six years in implementing new technologies in manufacturing drugs. In 1979 he set up Standard Organics and five years later, Dr Reddy's Laboratories. His group companies, DRL and Cheminor Drugs, now produce organic intermediaries, bulk pharmaceuticals and finished dosages with world class expertise. In 1991 he set up Dr Reddy's Research Foundation that truly makes him pioneer as far as pharma R&D in the country goes. His vision for the coming years is very straightforward: 'I expect to launch at least one major compound every year.'

▼ Constant R&D at Dr Reddy's Research Foundation has been a part of its corporate philosophy, with a current focus on a drug discovery programme for cancer and diabetes.

Raghupati Singhania shares Dr Reddy's concern for technology upgradation. 'We have invested heavily in our research and development activity, and are able to develop new products in a short time, based on customer needs. Constant upgradation of technology is another important prerequisite, apart from constant cost cutting measures,' he says.

Ajay Shriram views technology upgradation in the same vein, but is a man in a hurry. He says,

> instead of the long process of development, we are buying technologies outright and then balancing the existing equipment accordingly. The organization is moving towards setting up a world class IT system (at level with SAPR3, a German software) being installed across the board, in all the group companies.

In agreement with him is his cousin, Tilak Dhar, 42-year-old son of Lala Bansi Dhar and grandson of Lala Shriram. The Vice Chairman of DCM Shriram Industries, a group with interests in sugar, industrial alcohol, aromatic chemicals, drug intermediates, rayon tyrecord yard, shipping containers, and processed yarns, he says, 'The biggest step that the new generation of industrialists needs to take is to be innovative.'

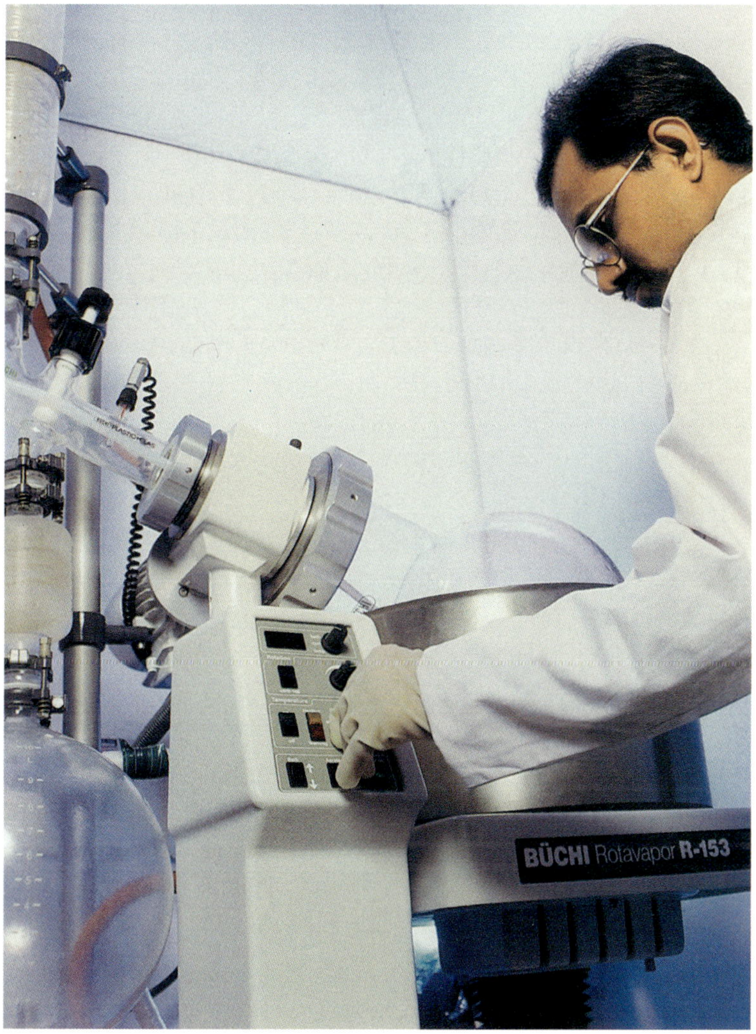

Premji has taken a more specific view of this requirement and incorporated it in the core values of his organization. 'Wipro's future will be charted by four core values, and innovative solutions will be one of them,' he says. 'These values manifest themselves in the new corporate identity, a unique symbol with a rainbow flower and the positioning statement, "Wipro Applying Thought".' Little wonder that Premji plans to invest Rs 350 m. a year towards R&D and supplement it with world leading technology partnerships where needed. In a similar environment, Satyam is one of the select ISO 9001 TickIT certified software solution providers in India. It has set up six development centres in India. One of its major achievements, through constant upgradation, is the development of its own Y2K solution, SOS 2000, which is the first Indian methodology to receive the coveted ITAA *2000 Certification.

In this context, credit is to be given to Dinesh Himatsingka, the MD and founder

▲ Rajendra Pawar heads a transnational IT services corporation, and says Indians will find success as long as they integrate their work with global standards of quality, cost and delivery.

▼ Harsh Neotia of Ganapati Greenfields and Gujarat Ambuja is truly concerned with the quality of life he can provide, not only for his colleagues, but also for the average Indian, and is making it his topmost priority.

of Himatsingka Seide Ltd, a fully integrated silk mill located just outside Bangalore, the largest producer of silk fabric in India, and certainly one of the most technologically upgraded. The HSL philosophy encompasses the concept of innovation, dedication, and commitment to quality. The machines used in the plants are all imported: winding and yarn twisting machines from Italy; the section wrapper from Switzerland. The team of qualified designers that aids Himatsingka, with CAD, to turn out his exquisite, exclusive silk tapestries, has earned him enviable international repute: his tapestries have been used by designers to furnish the Queen's apartments in London.

Innovation would hardly be possible without the concept of backward and forward integration that young industrialists in the country are now focusing on. Says R.V. Kanoria, 'We believe in complete integration technology.'

Most new generation industrialists are also concerned about the state of the environment, and its conservation. 'I have just one question: Would you let your children live in this environment?' asks R.V. Kanoria. 'If not, then do something about it.' His commitment has been translated into action at Renukoot where 2,50,000 trees have been planted. The water that is released from the manufacturing plant is treated to clean it of effluents, then used to water these trees. Environmental consciousness has also manifested itself in the housing projects Harsh Neotia is associated with, in the capacity of Managing Director of Bengal Ambuja Housing Development Ltd, a joint sector company involved in mass housing. The construction of family dwellings, particularly Udayan, has been targeted at providing maximum pollution-free housing space on the fringes of Calcutta. And, as Director of Ganapati Greenfields, he has promoted a resort with the Radisson chain at Shyamolima at Raichak, 50 km from Calcutta. Both projects aim at providing a wholesome, pollution-free environment for a choked urban populace.

The priorities are in position, but the Indian industrialist has another hurdle to overcome: the predatory MNC. How is he coping? The majority reaction opinion is a positive one, of healthy competition. 'The Indian manufacturers enjoy several advantages over their foreign counterparts. They have a better understanding of the structure and nature of Indian markets. Over the years they have built a well-developed sales and organization network and created their brands,' says Saroj Poddar optimistically. 'India is a large market and has a huge pool of resources. We are a much stronger nation in 1998 as compared to 1991–2 when the economic reforms process had just begun.' About his particular industry, he feels,

> Among shaving products, foreign brands provide healthy competition to

▲ Sanjeev Goenka believes that in the next millennium, India's business will increasingly focus on strategy-driven growth.

> *swadeshi* products through high performance, high value international standard products. But the lion's share of the market, over 75 per cent, is dominated by Indian products. Given the price sensitive nature of the Indian market, it will continue to be so.

Kanoria agrees with him. 'Why can't Indian companies deal with the onslaught of foreign competition? At KCIL, we are manufacturing chemicals that are world class. Besides, all our products have an ISO 9000 certification; we have nothing to fear the current situation.'

Sanjeev Goenka of the RPG Group with interests in power, tyres, telecommunications, financial services, and retailing businesses, has a confident and focused outlook. 'No business house afraid of tackling the international onslaught has any prospects of survival in India,' he feels; 'while the MNCs pose a considerable threat in some areas, Indian business houses also have certain competitive advantages.' RPG's business strategy, therefore, is a combination of international thinking and local experience. At home, the accent is on creating a manufacturing base which can withstand competition both from within and outside. This involved upgrading of production technology, reaching international size markets, and of course, exports.

Perhaps an even more comfortable situation has been created for his organization by Rajendra Pawar, CEO of NIIT, a global IT services corporation, founded in 1981 and today operational in twenty-five countries. Says Pawar,

> we see NIIT as a truly transnational corporation with its headquarters in New Delhi. We have set up subsidiaries and joint ventures abroad for our software trading operations. A half of NIIT's revenue comes from the rest of the world, while the other half is earned in India.

▼ Wipro is one of the leaders in the IT industry, and its growth has been based on Azim H. Premji's belief that people come first.

In this case, there can be no danger of foreign competition overwhelming the Indian organization. In any case, India provides the world's best systems and IT professionals, so NIIT has a definite edge even in the global market place. For, as Premji, another computer wiz, opines, 'What is important is that any product or service which benchmarks us should have global standards of quality, cost, and delivery.'

Typically confident is Raju, when he points out that

> Satyam's customers usually come from the Fortune 500 list. The company believes that its single-minded dedication to customer satisfaction and software engineering excellence has enabled it to build greater confidence amongst its customers. The market for software development is intensely competitive at an international level; competition for us usually comes from local companies.

Not surprising, with the superior software and IT resources pool available in India, this is one industry that has nothing to fear from outsiders.

▲▶ Dinesh K. Himatsingka *(above)* imported the technology and his plant for setting up a 100 per cent export company for producing silk upholstery. The plant has proved successful because it has remained true to its commitment towards excellence.

Raghupati Singhania goes a step further: 'The best known foreign brands have had decades to establish their presence in India,' he says, 'but we are not to be taken for granted.' He cites the example of JK steel radial tyres, 'We have built its brand presence even in the United States, it is considered a premium brand in the face of such international competition as Goodyear and Dunlop.' Sanjeev Goenka is more cautious: 'The question of brand enslavement does not arise. At the same time, there is no place for complacency. Eternal vigilance is the price for success.'

There are, of course, a few industrialists who are unhappy with the timing of this process of opening the Indian economy to foreign competition. Muses Raghupati Singhania,

> the competition is both inevitable and healthy, the question is only of time. Capable Indian companies should be given reasonable time to build on their strengths and gear up to effectively meet the MNC competition, particularly in the backdrop that Indian industry was hamstrung by over-regulations that even frowned upon growth. I feel that 'Indians' and not foreigners should be entrusted with the primary task of building India. After all, countries like Japan and Korea have done it.

Harsh Neotia has a similar outlook. Although the young industrialist supports a global economy, he calls for 'fair warning'.

> There is no way in today's world that any economy can continuously remain sheltered or protected. The world is getting increasingly globalized and in this context the trade barriers will have to fall. I do, however, feel that the liberalization process in India could have been adjusted to give time to the Indian industries to wake up to this new reality and readjust their priorities to face the onslaught of international competition.

▲▶ The Ffort Radisson complex *(left)* and Udayan condoville *(right)* are two of Harsh Neotia's pet projects that are indicative of his belief in providing a higher standard of living and lifestyle to the Indian people.

▲Like others of his generation, Ramalinga Raju believes that his strength and that of his software development firm, is his people, and this is one industry that has an edge in the global market place.

▼Subhash Chandra heads an entertainment conglomerate and believes that in the future, services and intellectual property businesses will be at the helm.

(facing page):

▲▼At the JK Organization *(above)*, Raghupati Singhania *(below)* is convinced of India's logical growth as an industrial giant.

He does not feel that Indian ability is short of international capability, only that it would be more realistic to face the fact of both the technology and financial crunch the country faces. Here, Dinesh Himmatsingka's view is more positive; 'globalization', according to him,

> ought to be a result of liberalization of our own economy. Far too many unnecessary controls and lack of basic infrastructure come in the way of ... our competing in the international situation. Once this point is addressed in a meaningful manner, globalization will happen as a logical next step.

Subhash Chandra also shares his concern with regard to the current state of affairs: 'I believe that the policies of anti-progress adopted during the British regime are still continuing ... if unfounded restrictictions are removed and we are freed of antiquated regulatory laws, I don't see why we can't face competition.' And adds caustically, 'If Indian business houses align their interests with those of the nation's ... they could look forward to better profit with more pride.' Essel group's vision, therefore, has acquired an acronym, TIMES, representing telecommunication, information technologies and services, media, entertainment, and social obligations. The future according to Subhash Chandra, 'will be good for services and intellectual property businesses'.

As for the vision this dynamic generation of industrialists shares, there is enough room for optimism. Harsh Neotia says, 'I am extremely optimistic for the Indian industrial scene over the next decade or so. I believe we will evolve as a major industrial power. As regards my companies, collectively we would like to be the best.' Premji is even more precise, when he says:

> We articulate a new vision for Wipro. Our mission quality, into its second year, is pursuing with enthusiasm the prioritized upgradation of our products. We will be enhancing our marketing and distribution investment by a large margin. But as we grow, we are committed to retain the sensitivity, leanness, simplicity, and speed of a small organization.

Sajjan Jindal, on the other hand, has commercially ambitious plans for his organization. Says he:

> The strategic focus is to make both companies, JISCO and VSL, fully integrated steel complexes, using state-of-the-art technology and cost reduction, making the unit the most competitive steel producer in the world ... to control the domestic market and to generate revenue in excess of 35 per cent from international business.

The same commercial ambitions prevail within the JK organization. Says Raghupati Singhania,

> India will become an industrial giant in the next decade. The Indian industrial sector will also be a major sourcing base for the global industry. With this vision we plan to grow and become not only the leader in our business but also create capacities and sharpen skills to become a viable, high quality and low cost world supplier.

In this ambitious scenario, RV adds another aspect: 'We are looking for complete automation. Our formaldehyde plant at Ankleshwar is already fully automated.' Sanjeev Goenka is confident, 'Today the RPG Group employs more than 50,000 people. It is one establishment which employs 20,000 women. There is no reason why we should not be able to meet the twenty-first century with confidence.' Or, as Harsh Neotia puts it, 'At the end of the day, as far as I can see it, it is not how much one did, but how well one did, and I think the quality of service would remain the topmost priority in the long term vision of our growth.'

Enterprise at Home and Abroad

Honed over centuries often against the greatest odds, Indian entrepreneurship has proved itself to the world. In most developed nations Indian businessmen today have not only made their fortunes but also their mark. As opportunities overseas grew, were offered to them, these were seized by Indian businessmen, and a slew of projects followed, often creating global empires. In fact, cut off from the sometimes obstructive regime of the home environment, they were often able to prove their mettle better, in a more competitive environment, both learning and teaching in the process, how wealth can be accumulated for social and personal benefit.

Not only have a large number of Indians formed their own corporations, a great many have risen to the very top as professionals in multinational companies. With their acumen, they head companies, shoulder immense responsibilities, and take decisions that affect thousands of lives, not just of those associated with their ventures but in society at large.

This pan-global achievement is the result not only of an inborn aptitude to excel, but also of a commitment to work that brings in its wake aspects natural to the Indian being of loyalty, honesty, and humaneness. This is layered with objectivity, analysis, even shrewdness. No wonder, where the climate has proved favourable in encouraging free enterprise, the Indian entrepreneur has not only excelled, he has done so with an insouciance and ease that is the envy of his colleagues.

▼ The role of the Indian community overseas is being recognized in which they reside. In London, the recently inaugurated Shri Swaminarayan Mandir is a tribute to the indomitable spirit of Indians who have contributed to the society in the UK.

An Experiment in Creating Wealth through Sweat Equity

N.R. Narayana Murthy

In the late 1970s and early 1980s, the concept of the creation of wealth by sweat equity was hardly known in India. In those days, financial strength was derived from being born with a silver spoon, and aspiring businessmen had to use the mantra of leveraging tariff barriers and government connections to keep competitors away. Certainly, there was no opportunity for information technology. Today, it is difficult to imagine a situation where a bureaucrat in Delhi decides whether a private company needs computers or not, and if so, what their configuration should be?

It was, however, in just such an environment that Infosys was founded as India's first software company of the professional, for the professional, and by the professional. But where was the market

▶ N.R. Narayana Murthy has proved that the spirit of enterprise can have its genesis in even the smallest seed. Infosys was begun with an initial capital outlay of Rs 10,000 in 1981, and is now a Rs 23,000 m. turnover company. Infosys has helped consolidate India's position in information technology around the globe.

▼ Work place at Infosys. The software company believes that the sharing of wealth with its employees is the key to achieving critical performance levels that will keep it on the cutting edge of competition.

and where was the money? Seven of us put together the Rs 10,000 we had borrowed from our wives. We were short on money but long on enthusiasm, energy, confidence, and hope. We decided that export would be our thrust: there was no market for our expertise in India. In any case, I believe India has to succeed in exports to be self-reliant. I define self-reliance as the ability of a nation to recognize and leverage its competitive advantages to earn enough global currency to import the best product from the global market.

We started Infosys from my apartment in Pune. As we had contacts in the US, we started our export operations with the rest of my colleagues going off to America to start the re-engineering of a package for a software house in New York. They also installed and supported this package at several customer sites on behalf of this software house. There was no way we could have added much value from India due to the low velocity of business here, and the poor infrastructure. There were no data communication facilities available at the time. Our customer was ready to loan us an expensive development machine to take up a large, IBM-mainframe-based project at Bangalore, but we could not even get a telephone connection for six months. The customer could wait no longer and we had to execute the project in the US.

Since our heart was in not in executing projects outside India, we floundered between 1981 and 1991. The liberalization package launched by Dr Manmohan Singh under the prime ministership of P.V. Narasimha Rao marked a watershed for entrepreneurial ventures like ours. Infosys symbolizes all the good that came out of the process.

Liberalization helped export companies in four significant ways. One, the velocity of business increased by an order of magnitude. Earlier, it would take six to eight months and 10–15 visits to New Delhi to get an import licence worth $1500; today it takes less than half a day and a single visit to the STP office, half a mile from our office at Bangalore, to import a machine worth several million dollars. Second, equity became a viable financing option, since the office of the Controller of Capital Issues was abolished, and market pricing of equities by the company became possible. The entry of foreign institutional investors provided a much needed source of capital. Third, the government removed restrictions on foreign exchange allocations for opening offices abroad and for hiring international consultants in quality and other areas. Finally, the opening up of the company brought several well-known multinationals like IBM, Digital, and ORACLE to open captive software development centres in India. This meant tremendous competition for the most precious asset in our business: professionals. It was very clear that the only way to succeed in the new paradigm was through agility, innovation, and adaptability to handle rapid changes in technology, and in preferences of customers, employees, and investors. Infosys seized this opportunity and has never looked back. It became the first Indian company to produce a highly transparent balance sheet and conform to US GAAP standards in disclosure; produce an audited quarterly balance sheet; create an Employee Stock Offer Plan (ESOP) for sharing wealth; create a world class, offshore software development centre with contemporary physical and technological infrastructure; get immediate certification to ISO 9001; and articulate the concept of twenty-four-hour workday for the benefit of our US customers. It is one of the few Indian software companies to get accredited to a coveted software quality standard called Level 4 of the CMM model.

The net result has been that Infosys has progressed from being a Rs 10,000 capital company in 1981 to a market capitalization of Rs 23,000 m. Sales have increased over eighteen-fold in the last five years. As a highly profitable company, it has created more than 600 rupee millionaires. It has grown from seven professionals in 1981 to over 2000 professionals in 1998.

There are several beliefs behind the progress of Infosys. Briefly articulated, these are: the creation of wealth legally and ethically;

Andhra Pradesh Inc.

Among those in the political firmament in India who have embraced computerization is Chandrababu Naidu, the CEO of Andhra Pradesh Inc. Andhra Pradesh, of course, is no corporation, and Chandrababu Naidu no corporator, but as Chief Minister of this southern state, he is leading a cyber revolution that portends the way Indians are beginning to think.

The Chief Minister uses a computer to stay linked with all developments in his state, whether at the grassroots level or in monitoring infrastructure. Officials feed data and update it constantly: the mercurial CM may want his information at any time, and he wants it all. Along with him, the way of documenting information is changing in the state, with Hyderabad, the capital, the only place Bill Gates of Microsoft has chosen to set up a manufacturing facility. As Hyderabad emerges as the world's most recent Silicon Valley, Naidu is concerned with the SMART way of running his government: that's Simple, Moral, Accountable, Responsive, and Transparent. His belief is that 'information technology ... allows delivery of government services in radically different ways, often direct to individuals and businesses, eliminating middlemen'.

Among his inventive use of IT is as 'one-stop non-stop services' for paying utility bills, getting certificates, permits and information from thirty government departments hooked online seven days a week, round the clock. Over time, Naidu hopes that every citizen in the state will be able to check on their property and tax status, register land sales, apply to engineering colleges and do the groundwork on developmental-projects online. 'Every citizen should feel like a stockholder in the state,' he says. He is working on in it, and the day every villager can go online, India's cyber state will become a reality.

the belief that a good night's sleep is worth a billion dollars; and the founders' need to share wealth with their employees since they believe that a small percentage of a growing pie is better than a large part of a shrinking one. Professionalism in the conduct of business has been made possible since every Infosys promoter believes in separating management from control, and in putting public good ahead of private good. The senior executives believe we are trustees of our shareholders and manage the company with a high level of transparency and integrity. We do it all for a very selfish reason: Infoscions know they will be better off this way. This is, indeed, the message of Infosys.

Indians in the United States

Abid Hussain

India's Kalpana Chawla, a NASA astronaut, reportedly said in an interview: 'Within an hour-and-a-half, we have gone around the whole planet. It is a very overwhelming realization that the earth is so small.' The earth feels especially small to the over one million Indians settled in the US. There seems to be an enduring bond between the two nations that has endured the travesties of time and vagaries of history. No matter what the status of diplomatic and strategic relations between the two, Indo-US cultural ties have always flourished and Indians in America have made outstanding contributions to virtually every profession in America and enriched its economy.

I am convinced of the pivotal role that Indians resident in America can perform in the modernization and creation of a renewed and vigorous India in the next century. Their technical expertise in a multitude of fields, and the capital at their disposal, can be usefully harnessed sustainably to benefit India's long-term development. India has NRI deposits worth approximately $13 bn in its banks, but most are in the form of company shares rather than being deployed for the creation of new assets or enterprises. With the opening of the Indian economy, I urge NRIs to participate more actively and play a more meaningful role in the Indian economy, and especially in the establishment of educational institutions equipped with all necessary resources.

Successful Indian professionals riding the crest of progress in the US are far too numerous to name, but those who spring to mind include IIT-trained Rajat Gupta, CEO of McKinsey and Co.; Vinod Gupta, founder and head of American Business Association, a company that grew from an initial investment of $ 100 (1972) with two part-time employees to an annual turnover of $ 110 m. (1996)

employing 1000 personnel; Sabeer Bhatia of BITS, Pilani, founder of Hot Mail; and Vijay Goradia who heads the Vinmar Group, an international marketing and distribution company in the area of chemicals and plastics with its office in Houston and twenty-one offices and agents around the world. There are others like Gopal Raju, editor and publisher of the highly circulated *India Abroad*; Shreedhar Menon, managing director of Lehman Brothers; Vijay Amritraj, former tennis star and now head of an entertainment conglomerate; Talat Ansari, partner in Kelley, Drye & Warren NY, who has developed a successful practice for the firm and has recently set up a Hong Kong office advising financial/infrastructure investments in India; and Damodar Reddy, CEO, Alliance Semiconductor Corporation with a company net worth of over $ 800 m. More names come to mind: Jayantilal K. Patel, Chairman Asian-Am Hotel Owners Association; Dr Bharat Shah, Atlanta-based realtor; and Amar Gopal Bose, audio-inventor and entrepreneur who has developed acoustic radio systems which are the world's most advanced (the Bose Corporation, founded in 1964, supplies acoustic radio equipment to leading institutions including the Voyager spacecraft).

The world of publishing has been enriched by the likes of Deepak Chopra who writes books that top the *NYT* bestseller lists, novelists Vikram Seth, Ved Mehta, Pico Iyer, Raja Rao, and Bharati Mukherjee. In the field of culture, sarod maestro Ustad Ali Akbar

▼ At a meeting organized by FICCI on Indo-US relations: Abid Hussain, former Ambassador of India to the USA, Frank Wisner, former Ambassador of the USA to India, and A.S. Kasliwal, past President of FICCI.

Khan is perhaps the greatest living exponent of Indian instrumental classical music, while Zubin Mehta has conducted the world's greatest orchestra and is Music Director for Life of the Israeli Philharmonic.

Even more important is the community's representation in the academic world. Among Indian stalwarts who continue to make valuable contributions to the US are Jagdish Bhagwati, Columbia University; T.N. Srinivasan, Yale; Amartya Sen, formerly at Harvard; Kaushik Basu, Cornell; and Raj Reddy, Carnegie-Melon. Hargobind Khurana, professor of biology and chemistry at MIT since 1971, was awarded the Nobel Prize for Physics and Medicine in 1968. Professr Jagdish Bhagwati is an Arthur Lehman Professor of Economics, and also Professor of Political Science, Columbia University. Professor Arun Gandhi runs the MK Gandhi Institute of Non-violence in Memphis, Tennesse, where he teaches the philosophy of non-violence.

The number of Indians studying in American universities has increased to over 16,000 in the last few years. Indians today have an impressive presence in the information technology industry, investment banking, corporate management and hotel business. This closeness should change the saying that 'foreign policy might change, but friends never change'.

Competing with the World

Swraj Paul

In the 1960s, there were few Indian businesses in the United Kingdom, and none of any significant size. Not many people thought that an Indian enterprise could compete in the Western world, especially in the manufacturing industries — operations largely regarded as obsolete. With God's blessings, a lot of hard work, and some nervous moments, I have been fortunate enough to preside over the Caparo Group, now one of the largest family-owned businesses in Britain with an annual turnover of about $ 1 bn. We have operations in five countries employing 4000 workers, and manufacture industrial products of world quality.

As I look around the British business scene today, I am struck by the dramatic change that the Indian community has experienced in the years since I came to London. Of course, not everyone has become prosperous but almost everyone makes a contribution to society. The community is now renowned for both its commercial efforts and its good citizenship.

Most of us are also very proud of our Indian traditions, and this gives us the strength to be good citizens anywhere. It also makes us want the best for our motherland, India. And here the data are quite compelling: about 20 m. people of Indian origin outside India produce as much as the entire Indian economy does each year. In short, there is another Indian economy overseas, a vast pool of capital and skills. Any link between these two economies will naturally benefit India.

To my mind, India is going through profound transition. The principal pillars of state policy, imperatives, and impulses that have served the nation long and well — the structure of democratic government, secularism, non-alignment in foreign policy and the planned economy are being directly or implicitly questioned. This is a process that takes place from time to time in the life of a nation. From it will come new ways of organizing government, of approaching society, and of solving problems of the society. Perhaps the most important of these re-examinations concerns the economy for this, after all, is how people live, work, eat, and survive. If we have the courage to apply to our economy the liberties we so cherish politically, if we can match political freedom with economic freedom, I believe the enormous entrepreneurial energies of the Indian people can be unshackled. What we see in Indians overseas will then take place in communities at home, bringing widespread prosperity and well-being to our multitudes. As we embark on the second half-century of our modern nationhood, all our people living in the country deserve no less.

▼ At the Ambika Paul Memorial at Caparo Steel, Farrell, Pennsylvania, USA, 1997. Swraj Paul, Chairman, Caparo Group Ltd, with sons Ambar Paul, Akash Paul, and Angad Paul.

The Credibility of Ethics

Raj Bagri

My emotional attachment to India serves as a source of profound and constant enrichment of life in Britain, whether it be in day-to-day business dealings in London, in public service, or at home through the enjoyment of classical Indian music, poetry, and literature. My faith in India is boundless. I am proud of my origins and intend ultimately to return to my roots. I recognize what has been achieved in the fifty years of Independence. In 1947, there were widespread doubts about India's survival as a single political entity given the differences in language, religion, culture, and geography, to say nothing of the problems posed by a huge and ever-increasing population. That India functions half a century later as a coherent nation is hugely creditable to its people.

▼ Raj Bagri and his wife Usha Bagri are flanked by Apurv Bagri and Alka Bagri, left, and Amita Birla and C.K. Birla, right.

But how much greater India could be today. Somewhere, somehow, we have failed to bring to fruition the ambitions of fifty years ago. India has the talent to do so much better. Throughout the world, people of Indian origin have made massive contributions to development and human good with creditable achievements in such diverse fields as trade, industry, medicine, banking, science, and the arts. Clearly, there is something of great value in the Indian personality.

People of Indian origin resident abroad, who as industrialists and entrepreneurs have succeeded in creating wealth and jobs in other countries, can play a significant role in helping India towards its rightful place in the modern international economy. We can offer business skills and experience, knowledge of how the global economy operates, and investment. It is, however, important that there be no discrimination against domestic Indian enterprises merely to attract non-resident Indians and foreign investors, all of whom should be expected to operate on a level playing field.

We have the size and the innate ability to make a far greater impact on the global economy than we have been making, but we must be bold. All my experience in international business and as chairman of the world's largest metal exchange, with a turnover currently running well over $ 10 bn per day reinforces my belief in the virtues of transparently open and fair trade, unencumbered by excessive regulation, bureaucracy, or undue state interference. Let us take that route and claim our birthright.

Off the Beaten Track

Lakshmi Mittal

The 1980s was a period of intense privatization in the steel industry. During this time the LNM Group experienced rapid expansion, leading to it becoming the world's fastest growing steel producer. I donot know of another company in the world that has participated in eight government privatizations in eight years. This was a route to growth that has enabled us to acquire excellent assets and infrastructure in companies that were under-performing, loss-making, and of little strategic importance to the seller.

The 1990s is an era of consolidation in the global steel industry that began in Latin America, Europe, and Africa and is only now beginning in the US where our acquisition of Inland Steel should rank the LNM Group as the world's third largest steel producer in 1998, based on current rankings and an estimated production of 19 m. t.

▼ Lakshmi Mittal is one name everyone associated with the steel industry is familiar with. Having successfully run mega-plants around the world, after acquiring them as sick units, he feels 'the Indian people hold the future of our nation in their hands'.

In India, prior to economic and industrial deregulation which began in 1991, the regulatory and licensing laws and the protectionist environment were obstacles to growth beyond a certain scale. Some of India's largest and most successful entrepreneurs had to diversify into non-core areas. While adhering to what you know best holds true, Indian entrepreneurs should not be too easily criticized for diversifying.

The government's need to source external finance for developing core infrastructure such as telecommunications, power, oil, and transportation also encouraged more private sector entry in these sectors. However, the development of these core areas has been slow, and unless the government channels the pace and scope of progress, the vital foundation for economy and industry to develop will remain weak.

The outlook for industries the world over has changed. The environment within which industry must operate has dramatically altered as governments are advancing their pace of economic development. Much of this has been accompanied by increased competition as trade barriers have declined. This is equally true for India, where we have seen a number of multinationals attempting to capture India's mass market potential and access its natural resources and skilled manpower. But as economic liberalization has attracted new competition into India from multinationals, it has failed to push Indian industry to go global. I believe that the opportunities to expand Indian industry both within and beyond the country's borders are boundless. Used to a protectionist environment, many in India viewed the government's efforts with scepticism, urging a slower pace of reform. With some exceptions, Indian enterprise has also failed to achieve the standards of performance necessary to compete globally. Only a few have grabbed the new opportunity and formed successful partnerships with multinationals.

I believe that the Indian people, whether they live and work in India or abroad, hold the future of our nation in

ASHOK LEYLAND

their hands. I believe the realization has dawned and India's journey has already begun. The creation of the world's most global steel company in an industry which until recently was national, has proved that it pays to sometimes deviate from the beaten track in order to create a new beginning.

Building Bridges

Srichand P. Hinduja

In the mission to promote business and humanitarian activities in India and abroad, our aim is to help build bridges between the past and present, between India and the world, and between the generations that are and the generations yet to come.

Built on the solid foundations laid by its founder, Parmanand Deepchand, the Hinduja group has constructed an edifice that is raring to seize the opportunities of the twenty-first century with the same zeal and foresight displayed by the group's founder at the beginning of the twentieth century. Globalization has opened the floodgates of business opportunities both in India and abroad. A global player even before India embarked on the path of economic liberalization, the Hinduja group has positioned itself strategically to seize the emerging opportunity. Based on its core competencies and internal synergies, the group has chalked out a gameplan which places its existing and planned businesses in eight major strategic areas: transportation, power, information technology and media, chemicals and pharma, trading, banking and finance, real estate development, and infrastructure projects. The Hinduja Foundations in the UK, the US and India are actively involved in philanthropic activities in the fields of health, education, sports, and culture.

◄▼ Srichand P. Hinduja *(below)* heads the Hinduja group in London, and has interests in India, which includes Ashok Leyland *(previous page)*. Closely linked with several philanthropic foundations, the Hindujas have retained a clear focus on their activities through which they hope to continue building a global empire.

NRIs have a critical role in creating the climate in India for investment and prosperity. India must continue the process of market liberalization. It is only through the free market that India will enjoy prosperity. India must remind the world that it is the world's largest democracy. And India should question why it is that a communist state like China can pursue market reforms better than a democratic nation.

Contributors

A brief introduction to the authors and members of the Editorial Board who have worked on the making of this book.

Achar, Suresh, is a consultant on public affairs and image management.

Aiyar, Swaminathan S. Anklesaria, is Consulting Editor, *The Economic Times.*

Arif, Nazeeb, is Secretary-General, Indian Chambers of Commerce, Calcutta.

Bagri, Lord Raj, Chairman, Metdist, London.

Baru, Dr Sanjaya, is Economic and Business Editor, Eenadu Group, and has formerly been with *The Economic Times* and *The Times of India.*

Bhattacharya, Dr Sabyasachi, is Professor, Centre for Historical Studies, School of Social Sciences, Jawaharlal Nehru University, New Delhi and was formerly Vice-Chancellor, Vishwa Bharati University, Shantiniketan.

Bose, Kunal, is Correspondent, *The Financial Times,* London and was formerly Resident Editor, *The Economic Times,* Calcutta.

Champakalakshmi, Dr R., is Consulting Member of Indian Council for Historical Research and University Grants Commission and was formerly Professor, Centre for Historical Studies, School of Social Sciences, Jawaharlal Nehru University, New Delhi.

Chandra Mohan, Dr N., is the Business Editor, *The Times of India,* New Delhi.

Chattopadhayaya, Dr B.D., is Professor, Centre for Historical Studies, School of Social Sciences, Jawaharlal Nehru University, New Delhi.

Chung, Prof. Tan, is Consulting Professor, Indira Gandhi National Centre for the Arts, and was Professor of Chinese Language, School of Languages, Jawaharlal Nehru University, New Delhi.

Dae-Hwa, Choi, is Ambassador of The Republic of Korea to India.

Damani, M.G., is former President of the Bombay Stock Exchange and is currently on its Governing Body.

Desai, Ashok V., is Consulting Editor, *Business Standard,* and was formerly Chief Consultant, Ministry of Finance, Government of India.

Devra, Prof. G.S.L., is Professor, Department of Indian Traditions and Culture, Kota Open University, Kota.

Dhar, Dr Jawahar, is Emeritus Scientist, CSIR and Coordinator, Science Education Programme, Indian National Science Academy.

Fischer, Tim, is Minister for Trade and Deputy Prime Minister of Australia.

Goswami, Kanika, is a freelance business writer, formerly with *Spectrum Magazines* as Correspondent with *Global Magazine.*

Hakeem, M.A., is Secretary-General, Standing Conference of Public Enterprise, New Delhi.

Hinduja, Srichand P., is Chairman, The Hinduja Group, London.

Hussain, Abid, is former Ambassador of India to the USA.

Jha, Prem Shankar, is an economist and columnist for *The Hindu.* He has been a Visiting Fellow, Centre for International Affairs, Harvard University, and a Visiting Professor at the University of Virginia.

Joshi, Jagatpati, is former Director-General, Archaeological Survey of India.

Kanoria, S.S., Chairman, Kanoria Chemicals, is a past President of FICCI, and has been associated with a recent two-volume publication on 'performing arts' of the Anamika Kala Sangam of which he is a Founder-President.

Kawamoto, Nobuhiko, is President, Honda Motor Co. Ltd, and Chairman, Japan–India Business Cooperation Committee.

Ketkar, Kumar, is Chief Editor, *Maharashtra Times,* The Times of India Group, Mumbai.

Mahadevan, Dr Raman, is economic historian, formerly at the Centre for Developing Studies, Trivandrum, and Consulting Editor, *Business India.*

Mahbubani, Kishore, is Permanent Secretary, Foreign Ministry, Singapore.

Mashelkar, Dr R.A., is Director-General, Council of Scientific and Industrial Research, and Secretary, Department of Scientific and Industrial Research, Government of India.

McGeever, Michael Barrie, is Ambassador, Delegation of the European Commission.

Mitra, Dr Amit, is Secretary-General, FICCI and was formerly Professor at Franklin and Marshall College, USA, and Visiting Professor, University of Virginia.

Mittal, Lakshmi, is Chairman, Ispat Group, London.

Moosvi, Dr Shireen, is Chairperson and Coordinator, Centre of Advanced Study, Department of History, Aligarh Muslim University.

Mukherjee, Dr Aditya, is Professor of Contemporary History, Centre for Historical Studies, School of Social Sciences, Jawaharlal Nehru University, New Delhi.

Murari, P., is Advisor to the President of FICCI. He was formerly Secretary to the Government of India and has also served as Secretary to the President of India.

Murthy, N.R. Narayana, is Chairman of Infosys Technologies Ltd.

Narasimham, M., is Chairman, Administrative Staff College of India, Hyderabad, and was formerly Finance Secretary to GOI, Governor, Reserve Bank of India and Vice-President, Asian Development Bank.

Paul, Lord Swraj, Chairman, Caparo Group, London.

Piramal, Dr Gita, is a writer and author of books on India's business families.

Rahman, A., is Consultant, Science and Technology Policy Planning and Management and is the former Advisor (Planning), CSIR and Founder-Director of National Institute of Science, Technology and Development Studies (NISTADS), New Delhi.

Rajivan, Dr Anuradha K., is a senior bureaucrat with the Indian Administrative Service.

Rangachari, Kokila, is a former Fellow at Indian Council for Historical Research, New Delhi, and American Institute of Indian Studies, Chicago, and has been a Research Associate at the Department of Chinese and Japanese Studies, University of Delhi.

Ray, Dr Himanshu P., is Assistant Professor, Centre for Historical Studies, School of Social Sciences, Jawaharlal Nehru University, New Delhi.

Sahai, Dr Sachchidanand, is Professor and Head of Department of Ancient Indian and Asian Studies, Magadh University, Bodh-Gaya.

Sengupta, Dr Nitish, is Director-General, International Management Institute, New Delhi, and was formerly Member-Secretary, Planning Commission, Government of India.

Shankardass, R.K.P., is Senior Advocate and former President, International Bar Association, Vice-President Bar Association of India, Commissioner and Panel Chairman at the UN Compensation Commission.

Singh, Kishore, is a Consulting Editor with *Business Standard,* and was formerly Executive Editor, *Spectrum Magazines* and Chief Editor, Roli Books.

Singh, S.K., is former Foreign Secretary, Government of India.

Srinivasa-Raghavan, T.C.A., is Consulting Editor, *Business Standard.*

Sundar, Pushpa, is Founder- Director, Indian Centre for Philanthropy, New Delhi and was formerly a member of the Indian Adminstrative Service and a development specialist.

Swaminathan, Dr M.S., is Chairman, M.S. Swaminathan Research Foundation, Chennai and holds the UNESCO Chair in Eco-Technology.

Tien, James, is Chairman, Hong Kong General Chamber of Commerce.

Topa, Vijay, is Additional Secretary-General, FICCI.

Tripathi, Dr Dwijendra, retired as Professor of Business History, Indian Institute of Management, Ahmedabad, and held the Kasturbhai Lalbhai Chair, IIM, Ahmedabad. He is the Founder-Editor of *The Journal of Entrepreneurship.*

Varadarajan, Dr Lotika, is Advisor-Consultant, National Institute of Science, Technology and Development Studies (NISTADS), and former Advisor (Planning), CSIR.

Wisner, Frank, is former US Ambassador to India.

Arrt Creations, Ritu Topa and Animesh Roy of Arrt Creations are designers who have done various projects involving design, photography and production.

Acknowledgements and Picture Credits

A large number of people have contributed to the visual making of this illustrated volume. All efforts have been made to provide due credit, but in some cases, because of the complex nature of the production effort, oversights may have occurred. The Federation of Indian Chambers of Commerce and Industry would like to convey its gratitude to the various individuals, institutions and organizations for the research that made these pictures, illustrations and other visual material possible. FICCI would also like to thank the authors who contributed pictures from various sources for the making of this book.

In particular, the Editorial Board would like to thank the following for their unstinting cooperation and support on the project: Dr S. Sarkar, Director-General, National Archives, New Delhi, Shanti Sarkar, Chief Librarian and Jagmohan Singh of the Department of Reprography, National Archives, New Delhi; Ms Kasturi Menon, Director-General, National Museum and Joint Secretary, Department of Culture in the Ministry of Human Resource Development; Prof. Naseem Akhtar and Jaideep Grover from the National Museum, New Delhi; Dr Hardev Sharma, Director, Nehru Memorial Museum and Library, Teen Murti; Dr Ravindra Kumar, former Director Nehru Memorial Museum and Library; Mr Ajai Shankar, Director-General, Archaeological Survey of India; Dr Dwijendra Tripathi for suggesting the title of the volume; Professor Vachaspati Upadhyaya Vice-Chancellor, Lal Bahadur Shastri Vidyapeeth, New Delhi, for providing the Sanskrit quotations used in the book; and industrial photographer S. Kumar; and last but not the least, the countless number of businessmen who gave freely of their pictures from their personal collection, brochures and books.

Photographers

Arrt Creations, Pictures on pages x, xvii, 9, 28, 32,33, 39(left), 41, 43, 44, 49, 51, 174, 176(top), 178(left), 180(top), 182-3, 203(below), 228, 231, 275, 286, 335
Chowdhury, Mona, Pictures on pages 88(below), 89(top)
Dutt, Provin, Pictures on pages 230, 234, 264, 265, 266
Ghosal, Kalyan, Picture on page 240
Kumar, S., Pictures on pages xviii, 148-9, 157(left), 158(top), 159, 162, 182, 184(below), 193, 195, 196(top), 198, 219, 239, 241, 242, 260(below), 288(top), 291, 296, 297, 299, 301, 307, 313, 320, 325, 342-3
Rakesh, Pankaj, Pictures on pages 125(both left), 126, 127, 128(below)
Sahai, Rakesh, Pictures on half title page, and pages vii, 156(below), 159, 163, 166(top), 167, 168, 169(top), 170, 171, 172(top), 177(below), 178, 179(right), 182, 190(right), 206(below), 221, 243(below), 245, 280, 283, 285, 286, 288(below), 290-1, 292, 293(below), 294, 304(below), 305, 306(below), 308(top), 314, 316, 319(top), 339, 363(left), 373(top), 374, 382, 389
Sahai, Sachidanand, Pictures on pages 56, 57, 58, 59, 60
Saili, Ganesh, Picture on page 39(right)
Singh, Hardev, Picture on title page, and pages 160, 175(left), 178(top), 183, 237, 262-3, 278, 282, 287, 337

Institutions, Organizations and Libraries

Ashutosh Museum, Calcutta
Archaeological Survey of India, New Delhi
Bourne and Shepherd, Calcutta
Federation of Indian Chambers of Commerce and Industry, New Delhi
National Archives, New Delhi
National Museum, New Delhi
Nehru Memorial Museum and Library, New Delhi
Ministry of Food Processing, Government of India
Ministry of Non- Conventional Energy Sources, Government of India

Photo Division, Ministry of Information and Broadcasting
Press Information Bureau, Ministry of Information and Broadcasting
State Bank of India, New Delhi
Textiles: The author, Lotika Varadarajan, would like acknowledgements specially made to the following: Murali Sari Emporium, Putupaka, Andhra Pradesh; K.R.T. Hardjonogo, Solo, Indonesia; Hindeloopen Museum, Netherlands; Sonobuduyo Museum, Yogyakarta, Indonesia; Museum of Mankind, London; National Gallery, Canberra; Victoria and Albert Museum, London; National Museum, Bangkok, Thailand.
The Asiatic Society, Mumbai

Publications

Several companies made their material freely available for the compilation of this book. The following books have been used for reference.

A Business of Her Own, East -West Books (Madras) Pvt. Ltd.
An Inspired Journey, Writers Workshop
B.M. Birla, His Deeds & Dreams, Arnold Heinemann
Bombay and Western India
Brand New– Advertising Through the Times of India, The Times of India Sesquicentennial
Business Today, Anniversary Issue, January 7 1998– February 6, 1998
Cotton Mills Of India 1854-1954, The Textile Association (India)
Cyclopedia Of India, vols I-III
Daily Life And Work In India, W.J. Wilkins
Dr Rajah Sir Muthiah Chettiar, Annamalai University
Dr Ramnath Anandilal Podar
Dunhuang Art, Abhinav Publications
Gandhi's Coolie, Life & Times Of Ramkrishna Bajaj, Allied Publishers Limited
G.D. Birla, A Biography, Vikas Publishing House Pvt Ltd
Godrej, A Hundred Years, Viking
History of The Reserve Bank of India(1935–51), RBI
Homage To Jamnalal Bajaj, Allied Publishers Private Limited
Indian Asia, Elsevier-Phaidon
Indian Textile Journal (Bombay) ibid
India's Contribution To World Thought And Culture, Vivekananda Rock Memorial Committee
India's Industrialists, Three Continents Press, Inc.
In Gandhi's Footsteps, The Life And Times Of Jamnalal Bajaj, Oxford University Press
In The Image Of Man: The Indian Perception Of The Universe Through 2000 Years Of Painting And Sculpture, Vikas Publishers
Jawaharlal Nehru, A Biography, Sarvepalli Gopal, Oxford University Press
Lakshmipat Singhania, His Concepts And Creations, Vikas Publishing House Pvt Ltd
Mahatma Gandhi, Publications Division, Ministry of Information and Broadcasting
Mildred Archers India And British Portraits
Miniatures of Baburnama, H. Suleiman, Tashkent
New Horizons For Business, R.G. Maheshwari & Co
Outlook, August 31, 1998
Paintings of Baburnama, M.S. Randhawa
Picturesque India, A Handbook For European Travellers, W.S. Caine
Remembering Lala Shri Ram, DCM Limited
Shri and Smt. B.M. Birla, A Profile In Pictures
Silver Jubilee Souvenir 1927-51, FICCI
Tata, A Chronicle Of His Life, Blackie & Son (India) Limited
The Art Of India, Calambur Sivaramamurti, India Book House
The Evolution of the State Bank of India. The Roots 1806–1876, Oxford University Press
The Evolution of the State Bank of India. Volume 2, Sage Publications
The Costume Of Hindostan, Edward Orme
The Library Of A. Chester Beatty: A Catalogue Of The Indian Miniatures, vol. II, London
The Route Of Buddhist Art, Silk Road Exposition, Nara, 1988
To A Gandhian Capitalist, Sevak Prakashan Bombay

Index

ERRATA

p. 399: The caption should read: Raj Bagri and his wife Usha Bagri are flanked by Apurv Bagri and Amita Birla, left, and Alka Bagri and C.K. Birla, right.

p. 403: The caption should read: Gopichand P. Hinduja *(below)*, brother of Srichand P. Hinduja, is the livewire of the Hinduja group in London. The group has interests in India which includes Ashok Leyland *(previous page)*. Closely linked with several philanthropic foundations, the Hindujas have retained a clear focus on their activities through which they hope to continue building a global empire.